The SOCIAL SIGNIFICANCE of SPORT

AN INTRODUCTION TO THE SOCIOLOGY OF SPORT

Barry D. McPherson, PhD
Wilfrid Laurier University

James E. Curtis, MA
University of Waterloo

John W. Loy, PhD
University of Illinois

Human Kinetics Books
Champaign, Illinois

Library of Congress Cataloging-in-Publication Data

McPherson, Barry D.
    The social significance of sport : an introduction to the
sociology of sport / Barry D. McPherson, James E. Curtis, John W.
Loy.
        p.   cm.
    Bibliography: p.
    Includes index.
    ISBN 0-87322-235-0
    1. Sports—Social aspects.   2. Sports—Social aspects—United
States.   I. Curtis, James E.   II. Loy, John W.   III. Title.
GV706.5.M37   1989
306'.483—dc19   89-1975
                                                          CIP

ISBN: 0-87322-235-0

Copyright © 1989 by Barry D. McPherson, James E. Curtis, and John W. Loy, Jr.

Developmental Editor: Jan Progen, EdD
Managing Editor: Christine Drews
Production Director: Ernie Noa
Copy Editor: Steve Otto
Assistant Editors: Valerie Hall, Robert King, and Holly Gilly
Proofreader: Linda Siegel
Typesetter: Impressions, Inc.
Text Design: Keith Blomberg
Cover Design: Jack Davis
Cover Photo: Wilmer Zehr
Illustrations By: David Gregory
Printed By: Versa Press

Printed in the United States of America   10 9 8 7 6 5

Human Kinetics
Web site: www.humankinetics.com

United States: Human Kinetics
P.O. Box 5076
Champaign, IL 61825-5076
800-747-4457
e-mail: humank@hkusa.com

Canada: Human Kinetics
475 Devonshire Road, Unit 100
Windsor, ON N8Y 2L5
800-465-7301 (in Canada only)
e-mail: hkcan@mnsi.net

Europe: Human Kinetics
P.O. Box IW14
Leeds LS16 6TR, United Kingdom
+44 (0) 113 278 1708
e-mail: humank@hkeurope.com

Australia: Human Kinetics
57A Price Avenue
Lower Mitcham, South Australia 5062
08 8277 1555
e-mail: liahka@senet.com.au

New Zealand: Human Kinetics
P.O. Box 105-231, Auckland Central
09-309-1890
e-mail: hkp@ihug.co.nz

Photo Credits

To
Gerald S. Kenyon
Athlete, scholar, mentor, friend, and critic
and
one of the founders of the sociology of sport
in North America

Contents

Preface

In contemporary society there are few individuals or groups who do not, directly or indirectly, encounter elements of sport in their daily social lives. Some people may be actively involved as participants in a sporting activity; others may be spectators at sport events or consume sport via the mass media; still others may volunteer to work as coaches, referees, or executive members of sport organizations.

There is also a segment of the population that is not particularly interested in sport. But even these individuals find that sport in some way is a part of their lives, through such regular occurrences as sport news and sport-oriented conversation in family or work settings or through the enthusiasm demonstrated by others about major sport events (e.g., the Super Bowl, the Olympic Games, or the Kentucky Derby). Clearly sport has significant direct and indirect influences on the lives of most children and adults throughout North America, and for much of the rest of the world.

As a result of this general involvement in sport—whether by participants, consumers, or idle bystanders—social scientists, and particularly sociologists, increasingly have studied the world of sport in the past 20 years. This research has yielded descriptions and explanations of many social dimensions of sport, including those that do not occur directly on the playing field. One outcome has been the refuting of many erroneous conventional wisdoms that have been created and perpetuated within the world of sport. Another by-product has been the development of more viable policies and programs within sport settings. Most important, a significant outcome has been the development of a sufficient body of knowledge for colleges and universities to offer courses in the sociology of sport, in various departments, including physical education, sociology, sport studies, and kinesiology.

This textbook, written for the undergraduate student in one of these courses, summarizes the results of sociological research and reflects on the various social dimensions of sport. The specific purposes of this book are to develop an awareness and appreciation of the social significance of sport in modern societies; to promote an understanding of the social structure, social relations, and social problems of sport; and to indicate how the theories and methods of the social sciences allow us to better understand sport and thereby provide us with a basis for developing policies to address the social problems of sport.

Although this book emphasizes the results of sociological research, the information is not based solely on such studies. We have drawn on theories and research from social psychology, anthropology, and the other social sciences, along with the insights and interpretations of journalists, educators, and those inside the world of sport. To have used materials from only one approach would have been too limiting for a survey textbook—insights important to a complete social understanding of sport would have been excluded. Indeed, the sociology of sport is a specialty that employs multiple theories and research approaches, each of which can help us understand different social dimensions of sport. Throughout this book you will be introduced to a variety of types of data and theories associated with the sociology of sport.

This book is based on the premise that sport is an integral aspect of society and culture that frequently and significantly affects individuals and groups. The degree to which sport affects people can vary considerably from one country to another, and from one region to another within a society. It is for this reason that you will read about sport in other countries and within different subcultures. Clearly the organization and meaning of sport differs in, for example, China and the United States, or the Soviet Union and Canada. Similarly, within the United States, basketball, football, and baseball are more highly valued in some parts of the country and by some segments of the population. Such cultural and subcultural variations in sport are emphasized in this volume.

Throughout, sport is viewed as a major social institution of society similar to the family, education, the mass media, the economy, or politics. Sport is similar to these other institutions in that each involves social organizations and culture (a set of values, beliefs, and norms), and each has an impact on the lives of many members of the society.

There is considerable interaction between sport and the other social institutions. This occurs when people move from one institution to another while carrying on their lives.

It also occurs when sport organizations intersect with those of the wider society and exchange goods and services of all kinds, as well as values, beliefs, and norms. In this text we show that these interrelationships between sport and society lead to three interesting patterns: (1) Sport *reflects* culture and society; (2) sport *reinforces* social inequalities; and (3) sport is a vehicle for *resistance* or social conflict.

The book is structured into an introduction and three major parts. The introduction (chapter 1) gives an overview of the field of study and defines *sport, society, culture,* and other key concepts. Evidence is presented to illustrate how sport is a significant social activity. Sport is also shown to be a cultural product that varies across societies. Finally, the reinforcement, reflection, and resistance patterns are described.

Part I consists of five chapters that consider how sport reflects other social institutions. The institutions considered are the family (chapter 2); school and youth groups (chapter 3); politics and law (chapter 4); the economy (chapter 5); and the mass media (chapter 6).

Part II describes how sport reinforces social inequalities. Chapter 7 discusses how sport fosters or reinforces social class and status inequalities. It considers the extent to which social mobility is possible through sport. Chapter 8 addresses racial and ethnic inequality in sport, and chapter 9 focuses on gender and age inequality. In other words, we show how our opportunities in the world of sport are influenced by aspects of our social backgrounds.

Part III contains two chapters that focus on sport as a potential arena of resistance. Social conflict as expressed in sport settings is emphasized. Attention is also given to whether sport may be a stimulus for social change beyond the world of sport. Chapter 10 considers how sport may lead to the creation of resistant subcultures, which either oppose the values of the wider society or pursue the interests of disadvantaged groups within sport. Chapter 11 discusses various forms of collective behavior in sport and documents how sport has changed and how it contributes to social change.

Each chapter begins with a general overview of the topic, including some of the questions that have stimulated research in the area. Throughout, we introduce concepts and theories that will help you understand the facts and patterns about sport described in the chapter. As much as possible, we have tried to present interpretations for the major findings addressed in the chapter. Each chapter includes a set of *highlights* to further illustrate certain aspects of sport. Most highlights summarize a single interesting study or synthesize a few studies that address the same topic. Each chapter concludes with a *wrap-up*, to use a sport media term, that summarizes the material covered in the chapter.

Key concepts and terms in each chapter are presented in bold type. These are defined in a glossary at the end of the book, and you should add them to your working vocabulary. Finally, we have provided a set of references with each chapter. These can serve as a starting bibliography if you are required to write a term paper on one of the topics discussed or if you simply wish to acquire more detailed information about a particular topic.

If you want to pursue a particular topic still further, you can find recent publications on many of the topics through general reference sources, such as *Current Contents* (published by the Institute for Scientific Information) and *Sociological Abstracts*. In addition, the Specialized Information Retrieval and Library Service, or SIRLS, contains more than 18,000 published and unpublished documents on the sociology and social psychology of sport. (Address: SIRLS, University of Waterloo, Waterloo, Ontario, Canada, N2L 3G1.) Most libraries should have copies of the major re-

search journals in the field: *Sociology of Sport Journal, International Review for the Sociology of Sport, Arena Review, The Journal of Sport Behavior, Quest*, and the *Journal of Sport and Social Issues*. These journals regularly publish research studies and discussions about important issues and theories in the sociology of sport.

To acquire a thorough understanding of sport as a social activity you must become an avid reader, and a critical thinker concerning what you read. Be thorough and wide-ranging in your reading. Discuss your ideas and views with your instructor, classmates, and others. Be skeptical in what you accept as fact and explanation.

As authors, we strongly believe that the best test of how well a text serves as a learning resource is whether students find the material easy to understand, interesting, useful, and comprehensive. The three authors of this book have, in total, more than 40 years of experience in teaching undergraduates about the sociology of sport. But we still have much to learn, because student audiences and the world of sport change continually. Thus we encourage you to provide us with critical feedback on this introduction to the sociology of sport. Please submit your comments through your instructor or by writing directly to one of the authors.

Now it is time to begin your journey into the social world of sport. As noted throughout this text, sport is a significant part of our lives. Therefore, even if you are never employed in a sport-related occupation, it is important that you appreciate and understand the significance of sport in the lives of yourself and your children. By the end of this course, we hope that you will have become a more critical observer of contemporary sport.

Barry D. McPherson
James E. Curtis
John W. Loy

Acknowledgments

Behind every author there are a number of colleagues and friends who provide direct and indirect support and assistance. In our case there have been many. First, the primary sources and documents required to write the text were retrieved by Ms. Betty Milman and her staff in the Information Retrieval System for the Sociology of Sport and Leisure at the University of Waterloo. Second, a number of graduate students and colleagues provided suggestions and critical comments on sections of the text at various stages. In alphabetical order, we express our sincere thanks for the contributions of Maria Allison, David Andrews, Barbara Brown, Jim Bryant, P. Chelladurai, Jane Colwell, Peter Donnelly, Wendy Frisby, Marc Gelinas, Michael Smith, Nancy Theberge, and Neil Widmeyer. Third, we are especially grateful for the thorough reviews of the entire manuscript provided by Garry Smith and Lee Vander Velden. Fourth, appreciation is extended to Janet Bannister, Beverly Brooks, and Gail Forsyth, who performed a variety of administrative and typing tasks as the manuscript was being prepared. In addition, we acknowledge the assistance of Rick Campbell at the *Waterloo Chronicle* and Arthur Stephen at Wilfrid Laurier University, for selecting and donating photographs used in this text, as well as Kent Brown at the University of Illinois Sports Information office and Frances Roehm at the Champaign County Historical Archives at the Urbana Free Library, for helping to select photographs used in this text.

Deserving of special mention is Lorraine Thompson, who sacrificed many hours to produce early drafts and the final manuscript. She is especially commended for her patience and skill in deciphering the penmanship of the second author and for remaining loyal and committed to the project when the first author changed institutions—around the eighth inning of this particular game.

Finally, we thank our many former undergraduate students who honestly told us what they liked and disliked in our sociology of sport classes and in our earlier text, *Sport and Social Systems*. Their insightful criticism is reflected in this text and contributes to future generations of students entering the world of the sociology of sport.

Introduction to Sport, Culture, and Society

You are about to embark on a reading journey that is both stimulating and frustrating. The intellectual stimulation will come from a critical examination of sport that is seldom presented, and then only in skeletal form, in the popular press. Rather than merely describing an event, process, organization, or problem in sport, as the popular press generally does, we seek to provide evidence of the extent to which, and under what circumstances, the phenomenon regularly occurs. We ask whether there is any *social pattern* to the phenomenon—does it occur on some regular, repetitive, predictable basis? We consider various explanations for why the phenomenon occurs. As much as possible, these explanations are based on the most recent research and interpretative analyses by scholars specializing in the study of sport.

The sociology of sport is still a relatively young area of sociology, and we often know far less about the social aspects of sport than we would like. The lack of complete facts or explanations may prove frustrating, although this frustration can stimulate us to ask questions and undertake further study.

The contents of this text and the lecture material provided by your instructor may both fascinate and shock you. You may be fascinated by the pervasiveness of sport in contemporary societies. For example, you will realize that sport behavior and conversation about sport can be found in a great variety of social settings—at work, in the home, in bars, at parties, in movies, on television, and even when astronauts explore the moon.

Sport is also an important theme in such aspects of our culture as poems, plays, short stories, novels, paintings, sculptures, and music.

You may also be shocked by what you learn during your visit to the *back regions* of sport. Here you will discover that sport—its rules of behavior and values, and the individuals and groups involved—is not as it often appears when portrayed by the mass media, parents, teachers, or coaches. Overly favorable myths often are created and perpetuated by these groups, for reasons we will discuss. There is a seamy side to sport that involves inequality, oppression, discrimination, scandal, deviant behavior, and violence. Often these situations warrant the label *social problem*, because they cause physical or emotional injury, or economic abuse, to a number of people.

For many years this seamy side of sport remained hidden. If known by a few, it remained undiscussed. From about the late 1960s on, though, sociologists and journalists have opened the back door of sport to describe, criticize, and seek explanations of the problems. Many of these social problems have occurred as sport has become increasingly embedded in the social life of the rest of society. The problems of sport are, in a real sense, a reflection of (and thus part of the problems of) society. We explore this situation throughout the text.

We offer this text as a guide to the social ramifications of sport. This volume invites you to be more critically and thoroughly informed about modern sport. You are asked to develop a *sociological consciousness*—a way of thinking that compels you to look beyond the obvious aspects of sport that you see on the field or in the mass media. You will be asked to search for deeper meanings and for underlying patterns of social behavior in sport. In this way you will begin to seek sociological interpretations for the observations

you and others make concerning sport. Whether you are employed in the world of sport or are a parent, sport fan, or sport volunteer, this book should help you become better equipped to recognize and deal with social problems that arise in sport in your local community.

SPORT IS PERVASIVE IN SOCIETY

During the present century, sport has become a social phenomenon of great magnitude and complexity. It has both positive and negative consequences for individuals and groups throughout the world. For example, the majority of North Americans—as active participants, interested spectators, or disinterested bystanders—encounter sport in some form nearly every day of their lives. Highlights 1.1 and 1.2 illustrate the variety of forms and the numerous social settings in which sport can enter our social lives. These examples should convince you that sport is a highly salient and pervasive part of our social lives. Indeed, sport seems to be an ever-present element of modern society. Speaking of American culture, Boyle (1963) observed that

> sport permeates any number of levels of contemporary society, and it touches upon and deeply influences such disparate elements as status, race relations, business life, automotive design, clothing styles, the concept of the hero, language and ethical values. For better or worse, it gives form and substance to much in American life. (pp. 3–4)

UNDERSTANDING SOCIOLOGY IN THE CONTEXT OF SPORT

Since this book presents the subject matter of the field of study known as the sociology

---

Highlight 1.1
Examples of Involvement in Sport

Participation in Sport

- Estimates of the number of people who actively participate in sport vary, but studies yield surprisingly high figures. The Miller Lite study in 1982 (Miller Brewing Company, 1983) found that the percentage of U.S. adults who participated at least once per week, in season, ranged from 6% for golf, to 12% for tennis, to 21% for softball/baseball, to 33% for swimming. The Canada Fitness Survey (1983), conducted in 1981, reported that among Canadians 10 years old and up, 38% bicycled, 36% swam in a pool, 31% jogged, 21% skated, 15% played tennis, and 13% golfed at least once in the 12 months preceding the survey.
- Well over 20 million children and adolescents in North America participate in organized, competitive sport programs such as soccer, basketball, gymnastics, and age-group swimming.
- Sport camps cater to the needs of children or adults who want to improve their skill levels. Moreover, adult fantasy baseball camps enable adults to work out and interact with former major league players, many of whom were their childhood or adolescent heroes. These camps come complete with uniforms, pregame meals, and intrasquad games (Brandmeyer & Alexander, 1986).

Attendance at Spectator Sports

- In recent years when there have been close pennant races, each major league baseball team has attracted more than one million spectators.
- The total annual attendance for 11 major spectator sports in North America has exceeded 427 million in recent years. The following chart shows the most popular spectator sports, with estimated annual paid admissions for 1987.

Sport	Estimated annual paid admission for 1987 (in millions)
Baseball	88.2
Automobile racing	78.2
Horse racing	73.5
Football	50.1
Basketball	45.1
Hockey	25.5
Wrestling	21.9
Soccer	6.4
Tennis	6.4

Note. Data from Waldman, 1988.

- Domed stadiums and their sky boxes make attending sports an opulent affair. In sky boxes spectators are fully protected from the weather as they watch the event, live or on television, and consume gourmet meals. Perhaps the most extreme example of opulent sport attendance is provided by The Skydome in Toronto, Canada. A hotel has been built as part of the stadium, and some of the rooms have windows that look out directly onto the playing field. The occupants do not even have to leave

(Cont.)

Highlight 1.1 Continued

their hotel room to go to the game. From these rooms, however, people are unlikely to be able to catch a souvenir ball, experience the odor of hot dogs and peanuts, actively participate with the crowd in cheering or booing the players or officials, or participate in a supportive "wave" with the home town fans.

Media Consumption of Sport

- The most popular section of most daily newspapers is the sport section. Because of this, businesses are willing to pay higher advertising costs for placing ads in this section.
- The weekly circulation of *Sports Illustrated* is over 3.5 million.
- In January 1989, a new monthly magazine, *Sports Illustrated for Kids*, was launched to appeal to the almost 20 million 8- to 13-year-old Americans.
- The major U.S. networks televise more than 1,400 hours of sport per year and more in an Olympic year.
- Cable or pay-television sport stations broadcast more than 8,000 hours of sport per year in North America.
- The worldwide viewing audience for the opening ceremonies of the 1984 Summer Olympic Games was estimated at 2.5 billion, and an estimated 2 to 3 billion people viewed the World Cup Soccer Final in June, 1986.
- The estimated television viewership, by gender, for some specific types of sport events indicates that (a) more males watch the popular team sports of football, baseball, and basketball, but the number of female viewers increases considerably for championship or special events (e.g., the Super Bowl, the Rose Bowl, the World Series); (b) there is little gender variation in viewing patterns for horse racing and bowling; (c) the events that attract the largest number of female viewers are the Super Bowl, horse racing, tennis, the Rose Bowl, and the World Series; and (d) the events that attract the fewest number of female viewers are college and professional basketball, auto racing, college and professional football, and boxing.

Sport in Nonsport Settings

- Sport is the subject of many collectors' items such as stamps, coins, baseball cards, team hats, buttons and pins with team logos, pennants, and so on. Pin collecting and trading was one of the favorite activities for spectators at the 1988 Winter Olympics in Calgary. For others, the production and marketing of these pins was a profitable enterprise.
- In bars and taverns large-screen television sets and satellite dishes provide sport shows to attract patrons and to stimulate conversation and increased drinking.
- Using free Washington Redskin tickets as bait, F.B.I. agents attracted and arrested 100 fugitives, including 2 individuals on the *10 most wanted list*. These individuals were arrested in December 1985 when they showed up at a free brunch to collect football tickets offered as prizes in a draw of citizens' names. A similar police ploy in April

(Cont.)

Highlight 1.1 Continued

1986 netted only 3 of 950 invited suspects to a Yankee pregame brunch and game. Perhaps the fugitives read the news and took heed, or maybe football is more appealing to fugitives than baseball!

---

of sport, it is essential to be clear about what constitutes the sociological approach. This section discusses some of the basic concepts that you will use throughout this text.

Defining Basic Terms

The science of **sociology** describes and constructs theories to explain the social relationships that make up a society. This apparently simple definition includes four important elements that must, in turn, be defined.

Science. The concept of **science** has a meaning for sociologists similar to that held by physicists or biologists. Namely, science is the careful description of the real world and the construction and validation of theories about the real world. In principle the goals of all sciences are the same: to describe and explain through the testing of theories.

Theory. For sociologists, as for physicists or biologists, a **theory** is a tentative explanation of observable reality and forms the basis for predicting future events. Each theory is judged against competing theories for thoroughness and economy of explanation. Researchers test and retest their theories with valid observational data in order to correct or fine-tune them.

Social relationships. The ways in which people's social actions affect others are termed **social relationships**. People are bound together by these relationships. Therefore, a subject matter of sociology is also the *social bonds* that connect individuals in groups and societies.

Society. A collection of social relationships represents a **society**. Sometimes the sum of these relationships in a group is called the *social structure* of the group. Society is made up of all the families, clubs, corporations, and other groups in which its members participate.

Boundaries of a Society

Seeing the boundaries of a given society is sometimes difficult, for many social relationships may span international borders, like the ones between the United States and Canada. Indeed, some writers have wondered whether Canada and the United States, which are certainly distinct nations, should be viewed as distinct societies. Others have wondered whether the two have distinct economies. These questions arise because of the close economic ties and the frequent flow of people between the two societies. Consider, for example, the way in which the personnel and other resources of some professional sport teams (e.g., the National Hockey League and in major league baseball) move freely across the U.S.-Canada border.

Yet *American* society and *Canadian* society are meaningful entities to sociologists be-

---

Highlight 1.2
Links Between Sport and Other Social Institutions

Economy

- The underground economy in ticket scalping in several sports can yield surprisingly large profits. For example, scalpers asked $1,500 for a seat originally priced at $75 for the January 1988 Super Bowl.

- A number of sport stars now earn more than $1 million per year in wages, plus bonuses. Kareem Abdul-Jabbar earned $4 million for his 20th NBA season in 1988-89. Even the average or marginal player, because of guaranteed minimum salaries, can earn more than $80,000 per year.

- Some investors in the stock market, looking for trends to give them an investment edge, have found that in the year a horse wins the Triple Crown, the Dow Jones average declines (e.g., in 1973, −16.6%; in 1977, −17.3%; and in 1978, −3.1%). Similarly, some investors have discovered that in 7 of the 8 years in which an NFC team has won the Super Bowl, the Dow Jones average has increased ("Scorecard," 1987). Although there is no logical explanation for such patterns, these examples show the extent to which sport influences even the financial decisions made by some individuals.

- In North America the fitness industry has become a billion dollar business that involves sales of membership fees, equipment, clothing, and diet foods, as well as salaries for fitness leaders and medical personnel (Brand, 1988).

Education

- Most high school trophy cases display more "silverware" honoring athletic prowess than intellectual achievements. Moreover, outstanding athletes are accorded more formal recognition, like medals and jackets, than are outstanding scholars.

Politics

- Politicians like to be visible. So they often phone or visit the locker rooms of championship teams. It is a tradition for the president of the United States to phone the winners of the Super Bowl. This is usually televised from the locker room. Politicians are also chosen to throw the first pitch at major baseball games.

Family

- Family meals and leisure pursuits may be regulated by the sport participation schedules of the children, and by the television times for major sport events.

---

cause the social bonds of Americans with other Americans differ from the bonds of Americans with Canadians (and vice versa). We need only consider the strong attach-

ments that Americans and Canadians do *not* share (e.g., national flags, the U.S. Congress vs. the Canadian Parliament, football and basketball vs. hockey) to know that we are speaking of two societies here. Most Americans share in the strong positive sentiments evoked by the idea of *American*; few Canadians would do so, and vice versa. The same is true of Americans' and Canadians' attitudes toward the Olympic teams of the two nations.

Defining Culture

Culture is another side of social life that must be understood at the outset. An adequate sociological study of sport cannot proceed without considering what exactly culture is. A classic definition, by the social anthropologist Edward Tylor, states that culture is "that complex whole which includes knowledge, belief, art, morals, law, custom, and any other capabilities and habits acquired by man as a member of society" (Tylor, 1913, p. 1). Thus, culture involves all *meanings* that people learn from one another. It includes ideas that are shared by society members.

Culture includes **beliefs**, both descriptive beliefs (e.g., ideas about what is, or was, or will be), and normative beliefs (e.g., ideas about what should be or ought to be). It includes **values**, which are general criteria by which we judge people's behaviors, and **ideologies**, which are emotionally charged sets of beliefs that people use to explain and justify how society is organized. And culture contains **norms**—rules, regulations, laws, and informal understandings about how to perform in particular situations. Norms are illustrated, for example, by the game plans followed by athletes, or the rules book of any organized sport.

Culture and Society

Culture and society are intimately linked. They are different sides of the same coin of social reality. Society, as we said above, is made up of sets of social relationships. Culture comprises the meanings that are developed by people in social relationships and that are taught and learned through social relationships. Culture also helps determine how social relationships take place, because these relationships are guided by shared norms, beliefs, values, and so on.

Because culture is shared by people, social relationships and society are possible. For one thing, people can act predictably with each other when they share the same culture. In automobile traffic, for example, drivers know what to expect of other drivers and pedestrians through commonly understood rules of the road. We can make reasonably accurate predictions about other drivers' behavior on the basis of the rules. Indeed we routinely stake our lives on these understandings. And the social relationships of traffic continually run more or less according to plan. Imagine traveling in an automobile across one of our cities if we did not share such understandings!

As another example, nearly every professional baseball game is played in a recognizable fashion and in a predictable way. There are nine or more innings (except for rainouts); nine players per team; and at each game spectators enter the stadium, take a seat, watch the game, and leave—all in an orderly fashion. They even stand and stretch, with or without cue, halfway through the 7th inning! These behaviors are the result of shared sport culture.

In Highlight 1.3, you will see another example of shared sport culture and its implications. The highlight shows how common understandings emerged to guide social relationships during recreational swimming sessions at a university pool.

We must be careful not to exaggerate the concept of shared culture, however. Not all parts of a culture are shared by all members of the society. Some aspects of culture are

Highlight 1.3
A Participant-Observation Study of the Social Order of Recreational Swimming

Most social behavior in group situations is orderly and follows recurrent social patterns. Sport settings are no exception. For example, consider recreational swimmers or weight lifters who work out in crowded facilities on a regular basis. Have you ever wondered how, in situations where there are few posted rules, few leaders, and little or no verbal contact, some degree of order is maintained? Have you ever noticed that an informal status hierarchy evolves among the regular participants?

As a 10-year veteran of recreational swimming sessions, the sport sociologist Howard Nixon decided to analyze the social order in the pool to better understand the pattern of social interaction that emerges among recreational swimmers. Based on past observations and on systematic notes he kept for a 2-month period, Nixon (1986) studied the interaction of the noon-hour faculty-staff swim period at his university. Most of the swimmers were relative strangers to each other (they didn't arrive in groups or engage in much conversation in or around the pool). There were about as many male as female swimmers.

He found that norms emerged concerning which lane to swim in; the direction to swim; where to rest; how to pass others (always on the left); how to avoid interfering with another swimmer who is about to begin a turn; and, because swimsuits are revealing, how to respect the privacy of others (one should not focus inordinate attention directly on others, especially members of the opposite sex). Nixon concluded that a *mini-max* principle of interaction emerges in the pool—minimize involvement and maximize order. People take each other into account to maintain order and to protect personal privacy.

Developing and maintaining social order in the pool involved establishing a status hierarchy of swimmers. People interacted according to their status, which was achieved by the frequency of attendance and by the intensity of involvement. The author, based on his observations, identified four types of status: serious-regular; serious-nonregular; casual-regular; and casual-nonregular. Once established, the status differential and related informal norms regulate social interaction in the pool. For example, others give the serious-regular swimmers more space and the fast or uncrowded lanes. Serious-regular swimmers also have more input into creating and legitimizing new, informal rules.

What happens when someone cannot maintain the pace in a fast lane and won't change lanes, or when strangers arrive who do not understand or accept the informal code of behavior? One outcome is hostile outbursts against the offender, because there is no one to enforce the informal rules. Some of these outbursts were ignited, for example, when women were touched or kicked by men, even accidentally. In some instances, these incidents were interpreted by women swimmers as sexual harassment.

In summary, regular attendees often establish and maintain social order in

(Cont.)

Highlight 1.3 Continued

crowded recreational sport settings where formal, prescribed norms are lacking. These participants establish a social code and become part of an informal status system that is based on frequency of participation. By effective, usually nonverbal socialization of new members, informal social control is created and maintained among a group of relative strangers. In this way our recreational social life proceeds in a regular, patterned, and orderly fashion.

learned and known by most of us, but other cultural items are shared by only a few. In addition to the rules of traffic, most of us know the meanings of such concepts as *money* (e.g., what a dollar will buy today), *work*, *family*, or *education*. Very few of us, however, are privy to the information shared in the owners' meetings of the National Football League or National Hockey League. And only some of us know much about power plays or penalty killing strategies for hockey; or how to throw or hit a curve ball and how to lay down a bunt.

In other words, for much of the culture that has been accumulated within a society, there are *subcultures*. These subcultures share some of the common culture with others, but not all of it. Also, these subgroups have a culture they do not share with the wider society. Without some shared culture, though, there would be no society, because we would no longer have the social relationships requisite for society. And without social relationships and society there can be no culture.

SOURCES OF DATA ON SOCIETY AND CULTURE

A basic goal of the sociology of sport is to describe and explain patterns, processes, and problems in the world of sport. To do so, the sport sociologist must employ valid and reliable quantitative and qualitative data. Many different sources may provide data. Any data source is appropriate if it has some bearing on social relationships or cultural patterns involving sport. Some of the basic forms of data used by sport sociologists are described below.

First, we may study existing records found in libraries or books. Examples are an examination of the record books for professional baseball to determine, over a period of time, the proportion of blacks among players and managers; a study of television ratings over time to analyze changes in the viewing preferences of males and females or of those in different age groups; and a review of microfilms of a local newspaper to determine the coverage of women's sport in the same newspaper over different time periods.

Second, we may use interviews or questionnaires to survey people. For example, owners, managers, and players in professional baseball may be asked about the process of selecting managers, in an attempt to understand why so few blacks have been employed. National surveys may ask adults about their extent of involvement in sport or physical activity, either as participants or spectators.

Third, we may collect observational data. An example would be when a sociologist lives and travels with a group of athletes and observes their lifestyles. An example of *participant observation* would be where the sociologist trades buttons and pins with other sport spectators to better understand the motivation, techniques, and meaning of this sporting hobby.

Fourth, we may undertake an historical study, perhaps by researching records to understand changes in the structure or regulations of a particular sport over time. For example, we may study the changing legal and informal definitions of professional versus amateur status. Or we may study the contents of the medical and physical education literature to explore changing definitions of the extent to which women should participate in "strenuous" sports.

Any of these research approaches—existing records, interviews, questionnaires, observation, and historical analyses—is fair game for the sociologist. The only requirement is that the information relates to the sociological problem under study. It must tell us something about the social organization or culture of sport. Any data source that does this will be helpful. The more different types of data we gather and compare, the better our understanding of sport. Each of the research approaches gives us a different and complementary slant on our topic.

SPORT AS A SOCIAL PHENOMENON

Despite the fact that **sport** is a salient part of our daily lives, it has, until recently, received little serious study by sociologists. Accordingly, there are few clear and compelling definitions and descriptions of sport as a social activity. Sport generally has been examined with a broad yet loose view, especially by the members of the mass media.

One only has to examine the content of the daily newspapers or televised sport shows to discover the vast variety of activities treated as sport. These activities range from those that can be considered core forms of sport to those that can be considered, at best, peripheral forms. First, there are many competitive physical activities universally viewed as sport. These include golf, karate, tennis, bowling, football, skiing, boxing, hockey, baseball, basketball, and many more. There are also relatively new physical activities or special combinations of traditional activities that most (but not all) would accept as sport, such as hang gliding, wind surfing, and the triathlon. There are largely entertainment activities that some consider sport and others view as pseudosport, including body-building contests, professional wrestling matches, and the recently popular truck and tractor pulls.

One finds the mass media often treating as sport such games as bridge, chess, Monopoly, and poker, although they do not require physical prowess. The mass media also often present as sport such recreational activities as birding, fishing, caving, and kite flying, although they usually do not involve a contest. Some activities depicted as sport by the media stretch any definition of sport to the extreme, such as the modeling of sport fashions, and contests to see how many groceries can be packed into a grocery bag within a limited time.

Given that the concept of sport is rather ambiguous, we note that no single definition of the term is likely to satisfy everyone. We suggest that sport is best considered from several points of view and describe it in four ways: (a) as a form of involvement; (b) as a ludic physical activity; (c) as a social institution; and (d) as a cultural product.

SPORT AS A FORM OF SOCIAL INVOLVEMENT

Earlier we gave several examples of participation in sport, attendance at spectator sports, media consumption of sport, and sport in nonsport settings. As well as showing that sport is pervasive in society, these examples illustrate that individuals are involved in sport in different ways and to varying degrees. In this section of the chapter, we discuss how individuals can participate in sport behaviorally, cognitively, and affectively. We define the degree of participation in terms of frequency, duration, and intensity; and we describe four main patterns of sport involvement.

Behavioral Involvement

Behavioral involvement in sport settings typically takes one of two forms: primary or secondary involvement. **Primary behavioral involvement** refers to participation in the sport as a player, not unlike the role of actors in the production of a film or play. More specific sport roles include, for example, starters, substitutes, superstars, and marginal or journeyman players. **Secondary behavioral involvement** refers to the many other forms of participation, including being involved, for example, as managers, player agents, owners, and spectators.

Sport producers are responsible for staging the event. Individuals involved with the actual production of a game or sporting event may be characterized as direct or indirect producers. Direct producers do not actually compete in a sport contest but perform tasks that have direct consequences for the outcome of a game. Direct producers include instrumental leaders, such as coaches, managers, and nonplaying captains; arbitrators, such as judges, umpires, and referees; and health service personnel, such as doctors and trainers.

Indirect producers are actively involved in a sport situation but have no direct or immediate impact on the outcome of a sport event. Indirect producers include entrepre-

Behavioral involvement in sport encompasses both primary involvement, such as these active karate students, and secondary involvement, represented here by the spectating parents.

neurs, such as owners, promoters, and sporting goods manufacturers; expressive leaders, such as cheerleaders, bandleaders, and mascots; technicians, such as broadcasters, photographers, reporters, and scorekeepers; and service personnel, such as concession workers, groundskeepers, program hawkers, and security guards.

Sport consumers are people who at any time consume sport, either directly, through attending an event, or indirectly, through exposure to some form of mass media. Although it is not possible to delineate all of the behaviors and expectations associated with the sport consumer, he or she can be expected to

- invest given amounts of time and money in various forms of direct and indirect secondary sport involvement;
- have varying degrees of knowledge concerning sport performers, sport statistics, and sport strategies;

- have an emotional involvement with one or more individuals or groups in sport;
- experience different mood states while consuming a sport event;
- discuss sport with friends and strangers; and
- arrange leisure-time activities to coincide with professional and amateur sport events.

The distinction between direct and indirect consumption becomes more clear when we consider that the spectator is part of the sport situation. He or she may have some immediate and spontaneous effect on the event (e.g., cheer, hurl objects, or yell advice to players or officials). Someone consuming sport via radio or television may be thousands of miles from the event and has no direct impact on the event.

Highlight 1.4 reports results from a national survey of American adults concerning what sports are watched and played. Notice the strong relationship between the two forms of involvement—people tend to watch what they play and play what they watch.

Cognitive Involvement

The amount of information made available by the mass media makes it almost impossible to avoid learning and knowing something about the world of sport. This behavior is called **cognitive sport involvement**. We learn about the history, organization, rules, strategies, and technical requirements of given sports and their environmental settings. We also learn about the successes and failures of particular players, teams, and leagues; the personalities and private lives of players; and the outcome of particular sporting events. This information is sometimes retained long after a specific event or a particular player's career is over. Extreme examples of cognitive involvement with sport are those individuals who have amassed highly detailed information and statistics about their favorite sport.

At this time little is known about the amount, variability, and source of such sport knowledge held by individuals or groups. This is a fertile field for research, particularly for those interested in the study of linguistics or mass communication.

Despite our limited knowledge of the cognitive dimensions of sport involvement, it seems clear that learning sport information depends on the nature of the social groups in which we participate. It also depends on our past experiences with sport. For example, as a college student it is difficult not to become cognitively, and perhaps emotionally, immersed in your school's football or basketball team. These teams' schedules probably shape your social life at certain times of the school year, because they are important to you or others around you. Whether the success of your college teams remains important to you after graduation depends on such factors as your later degree of involvement in other aspects of sport, the interests and experiences of your present and future peer groups, and future identification with your school.

Affective Involvement

Being involved as a participant in a sport is a sufficient but not a necessary condition for the development and demonstration of emotional or affective involvement. Just as people can think about sport without playing sport, people may become deeply involved emotionally without ever playing. There can be strong loyalties toward, or identification with, given players or teams. Extreme examples include the coach who loses emotional control and attacks (verbally or physically) an official or spectator, or the consumer who yells, "Kill the umpire!"—and then tries to do it!

Highlight 1.4
A U.S. National Sample Survey on the Most Popular Sports to Watch and Play

Recognizing that many sport-minded Americans consume beer and watch commercials, the Miller Brewing Company (1983) commissioned a survey of popular attitudes toward various sport issues, including the involvement of adults as fans, spectators, and participants; the participation of children in sport; the role of the media, businesses, drugs, betting, and violence in sport and in the Olympic Games; the role of sport in education; and the concerns about equal opportunity in sport. Telephone interviews were conducted with 1,139 adults selected to be represen-

tative on age, race, gender, and education characteristics as reported in census data. The questions on the survey were designed by an advisory panel of sport scholars and athletes.

The following chart shows what sports the adult sample preferred to watch more than any other, and what sports they enjoyed participating in most. Note that data were not gathered for both categories for all sports. However, one can still see that, with few exceptions, the favorite sports to play are also the favorite sports to watch.

Favorite sport to watch	Percent	Favorite sport to play	Percent
Football	28	Swimming	20
Baseball	18	Football	8
Basketball	8	Baseball	7
Gymnastics	5	Basketball	7
		Tennis	6
		Bowling	5
		Golf	5

Note. Data from the Miller Brewing Company, 1983.

Consumers who are emotionally as well as cognitively involved in a game can experience extreme mood shifts that coincide with the successes and failures of their favorite team or player. Many mood changes are accompanied by physiological changes (e.g., an increase in heart rate, a rise in blood pressure, or a heightened galvanic skin response). **Affective sport involvement** is also revealed

in the way people proudly wear their school colors or clothing that identifies their bowling team, softball team, or favorite professional sport team. Bumper stickers and personalized license plates may tout the car owner's favorite player or team.

In summary, sport attendance figures, the size of audiences for sport telecasts, and the sales figures for clothing and other items with

Spectators become emotionally, or affectively, involved in sport.

team insignias all provide indirect evidence that a large percentage of people hold strong attitudes and have deep feelings about sport activities. The agony and ecstasy of sport insure that spectators as well as athletes become affectively involved with sport.

Patterns of Involvement

We can expect to find considerable variation in the three types of involvement across the life cycle. For example, compare the typical behavioral involvement of adolescents with the elderly. Also, depending on the values and opportunities concerning sport that are available at different stages in the history of society, one generation of young people (e.g., current 18- to 25-year-olds) may be rather highly involved in sport; the preceding or following generation may be much less involved at the same age. Finally, within an age group there is often considerable varia-

tion in the degree of sport involvement according to gender, social class, race, ethnicity, and geographical location.

Degrees of involvement can be measured by frequency, duration, or intensity. *Frequency* refers to the rate of participation or consumption; for example, bowling twice a week or watching football on television three or more times a week during the fall season. *Duration* refers to the length of participation at a given time; for example, playing three sets of tennis each week or watching 5 or more hours of sport telecasts on Sunday afternoon. *Intensity* of involvement refers to the individual's commitment and investment of time, money, energy, and emotion in a sport situation. This is often measured by a combination of frequency and duration of involvement and often serves as an index of a person's affective involvement in sport.

We know that not everyone maintains the same level (frequency, duration, or intensity) of sport involvement over time and that individuals vary in their patterns of sport involvement. However, these four general patterns of sport involvement are commonly found (Kenyon & Schutz, 1970):

- normal involvement
- cyclical involvement
- divergent involvement
- withdrawal or noninvolvement

Normal involvement refers to individuals who participate regularly in sport and whose participation patterns are integrated into their lifestyles (e.g., the thrice-weekly set of tennis at noon). *Cyclical* involvement is characterized by sporadic participation (e.g., the person who skis only during his or her 2-week vacation).

Divergent involvement refers to individuals who become obsessed with sport to the point of addiction. An example of divergent primary involvement is the middle-aged academic or business person who leaves a career to devote his or her life to surfing, skiing, or sailing. Divergent secondary involvement includes those who consume sport to excess (i.e., sport addicts). An example is the person who experiences bankruptcy as a consequence of betting to excess at the racetrack. Another example is the couple who make a point of attending every game of their favorite basketball team.

Withdrawal, or noninvolvement, is the opposite of divergent involvement. It is represented by asportual individuals who abhor any association with sport. These individuals may never have been socialized into sport roles (see chapter 2). Alternatively, they may have been involved in sport at one time and become desocialized from sport because of a lack of opportunity, a declining interest, competing interests that took priority, or an unpleasant experience that led them to drop out of sport.

DEFINING SPORT

Often we think of sport as a set of specific competitive physical activities based on elements of play, games, and contests. From this perspective we formally define sport as a structured, goal-oriented, competitive, contest-based, ludic physical activity. As this definition is rather detailed, let us examine each of the five distinguishing features of sport.

Sport Is Structured

A fundamental feature of sport is that it is a structured physical activity. Even the most informal forms of sport are governed by rules and are limited in space and time. All sports have either written or unwritten codes of conduct. Most take place in a circumscribed space such as a basketball court, boxing ring, golf course, ski slope, or swimming pool. Fur-

ther, nearly all sports have fixed guidelines for determining the duration of a given event, including the tie-breaker and sudden-death procedures used to break a deadlock.

The most formal forms of sport are highly structured. For example, most intercollegiate and professional sport groups are large, complex organizations with a formal structure. Such organizations usually have an official statement of objectives, a clearly defined division of labor into specialized and coordinated tasks, a hierarchical administrative structure involving the delegation of authority, and both formal and informal channels of communication. This structure, combined with the size of the organization, governs decision-making, communication, conflict, efficiency, and effectiveness.

Sport Is Goal-Oriented

A second characteristic of sport is goal orientation. Nearly every sport situation offers various forms of contest and self-testing. All forms of sport involve achievement and goal-oriented behaviors. This is evidenced by the concern of athletes, coaches, and spectators with attributes of ability, competence, effort, degree of difficulty, mastery, and performance. It is for this reason that such detailed individual and team performance statistics are recorded and reported. Some common examples include batting and fielding averages in baseball, field goal and foul shooting percentages in basketball, percentage of successful first serves in tennis, and average strokes per round in golf.

Athletes and teams may have different goals, and a variety of standards of excellence may be established. But sport situations usually provide clear criteria for evaluating success and failure, whatever the particular goals or specific standards of excellence. Moreover, the element of competition and the determination of a winner and loser is usually involved in sport.

Sport Is Competitive

Like goals and standards of excellence, competition can take many forms in sport. For example, an athlete competing in a cross-country race may be competitively involved in the following ways: as an individual against another individual (e.g., the current record holder), as a team member against members of an opposing team, as a team member (e.g., rookie) against another team member (e.g., veteran), and as an individual or team member against some standard (e.g., an existing record).

Competition in sport takes one of three forms. First, there is *direct competition*, where two opponents (individual or team) confront one another. This is seen in all combative sports and nearly all court sports. Second, there is *parallel competition*, where contestants compete with one another indirectly by taking turns or contesting in separate areas, as in bowling, track events, golf, and swimming. Third, there is *competition against a standard*, as in archery, diving, gymnastics, figure skating, and trap shooting. Although these three forms of competition are not always mutually exclusive, they indicate that all sport is contest-based.

Sport Is Contest-Based

As Birrell (1978) has pointed out, the majority of sport forms are either sporting *contests* (e.g., bowling, golf, swimming, track) or sporting *games* (e.g., baseball, football, hockey, tennis). Sporting contests typically involve competition against a standard, parallel competition, or individual forms of direct competition (e.g., boxing, fencing).

Sporting games usually involve group forms of direct competition (e.g., baseball, soccer).

More specifically, as Weiss (1969) has observed in the context of athletics:

> Contests, whether they occur by themselves, or in games, usually pivot about the performance of individuals occupied with demonstrating their relative superiority in five areas—speed, endurance, strength, accuracy and coordination. (p. 100)

Clear examples of these basic types of physical prowess include speed in the 100-meter dash, endurance in the Marathon, strength in weight-lifting contests, accuracy in archery and trap-shooting competition, and coordination in diving and gymnastic events.

Sporting games often involve several separate but simultaneous contests within the larger contest of the games themselves. For example, the Olympic Games comprise many separate but often simultaneous contests conducted over a period of several days. Sporting games also represent **agonal contests**, where the honor of individuals, institutions, and even nations are at stake. To paraphrase Gouldner's (1965) account of the classical Greek contest system, the three fundamental rules of all agonal contests are the following:

- The goal of a contest is for an individual or team to win more personal honor or public prestige than their opponents.
- Honor and prestige are won by means of demonstrated superior physical prowess.
- The amount of honor and prestige that is won depends on several conditions, including (a) the importance of the contest to all members of a social system; (b) the importance of the contest to the particular peer group of participants; (c) the

status and ability of opposing contestants; (d) the degree of difficulty associated with a given form of competition; (e) the value of the prizes (symbolic or material); and (f) "The value of the stakes that the contestant risks and the extent of the risk to which these are subjected." (p. 49)

The application of these rules and conditions is well illustrated in the context of the Olympic Games. For example: (a) An Olympic gold medal is the most prestigious prize in all of sport; (b) the status and ability of opposing contestants is of the highest level; (c) the Games allow contestants to establish their world ranking in their respective athletic disciplines; and (d) the success of a nation's team is held to reflect national character and to serve as an index of moral superiority (Loy, 1981). An interesting feature of two of the last three Olympiads is that the boycotts by the USA, in 1980, and the USSR, in 1984, were viewed as having lessened the status and ability of opposing contestants and, more generally, having reduced the overall prestige of the Games. Thus, although sports can often serve instrumental and political purposes, they are fundamentally ludic in character.

Sport Is Ludic

The term *ludic* is derived from the Latin word ludus, meaning play or game. When we state that sport is a **ludic activity**, we imply that it is based on elements of play and games. We recognize that (a) not all sport is play, as there are professional forms of sport; (b) not all sports are games, (e.g., archery and swimming); and (c) not all contests are playful—war, for example, is a deadly, earnest contest. But we also recognize that as a playful contest (Birrell, 1978) sport shares at least two elements with all ludic activities: an uncertain outcome and sanctioned display.

As Goffman (1961) has shown, it is these two elements that make games and sport fun. With the outcome uncertain until the last minute, all types of ludic activities maintain suspense and the excitement of involvement. The sanctioned display gives participants "an opportunity to exhibit attributes valued in the wider social world, such as dexterity, strength, knowledge, intelligence, courage, and self-control" (Goffman, 1961, p. 68).

In sport, sanctioned display typically emphasizes the demonstration of physical prowess. The display of physical skills and abilities under conditions of high risk often is especially valued by athletic peers and sport spectators. Poise under pressure, as reflected in aesthetic athletic movements, is also greatly admired. As Bensman and Lilienfeld (1973) have observed, the athlete, like the performing artist,

> must produce a final, instantaneous and temporal image of the world as embodied in the score without error, with full mastery of highly developed technical means of performance, and with sufficient warmth, spontaneity, and freshness to involve an audience to suspend its awareness of all other worlds but the world framed by the score and created by the performance. (p. 61)

In summary, the combination of the competitive and ludic elements of sport involves athlete and spectator alike—affectively, behaviorally, and cognitively.

SPORT IS A SOCIAL INSTITUTION

We have discussed elements of sport and how it is a form of social involvement. This section examines more abstractly how sport can be considered a social **institution**.

The term *institution*

> denotes an aspect of social life in which distinctive value-orientations and interests, centering upon large and important social concerns . . . generate or are accompanied by distinctive modes of social interaction. Its use emphasizes "important" social phenomena; relationships of "strategic structural significance." (Schneider, 1964, p. 338)

We argue that the magnitude and pervasiveness of sport in society readily justifies its consideration as a social institution. As will be shown throughout this book, sport, like other social institutions, constitutes a distinctive kind of social organization; represents a unique form of social activity; provides a basis of social identity; serves as a link to other social structures; and acts as an agent of social control.

Institutionalization

One cannot fully understand sport as a social institution without addressing the issue of institutionalization and the potential issue of *de*institutionalization. Specifically, one must probe how sport became an institution; how this status is maintained; how it has changed; and how it might be destroyed.

The sociological concept of **institutionalization** in its simplest sense refers to the global process by which social units and social activities become organized in a relatively permanent and enduring way. A major outcome of the process in any particular case is that *one* way of doing something becomes *the* accepted way. For example, most of us are so accustomed to how we currently play

baseball in North America that it is difficult for us to imagine that the game was once played rather differently or to recognize that different cultures play other forms of baseball (e.g., Finnish baseball, the national game of Finland).

Modern sports are such readily accepted aspects of our daily lives that we rarely ask how they came into being. Yet to understand modern sports we need to know how they evolved from rudimentary ludic forms, folk games, religious rituals, military exercises, or early survival activities.

Ludic Institutionalization

Ingham (1978) describes the transformation of play and game forms into modern sport as the process of ludic institutionalization. Ingham suggests that the process

> can be comprehended most clearly in the form of a continuum upon which play and sport are the polar extremities. The continuum *per se* represents the degree to which "ludic" activity is regulated, formalized (or patterned), legitimated, and even ideologized. At the same time, the continuum represents the degree to which "ludic" activity is instrumentalized or made utilitarian. . . . The continuum represents the degree to which "ludic" activity is more or less voluntary and embodied or, conversely, more or less regimented and estranged. (p. 277)

Whether you are studying sport in general within a given society at a particular point in history or a specific sport in a particular culture, the following questions can be asked:

- What is the social distribution of the sport?

- What is the kind or degree of social participation in the sport?
- What is the social thought about the sport?
- What is the social structure of the sport?

Social Distribution. The question of social distribution tries to determine the social origin of a sport in terms of a particular time and place and to trace its pattern of **cultural diffusion**. It is fascinating to study how certain sports seem to have worldwide appeal while others are often restricted to national boundaries, and still others are only popular within certain regions of a country. The official sports and demonstration sports (e.g., baseball at the 1984 Los Angeles Summer Olympics, curling at the 1988 Calgary Winter Olympics, and tae-kwon-do at the 1988 Seoul Summer Olympics) within the Olympic Games illustrate the issue of the social distribution and cultural diffusion of sport.

Kind or Degree of Social Participation.
The question of social participation examines the number of people involved in a sport and how they are involved at different levels. It also analyzes the degree to which sport has become democratized (i.e., open to all regardless of age, class, education, ethnicity, gender, physical disability, race, etc.). A focus on the process of **democratization** in sport raises many issues and questions for serious study. Why were women not allowed as spectators at the original Olympic Games? Why were Jews barred from golf and country clubs in most of the United States before World War II? Why are no blacks presently head football coaches in professional football?

Social Thought. The question of social thought about a sport analyzes how a sport is perceived by different segments of the public and tries to determine its degree of **legitimation** (i.e., the extent to which it is held

to be a proper and respectable activity in the eyes of the general public). A focus on the process of legitimation in sport directs our attention to why some sports are legal and others illegal (e.g., cockfighting and bullfighting in North America); why some sports are viewed as proper for men to participate in but not for women (e.g., football and wrestling); and what reasons are offered to justify the importance of a sport (e.g., for education, entertainment, fitness and health, control of juvenile delinquency).

Social Structure. The question of social structure looks at a sport's structural elements and cultural components. Modern sport differs from earlier sport forms in the degree to which it has become rationalized (i.e., characterized by efficient means and a calculating spirit). A focus on the process of **rationalization** in sport demonstrates most clearly the nature of ludic institutionalization. That is, expressive and nonutilitarian activities have been transformed into instrumental and utilitarian activities (e.g., the evolution from creative playground free play to commercialized sport leagues).

Effects of Rationalization on Sport

Every structural element of sport is affected as sport is transformed from a largely informal to a basically formal ludic activity. Premodern sports, like modern sports, typically had some degree of organization, procedures, personnel, equipment, and athletic training; often there was some degree of sponsorship and concern for records and meeting the needs of various social groups. With the rationalization of modern sport, however, sport organizations have become bureaucratized; procedures formalized; personnel specialized; equipment technologized; training professionalized; sponsorship commercialized; and records quantified. Often the needs of spectators supersede those of participants in the decision-making process of modern sport.

SPORT IS A SOCIAL AND CULTURAL PRODUCT

As students of sport we need to go beyond a mere tabulation of the number of people involved or the amount of money expended and examine more qualitative dimensions of sport. We seek the *meaning* of sport—for individuals, for collective lifestyles, and for society. We begin the task here, and continue throughout this book.

The meaning of sport in a particular society is greatly influenced by the evolving economic and political organizations and the values of that society. Sport is a socio-cultural product. In one society the purpose and meaning of a sport may emphasize the values of competition, aggressiveness, and violence. This is true of most team sports in North America. Another society may stress cooperative social interaction, friendship, physical fitness, skill, and a respite from the stresses of daily life.

Over time, the values, purpose, and meaning of sport may change greatly (Guttmann, 1988). China, for example, first entered the international sport arena in the 1970s by engaging in "Ping-Pong" diplomacy. By 1984 athletes from China competed more seriously—and with great success—in the Summer Olympic Games. This success was duplicated in the 1988 Seoul Summer Olympics, where the Chinese did especially well in diving and volleyball.

Cultural Roots of Sport

Sport has become embedded in the social life of nations for a variety of reasons. In North America the consumption of sport is a modern equivalent of the live theater that used to be so popular. Like theater, sport stirs the emotions and often reaches an exciting and suspenseful climax. Clearly the division of play in sport into periods or halves, the presentation of half-time shows, the use of cheerleaders and bands, the adulation of heroes and heroines, and the wearing of distinct uniforms all parallel the traditional form of Western theater.

Modern sport also seems rooted in the early pagan festivals of Europe, which celebrated seasonal change. These ceremonies provided an annual calendar that functioned to "draw all people together to emphasize their similarities and common heritage; to minimize their differences; and to contribute to their thinking, feeling, and acting alike" (Warner, 1953, p. 4). Thus, in North America, we have our own ceremonial sport calendar: in the fall, the U.S. Open Tennis Championships, the World Series, football weekends (homecoming), and the Grey Cup (Canada); in the winter, College Bowls and the Super Bowl; and, in the spring, the Indianapolis 500, the Kentucky Derby, the Masters Golf Tournament, the NCAA and NBA Basketball Championships, and the Stanley Cup.

Interestingly, there are no major sport festivals in the summer, except for Wimbledon and the Summer Olympics. Perhaps this is because major sport events are used by consumers as a relief valve or escape from everyday life. In the summer, we have vacations and more outdoor social events to serve this purpose. Television and sport executives, knowing that the viewing audience is likely to be smaller in the summer, do not schedule major events in this period. The exception is events that have taken place during the summer since well before the advent of television, like the Summer Olympics or Wimbledon.

Interaction of Sport and Culture

Sport, like any other set of norms, beliefs, and values, may be exported to other soci-

The division of play into periods allows for half-time theater.

eties. The sport may retain its original meaning and form; more likely it will take on a different meaning and form that is more consistent with the new culture (Donnelly and Young, 1985; Fox, 1961; Riesman & Denney, 1951). For example, as Highlight 1.5 illustrates, in Japan, professional baseball reflects the traditional pattern of strong group loyalty in that society. As a result, the practice of trading players and firing managers is quite different from North America (Andreano, 1965; Benedict, 1946; Whiting, 1976).

Traditionally, basketball emphasizes the concepts of cooperation and competition. But as Allison (1980) reports, the particular type of competition and cooperation that emerges is defined by the value orientations of the larger culture. For example, Anglo coaches working on a Navajo reservation have reported that Navajo athletes appear to lack the drive for complete superiority and domination over an opponent (i.e., they lack the "killer instinct"); they compete more against themselves than against their opponents; and, unlike Anglo athletes, they shun public rec-

ognition for their individual performance (i.e., similarity of status is valued and maintained). All of these emphases help foster feelings of group solidarity among the Navajo.

To illustrate further, Ross (1985) suggests that American baseball is a pastoral sport that stresses harmony, the individual, a slower pace, and ritual. In contrast, football is a heroic sport that is more complex, violent, warlike, and reflective of a collective pattern of life. Ross suggests that with these attributes it is not surprising that football has become the more popular sport in North America. He believes that the characteristics of football are more representative of contemporary culture. Baseball survives, he says, because it is an established American tradition and reflects a past way of life that people are fond of recalling.

Finlay (1971) suggests another interpretation of the meaning of football and baseball, based on a comparison with other forms of football (e.g., soccer and rugby). He argues that football is the dominant spectator game in North America because it represents a "corporate sport" that is more attuned than baseball to our present stage of mature capitalism, with its large corporations. Finlay notes that baseball more closely matches the early stages of capitalism, with its stress on individual entrepreneurs.

Similarly, the increasing popularity of squash in North America has been attributed to its intensely competitive character. Aggressiveness, fitness, self-discipline, and domination of the opponent are essential for success in squash. The sport demands attributes similar to those required for success in today's business world; for this reason, it is argued, the game has become popular among higher status men and women.

National Sports. There are many examples of societies that value one sport more than others. Canadians value hockey so highly it

Highlight 1.5
Baseball as a Mirror of Japanese Society

In North America, professional and collegiate trainers, managers, and coaches are released, or fired, when their teams continually lose. Poor performance is much less likely to lead to firing in Japan, where the cultural norms of the wider society are different.

Japanese culture traditionally places a high value on personal loyalty. The culture is also more group-oriented. That is, smooth-running social groups with strong integration of everyone into the group are given higher priority than individuals. These values result in low player turnover in baseball. Players recognize that they should be loyal and that their popularity is closely tied to a particular team. And, owners are afraid of appearing improper and losing face if they trade players.

When someone's performance declines, Japanese teams employ a number of face-saving strategies. One strategy is the ritualized process of *Kyuyo*, meaning rest or recuperation. Whiting (1976) describes how *Kyuyo* temporarily relieves professional baseball managers of their responsibility.

> In baseball, it consists of the owner of a sagging team ordering his manager to take a rest for a month or so. Another coach is usually appointed acting manager, while the manager goes off by himself to meditate on the situation. The stated purpose of a *Kyuyo* is to "refresh the mood of the team," and the wise owner knows that it can be a useful device. He realizes that if the players really respect their manager, they will feel that they have let him down. His departure may be just the spark needed to ignite their flagging spirit to shame them into playing better baseball. Their shame—and the trauma of separation from the surrogate father—will end when play improves. . . . Inevitably, the *Kyuyo* is accompanied by a flurry of statements from the owner, the front office, the coaches and the top players to the effect that the responsibility for the slump lies with everyone, not just the manager. (p. 48)*

As poorly performing teams usually improve over a period of time, managers sometimes return to their teams with much fanfare. However, some managers are destined never to return, and the *Kyuyo* serves as an effective "cooling out" process before a permanent reassignment (Whiting, 1976).

> The manager who takes a sick leave and does not come back has not really been fired and he has not really resigned. He just isn't there anymore. (p. 53)*

*Note. Reprinted by the permission of Dodd Mead & Co. *The Chrysanthemum and the Bat: The Game Japanese Play*, Robert Whiting, copyright 1976.

has been called *Canada's culture*; the Chinese have swimming and Ping-Pong; the Spanish Basques, jai alai; the Japanese, baseball and sumo wrestling; and the British and Europeans, soccer. It is interesting to note that Eastern European countries do not appear to value one specific sport over others; they emphasize instead a set of sports, including many sports that involve international competition. The governments promote these sports and sponsor training programs in an attempt to obtain international prestige.

Regional Sports. Sports also vary in popularity within different regions of a particular country. Regions that value a specific sport tend to produce a greater number of high quality athletes for college and professional teams. Rooney (1974) analyzed the birthplace of college and professional athletes in the U.S. and found that a higher percentage of athletes in baseball were born in California and the south; more football players came from Texas, Ohio, and Pennsylvania; more basketball players from Illinois, Indiana, and Kentucky; more stock car racers from the Carolinas; and more soccer players from the Northeastern states.

Although national cultural forms tend to be relatively stable and enduring (e.g., baseball in the United States and hockey in Canada), regional differences seem to change rather quickly, because of shifts in migration patterns or changes in how sports are organized and funded. In a recent study of the production of football players, Rooney (1986) found that the dominance of Ohio and Pennsylvania in the north and Texas in the south declined during the 1970s. By the early 1980s Mississippi and Louisiana were the leading producers. The south, in total, was now producing twice as many college football players per capita as the north. Yet in basketball, despite increased opportunities for southern blacks to compete, the highest per capita pro-

duction of high school basketball players was still found in small towns in Illinois and Indiana. This is interesting because even though a career in professional basketball seems more likely if one is black, at the high school and college level basketball is still highly valued and salient in small midwestern towns, where there are fewer blacks.

As Wecter (1937) stated, long before the sociology of sport was envisioned, students of society should study

> . . . how cricket, with its white clothes and leisured boredom, and sudden crises met with cool mastery to the ripple of applause among the teacups and cucumber sandwiches, is an epitome of the British Empire. Or why the bull-fight with its scarlet cape and gold braid, its fierce pride and cruelty, and the quixotic futility of its perils, is the essence of Spain. Or that football with its rugged individualism, and baseball with its equality of opportunity, are valid American symbols. . . . Most of these things have been felt or hinted before, but their synthesis has never been made. (p. 428)

SPORT AS REFLECTION, REINFORCEMENT, AND RESISTANCE

The preceding section has shown how sport can reflect the values and norms of the wider society. A common approach in the sociology of sport is to view sport as a microcosm of society that enables us to study the structure, processes, and problems of contemporary society in a simpler context.

There are actually three basic patterns in the way sport relates to society and culture.

First, sport reflects society and culture. Second, sport reinforces social inequalities. These we call the **reflection thesis** and the **reinforcement thesis**. Sport is an instrument of the status quo in both of these instances; it helps things stay as they are.

A third pattern for the relationship between sport and society is called the **resistance thesis**. This has been proposed in recent years to emphasize that primary and secondary sport participants are sometimes in conflict with some of the basic norms and values of society.

Reflection Thesis

The reflection approach has been used to portray the positive aspects of society and sport. In the early 1960s sport was praised for its contribution to race relations and to international understanding. For example, although American blacks could not readily participate in some predominantly white social institutions (e.g., universities and corporate boards), professional baseball and football offered equal opportunities to blacks and whites, at least according to some journalists and team owners. Similarly, the Olympic Games were presented as a forum that promoted international understanding, peace, and goodwill.

Unfortunately, examining sport as a mirror of society reveals imperfections as well. Scholars and journalists examining sport quickly discovered that it was the *business* of college sport—more than the goal of providing players with a quality education—that explained the questionable athlete recruitment policies of some large university sport programs. Similarly, the Olympic Games have been subject to boycotts, politically inspired disagreements (even violence), and charges of biased officiating, along with their positive contributions.

In the reflection thesis, people find in sport the same values, beliefs, and norms that exist elsewhere in society. All members of sport are members of the wider society as well; their ways of thinking before they came to sport continue to influence them. Only if sport was very compelling in teaching alternative ways of doing things would we expect to find major differences from the wider society. Sport is apparently *not* this type of institution.

An example of the common pattern is when a successful business executive tries to make money with a professional baseball franchise. This person is not likely to forget his or her profit-making orientation in making decisions that affect players and fans.

Reinforcement Thesis

Just as society is stratified into those who have a great deal of what is valued (e.g., power, wealth, and prestige) and those who have little, sport has offered examples of marked inequality. It has become clear, for example, that some black athletes and some women athletes are disadvantaged, that the mass media and the owners of large corporations control professional and Olympic sport to their advantage (see chapter 5), and that player strikes occur because athletes sometimes work together to try to improve their earnings or their working conditions (e.g., free agency, length of season, pensions, and medical care).

In the case of reinforcement of social inequalities, sport gives yet another social setting in which the values, beliefs, and norms of the wider society supporting inequalities are allowed to persist. This happens because people in sport bring their self-interests and prejudice-supporting beliefs and values (e.g., against blacks, the disabled, women, or older people) with them when they come to the sport domain. People would have to leave self-interests and prejudices at the gate of the sport arena for there to be any hope of few inequalities. Some have thought this would occur, but it appears to have been only wishful thinking!

Resistance Thesis

Sometimes sport and sport participants are in conflict with the norms and values of society. Sport, in other words, can reveal social conflicts. One variant of the resistance thesis emphasizes how sport sometimes contains opposition by the disadvantaged groups within the sport setting. Here it is not an opposition between sport and those outside sport, but rather between vying interest groups in sport—between blacks and whites, athletes and their employers, and females and males. The resistance pattern differs from the reinforcement process in that the disadvantaged group seeks to change the status quo by achieving somewhat greater opportunity. Under the reinforcement process this does not occur. As we will show in chapters 10 and 11, resistance in sport may lead to changes in the wider society. In this way, sport may operate as a vehicle for broader social change.

Another variant of the resistance thesis is where involvement with sport by the disadvantaged group serves to partially defuse their dissatisfaction. Sport provides an avenue for venting frustrations. On the surface, this might seem simply to reinforce inequalities. This would be true if resistance stopped here, but it may continue. This means that there is potential for social change. The sport participants are dissatisfied, and, therefore, in conflict with the wider society. The question is whether sport can defuse the frustrations fully and for how long. The resistance thesis suggests that the defusing process will not be successful over the long term.

THE ILLUSION AND REALITY OF SPORT

As sport has become a more significant element in our lives, there has been increasing interest in understanding both the **front region** and the **back region** of this social activity. Scholars have recognized that there is a need to understand more than the readily visible side of sport. To thoroughly understand the meaning and impact of sport on our lives, we must not accept simple descriptions or explanations; rather, we must become more critical and analytical, and consider alternative explanations or interpretations. This involves the development of a sociological consciousness whereby we learn to discover and separate the *illusions* from the *realities* of this part of our social world.

Skepticism About Sport

A basic premise of sociology and the sociology of sport is that illusion and reality are the two basic levels of meaning for social events and social behavior. The second level—the realities—may be hidden, intentionally or unintentionally, by those responsible for reporting, promoting, or controlling a particular area of activity. Hence, the sociologist brings to the sport world a suspicion that all may not be as it appears. The sociologist is skeptical of simple, official explanations until he or she knows much more. In other words, the sociologist looks beyond the conventional wisdoms and the myths that often are created by officials and perpetuated by the media. Unfortunately, these assumptions, or wisdoms, usually are accepted without question by the public. Even educators and parents are involved in creating and maintaining some of these myths. Sport officials may find that certain myths support their interests and make their organizations look good. Others accept myths because they have no information to the contrary.

Some examples of the debunking of myths in the sociology of sport are studies that have addressed the following questions:

- Are professional athletes overpaid or underpaid by owners?
- Do college athletes receive a high-quality education that enhances their future opportunities?
- Does a professional sport career provide an avenue of social mobility for athletes?
- Are sport riots random, isolated events unrelated to the society at large?
- Do women and blacks, compared with men and whites, respectively, have an equal opportunity to participate and achieve their potential in all sport roles?

Highlight 1.6 gives some reasons why the myth that women have equality in sport should be questioned, and not accepted at face value.

The Darker Side of Sport

Society at large always has a darker side—deviance, crime, poverty, discrimination, and appalling working and living conditions (Berger, 1963). So, too, does sport have a darker side. Some owners and coaches have exploited athletes; some athletes and coaches engage in deviant or illegal behavior; not every adolescent has an equal opportunity to achieve his or her potential in the world of competitive sport; and not every person is treated equally—one's age, ethnic background, socioeconomic background, or gender still make a difference.

You will find that Highlight 1.7 shatters some illusions about college sport in the United States. It reveals selected examples of the seamier realities of the social and academic life experienced by some U.S. college "scholarship" athletes.

Lately there has been increased social awareness of the seamy side of sport—a development that has parallels in other areas of social life. Until about 20 years ago, the private lives of politicians, religious leaders, and sport heroes were not considered newsworthy. Widespread social dissatisfaction in the 1960s, expressed in part as disenchantment with the Vietnam War and the mobilization of the civil rights and women's movements, helped focus our attention on areas needing improvement. Public interest helped strengthen the field of investigative reporting, by journalists and sociologists, about all aspects of society. Competition increased among the growing number and kinds of mass media, and they began to explore new kinds of news.

In sport the media began to focus more on personalities, issues, and problems. This has meant a much closer scrutiny of athletes' private lives than ever before. This approach also has initiated a raised consciousness on the part of journalists and concerned citizens about the integrity and quality of social life in the sport domain.

CHANGING SPORT

Can we, as individuals, do anything to change aspects of sport that we would define as problems? In trying to answer this question we discover quickly that many problems are deeply rooted in traditional ways of living and often are supported and perpetuated by the vested interests of powerful groups. Often the problems are embedded in social structure and culture and, therefore, are difficult to change. So can an individual have an im-

---

Highlight 1.6
The Myth of Gender Equality in Sport

Although women are acquiring increased opportunities to participate in sport, they still have fewer opportunities than men do. This inequality is reflected in a number of ways.

- There are fewer teams and leagues available for women.
- The least desirable hours for the use of facilities are allocated to women.
- There are fewer events at the Olympic Games for women.
- Fewer women than men get involved as coaches and administrators of women's sport.
- Fewer funds are allocated to women's sport by community agencies, government agencies, and educational institutions.

Here are the results of some relevant research about the myth of gender equality in sport. Acosta and Carpenter (1985) found that in Iowa, where the state high school girls' basketball tournament attracts at least as many spectators as the boys' tournament, only 12% of the girls' basketball teams are coached by women. At higher levels of sport administration, Abbott and Smith (1984) reported, 86.5% of the NCAA athletic programs are administered by a male, and 38% do not have even one female involved at the administrative level. Similarly, by 1986 only about 16% of college athletic budgets were allocated to women's sports, and only three women sat on the 86-member International Olympic Committee.

Further studies (see chapter 9) have shown that female student-athletes participate in reduced league schedules and receive fewer athletic scholarships, despite recent legislation requiring equality; that prize money in women's professional and amateur tennis, golf, skiing, and track events is less than that for comparable men's events; that female athletes receive less media coverage and fewer opportunities for commercial endorsements; and that women are still actively discouraged from participating and striving for excellence in some sports, because of inaccurate beliefs that the sport (e.g., marathons) or the level of competition will be physiologically or medically detrimental to them. Thus, it is still a myth that women have equal access to all sport roles, at all levels of involvement. Herein lies a challenge for your generation!

---

pact on the future of sport? The answer, surprisingly, is yes.

It is an axiom of the sociological approach that we all affect our social environment and history while being shaped by it, however limited this effect may be. C. Wright Mills (1959), a major figure in North American sociology, summarized this issue:

> Every individual lives, from one generation to the next, in some society . . . lives out a biography and

Highlight 1.7
The Seamy Side of U.S. College Sport

For years college athletes and coaches were revered as role models for young athletes. They were seen as honest, intelligent, clean-cut, and hardworking amateurs who demonstrated complete loyalty to the team and institution. College sport has shown a seamy side recently, especially since the early 1970s, as it has changed from a form of entertainment for the players, student body, and alumni to a big business. Success is now so important that deviant practices have increased alarmingly. Unfortunately, in February, 1989, 25 institutions were under NCAA sanctions for various rule violations.

By engaging in illegitimate practices or by condoning the practices of alumni or local boosters on their behalf, athletic department officials have deceived their public and, more seriously, have cheated their student-athletes. The abuses often begin during recruiting, where reported and documented violations have included illegal gifts of money to recruits, promises of cars or other material gifts for those who sign letters of intent, and offers of sexual favors during weekend recruiting visits. During admissions procedures, abuses include creating and opening back doors for academically unqualified students who can help a team be successful on the field. Until 1986, when the NCAA introduced Proposition 48 (requiring all prospective college athletes to achieve a minimum grade point average in a core high school curriculum and a minimal score on a standard aptitude test), even illiterate athletes with little chance of achieving success in

the classroom were admitted to college. Some students were recruited for their athletic skills, and then given remedial courses to try to keep them eligible for 3 or 4 years of athletic competition.

Although Proposition 48 has reduced these academic violations, some problems still occur. Some of the alleged violations of academic and athletic regulations include receiving illegal payments from boosters; receiving payments from player agents who hope to represent the athlete in negotiations with professional owners; receiving academic credit for a class never attended; securing interest-free loans for relatives; getting free meals or clothing at local businesses; participating in gambling or point shaving to earn extra money; consuming illegal substances to enhance performance; receiving suspended or lighter than normal sentences when found guilty of theft, rape, assault, or selling or using illegal drugs; and living in special dormitories where athletes receive first class treatment compared with that provided students in other dormitories.

Athletes who are marginal students are sometimes exploited to serve the business interests of high-pressure college sport programs, where victories and national television exposure are required and expected at all costs. For these athletes, the costs are high—some are encouraged to enroll in the easiest courses, which are the least useful for later occupational success, and some have a considerably lower graduation rate than their classmates (see chapter 2).

(Cont.)

Highlight 1.7 Continued

Yet some people condone such academic abuse, neglect, and exploitation, believing that college administrators are providing the unqualified or ill-prepared student with a chance in life. To illustrate, in 1986 a remedial instructor who had been fired for speaking out against preferential treatment for athletes brought a civil suit against two university administrators. An attorney argued that while they could not make the athlete a perfect student, at least they could teach him to read and write so that he could obtain a respectable job after his athletic career was over.

Is the teaching of elementary school reading and writing really the mission of higher education?

Clearly there is a seamy side to college sport. Fortunately, abuses are still the exception, and where they occur they are being addressed by college administrators and the NCAA. But it may take years to restore the academic and athletic integrity of some college sport programs. Meanwhile we, as sport sociologists and as concerned citizens, need to study why and how these practices began and continue.

. . . lives it out within some historical sequence. By the fact of his living, he contributes, however minutely, to the course of its history, even as he is made by society and by its historical push and shove. (p. 6)

This alone is small consolation, though, for those of us who want substantially to shape the destiny of some aspect of sport. Fortunately Mills also emphasizes that one payoff from the "sociological imagination," or from coming to have an informed sociological understanding of society, is that

the individual can understand his own experiences and gauge his own fate only by locating himself within his period, that he can know his own chances in life only by becoming aware of those of all individuals in his circumstances. In many ways it

is a terrible lesson; in many ways a magnificent one. (p. 5)

Mills adds that "knowledge is power," if we choose to act on it. When we know what is going on in society and act accordingly, we stand some chance of maximizing our own opportunities and making a real impact on others. We can follow two broad strategies in acting on sociological understanding: individual coping procedures and group-based action.

Individual Action

Under the individual response, you act to "work the system" to your benefit. For example, if you learn about the negative effects of highly competitive sport on children, you can take this into account when introducing your own children to sport and steer them toward the best sport environment for their purposes. Or you can volunteer to help in the organization of a local team or sport and check it out before your child becomes involved. From this position you can lobby for specific changes.

A recent book by Robert Kennedy (1986), an American demographer, emphasizes that we all must make choices of this type. He says,

> Your power of choice means that while "society" or some mix of "social forces" may contain your options, they do not entirely determine your life. . . . What the individual chooses to do at certain points in life can make a differ-

ence—personal actions have consequences. Opportunities can be exploited or squandered, difficulties can be overcome or compounded. (p. 5)

Group Action

You can also consider getting involved in groups or organizations that are calling for changes in sport—this type of group is found in many communities. Here, too, knowledge of the social and cultural aspects of sport is a prerequisite for making decisions about

An involved parent can make a difference in the quality of a child's sport experience.

which organizations are most appropriate to your interests. Your values will also determine your choices of goals and organizations. For example, you may choose to support in your community the funding of highly competitive sport programs or work toward more low-intensity recreational sport opportunities; or choose to lobby for construction of a new hockey arena rather than a library.

History is made by people acting in groups and organizations. Be warned, though, that this strategy of political action through groups and organizations can be a frustrating, slow road. Many of your efforts may be blocked, for a variety of political, economic, or legal reasons (McPherson, 1986). Dominant interest groups opposed to social change are not likely to give ground easily, and they have considerable organizational power. Often money and status is on the line for those who own, manage, or volunteer in sport organizations. Sport reinforces social inequalities, as we have said.

Political struggles can be won, however. There are some recent examples from ongoing protest movements in the U.S. and Canada. The civil rights movement in the U.S., which we have already mentioned, led to breaking the barriers that kept blacks out of professional team sports. The women's movement has had partial success in pursuing equality of the sexes in sport. The labor movement in North American sport has brought better wages and job conditions for some sport employees (i.e., players), often by creating unions and going on strike. These developments should motivate us toward political action if we are interested in initiating changes.

WRAP-UP

This chapter has presented a sociological definition of sport that considers sport as a form of social involvement, a ludic physical activity, a social institution, and a cultural product. We have also suggested how significant sport is in our social life by describing the extent to which people are involved in sport.

We have discussed how sport is related to the wider society and culture in three different ways. First, sport *reflects* society and culture, its social patterns, and its values. Second, sport is an arena where social inequalities, which abound elsewhere in society, are *reinforced*. Third, sport not only reflects and reinforces social inequalities but is a setting in which disadvantaged groups will sometimes *resist* those with power and social advantage. Sport is an arena for struggle between contending social groups. These struggles may help initiate changes in the wider society and culture.

Finally, we stressed that there is both an illusion and a reality within the world of sport. Both need to be discovered and described, and the relationship between them understood. The sociology of sport can make an important contribution to this type of analysis. This is important if we are to arrive at valid knowledge of the sport world around us.

REFERENCES

Abbott, A., & Smith, D.R. (1984). Governmental constraints and labor market mobility: Turnover among college athletic personnel. *Work and Occupations*, **11**(1), 29–53.

Acosta, R.V., & Carpenter, L.J. (1985). Women in athletics: A status report. *Journal of Physical Education, Recreation and Dance*, **56**(6), 30–34.

Allison, M.T. (1980). Competition and cooperation: A sociocultural perspective. *International Review of Sport Sociology*, **15**(3/4), 93–104.

Andreano, R. (1965). Japanese baseball. In R. Andreano (Ed.), *No joy in Mudville: The dilemma of major league baseball* (pp. 61–76). Cambridge, MA: Schenkman.

Benedict, R.R. (1946). *The chrysanthemum and the sword*. New York: New American Library.

Bensman, J., & Lilienfeld, R. (1973). *Craft and consciousness*. New York: Wiley.

Berger, P.L. (1963). *Invitation to sociology: A humanistic perspective*. Garden City, NY: Anchor.

Birrell, S.J. (1978). *Sporting encounters: An examination of the work of Erving Goffman and its application to sport*. Unpublished doctoral dissertation, University of Massachusetts, Amherst.

Boyle, R.H. (1963). *Sport: Mirror of American life*. Boston: Little, Brown.

Brand, D. (1988, July 25). A nation of healthy worrywarts? *Time*, pp. 40–41.

Brandmeyer, G.A., & Alexander, L.K. (1986). "I caught the dream": The adult baseball camp as a fantasy leisure. *Journal of Leisure Research*, **18**(1), 26–39.

Canada Fitness Survey. (1983). *Fitness and lifestyle in Canada*. Ottawa: Government of Canada.

Donnelly, P., & Young, K.M. (1985). Reproduction and transformation of cultural forms in sport. *International Review for the Sociology of Sport*, **20**, 19–37.

Finlay, J.L. (1971). Homo ludens (Americanus). *Queen's Quarterly*, **78**, 353–364.

Fox, J.R. (1961). Pueblo baseball: A new use for old witchcraft. *Journal of American Folklore*, **74**, 9–15.

Goffman, E. (1961). *Encounters*. Indianapolis: Bobbs-Merrill.

Gouldner, A.W. (1965). *Enter Plato*. New York: Basic Books.

Guttmann, A. (1988). *A whole new ball game: An interpretation of American sports*. Chapel Hill: University of North Carolina Press.

Ingham, A.G. (1978). *American sport in transition: The maturation of industrial capitalism and its impact upon sport*. Unpublished doctoral dissertation, University of Massachusetts, Amherst.

Kennedy, Robert E., Jr. (1986). *Life choices: Applying sociology*. New York: Holt, Rinehart and Winston.

Kenyon, G.S., & Schutz, R.W. (1970). Patterns of involvement in sport: A stochastic view. In G.S. Kenyon & T.M. Grogg (Eds.), *Contemporary psychology of sport* (pp. 781–797). Chicago: Athletic Institute.

Loy, J.W. (1981). An emerging theory of sport spectatorship: Implications for the Olympic Games. In J. Segrave & O. Chu (Eds.), *Olympism* (pp. 262–294). Champaign, IL: Human Kinetics.

McPherson, B.D. (1986). Policy-oriented research in youth sport: An analysis of the process and product. In R. Rees & A. Miracle (Eds.), *Sport and social theory* (pp. 255–287). Champaign, IL: Human Kinetics.

Miller Brewing Company. (1983). *Miller Lite report on American attitudes toward sports 1983*. Milwaukee: Author.

Mills, C.W. (1959). *The sociological imagination*. New York: Oxford University Press.

Nixon, H.L. (1986). Social order in a leisure setting: The case of recreational swimmers in a pool. *Sociology of Sport Journal*, **3**, 320–332.

Riesman, D., & Denney, R. (1951). Football in America: A study in cultural diffusion. *American Quarterly*, **3**, 309–319.

Rooney, J.F. (1974). *A geography of American sport: From Cabin Creek to Anaheim*. Reading, MA: Addison-Wesley.

Rooney, J.F. (1986, September). The pigskin cult and other sunbelt sports. *American Demographics*, **8**, 38–43.

Ross, M. (1985). Football red and baseball green. In D.L. Vanderwerken & S.K.

Wertz (Eds.), *Sport inside out*. Fort Worth: Texas Christian University Press.

Scorecard. (1987, June 8). *Sports Illustrated*, p. 17.

Schneider, T. (1964). Institution. In J. Gould & W. Kolb (Eds.), *A dictionary of the social sciences* (p. 338). New York: Free Press.

Tylor, E.B. (1913). *Primitive culture: Research into the development of mythology, philosophy, religion, language, art and custom*. London: John Murray.

Waldman, L. (1988). *1987 survey on sports attendance*. Hightstown, NJ: Daily Racing Form.

Warner, W.L. (1953). *American life: Dream and reality*. Chicago: University of Chicago Press.

Wecter, D. (1937). *The saga of American society: A record of social aspirations, 1607–1937*. New York: Charles Scribner.

Weiss, P. (1969). *Sport—A philosophical inquiry*. Carbondale, IL: Southern Illinois University Press.

Whiting, R. (1976, May). Bowed but never bloodied. *Sports Illustrated*, 46–48.

Whiting, R. (1976). *The chrysanthemum and the bat: The game Japanese play*. Tokyo: Permanent Press.

P A R T   I

SPORT REFLECTS CULTURE AND SOCIETY

Part I examines the interrelationships between sport and some of the major social institutions in society—the family, education and youth groups, law, politics, the economy, and the mass media. These enduring societal systems are built on unique sets of norms, values, and beliefs. As central components of social life they are found in every society, although their form may vary in different cultures.

As modern sport has become more complex and bureaucratic it, too, has become an institution in most societies. Yet in comparison to the other social institutions, sport is often viewed as a trivial institution that has little consequence for the rest of social life. In reality, sport *is* a significant and enduring element in the social and cultural life of most modern societies. Just as the other social institutions are woven into a social fabric, so is sport an integral part of a society. Sport, whether amateur or professional, in some way interacts with all of our major social institutions. As you will learn in Part I, sport reflects and reinforces many of society's values, norms, and beliefs. In turn, sport influences the major institutional sectors of society.

Part I begins with two chapters that focus on the socializing institution of the family. Here we examine how individuals become socialized into sport within the context of the family (chapter 2) and of school and youth groups (chapter 3). Chapter 2 also considers how what we learn through sport involvement is reflected in other social contexts and examines the process by which we are desocialized from the world of sport as participants.

The remainder of Part I examines the interaction between sport and other institutions, such as politics and law (chapter 4); the economy (chapter 5) and the mass media (chapter 6). Specifically, we consider how and why a two-way interaction has evolved in the 20th century between sport and the economic, legal, political, and mass communication systems.

In general, the increasing interaction of these other institutions with sport has resulted from the rationalization and professionalization of sport and from the discovery that sport can generate profits, whether for the corporate sector or for cities, universities, and colleges. That is, sport reflects the basic economic structure that prevails at this time.

For each institution, we discuss the nature of the interaction with sport and the consequences of the linkage—for individuals and for sport organizations, communities, and nations.

C H A P T E R   2

Sport, Socialization, and the Family

Socialization is a complex developmental learning process that teaches the knowledge, values, and norms essential to participation in social life. First we learn how to be a family member. Then we learn how to fit into other social institutions. Through socialization we learn all types of social roles—sex roles, work roles, leisure roles—and develop a sense of self.

Not all individuals within a given **generation** and not all generations experience the same socialization process. Rather, we are exposed to different values, beliefs, norms, and opportunities because of variations in social class, ethnicity, race, and gender. Where we live (which region and whether it is urban or rural) and when we live in the history of a society are important factors. Despite the considerable variation that occurs within or between generations, we all learn common socially acceptable behaviors, beliefs, values, and norms. The acquisition and internalization of these basic teachings underlie whatever stability culture and society have across time.

Because societies constantly change, each new generation is socialized somewhat differently. People change the culture before passing it on to a new generation, who, in turn, do the same. The socialization process can thus lead to conflict between generations if ways of thinking and behaving differ significantly. A recent example from sport would be the relative decline in popularity of traditional team sports (e.g., baseball, football, basketball) in favor of more individual physical activities, such as running, cycling, windsurfing, or tennis. Another example would be the dramatic shift in this century in what sporting activities are considered socially acceptable for women (e.g., from spectating to participating, from jogging to competing in marathons).

APPROACHES TO THE STUDY OF SOCIALIZATION

A number of theoretical approaches for explaining the process of socialization have evolved (Bandura, 1977; Brown, 1982; Goslin, 1969; McPherson, 1981, 1986; Thornton & Nardi, 1975; Wentworth, 1980; Zigler & Child, 1969). Two of the most useful approaches in helping us to understand this process have been the social imitation and symbolic interaction perspectives.

Social Imitation

The **social imitation theory** argues that the individual is more or less passive and learns by observing and modeling the behavior and perceived values, beliefs, and norms espoused by others—the socializing agents. Models for this imitation process can be im-

mediate (e.g., parents, siblings, peers, teachers, coaches) or symbolic (e.g., television personalities or fictional characters with whom the individual does not have face-to-face contact).

It is important to recognize that socialization operates over the entire life cycle, and that while most of the learning occurs during childhood and adolescence we continue to be socialized in various ways throughout our adult life. As a college student, you might be socialized into a specific career. It is also important to understand that through socialization we may learn deviant as well as normative behavioral patterns. This depends on the models that are available and imitated.

Symbolic Interaction

According to the **symbolic interaction perspective**, people participate more actively in the social learning process. The individual defines and interprets the world through interacting with others. This communication between persons based on the symbols and meanings is called **symbolic interaction**. Sometimes the individual reinterprets the social setting and attaches new or different meanings to the learning situation. While relatively little of this reinterpretation occurs among children, from adolescence on we are more free to react to, interpret, and redefine our social world. For example, it is during adolescence that athletes begin privately or publicly to question the values and behaviors expected by coaches and parents. Similarly, during the 1960s some young adults reinterpreted the meaning of sport. Rather than viewing sport as a competitive, win-at-all-costs, team-oriented spectator activity, they played sport for the sake of personal enjoyment—without an audience and without caring who won, or even whether a winner was declared.

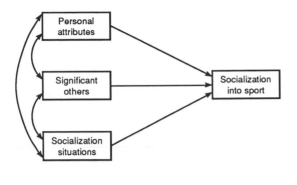

Figure 2.1   A model of factors involved in socialization into sport. *Note*. From "Becoming Involved in Physical Activity and Sport: A Process of Socialization" by G.S. Kenyon and B.D. Mc-Pherson. In *Physical Activity: Human Growth and Development* (p. 305) by G.L. Rarick (Ed.), 1973, Orlando, FL: Academic Press. Copyright 1973 by Academic Press. Reprinted by permission. Model in Rarick adapted from Sewell, 1963.

The symbolic interaction perspective argues that individuals acquire more or less shared meanings of the situation and a definition of the self. They then decide how to present themselves to others (through dress, behavior, and verbal conversation) in specific social settings. Thus, we learn ways of behavior that are situation-specific interactions. As university students you probably adhere to meanings of situations and to a definition of the self that leads you to present yourself differently to others, depending on whether you are at an 8:30 a.m. class, at a job interview, in a bar late at night, in a dormitory with your peers, at home with your parents, or visiting with your friends' parents.

Factors Involved in the Socialization Process

Sewell (1963) has summarized the factors involved in the socialization process. His model, depicted in Figure 2.1, suggests that over the

life cycle an individual with *personal attributes* (ascribed and achieved physical, sociological, and psychological characteristics), observes, imitates, or interacts with *significant others* found within a variety of *socialization situations* (e.g., the family, peer group, sport team or club, school, work group, or mass media).

Although Sewell's factors are important in the process of socialization, the process is not as automatic or deterministic as this model implies. We must recognize that individuals, regardless of the social setting, still partially create their own social and sporting lives. We are not all athletic robots stamped from the same machine. To illustrate, some children are exposed to sport environments and values early in life but decide not to participate. Others begin to participate as children but quit or avoid sport later in childhood. In some family settings, children are forced to participate in various forms of sport, whether they enjoy the activity or not. In contrast, some parents see sport involvement to be of little value and as an inappropriate form of leisure activity. Hence, they actively discourage or prohibit sport involvement by their children from an early age.

The degree to which each social institution affects the learning process depends on the role being learned, the sex of the person being socialized, and the person's stage in the life cycle. For example, the family and school are the most important settings for socialization during childhood; the peer group and the place of employment become more important during adolescent and adult years. Furthermore, the values learned in a particular institution may support, be indifferent to, or oppose the learning of a specific role from another institution.

To illustrate, if sport is not ranked highly in the leisure or career hierarchy of values held by parents, peers, or teachers; if positive reinforcement for participating and competing in sport is not received from significant others; or if opportunities are not created (e.g., equipment, coaching, and competition made available), then it is unlikely an individual will ever become involved in sport, regardless of how much natural athletic ability he or she may possess.

The dominant values and norms of the culture also greatly influence the sport behavioral patterns learned and whether they are continued later in life. If sport is not highly valued in a specific society or region, children are unlikely to be socialized into sport roles as part of their early experiences. It is important to consider the cultural context when studying the process of sport socialization as illustrated in Highlight 2.1. Here we learn how Navajo athletes are socialized by Anglo coaches into the game of basketball. However, different values than those inherent in the Navajo cultural system are stressed. In this example, we see that the Navajo culture contains values that have a strong integrity of their own, and that are at odds with the mainstream culture. As a result, while Navajo youth enjoy the game of basketball, they resist pressures from the dominant culture upon their basic values.

THE FAMILY AND SPORT SOCIALIZATION

The **nuclear family** is the most influential socialization institution in the early years. It is within this primary group that the infant or child learns to participate in social groups, both with siblings and with older adults. During childhood, the **family** provides economic and emotional support; role models for the internalization of values, knowledge, and norms; and the opportunity for involvement in voluntary associations (e.g., youth sport groups). By screening access to elements of the mass media, the family controls

the learning of the wider society's norms and values. In short, the family provides an initial frame of reference from which to view the social world—and the world of sport.

Later, other institutions such as education, the church, voluntary associations, the mass media, the peer group, and political and economic systems began to influence the socialization process. What is learned outside the family may be inconsistent with family socialization. If so, interinstitutional conflict may surface, particularly during the preadolescent and adolescent years when the individual encounters new reference groups (e.g., the peer group, school personnel). But the family's initial and strong effect on socialization strongly influences whether and how children and adolescents should be involved in sport.

How Parents Socialize Their Children

Many of the earliest parent-infant interactions are playful in nature. The child is thus first exposed to formal play and game experiences within the family unit. This exposure is closely related to the gender-role socialization process. Here, from an early age, boys and girls receive toys and games perceived by parents to be appropriate to their biological sex (Greendorfer, 1982).

In the most extreme and traditional form, a parent places a football in a son's crib and a doll in a daughter's crib. Such practices tend to continue throughout childhood, so that through direct and indirect teaching, sport is more likely to become part of the value system and social repertoire of males. Social values and norms can change, however, and some families are beginning to adopt more egalitarian views of child-rearing. An infant, regardless of gender, may now find a football *and* a doll in the crib. It will be interesting to

Highlight 2.1
Cultural Variation in the Process of Socialization Into Sport:
The Case of Anglo Versus Navajo Basketball

As the largest Indian tribe located on a U.S. reservation, the Navajo people have maintained a strong sense of cultural identification. Navajo culture reflects a cooperation-based society where group solidarity and homogeneity are highly valued. Yet, through the public schools, Navajo children have considerable contact with the individualism, competitiveness, and achievement orientation characteristic of the Anglo culture. Specifically within sport, Navajo athletes are taught by Anglo coaches. Thus, the child experiences two contrasting cultures—native at home, Anglo at school. Which set of values, attitudes, and orientations do the children assimilate as they are socialized into the role of basketball player (a sport the Navajos view as their national sport)?

Using participant observation and interviews with Anglo coaches and Navajo players and parents, Allison (1982) studied how views of what constitutes a good athlete vary for the two groups. She found three major differences. First, Navajo athletes did not enforce rules in their informal pick-up games to the same extent as their Anglo counterparts. Second, the Navajo athletes did not manifest the "killer instinct" Anglo coaches felt was essential to aggressive and win-oriented play. Although the Navajo athletes were quite competitive, the nature of their competitiveness was different from that of Anglo youth. The Navajo youth appeared more interested in competing with themselves than against others. Third, Navajo athletes shunned personal recognition and public reward.

The behaviors exhibited by the Navajo athletes are consistent with cultural values they learn at home. Even in a situation where socializing agents (e.g., Anglo coaches) have power and introduce conflicting values, athletes more clearly reflect the cultural values of their own society than those of the powerful outsiders.

see the effects of this practice on sport participation by gender in the next generation.

The importance of early symbols, beliefs, and practices in the family setting is illustrated by the frequent finding that those who later achieve at the highest levels in sport often began to participate as early as 5 or 6 years of age. Moreover, the initial interest in sport is most frequently fostered by the parents (Weiss & Knoppers, 1982).

Most studies of socialization into primary and secondary sport roles indicate that the family is the earliest and most persistent socializing agency, especially for females (Greendorfer, 1983; Higginson, 1985; Smith, 1979). A positive valuation of sport by parents is likely to encourage sport interests among the offspring. Moreover, children are more likely to consume and participate if the parents presently participate in sport or if they did so in the past; if parents attend sport events or regularly watch sport on television; if parents have expectations or aspirations for their children to achieve in sport; if parents actively encourage participation; and if sport is a common topic of conversation in the home. Highlight 2.2 reports the results of a study that illustrates how and why parents attempt to socialize children into different and distinct levels of competitive swimming.

How Children Socialize Their Parents

Although much of the socialization process is primarily one-way, from the parents to the child, reciprocal socialization can begin in later childhood and during the adolescent years (Hasbrook, 1982; Oliver, 1980; Snyder & Purdy, 1982). For example, the child who becomes socialized into sport primarily through the influence of the peer group and school may later socialize the parents, who perhaps never participated in sport themselves. Because of the child's involvement, the parents may begin to participate or spectate to varying degrees. They may also become involved in secondary roles (e.g., coach, manager, or executive).

Another example of reciprocal socialization involves immigrant parents who begin a family after their arrival in North America. We now see examples of Chinese or East Indian children playing on baseball, football, or hockey teams, and socializing their parents into the role of sport consumer.

Factors Affecting a Family's Attitude Toward Sport

Sport sociologists question why some parents value sport and others do not. That is, why are some children socialized in a family environment where sport is valued, thereby considerably increasing their chances of participating in sport? First, as the continuity theory of social behavior has suggested (McPherson, 1983), a lifestyle at one stage in life influences subsequent lifestyles. Parents who were socialized into one or more sport roles as children within their family units and who found the activities pleasurable are more likely to introduce the activity to their children. If it was *not* pleasurable, the chances of parents' promoting sport among their children would be low.

Second, members of the parents' reference groups who are involved in an activity provide role models and encourage similar behaviors. If other parents in the neighborhood introduce their children to sport activities, even parents who have never been directly involved may begin to steer the child in that direction.

Third, a deprivation hypothesis suggests that parents, especially fathers, may attempt to compensate for activities or experiences they missed during childhood. Hence, they actively socialize their offspring into as many sport activities as possible. The domination of children's sport by parents may result from this type of childhood deprivation or lack of success.

FAMILY, SPORT, AND GENDER DIFFERENCES

As part of the early gender-role socialization process, there are gender differences in toy selection, in play opportunities and preferences, and in the type and degree of involvement in formal and complex games (Branta, Painter, & Kiger, 1987; Lever, 1976, 1978; Lewko & Greendorfer, 1988). Despite the social change that has occurred with the women's movement, there are still major differences in the work and leisure roles of males and females. Not surprisingly, these differences extend into sport. For example, disproportionately fewer females are socialized into sport at both the recreational and competitive levels. Strong cultural prescriptions still gov-

Highlight 2.2
Parental Involvement in Socialization Into Age-Group Swimming

Sport experiences provided for young children in a community can range from the instructional level, to the recreational competitive level, to a highly competitive level that involves travel to other communities. Frequently, parents choose the child's level of competition. Age-group swimming, which began in the United States in 1952, has grown to become one of the largest of the youth competitive sport programs.

To what extent does the family determine which children participate in swimming and at what level of competition? In a study by Purdy, Eitzen, and Haufler (1982), the parents of 69 highly competitive swimmers and 53 summer recreational club swimmers were surveyed to determine the families' sport orientation and attitudes toward age-group swimming. Although there were no differences in the parents' degree or type of primary or secondary sport involvement, parents of the competitive swimmers reported significantly higher expectations for their child's involvement and achievement in swimming. Parents of competitive swimmers also held higher values for competition, viewed competition more positively, and felt that competition in sport was important training for a competitive society. In contrast, parents of the recreational swimmers viewed swimming as an activity where social skills could be acquired.

These results suggest that because they serve as indirect role models and pass on attitudes toward competition, specialization, and achievement, parents are critically important in determining whether a child is socialized into a competitive or recreational sport experience. The child's type and degree of sport involvement closely reflects the family's orientation to sport.

ern what is appropriate activity for males and females. Sport, to a great extent, is still more closely identified with the male role. Also, males control the decision-making process of most competitive sports. In short, play, games, and sport represent yet another domain where there is a gender-based double standard in terms of opportunities, values, and encouragement (see chapter 9).

Enhancing the Role of Women in Sport

To date, relatively little research has been completed concerning socialization into sport for females. We do know that if girls are to be socialized into this type of activity, specific opportunities and processes must be present (Greendorfer, 1982). First, if girls are to overcome the stereotypical socializing influences, they must be exposed to strong sources of positive influence, especially early in life within the family and later in adolescence in the peer group (Lewko & Greendorfer, 1988).

Given the current societal norms that discourage female involvement, unless girls receive encouragement from *both* the mother and the father they are unlikely to become more involved in sport, especially at the competitive level. Furthermore, they must be part

With recent social change due to the women's movement, young girls today have more sport opportunities than did their mothers.

of a family that values sport highly, they must associate with same-sex peers who are involved, and they should not be discouraged by teachers. In addition, a girl is more likely to be socialized into sport activities if her mother was or is physically active. Similarly, physical education teachers and coaches during the late elementary school and high school years must provide encouragement and opportunities and serve as athletic role models. This support becomes even more essential if a female is to be socialized into nontraditional female sports such as golf, soccer, ice hockey, squash, or rugby.

Prevailing regional differences in cultural values attached to specific sports may also make it easier for a female to become involved in a specific sport role in one region than in another. A good example of how historical and regional value systems can facil-

itate the socialization process of women into sport is the situation of girls' basketball in Iowa. Girls have *always* played basketball in Iowa. Indeed, the high school state championship for girls' basketball generally attracts more spectators and media coverage than the boys' tournament. Hence, a social environment is created for young girls where mothers have perhaps played the game, where fathers see the activity as gender-appropriate, where numerous opportunities to play are provided early in life, where male and female age-peers provide encouragement, and where the media provides additional support and recognition. Thus, regional values, norms, and opportunity sets can significantly influence whether a girl is socialized into a particular sport.

Sibling Influences

In addition to the influence of the parents, **siblings** can facilitate or inhibit socialization into sport roles (Sutton-Smith & Rosenberg, 1970). Because much of our socialization occurs through imitation, the older child can serve as either a positive or a negative role model. Interaction with siblings can also teach and provide experience with cooperation, competition, or conflict. In contrast, a child without siblings is not as likely to be exposed to these experiences early in life, but may learn them somewhat later through peer group relationships.

Some factors that influence patterns of sibling interaction are family size, ordinal position (i.e., birth order), gender and age differences among siblings, and differences in parental interaction with different siblings. To date, birth order or ordinal position effects have received the most attention from social scientists. This has occurred partly because this is an easy concept to measure and partly because such concepts as the *only child*, the *oldest child*, and the *youngest child* have suggested differences in life chances and behavior, including for involvement in sport.

The Only Child. One social view holds that the only child is advantaged because of the rich social environment in which he or she is socialized. Lacking siblings with whom to interact, an only child becomes adult-oriented or self-centered earlier in life and to a greater degree. A psychological perspective suggests that parents are more overprotective, anxious, and indulgent with the first-born child. Thus, the child becomes more dependent. However, this may apply solely to only children, because once a sibling arrives to compete for attention the first born receives less attention.

Birth Order. Different theories have been postulated to account for how birth order makes a difference. The physiological theories argue that first borns are healthier and have greater intelligence because of a more nutritious uterine environment. A contrasting view holds that later-borns are advantaged because subsequent deliveries are easier, forceps are less likely to be used at birth, and there is less likelihood of cerebral damage during birth.

Ordinal position may influence the socialization process in that first-borns serve as positive or negative role models. First-borns do not experience this advantage and, therefore, may have different life chances than later-borns. For example, it has been found that first-borns are less likely than later-borns to participate in sports considered more dangerous, such as hockey, football, and wrestling (Gould & Landers, 1972; Nisbett, 1968), supposedly because they have less freedom in selecting activities and are more psychologically dependent on adults. Similarly, some studies have shown that second-born siblings are overrepresented in sport. To illustrate, De Garay and his colleagues (1974), in

their study of 1,200 athletes who competed in the 1968 Olympic Games, found that second-born individuals were markedly overrepresented among the athletes who competed.

Gender and Age Differences Among Siblings. Sutton-Smith and Rosenberg suggest that first-born siblings interact with and serve as role models and competitors for younger brothers and sisters (1970). This implies a one-way process of socialization into sport, where the behavior of later-borns is primarily accounted for by the presence of older siblings. Birth order, in this approach, is usually considered in conjunction with the sex of the older sibling. Thus, a male later-born with an older brother will have a different learning environment than a male later-born with an older sister. This occurs because of different parental expectations and because a different modeling and interaction process may operate within the family. This latter theoretical framework has been utilized most frequently by those interested in explaining involvement in sport on the basis of birth order and sibling-sex.

It has been hypothesized that the sex of the older sibling in relation to that of the younger sibling would influence the type and frequency of sport involvement by the latter. To date, the research evidence is conflicting in that the *sibling-similarity* and *sibling-opposite* hypotheses have been either supported in different studies or rejected (Adams, 1972; Landers, 1979; Petrie, 1982). That is, it can *not* be predicted with certainty that a second-born male with an older brother will more likely be involved in sport, or that a female with an older brother will be more involved than her age-peers from other family configurations.

First-borns, especially if female, are also hypothesized to be the conservators of tradition within the family, in that they are more likely to assume traditionally defined occupational and leisure roles (Edwards & Klemmack, 1973). For example, Schacter (1959) noted that later-borns are overrepresented among professional baseball players. Schacter argued that first-borns are more likely to internalize parental educational and occupational expectations.

Effects of Sport on the Family

Based on current research evidence, the family provides the main social context in which initial sport and leisure role socialization takes place. Furthermore, an interest in sport that is generated in childhood within the family is likely to persist or to be reactivated at later stages in the life cycle (Kelly, 1974). If children are socialized into sport so that participation or consumption becomes an integral facet of their lifestyles, this will likely persist into and through the adult years. There may be a shift, however, from participation in the traditional team sports to individual sports, or a shift from active participation as a player to involvement in secondary sport roles (e.g., consumer or Little League coach).

The family has the potential to socialize individuals into sport and to provide a supportive environment for involvement. However, it, in turn, can be affected by the process of involvement in sport, particularly if the degree of involvement is high. For example, the interaction of sport and family life have the potential both for enhanced family solidarity and integration and for family conflict. Proponents of the integration and solidarity outcome have argued that "the family that plays together stays together." To date, there is no research evidence to support the view that sport is a major factor in the cohesiveness or stability of family units, at least not to any greater extent than other leisure interests. Rather, there is some research evidence (Highlight 2.3) and increasing anecdotal evidence, to suggest that heavy sport involvement by children, or by one or more parents, may be a source of tension and conflict in the family.

An excessive amount of sport consumption by a husband or wife can create conflict with family meal schedules, intimacy, and responsibility. Many jokes are based on the situation of the football, golf, or jogging widow or widower. This situation is occasionally cited as a factor in marriage breakdowns. However, most articles suggest that sport brings underlying stresses to the surface, and may reflect how some people cope with major changes in their lives. The sport activity, rather than some other activity, may help them to cope with these changes.

High separation and divorce rates among professional and top-level amateur athletes stem partly from the disruption to family life by excessive travel and seasonal absences. Moreover, a high percentage of wives may live in cities other than where their husbands play.

There have been reports that incidents of wife abuse increase following major sporting events. If this is true, sport may be the catalyst that induces drinking and excessive disappointment over a losing team, which in turn increases the propensity for violence in an already deteriorating and mentally abusive relationship.

Spousal conflict, or parent-child conflict, may arise over the relative importance of little league sport involvement compared to family, education, and other leisure responsibilities or commitments. In some families, parents' schedules are dictated by the practice and game schedule of their child's involvement in youth sport. This can be particularly stressful in highly competitive elite programs such as swimming, track, figure skating, and gymnastics. Here the child, and the parent, may have a 20- to 30-hour com-

---

Highlight 2.3
Running Miles or Running Households?

Running or jogging is one of the most frequently reported adult leisure activities. Yet it apparently is not practiced without some costs. Periodically the popular press has reported stress in marital relationships when one spouse invests a considerable amount of time and emotion in running or when running disrupts the lifestyle, eating patterns, and social friendships that prevailed before the commitment to running. Some authors have argued that running attracts few women and few married persons, because it demands a high level of time and emotional commitment, especially for marathoners and competitive runners.

Brown and Curtis (1984) studied these issues. In a national sample of 3,481 adults who reported jogging or running in the previous month, they found that 61% were males and 39% were females. Among these runners, 67% of the males and 70% of the females were married. Controlling for age, education, and gender, the data provided strong support for a pattern where married people are underrepresented among joggers and runners compared with the general population. Also, when the runners were grouped in terms of high or low commitment to running (more than or less than 60 minutes per session), married persons were underrepresented. Similarly, among both high frequency (more than 28 times per month) and low frequency (less than 28 times per month) runners, fewer runners in comparison to the general population were married.

In short, there is a strong relationship between being married and not running, for both males and females. This difference is even more marked for those with a high degree of commitment and frequency. Because running is a time-consuming and often solitary activity, those with marital and parental responsibilities may find that they have little time for a serious commitment to running.

---

mitment for 6 or 7 days of the week, for 10 or 11 months of the year, for 8 or 10 years.

The increased socialization of young girls and women into sport and physical activity, and the greater likelihood of women working full time, has added another potential strain to marriages, especially if there are young children in the family. Already faced with the time and energy demands of working and raising a family, a woman may have difficulty finding time for her own activity involvement. Moreover, within the family hierarchy she may find herself at the bottom with respect to support and assistance from others if she wants to be involved in sport pursuits. This problem of time management and lack of family support is more likely to be encountered by women from lower-income families, where sport for women is generally less highly valued.

SOCIALIZATION INTO SPORT

Research on the topic of **socialization into sport** has been guided by the search for answers to the following questions:

- Why and how do some individuals become socialized into sport while others with apparently similar physical and social characteristics do not?
- Why are some individuals socialized into specific sports rather than into other sports?
- How does the process of sport role socialization vary by gender, social class, race, age, and culture?

Formally and informally, individuals can be socialized *into* sport roles. This process concerns who gets involved in sport, and how individuals learn sport roles and at what stages in life. The process also identifies when individuals receive the opportunity to become involved in specific sport roles or ultimately to perform at an elite level.

The physical sciences may be able to describe physical differences between those who are involved in sport and those who are not and between athletes who are successful and those who are not. But they cannot explain fully why some individuals are involved in specific sport roles, or why some attain elite levels of performance and others do not. Furthermore, the physical sciences cannot totally explain why individuals from one country are more involved or successful in a particular sport role than those in other countries with a similar population or geographical area; or why one region of a country produces more elite athletes in a specific sport than another region (Rooney, 1974). We need to understand how the process of socialization into sport varies in different social and cultural environments.

Because the socialization process may occur in a variety of social institutions throughout the life cycle, it can vary by gender, age, social class, ethnic background, and nationality. Throughout this chapter you should be alert to sociodemographic variations that can influence the values, beliefs, opportunity sets,

and past experiences of both the person being socialized and the socializing agents. For example, differing values and beliefs of parents concerning gender role identification can greatly influence the socialization process and opportunity set to which females are exposed, both across societies and within a society.

Becoming an Athlete

Most of our knowledge about the socialization process within sport is derived from retrospective surveys of elite athletes. In this approach, successful athletes have been asked to recall their early years and to describe the opportunity set, the significant others, and the socialization situations that enabled them to become involved and achieve success. Obviously this method has a number of limitations—some are unable to recall all pertinent facts, the views of those who were socialized to some degree and then withdrew from sport are not obtained, and age-peers who never became socialized into sport are not available for comparison as a control group.

The ideal study to answer these research questions would be a longitudinal study of a large sample of people that followed them from about the age of 5 until they reach 20 to 25 years of age. Sociodemographic and regional factors could thus be controlled, and the situation of those who did and did not become socialized into sport could be compared.

Since this type of study is costly, and therefore unlikely to be initiated in the near future, we are dependent for information on retrospective cross-sectional studies of children, adolescents, and young adults who are or are not involved in sport. As we summarize the current state of knowledge, think of your own life history and why and how you did or did

Your opportunity set and significant others are among the factors that influence your socialization into sport.

leaders in voluntary sport associations in the community. By late elementary school and during high school and college, the peer group and teachers and coaches at school become more influential sources of social support.

The process by which elite athletes (i.e., college, Olympic, or professional athletes) become interested and involved in sport begins early in life, often before the age of 6 or 7. This initial interest is stimulated in the home, neighborhood, and school and normally involves exposure to one of the traditional team sports such as baseball, basketball, hockey, or football. Later, through either the school or voluntary associations, interest and participation in individual sports such as track and field, gymnastics, wrestling, and tennis may occur.

Many elite athletes participate in a number of sports before they begin to specialize, and often their early experiences result in a high level of success. Moreover, combined with a favorable opportunity set (such as living close to a sport facility), at specific stages in the life cycle they receive support from a variety of significant others, of which the family, peer group, and coaches appear to be the most influential. Many of these role models competed, or still compete, in one or more of the sports being learned by the aspiring athlete. Thus they serve as direct role models in addition to providing verbal, emotional, or financial support. Finally, although the general sport role socialization process has a number of common elements, there are unique differences in the process that vary by sport, social class, gender, race, and stage in the life cycle.

Some sport opportunities are more likely to be provided by the family, others by the school, and still others by voluntary associations in the community. To illustrate, the family can provide opportunities for individual sports but usually not team sports; the elementary school encourages intramural

not become involved in sport (in general, or in a sport in which you specialize) as a participant or consumer. Specifically, compare the research findings with your own opportunity set, the availability and importance of significant others who provided you with encouragement or discouragement, and your personal social attributes that may have enhanced or inhibited your sport interest and opportunities.

One consistent research finding is that there is a positive relationship between the amount of social support received from significant others and the degree of participation in sport roles. Specifically, those individuals who receive positive reinforcement for sport participation are more likely to become and remain involved than those who receive neutral or negative messages. In the early years, most of this support comes from the family or from sport; and volunteer community groups provide competitive team sport opportunities during childhood (e.g., Little League baseball, all-star hockey, and soccer). During adolescence, the high school encourages team sports and spectating, and additional opportunities in some sports are provided by volunteer associations or private clubs.

Similarly, the affluence and location (rural vs. urban) of a neighborhood or community can influence the type of athletic opportunity set provided to aspiring athletes (e.g., facilities, coaches, leagues). Few rural residents ever have the opportunity to become involved in competitive swimming, squash, or gymnastics because the equipment, facilities, or coaching are seldom available. Similarly, those who grow up in an inner-city environment are less likely to be socialized into competitive golf, tennis, swimming, hockey, or skiing. Depending on local cultural, ethnic, and social values, basketball, track, soccer, and baseball are more likely to be the sport opportunities presented to youngsters living in the urban core of large cities.

Becoming a Sport Consumer

Throughout this book we note the extent to which youth and adults consume sport directly at a stadium, arena, or field; indirectly, via television, radio, newspapers, and magazines; or indirectly, by discussing sport topics in a variety of social situations. In short, many citizens in most modern industrialized nations are sport consumers.

This interest in sport consumption is easily documented by attendance figures for events like the Super Bowl, the World Series, the Olympic Games, the World Cup of Soccer, the bowl games in college football, and for any other special sport event successfully marketed; by television ratings for sport events; and by subscription and over-the-

Sport consumers range from casual spectators, to moderately interested sport fans, to highly involved sport fans, to addicted sport fans.

counter sales of sport magazines. What cannot be documented is the amount of work and leisure time allocated by individuals to reading and to thinking about or discussing sport.

Anyone may be a casual or passive spectator at a sport event. One becomes a *fan* when the degree of interest and feeling for an athlete, sport, or team becomes internalized, intensified, and consistent. Specifically, as we suggested in chapter 1, a sport fan might be socialized to

- invest considerable amounts of time and money in numerous forms of direct and indirect secondary sport involvement;
- have knowledge of sport performers, sport statistics, and sport strategies;
- have an affective (emotive) involvement with athletes or teams;
- experience changed mood states while consuming sport events;

- use sport as a major topic of conversation with peers and strangers; and
- arrange leisure time around professional and amateur sport events.

Smith and his colleagues (1981) established the following minimal criteria by which an individual could be labeled a *deeply committed sport fan*:

- reading about sport in the newspaper every day;
- reading at least three different sport periodicals per month;
- watching an average of eight hours of sport per week on television;
- attending an average of at least one live sporting event per month where an admission is charged; and
- talking about sport every day.

By employing these criteria, along with other measures of time and money spent on sport consumption, it would be possible to identify consumers along a scale from casual spectators, to moderately interested sport fans, to highly involved sport fans, to addicted sport fans. Sport addicts typically display a passionate loyalty to one team, may gamble heavily on sport outcomes, and may invest a large proportion of their income and time to attend sport events.

Similar to the learning of primary sport roles, socialization into the role of sport consumer is a complex process that begins early in life. Children observe the degree to which parents and older siblings watch, read, or talk about sport. They may be taken to sport events as a special or regular family outing. Parents may spend large amounts of their leisure time watching the child compete in sport, sometimes to the point that they have no time to participate themselves. A child may be encouraged to read and think about sport in order to participate in family discussions.

This process of socialization into sport consumption is further reinforced by the media, which provide knowledge and an opportunity set; by the peer group, which may highly value sport involvement; and by the school, which encourages spectator support of school teams through pep rallies, bus trips to away games, dances following games, and the cancellation of classes to attend sport events. The net effect of the socialization process is that sport consumption is perceived by many to have high social value. Many, especially males, find that social interaction with others is easier if they can "talk sport."

Unlike primary sport role socialization, which tends to occur during childhood, adolescence, or early adulthood, the process of learning secondary sport roles can occur at any stage of the life cycle. It appears, though, to depend highly on the degree of socialization that has occurred at earlier stages. That is, there appears to be greater continuity or stability in the consumption of sport than in the degree of participation in active sport roles. Once learned, the role tends to carry forward much later into life than the role of athlete. Moreover, early involvement as a consumer can lead to later involvement as a participant (Yamaguchi, 1984).

SOCIALIZATION VIA SPORT

An examination of **socialization via sport** concentrates on the degree to which skills, traits, values, beliefs, and norms learned in sport settings can be generalized to other social institutions. For example, for many years competitive sport and physical education have been considered essential components of leisure and education during childhood and adolescence. Teachers, coaches, and the members of the mass media claimed that ideal character and moral traits (e.g., sportsmanship, honesty, courage, citizenship, cooperation, and achievement orientation) can be learned by children and adolescents who participate in physical education classes or in sport.

And many people believe that sport and games are the best or only setting where these desired attributes can be learned. Part of the rationale for the socialization *via* sport argument is the belief that play and games are an essential component of the early childhood socialization process, and therefore necessary as part of the school curriculum.

Scholars and journalists have noted the conspicuous presence of play and games during infancy and childhood. They have suggested that play and games resemble experiences in the larger society and are therefore an essential component of the early socialization processes. Imitative play thus serves to teach children the ways of life of the society and the interpersonal and survival skills they will need later. As Denzin (1975) noted, "all forms of play teach or socialize young children into the illusory worlds of social reality" (p. 476).

Although participation in games may be a universal phenomenon, the type of game found in a particular society is related to its culture. To illustrate, Roberts and Sutton-Smith (1962) found (a) that games of strategy are more likely to be found in structurally complex societies and are linked directly with obedience training and (b) that games of chance are more likely to be found where a culture's religious beliefs emphasize the benevolence or coerciveness of supernatural beings and are linked with training for responsibility. Games of physical skill (e.g., sport) are more conspicuous when the culture places a high value on mastery of the environment and personal achievement. Sutton-Smith (1973) suggests that games foster an "enculturative outcome so that after many years of gaming, players ultimately become persons with wide repertoires of adaptive

skills . . . relevant to the matters of crisis that concern the larger culture" (p. 2).

The argument for sport programs for children often has been based on the untested assumption that participation in sport is an essential element of the overall socialization process. As such, sport is thought to be an essential contributor to the mental and social development of youth, especially males. More specifically, it has been argued that there are psychological, behavioral, and attitudinal outcomes derived from involvement in competitive sport programs.

Research Evidence

Little research evidence supports the claim that sport involvement is essential for successful or complete socialization during childhood and adolescence. The studies have been correlational in nature, cross-sectional rather than longitudinal, and unable to establish a cause-effect relationship. For example, although some studies have found personality differences between athletes and nonathletes, among athletes of different ability, and among athletes in different sports, other studies have been unable to demonstrate personality or character differences among individuals in the various sport groups.

The empirical evidence, to date, also provides little support for the socialization *via* sport hypothesis, at least for specific types of outcomes. For example, several research reviews (Loy & Ingham, 1973; McPherson, 1981; Ogilvie & Tutko, 1975; Stevenson, 1975, 1985) have all concluded that there is little, if any, valid evidence that participation in sport is an essential element in the socialization process. Nor is there strong evidence, as conventional wisdom would argue, that involvement in sport teaches specific outcomes, such as character building, moral development, a competitive or a cooperative orientation, good citizenship, or certain valued personality traits.

The argument that what is learned in sport will be transferred directly to another institution—like the workplace—has not been documented. Indeed, it seems a low probability of transference occurs, because the child is not exposed just to sport but to many social settings that could have an influence on social learning. It is difficult, therefore, to isolate the learning that takes place in any given setting. Finally, there is considerable anecdotal evidence to support the view that participation in competitive sport as an adolescent is not essential to adult career success. Many leading figures in a variety of professions were never members of athletic teams earlier in life. This is especially true of women, many of whom were deprived of the opportunity to compete in sport.

Sport As a Positive Influence

Some studies have shown that athletes compared to nonathletes have higher grade point averages, are less delinquent, or demonstrate highly valued social or personality traits (e.g., achievement values, sportsmanship); other studies have failed to find differences. One reason athletes may be better students or less delinquent is that a selection process operates within sport. Thus, coaches eliminate the weaker students and the nonconformers before researchers begin to study athletes.

Armstrong (1984), based on an analysis of boarding schools in England and the United States, argues that this particular educational setting has an impact on the lifelong values that can be learned from sport. In this setting, some degree of sport participation is compulsory for all students. He argues, without presenting research evidence, that this particular type of environment helps teach team-

work, fair play, legitimate behavior, and the concept of a *gentleman*. In reality, it may be that these schools ensure access to lifelong networks for the sons and daughters of the social elite. In effect, the values and behaviors are learned because of attendance at the school per se and because of participation, whether required or voluntary, in extracurricular activities. It probably does not matter whether they play on a sport team or are members of the debating team, the computer club, or the math team.

In one of the few recent research studies completed on this topic, Dubois (1986) studied the traits and values developed in children 8 to 10 years old who competed in either an instructional or competitive soccer league over two seasons. He found that the value orientations of young athletes do change, at least temporarily, over the season. Not only were there differences between the two levels of involvement, but such values as competing, good sportsmanship, improving fitness, and improving social status were more highly valued by the competitive athletes by the end of the season. However, given the age of subjects in this sample, we ought not to suggest that these changes in value orientations persist when they enter other social settings or that they are retained throughout adolescence and adulthood.

At the college level, Stevenson (1985) notes that athletes in major compared with minor sports, and starters compared with substitute players, are less likely to exhibit good sportsmanship. Again, we do not know whether these behaviors and values persist beyond the season, or whether they are transferred into other sport or nonsport social settings.

Sport As a Negative Influence

In contrast to the arguments just described, others have argued that sport fosters the learning of undesirable or dysfunctional skills, values, and traits. To illustrate, Bredemeier and her colleagues (1986) concluded that "involvement in sports characterized by a relatively high degree of physical contact may be developmentally counterproductive for most preadolescent children" (p. 316). Specifically, they found that boys participating in high-contact sports and girls participating in medium-contact sports exhibited less mature moral reasoning and greater tendencies toward aggression in both sport and everyday life (Bredemeier, 1985; Bredemeier, Weiss, Shields, & Cooper, 1986). Highlight 2.4 provides observational evidence that competitive sport programs may contribute little to the socialization process and may, in fact, be detrimental to the individual.

We still need valid, consistent empirical evidence, gathered over a period of time from a number of social settings, before we can conclude whether socialization via sport does or does not occur. Until then, parents, children, physical educators, coaches, and administrators should seriously question attempts to justify a sport program by its inherent socializing value or hypothesized socialization outcomes.

DESOCIALIZATION FROM SPORT

Inevitably, at some stage in the life cycle, involved individuals leave competitive athletics. For some this occurs voluntarily in childhood or early adolescence, when they decide to pursue other forms of social participation (Gould, 1987). For others the change does not occur until early adulthood, when they graduate from college or retire from a career as an elite amateur or professional athlete. For many athletes, this withdrawal can occur quite suddenly and involuntarily through, for example, serious injury or being released from a team.

Voluntary or involuntary, withdrawal from sport can occur at any age and for a variety of reasons. Reaction or adjustment to this transition can range from satisfaction and anticipation of new opportunities, especially where the exit is voluntary and planned, to experiencing psychological stress and adjustment problems, especially where the process is involuntary and unexpected. In many situations the adjustment depends on such sociodemographic factors as age, gender, class, and educational attainment; other work opportunities available in the labor force; the degree to which sport has been a central part of self-identity; the amount of preplanning or socialization for alternative roles; and the support system available from family and friends for **desocialization** from the sport role.

Interest in the process of withdrawal from sport has been stimulated by journalistic and anecdotal accounts of former professional or Olympic athletes who experienced difficulty adjusting to life away from sport. Accounts have tended to highlight such problems as poverty, alcoholism, marital breakups, unemployment or unemployability, criminal activity, isolation from friends, identity crises, and suicide. The reports have helped to create and perpetuate the belief that athletes are not prepared for retirement and experience trauma in adjusting to life outside the world of sport. In the 1980s, many studies and scholarly papers concern retirement from sport (Blinde & Greendorfer, 1985; Brown, 1985; Coakley, 1983; Greendorfer & Blinde, 1985; McPherson, 1980; Rosenberg, 1984).

Rather than approaching the topic from the problem-oriented perspective of journalists, most of the literature in the sociology of sport has focused either on the process of desocialization or on the outcome, and whether it leads to a positive or negative adjustment.

Highlight 2.4
Some Negative Outcomes of Little League Baseball

For 2 years, sociologist David Voigt kept a diary based on his observations while serving as a manager of a Little League baseball team. He found that youth sport may not be the ideal environment in which to learn values and ethics. The following excerpts from his diary illustrate this point.*

A player berating his own team mate underscores the seamy side of little league baseball. I personally felt the ugly emotion of hate, a surge of uncontrollable rage tempting me to lash out at my players and my gloating rivals. . . . It is this kind of emotional reaction that is so often cited in the charges against the character-building claims of little league baseball. . . . I now confess that my Brockton team experience affords no evidence that any of these character-building virtues gets into my players. (p. 40)

As for sportsmanship, it was lacking from the start. . . . The plumbers suffered the most, being treated by the regulars as incompetents, which says little for baseball's claim for inculcating brotherhood or community solidarity. (p. 41)

Nor did parents set examples. . . . Parents of rivals constantly hassled us. . . . At home, our supporters returned rivals the same kind of treatment. That our parents gave a bit less . . . owed simply to . . . our big leads and heavy hitting. . . . If there is a point in all of this, I think it demonstrates the fact that in baseball, sportsmanship and good character go mostly to the winners and regular players and only slightly to benchwarmers. (p. 42)

I conclude that little league baseball is no shaper of lofty values or ethics. Rather it merely provides one setting for the playing out of norms and values already embedded in our culture. (p. 42)

---

*Note. From *A Little League Journal* (pp. 40-42) by D.Q. Voigt, 1974, Bowling Green, OH: Bowling Green University Popular Press. Copyright 1974 by David Q. Voigt. Reprinted by permission.

The literature distinguishes between the retirement of professional athletes from a career in sport and the withdrawal of amateur athletes from youth sport and interscholastic or intercollegiate sport, where participation is largely a leisure activity.

Withdrawal From Sport as a Leisure Role

Many youth are socialized into sport roles during childhood but relatively few still compete by the age of 20; most withdrawal occurs during adolescence or early adulthood. Much of this withdrawal is involuntary and occurs when an individual is not selected to play for a team at a higher age or skill level. Some who experience involuntary withdrawal may have difficulty adjusting to the loss of a major leisure role. They may experience an identity crisis and loss of peer status or have difficulty finding a substitute activity or a new peer group. Most people can adjust by continuing to participate in the sport at a lower level, participating in another sport, or placing a lower priority on sport involvement compared with other activities, such as education, work, or dating (Curtis & Ennis, 1988). In short, their leisure interests and lifestyles become similar to the majority of their age-peers, and they experience a "rebirth" (Coakley, 1983) or **resocialization** rather than a "social death" (Lerch, 1984).

Many youth voluntarily withdraw from sport before they attain their peak learning or performance potential (Brown, 1985). This tends to occur more among females, often because they see no further opportunities or social support. For most voluntary retirees, the process of adjustment is *not* traumatic, largely because it has been a rational decision that is usually supported by significant others. Among the reasons frequently cited for withdrawing from competitive sport roles are

- a desire to spend more time with friends who are nonathletes;
- a shift in the relative importance of sport compared with other age-appropriate activities (e.g., part-time work, achievement in the classroom, dating),
- a declining level of success as peak potential or desire is attained,
- encouragement from significant others (e.g., parents) to become involved in other age-based activities;
- a decline in encouragement for the sport role from significant others; and

Females are much more likely than males to voluntarily withdraw from sport before they attain their potential.

- a decline in the importance of the athletic role in one's self-identity.

Thus lack of success is not the only or major factor in withdrawal. Rather, a variety of "push" and "pull" factors interact to affect the transition. The decision and desocialization process usually is not sudden, but evolves gradually as other interests are identified and become more attractive. This is especially likely if parents and peers offer support for nonsport involvement.

Retirement From Sport as Work and Career

Athletes are unusual members of the labor force in that they retire early from their first careers (usually in their late 20s or early 30s). They must then find and begin other careers at a time when their peers are well along in their own careers. Athletes competing in professional sport also constantly face the possibility of sudden failure and retirement because of injury, declining ability, or personality conflicts with coaches.

An athlete forced to retire usually needs a period of adjustment to cope with a new lifestyle, a new image or identity, a new **social identity**, and possible loss of economic status. Most eventually adjust to the new situation and accept employment at a level commensurate with their education and ability. Some athletes wish to retire and get on with a normal adult life. For example, Allison and Meyers (1988), based on interviews with retired female professional tennis players, reported that many respondents had never planned to pursue a career in professional sport. The players were not happy with the traveling or with the pressures, loneliness, and frustrations of the life; they were eager to retire and lead more ordinary lives.

Kearl (1986) has argued that there are good and bad role or career endings. A good conclusion provides personal satisfaction and social order in one's life and to significant others. Satisfaction may be related to whether one was a starter or a nonstarter on the team during the last year and whether one was healthy or injured. A study of 426 former intercollegiate football and basketball players found that athletes who sustained career-ending injuries in their last year reported lower levels of life satisfaction (Kleiber, Greendorfer, Samdahl, & Blinde, 1987).

With respect to bad endings, the process of retirement is often most traumatic for those professional athletes who have been the most visible, have earned high incomes, and have little formal education and few job skills to transfer to a nonsport occupation. Moreover, former athletes often receive little social or emotional support from family and friends and have few friends or contacts outside the world of sport who can provide new job opportunities (Coakley, 1983). These former athletes often resort to accepting relatively low-income employment as minor league players or as scouts, assistant coaches, or trainers within the familiar world of sport. The former superstars may be the athletes most vulnerable to stress and dissatisfaction following their playing careers. Normally it is these athletes, when they fail in the world outside sport, who are featured in news reports. In short, athletes in these situations perceive retirement as a crisis rather than as a natural and inevitable role transition that happens to all athletes in early to middle adulthood.

Failure and Desocialization From Sport

Not every player or team can succeed in sport. In fact, most players and teams experience failure to varying degrees, as there can really only be one winner at the end of a game or season. To illustrate, a report in the January 18, 1985, *Globe and Mail* (Campbell) indicated the prevailing job insecurity in the National Hockey League. Of the 420 players who were in the NHL in the 1979-80 season, only 175 were employed in the NHL during the 1984-85 season; only 64 were still employed by their original team. Two teams had a 100% turnover of players over the five seasons. Moreover, of the most successful players in the 1979-80 season (the 12 players on the first and second all-star teams), only 5 were members of the same team 5 years later.

An analysis of failure in sport by Ball (1976) indicates that the process includes both the reaction of the individual to her or his failure and the reaction of members of the former group. The reaction of the group involves either degradation, where the player is ignored, or cooling out, where sympathy and rationalizations are extended, expected, and accepted. The person who fails is embarrassed by his or her unfulfilled expectations;

he or she must face significant others who know, in detail, these aspirations or career plans.

Coping as an Individual.
One coping mechanism is to apply new frames of reference. If, for example, the player is demoted to a lower level of classification, the player may join cliques on the new team. This new frame of reference consists of others who have failed within the organization or sport.

Ball (1976) suggests that the reaction to failure varies according to the structure of the sport. In baseball, a two-tiered system consisting of major and minor leagues, players who fail at the major league level are usually *sent down* to a minor league affiliate (that is, they experience downward mobility). But they are still in the system and can be seen by the public and by their former playing peers—a constant reminder of their second-class status. Jim Bouton (1970), a major league pitcher, said the following when he was demoted to a minor league team (cited in Ball, 1976): "As I started throwing stuff into my bag, I could feel the wall, invisible but real, forming around me. I was suddenly an outsider, a different person, someone to be shunned, a leper" (p. 731).

These processes of status differentiation and degradation seem to operate in sports such as hockey and professional baseball, where there is an extensive minor league system, and perhaps in tennis and golf, where there are satellite tours.

Alternatively, sports such as football and basketball have no formal minor league structure. Players who fail are released outright or remain on a "taxi squad." They are thus removed from public visibility and do not experience the public embarrassment of being seen in a marginal role. Many of the failures in these systems are rookies and may have a college education and more career alternatives outside the sport. Ball (1976) sug-gests that a cooling out mechanism operates in this type of sport structure, because there are alternatives. Furthermore, because there is no lower level of play, there is a higher expected rate of failure. Failure is thus less traumatic.

Some athletes may view failure as a form of premature death, because so much of their self-image and self-esteem is related to being successful. An ego so tied to sport often cannot cope with failure. This may lead to excessive use of drugs or alcohol, marital breakdown (Highlight 2.5), chronic unemployment, a psychiatrist's couch, or even suicide.

In general, the process of occupational and psychological adjustment to retirement from professional sport roles is influenced by four major factors: the early life socialization process into the career; the pattern and contingencies of the career; whether the decision to retire is voluntary or involuntary; and the extent to which athletes are desocialized from one career and resocialized into another (McPherson, 1980). Specifically, individuals are more likely to experience adjustment difficulties if they

- have failed to attain a high school or college diploma while being socialized into elite sport roles;
- have defined the self primarily as an athlete;
- have been idolized and perceived as a hero or someone special by friends and the general public;
- have failed to use the off-season to pursue alternative job experiences or to plan for the post-sport years;
- have experienced a sport career characterized by injuries or by frequently being demoted or traded, so that they complete their sport career on a downward slide in the minor or *bush* leagues;
- are forced to retire involuntarily by a coaching decision or an injury; or

---

Highlight 2.5
Life After Professional Sport

It is not only the athlete who experiences the stress and trauma of withdrawal from a career in professional sport. The spouse and family may also suffer. The lack of preparation for a post-career life is aptly illustrated in the words of one ex-wife (Christie, 1983):*

At the point hockey was over for him, he hadn't projected himself beyond hockey. His goal was always to be facing off against the Jean Beliveaus. My goal was to operate my own advertising company by the time I was 45. I had married a man whose only goal was to be what he was when he was 20. At the time he was going down, I was just finishing school and was ready to take off and pursue a career. We were at two totally differ-

ent spots in our lives. It was tough for him to pat me on the shoulder and say "run with it" when he was drowning in self pity. He wasn't coping with a new life. He had no pride left anymore in something that he could do. But then, hockey players are not taught to think about anything but hockey. If they did, they probably wouldn't stay with the game. I don't think that in the NHL anyone gives a damn what happens to the players when it's all over. (p. S1)

---

*Note. From "After Hockey: Anger, Unemployment" by J. Christie, 1983, March 26, *The Globe and Mail*, p. S1. Copyright 1983 by The Globe and Mail, Toronto. Reprinted by permission.

• do not receive social and emotional support from family and friends during the postretirement period of adjustment.

Fortunately, most former college, professional, and Olympic athletes adjust and cope with life away from the spotlight. This adjustment has been greatly facilitated by pension and disability programs, preretirement counseling and planning, and the increasing recognition that a college education or some other type of career training must be completed to maintain the expected lifestyle.

Coping as a Team. A team must deal with an image of failure if it experiences a pro-

longed losing streak within a season or over a few seasons. This can affect fans, who cease to attend games or to view or listen to the games; the owner, who loses revenue; the coach or manager, who may lose his or her job; the image of the city or college in the eyes of residents and nonresidents; and interpersonal relations among team members. Failure may also lead to the search for scapegoats, especially where the team was expected to win. This can create intense and long-lasting interpersonal conflict within the team or organization.

WRAP-UP

Individuals are socialized into, via, and out of sport roles at various stages in the life cycle. The process is complex and is influenced by one's gender, class, ethnicity, race, and nationality. These factors shape values, beliefs, norms, and opportunities in the world of sport. The process of socialization into primary sport roles also varies by sport and by stages in the life cycle.

While much of our primary sport role socialization occurs in childhood and adolescence, socialization into the role of sport consumer, sport official, or sport spectator can occur during adolescence, early adulthood, and even into the middle or later years of life. For young girls to be socialized into sport, same-sex role models and strong reference-group support, especially from parents, must be available. Clearly the family is the most important sport role socialization setting in early life. Nonetheless, excessive or unusual patterns of sport role socialization can compound family conflict.

While it frequently has been argued or accepted as conventional wisdom that socialization via sport is necessary and essential for one's social development as a mature adult, there is little valid evidence that essential social skills and values are best or only learned in a sport setting. Moreover, there is evidence that involvement in highly competitive sport can be detrimental to the social development of an individual.

Finally, athletes experiencing the most difficulty coping with the process of desocialization from sport usually are those with little education or training for other occupations, those with underlying personality or emotional problems, and those (often superstars in their playing careers) who have been forced to retire suddenly from a world in which they have felt secure for most of their adolescent life and all of their adult life. These former athletes often remain in the secure world of sport, as coaches, media personnel, or scouts.

REFERENCES

Adams, B.N. (1972). Birth order: A critical review. *Sociometry*, **35**, 411–439.

Allison, M.T. (1982). Sport, culture and socialization. *International Review of Sport Sociology*, **17**(4), 11–37.

Allison, M.T., & Meyers, C. (1988). Career problems and retirement among elite athletes: The female tennis professional. *Sociology of Sport Journal*, **5**, 212–222.

Armstrong, C.F. (1984). The lessons of sport: Class socialization in British and American boarding schools. *Sociology of Sport Journal*, **1**, 314–331.

Ball, D.W. (1976). Failure in sport. *American Sociological Review*, **41**, 726–739.

Bandura, A. (1977). *Social learning theory*. Englewood Cliffs, NJ: Prentice-Hall.

Blinde, E.M., & Greendorfer, S.L. (1985). A reconceptualization of the process of leaving the role of competitive athlete. *International Review for the Sociology of Sport*, **20**, 87–93.

Bouton, J. (1970). *Ball four: My life and hard times throwing the knuckleball in the big leagues*. New York: World.

Branta, C.F., Painter, M., & Kiger, J.E. (1987). Gender differences in play patterns and sport participation of North American youth. *Advances in Pediatric Sport Sciences*, **2**, 25–42.

Bredemeier, B.J. (1985). Moral reasoning and perceived legitimacy of intentionally injurious sport acts. *Journal of Sport Psychology*, **7**, 110–124.

Bredemeier, B.J., Weiss, M.R., Shields, D.L., & Cooper, B.A.B. (1986). The relationship of sport involvement with children's moral reasoning and aggression tendencies. *Journal of Sport Psychology,* **8**, 304–318.

Brown, B.A. (1982). Female sport involvement: A preliminary conceptualization. In A.O. Dunleavy, A.W. Miracle, & C.R. Rees (Eds.), *Studies in the sociology of sport* (pp. 121–138). Fort Worth: Texas Christian University Press.

Brown, B.A. (1985). Factors influencing the process of withdrawal by female adolescents from the role of competitive age group swimmer. *Sociology of Sport Journal,* **2**, 111–129.

Brown, B.A., & Curtis, J.E. (1984). Does running go against the family grain? National survey results on marital status and running. In N. Theberge & P. Donnelly (Eds.), *Sport and the sociological imagination* (pp. 352–367). Fort Worth: Texas Christian University Press.

Campbell, N. (1985, June 18). Rosters prove NHL job security fleeting [In *By the numbers*]. *The Globe and Mail,* p. 13.

Christie, J. (1983, March 26). After hockey: Anger, unemployment. *The Globe and Mail,* p. S1.

Coakley, J.J. (1983). Leaving competitive sport: Retirement or rebirth? *Quest,* **35**, 1–11.

Curtis, J.E., & Ennis, R. (1988). Negative consequences of leaving competitive sport? Comparative findings for former elite-level hockey players. *Sociology of Sport Journal,* **5**, 87–106.

De Garay, A., Levine, L., & Carter, J.E.L. (Eds.) (1974). *Genetic and anthropological studies of Olympic athletes.* New York: Academic Press.

Denzin, N.K. (1975). Play, games and interaction: The contexts of childhood socialization. *Sociological Quarterly, 16,* 458-478.

Dubois, P.E. (1986). The effects of participation in sport on the value orientations of young athletes. *Sociology of Sport Journal,* **3**, 29–42.

Edwards, J.N., & Klemmack, D.L. (1973). Birth order and the conservators of tradition hypothesis. *Journal of Marriage and the Family,* **35**, 619–626.

Goslin, D.A. (Ed.) (1969). *Handbook of socialization theory and research.* Chicago: Rand McNally.

Gould, D.R. (1987). Understanding attrition in children's sport. In D.R. Gould & M.R. Weiss (Eds.), *Advances in pediatric sport sciences* (Vol. 2, pp. 61–85). Champaign, IL: Human Kinetics.

Gould, D.R., & Landers, D.M. (1972, March). *Dangerous sport participation: A replication of Nisbett's birth order findings.* Paper presented at the North American Society for the Psychology of Sport and Physical Activity Conference, Houston.

Greendorfer, S.L. (1982). Gender differences in play and sport: A cultural interpretation. In J.W. Loy (Ed.), *The paradoxes of play* (pp. 198–204). Champaign, IL: Leisure Press.

Greendorfer, S.L. (1983). Shaping the female athlete: The impact of the family. In M.A. Boutilier & L. SanGiovanni, *The sporting woman* (pp. 135–155). Champaign, IL: Human Kinetics.

Greendorfer, S.L., & Blinde, E.M. (1985). Retirement from intercollegiate sport: Theoretical and empirical considerations. *Sociology of Sport Journal,* **2**, 101–110.

Hasbrook, C.H. (1982). The theoretical notion of reciprocity and childhood socialization into sport. In A.O. Dunleavy, A.W. Miracle, & C.R. Rees (Eds.), *Studies in the sociology of sport* (pp. 139-151). Fort Worth: Texas Christian University Press.

Higginson, D.C. (1985). The influence of socializing agents in the female sport-participation process. *Adolescence,* **20**(77), 73–82.

Kearl, M.C. (1986). Knowing how to quit: On the finitudes of everyday life. *Sociological Inquiry*, **56**, 283–303.

Kelly, J.R. (1974). Socialization toward leisure: A developmental approach. *Journal of Leisure Research*, **6**(3), 181–193.

Kenyon, G.S., & McPherson, B.D. (1973). Becoming involved in physical activity and sport: A process of socialization. In G.L. Rarick (Ed.), Physical activity: Human growth and development (pp. 303–332). Orlando, FL: Academic Press.

Kleiber, D., Greendorfer, S.L., Samdahl, D., & Blinde, E.M. (1987). Quality of exit from university sports and life satisfaction in early adulthood. *Sociology of Sport Journal*, **4**, 28–36.

Landers, D.M. (1979). Birth order in the family and sport participation. In M.L. Krotee (Ed.), *The dimensions of sport sociology* (pp. 140–167). Champaign, IL: Leisure Press.

Lerch, S.H. (1984). Athletic retirement as social death: An overview. In N. Theberge & P. Donnelly (Eds.), *Sport and the sociological imagination* (pp 259–272). Fort Worth: Texas Christian University Press.

Lever, J. (1976). Sex differences in the games children play. *Social Problems*, **23**, 479–487.

Lever, J. (1978). Sex differences in the complexity of children's play and games. *American Sociologial Review*, **43**, 471–483.

Lewko, J.H., & Greendorfer, S.L. (1988). Family influences in sport socialization of children and adolescents. In F.L. Smoll, R.A. Magill, & M.J. Ash (Eds.), *Children in Sport* (pp. 287–300). Champaign, IL: Human Kinetics.

Loy, J.W., & Ingham, A. (1973). Play, games, and sport in the psychosocial development of children and youth. In G.L. Rarick (Ed.). *Physical activity: Human growth and development* (pp. 257–302). New York: Academic Press.

McPherson, B.D. (1980). Retirement from professional sport: The process and problems of occupational and psychological adjustment. *Sociological Symposium*, **30**, 126–143.

McPherson, B.D. (1981). Socialization into and through sport involvement. In G.R.F. Luschen & G.H. Sage (Eds.), *Handbook of social science of sport* (pp. 246–273). Champaign, IL: Stipes.

McPherson, B.D. (1983). *Aging as a social process*. Toronto: Butterworths.

McPherson, B.D. (1986). Socialization theory and research: Toward a "new-wave" of scholarly inquiry in a sport context. In C.R. Rees & A.W. Miracle (Eds.), *Sport and social theory* (pp. 111–134). Champaign, IL: Human Kinetics.

Nisbett, R.E. (1968). Birth order and participation in dangerous sports. *Journal of Personality and Social Psychology*, **8**, 351–353.

Ogilvie, B., & Tutko, T. (1975, October). Sport: If you want to build character, try something else. *Psychology Today*, pp. 61–63.

Oliver, M.L. (1980). The transmission of sport mobility orientation in the family. *International Review of Sport Sociology*, **15**(2), 51–75.

Petrie, B.M. (1982). Birth order and sibling sex-status: Neglected variables in the study of socialization into sport. In A.G. Ingham & E.F. Broom (Eds.), *Career patterns and career contingencies in sport* (pp. 238–257). Vancouver: University of British Columbia Press.

Purdy, D., Eitzen, S., & Haufler, S. (1982). Age-group swimming: Contributing factors and consequences. *Journal of Sport Behavior*, **5**, 28–43.

Roberts, J.M., & Sutton-Smith, B. (1962). Child training and game involvement. *Ethnology*, **1**, 166–185.

Rooney, J.F. (1974). *A geography of American sport: From Cabin Creek to Anaheim*. Reading, MA: Addison-Wesley.

Rosenberg, E. (1984). Athletic retirement as social death: Concepts and perspectives. In N. Theberge & P. Donnelly (Eds.), *Sport and the sociological imagination* (pp. 245–258). Fort Worth: Texas Christian University Press.

Schachter, S. (1959). *The psychology of affiliation: Experimental studies of the sources of gregariousness.* Stanford, CA: Stanford University Press.

Sewell, W.H. (1963). Some recent developments in socialization theory and research. *The Annals of the American Academy of Political Science,* **349**(September), 163–181.

Smith, G.J., Patterson, B., Williams, T., & Hogg, J.M. (1981). A profile of the deeply committed male sport fan. *Arena Review,* **5**(2), 26–44.

Smith, M.D. (1979). Getting involved in sport: Sex differences. *International Review of Sport Sociology,* **14**(2), 93–101.

Snyder, E.E. & Purdy, D.A. (1982). Socialization into sport: Parent and Child reverse and reciprocal effects. *Research Quarterly for Exercise and Sport,* **53**, 263–266.

Stevenson, C.L. (1975). Socialization effects of participation in sport: A critical review of the research. *Research Quarterly,* **46**, 287–301.

Stevenson, C.L. (1985). College athletics and character: The decline and fall of socialization research. In D. Chu, J.O. Segrave, & B.J. Becker (Eds.), *Sport and higher education* (pp. 249–266). Champaign, IL: Human Kinetics.

Sutton-Smith, B. (1973). Games: The socialization of conflict. *Canadian Journal of History and Physical Education,* **4**(1), 1–7.

Sutton-Smith, B., & Rosenberg, B.G. (1970). *The sibling.* New York: Holt, Rinehart and Winston.

Thornton, R., & Nardi, P.M. (1975). The dynamics of role acquisition. *American Journal of Sociology,* **80**(1), 870–885.

Voigt, D.Q. (1974). *A Little League journal.* Bowling Green, OH: Bowling Green University Popular Press.

Weiss, M.R., & Knoppers, A. (1982). The influence of socializing agents on female collegiate volleyball players. *Journal of Sport Psychology,* **4**, 267–279.

Wentworth, W.M. (1980). *Context and understanding: An inquiry into socialization theory.* New York: Elsevier.

Yamaguchi, Y. (1984). A comparative study of adolescent socialization into sport: The case of Japan and Canada. *International Review for the Sociology of Sport,* **19**, 63–82.

Zigler, E., & Child, I.L. (1969). Socialization. In G. Lindzey & E. Aronson (Eds.), *The handbook of social psychology,* (Vol. 3, pp. 450-589). Reading, MA: Addison-Wesley.

C H A P T E R 3

Sport, Education, and Youth Groups

By the late 1800s, employers began to require complex, specialized skills of their workers. It became clear that families alone could not fully prepare their children for these new adult roles. Accordingly, the elementary and secondary educational system expanded to teach the skills that would be needed in a rapidly changing society. Higher education, in turn, developed to provide either a general liberal education or highly specialized training for specific occupations. The educational system is now a major partner in socializing children and adolescents.

Through teachers, coaches, textbooks, and classmates, a student acquires skills, knowledge, and values. A student also gains essential interpersonal skills and a sense of identity. Schools and community youth groups offer sport experiences because they are thought to contribute to this process of socialization.

Physical education classes and intramural and interscholastic competition were introduced into the British and North American curricula to (a) promote health through fitness, (b) socialize youth into sport skills, and (c) teach values and character traits deemed essential by society. Europe, in contrast, developed neighborhood and community sport clubs for the entire family.

SCHOOL AND SOCIALIZATION

To understand the role of sport in the educational system, we must address the purpose of **education**. One view holds that education should be designed for **enculturation**; that is, children must learn and internalize the prevailing cultural values and the accepted behavioral patterns of adulthood. The main role of education is thus to guarantee that individuals have sufficient social and vocational skills to fit successfully into the existing social structure. In this approach to education, the teaching is authoritarian, and the student passively accepts the information presented.

An alternative view holds that the educational system should help individuals become independent and effective decision-makers. Here the individual is given responsibility for his or her own opportunities. The student is encouraged to experiment and to question the self, others, and accepted views.

To date, enculturation has been the preferred model within the public educational system in North America. Interscholastic athletics have been used to reinforce enculturation. It has been argued that a high school sport program teaches the dominant community values and limits the opportunity to question the existing values or experiment with alternative approaches. Although only a few highly skilled athletes participate, many students support the school team as specta-

tors. It is argued that they thus learn, indirectly, the values promoted by sport.

Until recently, most sport opportunities in schools were restricted to male students. Women's participation in high school and college sport did not increase dramatically until the 1970s; the increase was related in part to passage of Title IX in the U.S. Higher Education Act of 1972. Title IX prohibited sex discrimination in all educational institutions that receive federal grants (Boutilier & San-Giovanni, 1983). Table 3.1 shows a 540% increase over 7 years in the number of female participants in 10 high school sports. Today, it is estimated that girls now comprise about 35% of all high school athletes (Melnick, Vanfossen, & Sabo, 1988).

The past few years have brought a considerable increase in the diversity of sports offered to female competitors and in the number of sex-integrated sport teams. Sport opportunities for women within the educational system have improved and are improving, although gender equality has not yet been attained. Thus, the school system has become an influential setting for the socialization of females into sport. To illustrate, Higginson (1985) found that girls over the age of 13 years believed that teachers and coaches provided the most important encouragement and reinforcement for their sport involvement. Thus, just as sport is becoming a more socially acceptable activity for adolescent females, the school is becoming more significant in socializing women into competitive sport roles.

SCHOOL AND SPORT SOCIALIZATION

The educational system in the United States, along with the family and peer group, is an influential institution in the process of sport role socialization. Similar to other social sys-

Table 3.1   The Number of Participants in U.S. Girls' High School Sport, 1970–1977

Sport	Number of participants		
	1970–1971	1972–1973	1976–1977
Track and field	62,211	178,209	395,271
Basketball	132,299	203,207	387,507
Volleyball	17,952	108,298	245,032
Softball	9,813	81,379	133,458
Tennis	26,010	53,940	112,166
Swimming and diving	17,229	41,820	85,013
Gymnastics	17,225	35,224	79,461
Field hockey	4,260	45,252	59,944
Golf	1,118	10,106	32,190
Cross-country	1,719	4,921	30,798
Total	289,836	762,356	1,560,840

Note. From *The Sporting Woman* (p. 164) by M.A. Boutilier and L. SanGiovanni, 1983, Champaign, IL: Human Kinetics. Copyright 1983 by Mary A. Boutilier and Lucinda SanGiovanni. Reprinted by permission.

tems, the role of the educational system varies—by sport, by roles within sports, by sex, and by stage in the life cycle (Howell & McKenzie, 1987; Snyder & Spreitzer, 1981; Snyder, 1985).

Elementary Schools

The public elementary school system seems to play a minor role in sport socialization. Rather, the family, neighborhood, peer group, and voluntary sport association play the major roles. This is not surprising considering that sport is not considered an important part of the curriculum in most elementary schools. A frequent exception is private schools or boarding schools, where some level of sport participation is required for all students (Armstrong, 1984).

Secondary Schools

In secondary schools, sport is an integral part of the youth subculture and is highly valued

by students, parents, and teachers. Adolescents thus have both opportunity and impetus to participate in sport. Highlight 3.1 indirectly illustrates the extent to which a high school sport is highly valued. Here, we learn of an annual ritual perpetuated from class to class.

Sport participants in secondary schools are likely to find role models and reinforcement from significant others; elementary schools, again, are not likely to provide this kind of support. For example, in sports such as gymnastics, wrestling, and track and field, champion athletes frequently report that their interests were aroused during high school. Many Olympic athletes report that they attended high schools where the students and teachers considered their particular sports to be among the most important extracurricular activities.

Colleges and Universities

At the college or university level, a socialization process operates in sports such as

---

Highlight 3.1
A High School Ritual: The Senior Ceremony

Rituals help to promote and reinforce important values and sentiments surrounding sport. This is aptly illustrated by the annual ceremony at the last practice for a southern high school football team. Attending this "Senior Ceremony" are parents, members of the athletic association, cheerleaders, and band members. While the band plays taps, the seniors on the team run through a gauntlet of underclassmen, symbolically hitting the blocking sleds at the goal posts for the last time. Dunleavy and Miracle (1979) describe the remainder of the ritual as follows:

... the seniors each made a farewell speech, and they were then saluted by representatives from the 11th and 10th grade players as well as by each coach. The head coach was last, and as he began to speak he broke into tears, and began hugging each player and shaking each one's hand. Most of the seniors also were crying, as were all of the cheerleaders and many parents. The seniors then formed a huddle and gave a cheer. The underclassmen cheered the seniors, as a parent consoled the coach who was still wiping the tears from his eyes. All of the players ran the full length of the field, and were joined by the coaching staff as the parents left. Practice resumed. (p. 21)

---

football and basketball to prepare elite athletes for careers in sport. At this stage an athlete learns the values and skills needed to succeed in professional or Olympic sport. This period of socialization involves learning and repeated testing against other elite athletes.

Similar to secondary schools, universities encourage students to become sport consumers, especially to become consumers of football and basketball. The adults most likely to consume professional football regularly are those who have attended college. Of these, football fans are more likely to have graduated from a college where attending football games was an integral part of the social scene. Thus, student spectators of football are likely to incorporate watching football into their adult leisure.

IMPACT OF SPORT ON EDUCATION

Even casual observation of high schools and colleges demonstrates that sport is an important part of their value systems. This is shown by the

- size of athletic facilities;
- wearing of school jackets by athletes and other students;
- number of pages and photographs devoted to sport in school yearbooks;
- prominent placement (often in the main lobby of high schools) of trophies awarded for athletic prowess;
- high status allocated to athletes in the peer status system;

- extensive media coverage of high school and college sport;
- social importance of sport activities of a school; and
- size of the athletic budget compared with budgets for (a) other student activities and (b) research or academic pursuits of the faculty.

For example, some American universities allocate more money to athletic budgets than to academic ones; some football coaches earn salaries greater than university presidents.

Competitive sport is valued as an essential and desirable part of the educational system. It is an activity that many believe students should experience. Some educators have long claimed that sport serves a number of utilitarian functions. Specifically, they have argued that sport in the high school and college setting

- teaches self-control and self-discipline, and thereby serves as a mechanism of social control;
- teaches principles of fair play, sportsmanship, achievement-orientation, and cooperation—lessons important for a successful adult life;
- encourages physical well-being;
- raises the educational aspirations and academic achievement levels of athletes;
- helps to integrate the student body and builds school spirit, morale, and cohesion;
- provides formal occupational socialization for those aspiring to professional sport careers;
- encourages so-called appropriate sex-role behavior (in the past, the role of athlete for males and the role of cheerleader for females were the major or only options provided); and
- develops loyalty to the college, which enhances alumni donations and helps to recruit future students.

Universities in the United States actively promote the consumption of sport.

Despite the almost total lack of supporting evidence, these claims are advanced regularly—in preparing and defending annual athletic budgets, following a sport scandal or riot, or in response to a report on the low graduation rate of athletes compared with nonathletes. We still do not know if interscholastic or intercollegiate sport helps meet educational goals. Nor do we know what educational impact, if any, sport has on the individual athlete, on the individual student who does not participate in sport, on the general student population, on alumni, on the image of the institution, or on the community in which the institution is located.

Educational Attainment of Athletes: Achievement or Failure?

In 1934, Davis and Cooper reported that nonathletes perform better in the classroom than athletes. This little-known study, rediscovered in the 1960s, has led to a large amount of research on the relationship between sport participation and academic achievement at the high school and college level. Most studies compare the grade point average (GPA) of high school or college athletes with nonathletes at one time and across various school sports. At the college level, studies compare the graduation rate of athletes with nonathletes or compare the graduation rate of athletes across sports, across institutions, or across athletic conferences.

Many of these studies indicate that involvement in sport affects athletes' levels of academic achievement. Only a few longitudinal studies assess whether grades improve or deteriorate with greater or lesser athletic involvement. And few studies examine whether grades change when an athlete does *not* participate in a varsity sport (e.g., during the off-season). Unfortunately, most studies do not include the grades of athletes (especially at the high school level) dropped from teams because of failing grades. Notwithstanding these methodological inadequacies (Baumann & Henschen, 1986), a large body of research literature indicates that at the high school level in the United States the academic performance of athletes equals or betters that of nonathletes, although the relationship varies by social class, race, and gender (Snyder & Spreitzer, 1981; Snyder, 1985).

At the college level, the relationship is less clear. Some studies show a positive relationship; others, a negative relationship; and still others, no relationship at all. We *can* conclude that at the college level in the United States there is more variation in the relationship, and that more studies seem to find a negative relationship between athletic participation and academic achievement. The academic performances of athletes might be classified in three general patterns: *passing*

easily, getting by, and *struggling along* (Brede & Camp, 1987). An athlete struggling along may pass less than half of her or his credit hours. To remain eligible, the athlete may take intersession courses to pick up credit hours and correct GPA deficits. In Table 3.2 we see that the 167 football and basketball players at one institution registered for about the same number of credit hours in the fall semester. The athletes' academic performance differed considerably at the end of the fall semester. At the end of the academic year, the GPA for all groups increased; the increase may have resulted from completing assignments or resubmitting earlier assignments for regrading. Nevertheless, there is still considerable variation within an institution, with about 25% of the athletes struggling to remain eligible for the next season.

Some variation in college athletes' academic achievement can be accounted for by philosophical differences among sports and among institutions. Academic performance can be greatly influenced by

- admission standards;
- recruitment practices;
- quality and demands of the academic courses and programs in which athletes are registered;
- time commitment and pressures to win, which vary by sport and by college;
- value different coaches place on an education; and
- perceived relative importance of men's and women's sports.

With regard to the final point, most studies have found that the grades of female athletes are *not* lower than those of nonathletes. The recent increases in the visibility and importance of women's sport on college campuses may increase the possibility of lower grades (Boutilier & SanGiovanni, 1983; Purdy, Eitzen, & Hufnagel, 1985). This decrease in ac-

Table 3.2   Academic Performance of Student-Athletes

Category	N	Average fall semester credit hours		GPA	
		Attempted	Passed	Fall semester	Academic year
Passing easily	31	13.3	12.6	3.21	3.43
Getting by	92	13.5	10.3	1.93	2.13
Struggling along	44	13.6	5.1	1.09	1.96

Note. From "The Education of College Student-Athletes" by R.M. Brede and H.J. Camp, 1987, *Sociology of Sport Journal*, **4**, pp. 245–257. Copyright 1987 by Human Kinetics Publishers. Adapted by permission.

ademic performance may be caused by longer schedules, lowering admission standards, a win-at-all-costs approach to the sport, and other negative factors now seen mainly in men's sport.

A number of explanations have been proposed to account for either the positive or negative relationship between athletic involvement and academic performance. Generally it has been suggested that the positive relationship can be attributed to (a) an already strong relationship between mental and physical ability, (b) coaches' selecting the better students for high school teams, or (c) the tendency for better students to pursue more extracurricular activities, including sport.

In a more detailed explanation, Schafer and Armer (1972) suggested eight possible reasons that athletes tend to be better students.

- Teachers grade more leniently.
- Values acquired in sport are transferred to the classroom.
- Superior physical conditioning improves mental performance.
- Athletes study more than nonathletes in order to remain eligible.
- Athletes make more efficient and effective use of their limited study time.

- High school athletes need good grades to be eligible for a college athletic scholarship.
- Athletes obtain extra tutoring and advice from peers, coaches, and teachers.
- Prestige earned in athletics provides a better self-concept and promotes higher aspirations in other domains.

A more analytical explanation by Rehberg (1969) argued that five intervening factors explain why athletes perform as well or better than nonathletes in the classroom. These include suggestions that athletes

- associate with highly achievement-oriented peers;
- transfer achievement values learned in sport to the classroom environment;
- acquire an increasing self-esteem that creates higher levels of aspiration in other domains;
- respond to pressure from coaches and others to consistently present themselves as successful; and
- receive more scholastic and career guidance from adult **significant others**, especially those within the school.

Contrasting theories suggest that athletic involvement may interfere with academic achievement. Possible explanations are that

- because sport is so highly valued, scarce time and energy must be focused on sport and away from academic pursuits (e.g., reading, studying, and attending classes);
- parent, coach, and alumni encouragement rewards athletic performance more than academic performance;
- because some schools plan to make money on sport (at the college level) their recruitment of athletes may not emphasize academic talent or a balanced commitment to academics and athletics (Sack & Thiel, 1985; Snyder, 1985); and
- athletic involvement in college is narrowly perceived as career preparation for a professional athlete rather than as general preparation for adulthood or for an occupation after a professional sport career.

To summarize, high school athletes appear to receive grades at least as high as, and perhaps higher, than nonathletes—if they stay in school. But, it is not known how many high school athletes have been eliminated from these studies because they were academically ineligible to be a member of the team that was being studied. At the college level, many studies suggest that athletes receive lower grades than nonathletes, especially if involved in a major sport like football or basketball (Baumann & Henschen, 1986; Figler, 1984; Kiger & Lorentzen, 1986).

Some of the factors we have discussed differ in other cultures. For example, Canadian universities have not been allowed to offer grants-in-aid to athletes. There is little recruiting by coaches, because they have little to offer that differs from another university except location, lifestyle, and quality of coaching. Similarly, alumni are less likely to be involved in the athletic program. As a result, Canadian athletes must gain admission to a university and remain eligible through academic merit. As students, they are per-

haps more likely to achieve at a level similar to that of nonathletes.

Without conclusive evidence, perhaps the best conclusion we can draw is a general one: An athlete's academic achievement reflects his or her intellectual ability and commitment to long-term educational goals. And this commitment will be influenced by the attitudes of the school, coach, and peers.

Aspirations and Career Attainment of Athletes

An early justification of interscholastic athletic programs was that being on high school teams motivates athletes to attain higher levels of education than they might otherwise. The argument suggests that educational goals and expectations are not taught by other high school extracurricular activities.

Since the 1960s, a number of studies have found a positive relationship between being an athlete and expecting to attend college, especially among male athletes (Snyder & Spreitzer, 1981). Detailed analyses have suggested that the relationship is more likely to hold for athletes with less favorable sociodemographic characteristics and for those who participate in specific athletic environments. The relationship appears to be *stronger* for boys with a lower social status, with a history of low academic performance, who lack parental encouragement for academic advancement, and who live in a rural area.

Studies have also indicated that this relationship may be stronger among athletes attending high schools where sport generates more status in the peer group than academics. Many black high school athletes believe that college is a prerequisite to a professional sport career; because they value a sport career highly, they report high expectations to attend college.

Researchers have proposed a number of explanations for the positive relationship between sport participation and academic expectations (Rehberg & Schafer, 1968; Snyder & Spreitzer, 1981). The orientation to continue in school may come in part from peers who are college-oriented, either because of their ability or their parents' encouragement. Athletes may also receive considerable encouragement from adult significant others (e.g., coaches) at their high schools or colleges. Athletes often report that their high school coach was instrumental in their decision to attend college.

One outcome of this apparent relationship between being a high school athlete and wanting to attend college is unrealistic educational and career goals. The inflated aspirations induced by social pressure may not jibe with actual ability or academic motivation. cademic difficulties may arise where there is a lack of ability or a lack of intrinsic motivation or encouragement. Such deficiencies are magnified if senior members of the team (who serve as role models) stress how to beat the academic system and still remain eligible.

Sport sociologists have recently questioned whether involvement in high school sport has *any* long-term benefits in career mobility or later-life earnings (Howell, Miracle, & Rees, 1984; Okihiro, 1984; Otto & Alwin, 1977; Picou, McCarter, & Howell, 1985; Sack & Thiel, 1979). Strong evidence gathered over a long period of time is still lacking. The few available studies suggest that many who remain involved in sport throughout high school and college attain a higher occupational status than might otherwise be expected. These studies have not demonstrated a consistent positive relationship between high school sport participation and later-life earnings, partly because there are so many possible confounding effects. However, as Highlight 3.2 describes, there is some evidence from one study of college football players that suggests that those successful in sport have

greater career mobility than those who participated in sport but were less successful.

One plausible explanation for the success of athletes in finding and holding jobs is that they have learned to interact well with people. Many former athletes are employed successfully in people-oriented jobs (Okihiro, 1984).

COLLEGE SPORT AS A SOCIAL PROBLEM

Particularly in the United States, intercollegiate sport has become an important economic and social element of higher education (Smith, 1988). Students originally organized their own sport programs to provide recreation. However, with the increasing interest of spectators and with a greater emphasis on winning, institutions began to provide facilities and full-time coaching personnel. Ultimately, the NCAA was established; it has grown into a large bureaucracy that administers college sport.

The basic mission of a university is to generate and transmit knowledge. But the promotion of athletic excellence has also become a major goal—one that is perceived by some as equally important. Where this perception holds, athletic departments have been required to justify their intensity and mission to the board of governors, to the president, to the faculty, or to the public. In response, they have claimed that sport makes a positive contribution to the social life of the student body, to the educational mission of the university, and to the economic stability of the institution.

It has been argued that a successful intercollegiate program

- contributes to character building, as illustrated by the numerous corporate and

---

Highlight 3.2
Participation in U.S. College Football and Later Career Mobility

Many case studies have documented the rags to riches story of a star college athlete from a ghetto or impoverished background. Seldom, however, are these individual athletes studied later in life. Although it is frequently argued that participation in high school and college football may be an effective avenue for upward mobility, there is only limited evidence that sport success in early adulthood has a carry-over influence on life after sport.

In a study of 218 football players and 264 randomly selected nonfootball players at Notre Dame, Sack and Thiel (1979) found that the football players came from somewhat lower socioeconomic backgrounds than the average student. Both groups, however, experienced considerable occupational status mobility. Athletes and nonathletes got better jobs than their fathers had. The athletes were neither more nor less mobile than the nonathletes. Also, there was very little difference in income attainment.

Among the athletes, 41% of those who played on the first team were earning $50,000 or more at the time of the survey, compared with 30% of those from the second team and 13% of the reserves. Similarly, of those who reported being a top executive in their company, 34% had played on the first team in their senior year, 13% were on the second team, and 14% were reserves. Whether these differences by playing ability are due to differences in status as a player, interpersonal skills, competitiveness, or postplaying career sponsorship remains to be determined.

Note. Adapted from Sack and Thiel (1979).

---

political leaders who were former intercollegiate athletes;
- provides a unifying element to generate school spirit or institutional loyalty, as evidenced by continued alumni interest in attending games and contributing money;
- serves a public relations function, as evidenced by the number of high school students who report that they select a university partly on the basis of the success of the football or basketball team—despite the finding of a strong negative relationship between the national academic ranking of an institution and the ranking of the football team (Roper & Snow, 1976);

- provides student-athletes with an opportunity to become well-rounded individuals, because athletes are expected to be students first and athletes second, as evidenced by athletes on Dean's lists, who become Rhodes' scholars, or who succeed in graduate school, law school, or medicine; and
- contributes to the income of the university and the local community by attracting spectators to home games. For example, on a football weekend tourists may generate an unusual amount of business.

The growing importance and increasing complexity of college sport has led to a num-

The size of athletic facilities and the popularity of sport events illustrate the emphasis schools place on sport.

ber of negative outcomes. Moral and economic abuses seem to increase (or are detected and reported more frequently) as success on the playing field increases. Success generates more revenue for recruiting and raises expectations of continued success. To remain successful, colleges and universities may change their recruiting practices and educational standards. One outcome is the loss of autonomy and freedom by individual student-athletes, who may be viewed less as students and more as investments or commodities to be exploited by the university for profit. Because some programs view athletes this way (the argument goes) every institution must respond similarly to compete successfully on the field. The NCAA appears unable or unwilling to deal with these problems, either to identify the violations or to enforce the many rules in their rule book (Stern, 1981).

The following subsections describe a number of recent abuses associated with this heightened emphasis on achieving and maintaining a successful athletic program. Although we focus here on negative consequences, the positive consequences must not be overlooked. In Table 3.3, the number of hypothesized or alleged positive outcomes clearly outweigh the negative outcomes. But only a few negative outcomes can tarnish or destroy an athlete or an athletic program.

Educational Abuses

Journalistic reports in the print and electronic media (Underwood, 1980; Kirshenbaum,

Table 3.3   Positive and Negative Outcomes of Intercollegiate Athletics

Individual or group affected	Outcome	
	Positive	Negative

Education system	Integration of student body
	Reduction of conflict
	Unity of members across class lines
	Social control
	  Displace aggression
	  Norm affirmation
	Prestige
	Community visibility
	Academic communities' visibility
	Generalized political and economic influence/support
	Informal membership retention and support beyond formal break (i.e., graduation)
	Attraction of membership
	Promotion of "town and gown" affiliation
		Detraction from educational mission
		Promotion of hostility/conflict

Athlete	Character development (e.g., courage, humbleness) Acquisition of social skills Tension release Education attainment Occupational attainment Occupational success Educational opportunity Physical fitness Prestige Tension/excitement Identity formation Affective association	Character detraction Negative aggression Educational detraction Exploitation of larger subsystems (i.e., powerlessness) Role conflict and stress Dehumanizing and delusionary Value distortion

Community	Unity of members across social categories
	Democratization of interpersonal relations—"talking sports"
	Social control
	  Displace aggression
	  Norm affirmation
	  Safety valve/tension management
	Entertainment—tension excitement
	Economic—flow of new capital
	Opportunity for association with political and economic elite
	Identity and visibility via boosterism
	Community legitimacy—"big league"
		Creation of false consciousness
		Diversion of attention from social problems
		Reinforcement of class distinctions
		Promotion of hostility and conflict

(Cont.)

Table 3.3   (Continued)

Individual or group affected	Outcome	
	Positive	Negative
Society	Socialization of accepted values, norms (e.g., conformity)	Socialization to norms and behavior which are demeaning or potentially disruptive (e.g., dishonesty, circumventing rules)
	Safetly valve/tension release at class level	Intergroup/class hostility
	Ritualistic expression of American life—norm and value affirmation	Diversion of attention from exploitive social structure
	Reinforcement of sex, age, and racial role allocations	Reinforcement of sexism, racism, and unequal distribution of resources

Note. From "College Athletics: Problems of a Functional Analysis" by J.H. Frey. In *Sport and Social Theory* (pp. 206–207) by C.R. Rees and A.W. Miracle (Eds.), 1986, Champaign, IL: Human Kinetics. Copyright 1986 by Human Kinetics Publishers, Inc. Adapted by permission.

1989; Reilly, 1989; Telander & Sullivan, 1989) and increasing scholarly interest in the problems of intercollegiate sport (Chu, Segrave, & Becker, 1985; Figler, 1984; Frey, 1982, 1986; Marmion, 1979; Nixon, 1982), have identified a number of abuses. If indeed they are present, these issues must be addressed by the academic institution before they begin to detract from the quality of education provided to the athlete and perhaps even the nonathlete.

Who is to blame for these abuses? The institution? The alumni? The media? A partial answer is found in a four-year participant-observation study of the academic goals and beliefs of athletes in a major college basketball program (Adler & Adler, 1985). The researchers found that athletes enter college with idealistic goals of academic achievement; their perspective changes, however, as they move toward their senior year. They became cynical about and detached from the academic part of college life. They lose interest and expend little effort on academic pursuits. Those who reach their senior year

and have professional sport aspirations often abandon the classroom as soon as they complete the last game of the season.

Adler and Adler (1985) attribute these behavioral and attitudinal changes to the structure of large college athletic programs. The crucial factors are

- intense demands to perform as athletes, which sap their energy and concentration and distort their perceptions and values;
- the degree to which they are socially isolated (e.g., in athletic dormitories) from the student body, especially if they are minority athletes with different cultural experiences; and
- a gap between the athletes' academic qualifications and the universities' expectations; this gap can lead to frustration, failure, and further alienation from the peer subculture and the goals of academia.

Recruiting Practices.   To recruit athletes, university representatives in the United States are permitted, depending on the sport, two or three visits to an athlete's home; the athlete is permitted only one expense-paid visit to each campus, and no more than five expense-paid visits in total. Only full-time employees of the university may contact athletes. Recruiting violations have included, however, having alumni (*boosters*) entertain prospects, offer gifts or money, promise favors if they attend the university, and visit the athletes in their hometown. Another abuse involves encouraging academically weak students to enroll in a junior college for a few semesters before transferring to the major college—this kind of farm system is illegal. Coaches are also reportedly dishonest in telling high school players when and where they will play. These recruiting violations may be increasing in frequency, because the competition for scarce talent is intense. Once the search for talent was generally restricted to a given region; many colleges now search the nation for athletic talent (Rooney, 1980).

Admission Standards and Practices.

Universities have been known to ignore or lower their usual standards if a highly talented athlete cannot meet the minimum admission criteria. In recent years some colleges have actually condoned such practices as altering and falsifying high school transcripts; admitting functionally illiterate athletes; and sending players to junior colleges for easy credit courses (sometimes the athletes do not even attend these classes) that will raise their GPAs to some minimum level.

To standardize and strengthen basic admission requirements, the NCAA introduced Proposition 48. This rule, which took effect on August 1, 1986, states that freshman athletes must attain at least a 2.0 GPA in 11 core high school courses (including three years of English, two of math, two in the social sciences, and two in the natural or physical sciences); must maintain this GPA in college;

and must achieve a combined score of 700 on the Scholastic Aptitude Test (SAT) or 15 on the American College Test (ACT). The rule had an immediate impact: In September 1986, an estimated 200 freshmen athletes with scholarship offers were declared ineligible. Most of these athletes had been recruited by Division I-A schools. These regulations were further tightened with the introduction of Proposition 42 in 1990.

Many have argued that these rules are culturally biased and discriminates against blacks (Hanford, 1985) and foreigners, who may not perform as well on standardized tests (i.e., SAT or ACT). The rules are intended to ensure that all college athletes have a chance to earn an education and to graduate.

Registration and Grading Discrepancies.

Once admitted to a college, athletes may be steered by counselors into easy courses (e.g., Food I, Beginning Football, Film Projector I, Music Listening) or encouraged to take the minimum number of courses per semester. Sometimes an athlete is enrolled in remedial courses and can play for 2 years without taking a college-level course. Sometimes advisers do not explain that specific courses are required for graduation; 4 years after admission an athlete may not have a major or may lack specific required courses. Athletic staff may pressure faculty to change a failing grade to an Incomplete or a Pass or to give credit for a course the athlete has not attended. Athletes may be encouraged, as well, to cheat on exams or copy term papers in order to remain eligible.

These practices ultimately punish athletes by depriving them of a quality education. Moreover, athletes may come to believe that their major role on campus is to perform on the field rather than in the classroom. Indirectly, this encourages poor attendance of classes and may lead to deviant behavior. Because of lowered admission and ethical standards, some college athletes enter an educational environment without the skills they need to succeed, regardless of how much remedial work they undertake. Some athletes have been unable to read the questions on examinations!

Graduation Rates. In recent years a number of newspaper articles and research reports have revealed that graduation rates for athletes are quite low. The rate tends to be consistently lower at some institutions. Within a particular institution, the rate may vary by sport, by the race of the athlete, or by gender. One type of study has reported the percentage of players in a professional sport league that graduated of those that attended college. In professional football and basketball, the number of players *without* a degree has ranged from 33% to 80%. Moreover, many athletes do not graduate in the normal 4 or 5 years but must return in the off-season to complete the degree requirements at their own expense.

Another type of study has examined graduation rates at specific colleges for a specific period of time (Curtis & McTeer, in press; Figler, 1984; Henschen & Fry, 1984; Kiger & Lorentzen, 1986; Messner & Groisser, 1982; Shapiro, 1984). These studies usually compare the rates for athletes versus nonathletes; black athletes versus white athletes; male athletes versus female athletes; and athletes in major sports versus athletes in minor sports (see Highlight 3.3). Lower graduation rates for athletes are assumed to reflect varying levels of indirect or direct exploitation of the scholarship athlete. In effect, a lower graduation rate for athletes may indicate that these students are pursuing goals other than those of the academic institution. It may also indicate that unqualified students are being admitted.

Combating Abuses. Ultimately these abuses result in stiffer penalties, tighter rules,

and increased enforcement procedures, initiated by the NCAA. As a result, the number of institutions placed on probation has increased, mainly because coaches, professors, or alumni have been found guilty of such practices as improper recruiting, awarding unearned grades, providing extra benefits to athletes, or using academically ineligible athletes. For example, Rooney (1985) reported that two thirds of the institutions of higher learning affiliated with the NCAA have engaged in some form of cheating in recent years.

The number and severity of measures to prevent abuses is also increasing. These methods include

- visiting campuses to inform athletes about the intent of NCAA rules and about their personal rights;
- encouraging more high school athletic associations to raise and enforce academic requirements (for example, Bill 72 in Texas initiated the "No Pass, No Play" rule: every high school student must pass *every* subject during a 6-week grading period or be declared ineligible for extracurricular activities for the following 6 weeks);
- enacting and actually invoking the "death penalty," which punishes repeated rule violations within a 5 year period with cancellation of playing seasons for up to 2 years (the most severe "death penalty" to date was invoked against the football program at Southern Methodist University in February 1987; this decision prevented the school from fielding a team during the 1987 season, they were limited to seven games in 1988, and other sanctions were imposed on recruiting practices and the size of the coaching staff until the fall of 1990); and
- implementing new rules to discourage recruiting violations (for example, the

Highlight 3.3
Graduation Rates of U.S. College Athletes

In recent years, people concerned about college athletics have argued that athletes are hired as laborers to perform on the field. Performance in the classroom is merely an added bonus. This view has been reinforced by anecdotal stories and by a few research studies that show that somewhere between 25% and 69% of NCAA athletes graduate (Henschen & Fry, 1984; Kiger & Lorentzen, 1986; Shapiro, 1984).

Some of these recent studies have indicated that the graduation rates of college athletes are lower

- in more recent decades as the level of competition has increased;
- for black athletes;
- for athletes in major sports;
- for male athletes;
- for female athletes since the introduction of Title IX;
- for athletes who are drafted by a professional sport team; and
- for teams that strive to compete at the national rather than the regional level.

Yet some of the studies have shown that, on average, male and female athletes are more likely to graduate than nonathletes within the same university.

Graduation rates among athletes have also been found to vary greatly from one institution to another, perhaps because of variations in academic support (e.g., tutoring, course counseling), in admission procedures, in the level of competition, and in the amount of financial and moral support offered by the athletic department to athletes when their academic eligibility expires.

More student-athletes will graduate when only academically qualified students are admitted, when athletes themselves are intrinsically motivated to achieve in the classroom, and when institutions provide guidance, encouragement, and financial support to ensure that every athlete has a fair and reasonable opportunity to graduate within a 5-year period.

NCAA has discussed the possibility of initiating a rule that would link the number of football and basketball scholarships a university may offer to the graduation rates of athletes on each team).

Individual Abuses

If athletes do not have the skill or interest to engage in academic pursuits, they may be more likely to engage in deviant behavior. To illustrate, in recent years athletes have been charged with theft, attempted bribery of arresting police officers, assault, rape, shoplifting, scalping complimentary tickets, selling or using drugs, drinking and driving, gambling, point shaving, and signing a contract with a sport agent, often in return for a financial signing bonus. These acts are ultimately the responsibility of the individual athlete. But the system, including coaches, alumni, local boosters, and the peer group, must take some responsibility for failing to supervise or guide the athlete or for directly or indirectly encouraging the deviant behavior. Of course nonathletes also engage in deviant acts. But the amount of deviance by athletes seems to be increasing, perhaps because they are no longer immune from the legal system and are being charged with offenses rather than being ignored. Another possible explanation is that the media now give more attention to the deviant actions of athletes or former athletes.

The Future of College Sport: Athletics or Academics?

There appears to be a discrepancy between the quality of education that universities are supposed to be offering student-athletes and the quality and quantity of education they are actually receiving. Although many moral and ethical abuses have been identified in college sport, other abuses may remain unidentified and go unpunished. These abuses have arisen partly because college sport has become both a farm system for professional football and basketball and a major entertainment business, where patrons demand excellence.

Rooney (1985) has suggested that in the future college sport must decide which of two models to pursue, then enforce ethical and moral rules to achieve the desired end. The *total professional entertainment model* would apply mainly or only to college football and basketball. Here, high school players would be drafted instead of recruited; they would be paid by the university according to a league-initiated salary schedule; and they could attend classes in the off-season, if academically eligible. In effect, the athletic department would be operated as a small profit-oriented business similar to any professional sport franchise. In contrast, the *total amateur model* would be controlled and funded by the central university administration, similar to any other academic department. In this system, every athlete would have to be a full-time student, and none would be subsidized unless he or she earned an academic scholarship or bursary. Most importantly, an athlete would have to meet the same yearly academic standards for promotion as any other student in order to remain eligible for athletic competition. This latter model has been employed in Canadian universities for decades.

Since neither of these models is likely to be adopted by existing large athletic programs, there is an urgent need for a compromise between the two positions. Athletics and academics can be intimately integrated within the world of higher education. Picou and Wells (1987) have proposed a number of changes to reach this ideal state, and to restore the integrity of intercollegiate sport.[1]

- Student athletes must become more sensitive to the importance of academic achievement and less oriented toward the fantasy career of professional sport.
- Coaches must become aware of the career and academic needs of student-athletes and must establish a set of ethics for their profession.
- Both coaches and student-athletes must be given greater job security. This would help to avoid the form of competitive neurosis that fosters the bending or breaking of recruiting, eligibility, and academic rules.

[1]*Note.* From "Rewrite the Book on College Sports" by J.S. Picou and R. Wells, 1987, March 22, *The Houston Chronicle.* Copyright 1987 by The Houston Chronicle. Adapted by permission.

- University faculty must eliminate prejudicial attitudes and discriminatory behavior directed toward college athletics and must provide intellectual and moral leadership to organize intercollegiate sports in terms of the academic values they represent.
- University presidents need to play a leadership role in preserving the academic integrity of their institutions. They must take responsibility for eliminating the abuses in athletic programs.
- Influential alumni must learn that the university is an academic community for developing resources and knowledge—not an athletic playpen where they can reap prestige and foster bragging rights.
- The university system must provide student-athletes with academic resources and coaches with both professional training and professional commitments.

YOUTH GROUPS AND SPORT SOCIALIZATION

Given freedom and encouragement to venture from the home during the early school years, children begin to participate first in peer groups within the neighborhood and school and later in age-based voluntary sport groups. These new social groups have a more informal structure than the family and school systems. And unlike ascribed membership in the family and school, membership in youth groups is voluntary. An individual may belong to one or more groups at the same time, and membership in a given group may vary over time in degree of interest.

The Peer Group as an Informal Socializing Setting

The peer group frequently becomes a socializing agent before the child begins school. In

Many children begin participating in sport via youth groups.

school, these groups reinforce or oppose the ideas, values, attitudes, behavioral patterns, and skills learned in the home and in the school. During childhood, the peer group teaches interactive social skills in a relatively egalitarian environment. Children learn about taboo subjects; gain independence from parents and other authority figures; and acquire ideas, values, and experiences that may not be taught or observed in their family. Later in life, and especially during the adolescent years, one's peer group provides opportunities to engage in decision-making processes: to lead and to follow; to ignore the influence of the family, especially when the individual is integrated into a highly cohesive age-graded subculture; and to experience and cope with rejection and failure in a world outside the family. For example, sport teams provide a setting for experiencing success, leadership, failure, rejection, and power.

An interesting aspect of peer groups is their increasing variation of values and interests as one gets older. During childhood, peer groups in the immediate neighborhood tend to hold somewhat similar values to those taught in the home. During adolescence, peer groups (a youth subculture) at the high school or in community youth sport organizations may introduce different values, opportunities, and interests. During adulthood, an influential peer group, often comprised of peers in the workplace, can provide an even greater source of variation in interests and values concerning sport. Despite this possible variation in influence throughout the life cycle, we do not know whether people gravitate toward a peer group that fits their previously established lifestyle, values, and interests, or whether they experience dramatic changes in lifestyle and values because of the influence of new peer groups.

Effect of Peer Groups on Sport Involvement

Although an initial interest in sport is often stimulated in the home, peer groups can reinforce or inhibit subsequent development. The research evidence overwhelmingly supports the importance of peer group support for involvement and success in sport. Without a sport-oriented peer group, children often reduce their involvement in sport, especially as participants.

During childhood and early adolescence most of the peer influence comes from same-sex peers, especially among males. However, many female athletes report having been a member of a male-dominated peer group in early to middle childhood. During high school, female athletes report receiving more support from female friends than from male friends (Snyder & Spreitzer, 1976). Later in life, and especially after dating begins or after marriage, opposite-sex peers may become more influential in encouraging or discouraging various forms of sport involvement for females.

Voluntary Sport Associations

By the early 1900s, most sport for children and adolescents was organized within the school system. However, as Berryman (1975) notes, the philosophy of highly organized sport competition for pre-adolescents was questioned in the 1930s. The educational system subsequently ceased to provide sport competition in the elementary schools. Yet at this same time, there was a growing desire by parents to provide varied sport opportunities so their children could develop and realize their full athletic potential. As a result, many boys' clubs were formed to organize sport competition for children and adolescents (Fine, 1987; Wiggins, 1987). Thus, when the educational system renounced competition for boys, the voluntary sector, comprised mostly of parents, took control. Later, especially following World War II, sport leagues were created to provide more competitive opportunities in specific sports.

All of these factors resulted in the growth of highly bureaucratized formal organizations that provide competition for children and adolescents (Ralbovsky, 1974a, 1974b). Many of these organizations are no longer truly voluntary associations. Rather, they employ professional, full-time workers, they have complex organizational structures that are national or international in scope, and they operate with large, fixed incomes. For example, Little League baseball, formed in 1939, has become an incorporated business organization with a head office and a large, fixed budget.

Currently, an estimated 20 million children in North America are involved in competitive sport programs (Martens, 1986); many join as early as 5 or 6 years of age. These voluntary organizations are a significant socializing institution for children and a major source of social involvement for adults. In these organizations children can experience

By the age of 5 or 6, many North American children are eager to join voluntary sport organizations.

and learn sport roles and model their behavior after their teachers or coaches. Many parents become psychologically and emotionally involved (e.g., as coaches, executives, or spectators) and strongly support and encourage their childrens' involvement.

Voluntary sport associations are viewed as a setting where children can be socialized into desirable values and characteristics. But youth sport can also inhibit a child's personal growth and lead to the emergence of intolerable social conditions in the child's environment.

YOUTH SPORT: A SOCIAL PROBLEM?

Since about the mid-1970s, journalists and sport scientists have increasingly identified, described, and studied a number of negative outcomes associated with voluntary sport associations (Brown & Branta, 1988; Coakley, 1986a, 1987; Colburn, 1985; Fine, 1987; Malina, 1988; Martens, 1978; McPherson, 1986; Ralbovsky, 1974a; Smoll, Magill, & Ash, 1988; Voigt, 1974; Weiss & Gould, 1986; Weiss & Sisley, 1984; Yablonsky & Brower, 1979). Some of these problems are dramatically illustrated in newspaper headlines.

- Some "Sports Parents" Behave Like Fools
- Violence; Expense Hits Minor Hockey
- Don't Let Your Son Play Smallfry Football
- Ban Parents From Sport Events
- Referee Files Charge Against Fan
- Manager Assaults Umpire With Bat
- It's Fun for Adults, Heartbreak for Kids

Some of these evils result in a high withdrawal rate from youth sport and in fewer participants in some of the traditional team sports. The decline in participation rates can be accounted for, at least partially, by lower birth rates. But even so, a smaller *proportion* appears to be participating, particularly among males who might have participated in the traditional team sports of football, in the United States, and hockey, in Canada.

Unrealistic Hopes for Professional Sport Career

Well-meaning parents can provide excessive encouragement for a child to aspire to a career in professional or elite amateur sport. Unfortunately, the success ratio for this type of career is relatively low considering the numbers who participate at the youth level. For example, only about one in 20,000 Little League baseball players earn even a try-out with a major league team; 29 out of 30 high school basketball players will not be selected to play for a college team. A recent study estimated the odds of American youth becoming a professional athlete at 4 per 1,000,000 for females and 7 per 100,000 for males (Leonard & Reyman, 1988). And these odds decrease significantly by race. For example, the odds for black females and males, respectively, were calculated as 4 per 1,000,000 and 2 per 100,000. Parents should recognize that there are only about 3,000 positions available in all North American professional sport. With a relatively low annual turnover rate, few professional opportunities are available for graduating seniors.

Parents must learn to encourage their children to achieve in both the educational and sport domains. Children will thus have viable career options when they must leave sport, whether voluntarily or involuntarily. As Conacher (1971) observed, "with an education, sport will always be a thing of choice, rather than a necessity" (p. 20). Similarly, Arthur Ashe (1977) recommended that black parents send their children to the libraries to instill a desire for learning. This will lower the school drop out rate, and children will have a range of choices when their dream of a sport career suddenly ends.

Excessive Parental Involvement

Another problem in children's sport is the increasing tendency for adults to control the children's play activity. Adults who organize youth sport programs become involved for a variety of reasons—to vicariously experience success, to seek prestige or status that is lacking in their own occupational or leisure world, or, in some cases, to protect their child from the coaching practices and values of other adults. One possible consequence is that adults expect more than children can give. Expectations for success and the motivation to participate may be forced on the child by an adult. As a result, the child has no motivation of his or her own. This often leads

to unrealistic norms, goals, and practices within the sport system, especially where the child's age is ignored. For example, some adults verbally abuse young children for failing to perform well. Or they demand performances that are not possible given the physical or social maturation level of the child. Thus, adults, by invoking unrealistic expectations, may ruin the fun inherent in organized sport.

The emphasis on winning and the need for competition introduced by adults can lead to

- all-star competition, with considerable travel and financial commitments required for participation;
- children sitting on the bench throughout games or seasons;
- recruiting beyond the immediate community for more highly skilled players;
- an escalation in the number of games played and the length of the season; and
- the professionalization of youth coaching, which has occurred in swimming, gymnastics, track, and figure skating (i.e., the hiring of full-time, high-salaried coaches who demand 30- or 40-hour work weeks from their young athletes).

One outcome of some of these perceived problems is that fewer children register for competitive sport programs at a very young age. Not only are children dropping out of organized sport programs but more parents are steering their children away from community sport programs, especially team sports. Maybe they have heard about the negative aspects of youth sport from other parents or have seen the problems themselves through the experiences of their older children. Many children who want to remain involved are forced out of competitive sport by coaches who think they are not good enough. As coaches often state when they cut a player, "You don't fit into *my* plans."

More recently, interest in the adult domination of youth sport has focused on the potential for child abuse. This is more likely to occur in highly competitive training programs such as swimming, gymnastics, track and field, and figure skating. These intense and demanding activities may require 20 to 30 hours of practice per week. These athletes, who have been labeled *child athletic workers* (Cantelon, 1982), may become victims of the *lost childhood* or *lost adolescence* syndrome (Donnelly & Sargent, 1986). Grupe (1985) argues that such child athletes

- are not allowed to be children;
- are abandoned by adults when they retire from competition;
- lose important social contacts and experiences while growing up;
- are subject to excessive psychological and physiological stress;
- are victims of a disrupted family life;
- face the risk of an endangered intellectual development; and
- may become totally focused within the sport context and thereby lose contact with the larger society.

If rejected or labeled failures, many children never regain interest in organized sport. Because there is considerable variation in youth and maturation rates (Malina, 1988), children must have the opportunity to remain involved in sport at a level that matches their ability. For example, children cut from a team at 11 or 12 years of age could simply be late maturers; they may become more highly skilled athletes at age 15 or 16 than their age peers. Michael Jordan, an NBA all-star, was cut from the high school basketball team in his sophomore year.

As Devereux (1976) noted, we must show an increasing concern for "what the ball is doing to the boy rather than what the boy is doing to the ball" (p. 54). To meet this concern, we must reduce the degree of adult involvement, modify the playing rules, reduce the size of the playing area for the youngest age groups, and evaluate the process and outcomes of youth sport programs (Coakley, 1986b; Martens, 1978; Martens, Rivkin, & Bump, 1984; McPherson & Brown, 1988; Orlick & Botterill, 1975).

To illustrate how much child athletes wish to be treated as children and to help adults remember this right and principle, consider the implications of the letter in Highlight 3.4 and the parent's code of ethics in Highlight 3.5.

WRAP-UP

Sport has almost always been a part of the educational system, and therefore an important agent of socialization. In school and in the community, sport is also an important element of the youth subculture, whether for participants or spectators. Indeed, some high schools and colleges seem to value excellence in sport more than academic excellence.

Given the prominence of sport in the educational system, the casual observer might assume that sport is a necessary component of the curriculum. But little research evidence supports the view that sport participation contributes directly either to individual academic attainment or to achieving the educational goals of the school or college. At the college level, the relationship between athletic participation and scholastic success is irregular, at best. Some athletes pass regularly, some get by, and some struggle. The strugglers are most frequently described in the popular press.

Closer analysis often reveals that many, if not most, of these struggling student-athletes are ill-prepared for the academic rigors of college life. The inability of such athletes to perform in the classroom is an example of how

Highlight 3.4
A Child's Letter on Parents and Sport

Some parents let their emotions run wild during their child's sport activity. The following anonymous letter (Ontario Hockey Council, 1982), written by a young hockey player, expresses a child's view of how parents can detract from the child's enjoyment of sport.*

Dear Mom and Dad:

I hope that you won't get mad at me for writing this letter, but you always told me never to keep anything back that ought to be brought out into the open. So here goes.

Remember the other morning when my team was playing and both of you were sitting and watching. Well, I hope that you won't get mad at me, but you kind of embarrassed me. Remember when I went after the puck in front of the net trying to score and fell? I could hear you yelling at the goalie for getting in my way and tripping me. It wasn't his fault, that is what he is supposed to do. Then do you remember yelling at me to get on the other side of the blue line. The coach told me to cover my man, and I couldn't if I listened to you, and while I tried to decide they scored against us. Then you yelled at me for being in the wrong place. You shouldn't have jumped all over the coach for pulling me off the ice. He is a pretty good coach, and a good guy, and he knows what he is doing. Besides he is just a volunteer coming down at all hours of the day helping us kids, just because he loves sports. And, then neither of you spoke to me the whole way home, I guess you were pretty sore at me for not getting a goal. I tried awfully hard, but I guess I am a crummy hockey player. But, I love the game, it is lots of fun being with the other kids and learning to compete. It is a good sport, but how can I learn if you don't show me a good example. And, anyhow I thought I was playing hockey for fun, to have a good time, and to learn good sportsmanship. I didn't know that you were going to get so upset because I couldn't become a star.

Love,

Your son

*Note. From You and Your Child in Hockey by the Ontario Hockey Council, 1982, Toronto: Ontario Ministry of Tourism and Recreation. Copyright 1982 by the Ontario Ministry of Tourism and Recreation. Reprinted by permission.

college sport has become a social problem. Problems have also increased as the need to win has increased, whether for prestige or economic gains. This increased pressure to win has introduced other abuses, such as illegal recruiting, lowering or ignoring admission standards, improper registration for classes, using player agents, and discrepancies in grading practices.

Youth sport groups organized outside the school system also serve as socialization agents before and during the school years.

Highlight 3.5
Parents' Code for Sport

The National Task Force on Children's Play (1979) has written a set of fair play codes for persons involved in children's sport. This is intended to educate parents and to make youth sport more enjoyable and satisfying for children. This code has been posted in a number of youth sport facilities throughout Canada.*

Parents' Code

1. Do not force an unwilling child to participate in sports.
2. Remember children are involved in organized sports for their enjoyment, not yours.
3. Encourage your child always to play by the rules.
4. Teach your child that honest effort is as important as victory so that the result of each game is accepted without undue disappointment.
5. Turn defeat to victory by helping your child work towards skill improvement

and good sportsmanship. Never ridicule or yell at your child for making a mistake or losing a competition.
6. Remember that children learn best by example. Applaud good plays by your team and by members of the opposing team.
7. Do not publicly question the official's judgement and never their honesty.
8. Support all efforts to remove verbal and physical abuse from children's sporting activities.
9. Recognize the value and importance of volunteer coaches. They give of their time and resources to provide recreational activities for your child.

---

*Note. The parent code is reprinted with permission of the Canadian Council on Children and Youth, 1979, publishers of the FAIR PLAY CODES FOR CHILDREN IN SPORT. Canadian Council on Children and Youth, 2211 Riverside Drive, Suite 14, Ottawa, Canada K1H 7X5.

However, in recent years the sport leagues and opportunities provided for preadolescents by volunteers, parents, or full-time coaches (e.g., gymnastics, track, swimming) have generated problems. Specifically, with adult domination of children's leisure, dropout rates have increased, violence has increased, parental spectators have become more obnoxious, and incidents of indirect verbal and physical abuse by coaches against children have increased. In addition, winning has been emphasized at the expense of participating for fun, for the learning of important social skills, or for social interaction.

In this chapter we have seen how many of the decision-makers in two socialization settings—the educational system and voluntary community sport organizations—have lost control of the process of sport. The intended ends are not being met well. Many people are beginning to question whether youth sport in these settings involves more problems than it is worth. Yet few are addressing the issues or proposing initiatives to try to change children's sport. Clearly some degree of reform is needed to introduce different structures or philosophies that may be more appropriate to the needs, interests, and abilities of the child and adolescent. Here lies yet another challenge for your generation, which will soon be the parents of potential Little Leaguers and young Olympians. What type of sport environment do you want for your daughter or son?

REFERENCES

Adler, P., & Adler, P.A. (1985). From idealism to pragmatic detachment: The academic performance of college athletes. *Sociology of Education, 58,* 241–250.

Armstrong, C.F. (1984). The lessons of sport: Class socialization in British and American boarding schools. *Sociology of Sport Journal, 1,* 314–331.

Ashe, A. (1977, February 6). Send your children to the libraries: An open letter to black parents. *New York Times,* Section 5, p. 2.

Baumann, S., & Henschen, K.P. (1986). A cross-validation study of selected performance measures in predicting academic success among collegiate athletes. *Sociology of Sport Journal, 3,* 366–371.

Berryman, J.W. (1975). From the cradle to the playing field: America's emphasis on highly organized competitive sports for preadolescent boys. *Journal of Sport History, 2*(2), 112–131.

Boutilier, M.A., & SanGiovanni, L. (1983). *The sporting woman.* Champaign, IL: Human Kinetics.

Brede, R.M., & Camp, H.J. (1987). The education of college student-athletes. *Sociology of Sport Journal, 4,* 245–257.

Brown, E.W., & Branta, C.F. (Eds.) (1988). *Competitive sports for children and youth.* Champaign, IL: Human Kinetics.

Cantelon, H. (1982). High performance sport and the child athlete: Learning to labour. In A.G. Ingham & E.F. Brown (Eds.), *Career patterns and career contingencies in sport* (pp. 258–286). Vancouver, BC: UBC Press.

Chu, D.B., Segrave, J., & Becker, B.J. (Eds.) (1985). *Sport and higher education.* Champaign, IL: Human Kinetics.

Coakley, J.J. (1986a). Socialization and youth sports. In R. Rees & A. Miracle (Eds.), *Sport and social theory* (pp. 135–143). Champaign, IL: Human Kinetics.

Coakley, J. (1986b). When should children begin competing? A sociological perspective. In M.R. Weiss & D. Gould (Eds.), *Sport for children and youths* (pp. 59–63). Champaign, IL: Human Kinetics.

Coakley, J. (1987). Children and the sport socialization process. *Advances in Pediatric Sport Sciences, 2,* 43–60.

Colburn, K. (1985). Honor, ritual and violence in ice hockey. *Canadian Journal of Sociology, 10*(2), 153–170.

Conacher, B. (1971). *Hockey in Canada: The way it is.* Richmond Hills, ON: Gateway.

Curtis, J.E., & McTeer, W. (in press). Sport involvement and academic attainment in university: Two studies in the Canadian case. *Psychology and Sociology of Sport.*

Davis, E.C., & Cooper, J.A. (1934). Athletic ability and scholarship. *Research Quarterly, 5*(4), 68–78.

Devereux, E.C. (1976). Backyard versus Little League baseball: The impoverishment of children's games. In D.M. Landers (Ed.), *Social problems in athletics: Essays in the sociology of sport.* Urbana, IL: University of Illinois Press.

Donnelly, P., & Sergeant, L. (1986, October-November). *Adolescents and athletic labour: A preliminary study of elite Canadian athletes.* Paper presented at the Seventh Annual Meeting of the North American Society for the Sociology of Sport, Las Vegas, NV.

Dunleavy, A., & Miracle, A. (1979). Understanding ritual and its use in sport. In W.

Morgan (Ed.), *Sport and the humanities: A collection of original essays* (pp. 15–26). Knoxville, TN: The Bureau of Educational Research, University of Tennessee.

Figler, S.K. (1984). Measuring academic exploitation of college athletes and a suggestion for sharing data. *Sociology of Sport Journal*, **1**, 381–388.

Fine, G.A. (1987). *With the boys: Little League baseball and preadolescent culture*. Chicago: University of Chicago Press.

Frey, J.H. (Ed.) (1982). *The governance of intercollegiate athletics*. Champaign, IL: Leisure Press.

Frey, J.H. (1986). College athletics: Problems of a functional analysis. In R. Rees & A. Miracle (Eds.), *Sport and social theory* (pp. 199–209). Champaign, IL: Human Kinetics.

Grupe, O. (1985). Top-level sports for children from an educational viewpoint. *International Journal of Physical Education*, **22**(1), 9–16.

Hanford, G.H. (1985). Proposition 48. In J.O. Segrave & B.J. Becker (Eds.), *Sport and higher education* (pp. 367–372). Champaign, IL: Human Kinetics.

Henschen, K.P., & Fry, D. (1984). An archival study of the relationship of intercollegiate athletic participation and graduation. *Sociology of Sport Journal*, **1**, 52–56.

Higginson, D. (1985). The influence of socializing agents in the female sport-participation process. *Adolescence*, **20**(77), 73–82.

Howell, F., Miracle, A., & Rees, R. (1984). Do high school athletics pay? The effects of varsity participation on socioeconomic attainment. *Sociology of Sport Journal*, **1**, 15–25.

Howell, F.M., & McKenzie, J. (1987). High school athletics and adult sport-leisure activity: Gender variations across the life cycle. *Sociology of Sport Journal*, **4**, 329–346.

Kiger, G., & Lorentzen, D. (1986). The relative effects of gender, race and sport on university academic performance. *Sociology of Sport Journal*, **3**, 160–167.

Kirshenbaum, J. (1989, February). An American disgrace. *Sports Ilustrated*, pp. 16–19.

Leonard, W.M., & Reyman, J. (1988). The odds of attaining professional athlete status: Refining the computations. *Sociology of Sport Journal*, **5**, 162–169.

Malina, R.A. (Ed.) (1988). *Young athletes: Biological, psychological, and educational perspectives*. Champaign, IL: Human Kinetics.

Marmion, H. (1979). On collegiate athletics. *Educational Record*, **60**, 341–539.

Martens, R. (Ed.) (1978). *Joy and sadness in children's sports*. Champaign, IL: Human Kinetics.

Martens, R. (1986). Youth sport in the USA. In M.R. Weiss & D. Gould (Eds.), *Sport for children and youths* (pp. 27–33). Champaign, IL: Human Kinetics.

Martens, R., Rivkin, F., & Bump, L.A. (1984). A field study of traditional and nontraditional children's baseball. *Research Quarterly for Exercise and Sport*, **55**, 351–355.

McPherson, B.D. (1986). Policy-oriented research in youth sport: An analysis of the process and product. In C.R. Rees & A.W. Miracle (Eds.), *Sport and social theory* (pp. 255–287). Champaign, IL: Human Kinetics.

McPherson, B.D., & Brown, B. (1988). The structure, processes, and consequences of sport for children. In F.L. Smoll, R.A. Magill, & M.J. Ash (Eds.), *Children in sport* (3rd ed., pp. 265–286). Champaign, IL: Human Kinetics.

Melnick, M., Vanfossen, B., & Sabo, D. (1988). Developmental effects of athletic participation among high school girls. *Sociology of Sport Journal*, **5**, 22–36.

Messner, S.F., & Groisser, D. (1982). Intercollegiate athletic participation and academic achievement. In A.O. Dunleavy, A.W. Miracle, & C.R. Rees (Eds.), *Studies in the sociology of sport* (pp. 257–270). Fort Worth: Texas Christian University Press.

National Task Force on Children's Play. (1979). *Fair play codes for children in sport*. Ottawa: Canada Council on Children and Youth.

Nixon, H.L. (1982). The athlete as scholar in college: An exploratory test of four models. In A.O. Dunleavy, A.W. Miracle, & C.R. Rees (Eds.), *Studies in the sociology of sport* (pp. 239–256). Fort Worth: Texas Christian University Press.

Okihiro, N.R. (1984). Extracurricular participation, educational destinies and early job outcomes. In N. Theberge & P. Donnelly (Eds.), *Sport and the sociological imagination* (pp. 334–349). Fort Worth: Texas Christian University Press.

Ontario Hockey Council. (1982). *You and your child in hockey*. Toronto: Ontario Ministry of Tourism and Recreation.

Orlick, T., & Botterill, C. (1975). *Every kid can win*. Chicago: Nelson Hall.

Otto, L.B., & Alwin, D.F. (1977). Athletics, aspirations and attainments. *Sociology of Education*, **42**(2), 102–113.

Picou, J.S., & Wells, R. (1987, March 22). Rewrite the book on college sports. *The Houston Chronicle*.

Picou, S., McCarter, V., & Howell, F. (1985). Do high school athletics pay? Some further evidence. *Sociology of Sport Journal*, **2**, 72–76.

Purdy, D.A., Eitzen, D.S., & Hufnagel, R. (1985). Are athletes also students? The educational attainment of college athletes. *Social Problems*, **29**, 439–448.

Ralbovsky, M. (1974a). *Destiny's darlings: A world championship Little League team twenty years later*. New York: Hawthorn Books.

Ralbovsky, M. (1974b). *Lords of the locker room: The American way of coaching and its effects on youth*. New York: P.H. Wyden.

Rehberg, R.A. (1969). Behavioral and attitudinal consequences of high school interscholastic sports: A speculative consideration. *Adolescence*, **4**(April), 69–88.

Rehberg, R.A., & Schafer, W.E. (1968). Participation in interscholastic athletics and college expectations. *American Journal of Sociology*, **73**, 732–740.

Reilly, R. (1989, February). What price glory? *Sports Illustrated*, pp. 32–34.

Rooney, J.F. (1980). *The recruiting game: Toward a new system of intercollegiate sports*. Lincoln, NE: University of Nebraska Press.

Rooney, J.F. (1985). America needs a new intercollegiate sports system. *Journal of Geography*, **84**(4), 139–143.

Roper, L.D., & Snow, K. (1976). Correlation studies of academic excellence and big-time athletics. *International Review of Sport Sociology*, **11**(3), 57–69.

Sack, A.L., & Thiel, R. (1979). College football and social mobility: A case study of Notre Dame football players. *Sociology of Education*, **52**(1), 60–66.

Sack, A.L., & Thiel, R. (1985). College basketball and role conflict: A national survey. *Sociology of Sport Journal*, **2**, 195–209.

Schafer, W.E., & Armer, J.M. (1972). Athletes are not inferior students. In G.P. Stone (Ed.), *Game, sport and power* (pp. 97–116). New Brunswick, NJ: Transaction.

Shapiro, B.J. (1984). Intercollegiate athletic participation and academic achievement: A case study of Michigan State

University student athletes, 1950–1960. *Sociology of Sport Journal, 1*, 46–51.

Smith, R. (1988). *Sports and freedom: The rise of big time college athletics*. New York: Oxford University Press.

Smoll, F.L., Magill, R.A., & Ash, M.J. (Eds.) (1988). *Children in sport* (3rd ed.). Champaign, IL: Human Kinetics.

Snyder, E.E. (1985). A theoretical analysis of academic and athletic roles. *Sociology of Sport Journal, 2*, 210–217.

Snyder, E.E., & Spreitzer, E.A. (1976). Correlates of sport participation among adolescent girls. *Research Quarterly, 47*, 804–809.

Snyder, E.E., & Spreitzer, E.A. (1981). Sport, education and schools. In G.R.F. Luschen & G.H. Sage (Eds.), *Handbook of social science of sport* (pp. 119–146). Champaign, IL: Stipes.

Stern, R.N. (1981). Competitive influences on the interorganizational regulation of college athletics. *Administrative Science Quarterly, 26*(March), 15–31.

Telander, R., & Sullivan, R. (1989, February). You reap what you sow. *Sports Illustrated*, pp. 20–31.

Underwood, J. (1980, May). The writing is on the wall. *Sports Illustrated*, pp. 36–72.

Voigt, D.Q. (1974). *A Little League journal*. Bowling Green, OH: Bowling Green University Press.

Weiss, M.R., & Gould, D.R. (Eds.) (1986). *Sport for children and youths*. Champaign, IL: Human Kinetics.

Weiss, M.R., & Sisley, B.L. (1984). Where have all the coaches gone? *Sociology of Sport Journal, 1*, 332–347.

Wiggins, D.K. (1987). A history of organized play and highly competitive sport for American children. *Advances in Pediatric Sport Sciences, 2*, 1–24.

Yablonsky, L., & Brower, J.J. (1979). *The Little League game: How kids, coaches and parents really play it*. New York: Times Books.

Sport, Law, and Politics

As sport has become more bureaucratized, professionalized, and rule-bound, the regulative influence of the legal and political systems has increased. This is evident in the increased number of sport disputes brought to the courts, especially in North America. Here, the sport industry has a significant influence on the economy, and the ideological system stresses equality, justice, and fair competition. Moreover, the legal and political systems are closely interrelated. Political decisions become laws, and laws are invoked to condemn behavior within a sport setting (e.g., an assault against another player during a game). Throughout this chapter you will find numerous examples of legal and political events in our daily lives being reflected in sport.

THE LAW AND SPORT

Early sport-related uses of the **legal system** in North America involved tort liability (e.g., an individual seeking damages for an injury sustained in a sport setting) and challenges to the antitrust laws of the United States and Canada. To illustrate the latter, the reserve clauses in the contracts of most professional athletes bind players to one team for life.

Teams cannot negotiate for other teams' players. Professional athletes have challenged this clause by claiming that it violates antitrust laws.

How Do Courts Affect Sport?

Many segments of our society increasingly are using the courts to resolve conflicts and address perceived injustices. Athletes, owners, leagues, and politicians also have sought resolutions to sport issues through the legal system. Although owners tend to argue that sport should be immune from the legal system and should settle its own disputes, aspects of sport are increasingly regulated by **law**.

- With the appearance of pay TV, VCRs, and satellite television, courts are having to address the question of who owns sport broadcasts.
- Class action suits have been initiated to block the television blackout of home games.
- Malpractice suits against team physicians or team owners for negligent behavior are seeking damages for career-ending injuries or for requiring players to compete while still injured.
- Players are prosecuted for "fixing" games.
- Women are seeking the opportunity to compete in exclusively male sport leagues (see chapter 9).
- Civil suits are filed to reduce discrimination against minority groups.
- Players or spectators who behave violently are charged with criminal acts (see chapter 11).
- The Baseball Players' Association is appealing to the U.S. Supreme Court for legal rights to the revenue from all televised games.
- Team owners are appealing tax decisions concerning their right to depreciate the value of player contracts.

- Local governments are questioning the right of team owners to relocate a sport franchise to another city.
- Manufacturers are being charged with copyright violations if they have not paid a royalty to use a team's slogan or logo on their products.
- Athletes are suing the manufacturers of sport equipment (e.g., football helmets) following injuries.

What's Behind the Emphasis on Legal Issues?

The legal system has become more involved at all levels of sport for a variety of reasons. First, increasing violence in our society has brought greater public awareness and concern which spills over into sport. Second, our citizens know more about their rights—particularly their civil rights—and are more willing to seek fundamental freedoms and equality through the courts. Third, the rules and organization of sport have changed—new leagues challenge existing monopolies, players have more freedom to move from one team to another, leagues expand and merge, franchises move, and players and officials form unions that lobby for change. These events raise legal questions that must be resolved to maintain order, equity of competition, and civil or constitutional rights.

Finally, laws and the interpretation of laws are constantly in flux. A more informed public, along with players and owners, continually raises new legal questions concerning amateur and professional sport. This increased legal intervention in sport can, for example, seek interpretations of existing or new rules, introduce social control, guarantee individual rights and freedom, and protect players, owners, and fans from economic exploitation.

Sport as a Legal Specialty

The increased interaction between sport and the law has led to sport becoming a subspecialty of law. For example, numerous lawyers now serve as player agents, executive directors of players' associations, commissioners or presidents of leagues, negotiators in labor disputes within sport, and organizers and promoters of international sport events. Many law schools offer courses on law and sport or discuss sport cases in courses pertaining to contract, tort, taxation, corporate, or criminal law. The aspiring or practicing sport lawyer now has access to specialized texts (Barnes, 1983; Hoch, 1985; Yasser, 1985), law journals, and other professional resources (e.g., the Center for Law and Sports at Indiana University) that help address more and more complex legal questions.

ANTITRUST LAWS AND SPORT

To ensure free competition within an industry, the United States and Canada passed legislation outlawing monopolies (the Sherman Antitrust Act of 1890 and the Combines Investigation Act of 1966, respectively). In recent years, players, owners, and leagues have argued that existing sport laws and practices violate these antitrust laws (Friedman, 1987). Players claim that the universal draft system and the reserve clause restrict their right to sell services in a free market. Owners have responded with the argument that sport is a unique industry that requires monopolistic practices to preserve fair competition.

Free Agency

For years courts in the U.S. have repeatedly declared professional baseball exempt from the antitrust laws (Michener, 1976). In contrast, basketball, football, and hockey have been found in violation of antitrust laws. Players in these professional team sports are no longer required, technically, to sign with the team that originally drafts them, and free-agency and option clauses are allowed. But athletes still do not have the same freedom to select or change employers that employees enjoy in other industries. Free agency as a principle is not working as intended, either because the owners agree not to sign free agents or because owners cannot agree on the compensation (e.g., players or draft choices) to be awarded for losing a player in the free-agent market. Labor law appears to be the only effective means for professional athletes to gain increased contractual freedom. Conflicts are thus resolved within labor law procedures and through union and management negotiations, strikes, grievances, and binding arbitration (Berry, Gould, & Staudohar, 1986).

Franchise Relocation

Other recent antitrust actions have involved franchise relocations (Johnson, 1983; Staudohar, 1985). Judges are being forced to make decisions as to whether a franchise relocation is fair to sport fans or not. In 1982 the Oakland Raiders moved to Los Angeles without the required approval of the NFL Council. The NFL tried to block the move in court, but was found in violation of antitrust laws. The Los Angeles Raiders were awarded $49 million in damages.

Broadcast Rights

In a dispute over the ownership of broadcast rights, two universities claimed that the NCAA violated antitrust laws by preventing them from negotiating their own contracts for television rights to their football broadcasts (Gulland, Byrne, & Steinbach, 1984; Pacey,

Highlight 4.1
A Football Civil Suit: USFL versus NFL

The most famous sport antitrust lawsuit in recent years was filed by the now defunct United States Football League (USFL) against the National Football League (NFL). The USFL sought $1.69 billion in damages by arguing that the contracts signed by the NFL with the three major television networks (all signed before the USFL came into existence) were illegal, because they constituted a monopoly. That is, unless the NFL was restricted to signing contracts with only two networks, the USFL could not meaningfully negotiate with a major television network for a contract that would ensure a fair chance for economic survival. The USFL also charged that the NFL had pressured the networks to deny the USFL a contract when it decided to switch from a spring to a fall schedule.

After an 11-week court case, the jury ruled that the NFL had violated antitrust laws, but the USFL was awarded only $1.00 in damages, which by antitrust laws was tripled to $3.00 in favor of the plaintiff (the USFL). This decision showed that the court believed that the NFL is a monopoly. But because the USFL was awarded only $3.00 rather than millions, the court condoned the practice. As a result of this historic decision, the USFL was forced to disband within a few months. It could not remain economically viable without access to a major television contract.

1985). Their claim was upheld by the Supreme Court, and universities are now free to sell their local broadcast rights without NCAA involvement or control. Highlight 4.1 describes the most significant sport-related antitrust case in recent years.

CIVIL RIGHTS AND SPORT

Since the 1970s, issues involving civil or constitutional rights have been raised frequently in sport. For example, before passage of Title IX of the U.S. Education Amendment Act of 1972 and before more general civil rights' legislation was passed in a number of jurisdictions, young girls and women often had to resort to civil suits to participate in male-dominated sport leagues or sport contests.

Many cases involved Little League baseball, in the United States, and minor hockey, in Canada (see Highlight 9.7).

Other civil cases have involved parents' seeking the right for their children to choose teams and not be assigned arbitrarily by a league's rules. To circumvent league rules, some parents in Canada have established legal guardians in other communities for their sons or daughters (who are often 10 to 14 years old) so that they can join more prestigious or successful minor hockey teams or swim clubs. Hockey superstar Wayne Gretzky was involved in one of the most famous legal guardian disputes, when he left home in his early teens to play hockey in another town.

More recently, civil suits have challenged the right of the NCAA to administer Proposition 48 and to require urine testing of athletes for drug use. Proposition 48 is said to be especially discriminatory against some black athletes who reportedly do not score as well on the SAT or ACT because of cultural biases in the questions. Urine testing, it is argued, represents an unconstitutional invasion of privacy. Like challenges to mandatory sex tests at the Olympics, decisions for or against the plaintiff are always considered in light of two principles: What is best for the sport or the public (i.e., the greater-good doctrine) and what best protects the privacy and rights of the individual. Often the decisions depend as much on philosophical and moral arguments as on legal rights.

THE LAW AND VIOLENCE IN SPORT

Sport leagues argue that they should be responsible for policing and enforcing the rules of their business and that sport should be exempt from the moral and legal jurisdiction of civil or criminal law. But some sport leagues have not been able or willing to control violence in their games (e.g., professional hockey and soccer), and civil or criminal laws have been invoked to protect players and spectators.

Violence is not a new issue in sport. Cases involving player violence entered the British courts as early as 1878 (Gulotta, 1980). One particular case involved a soccer player accused of manslaughter after he charged and collided with an opposing player, killing him in an action deemed beyond the spirit and intent of the rules. Lord Justice Bramwell instructed the jury that no rules or practices of a game can make something lawful if it is not lawful in the country. Yet, like most recent court decisions in North America, the defendant was acquitted.

In North America, crown attorneys or public prosecutors have tried to introduce some

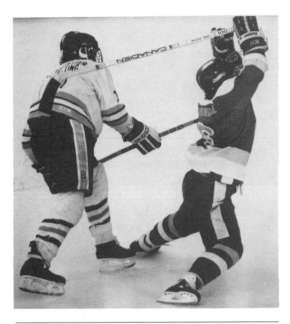

The organizers of some sport leagues have not been able or willing to control violence in their games.

element of social control to professional sport, particularly to hockey (Watson & MacLellan, 1986). Professional athletes have been indicted on charges of aggravated assault and assault with a dangerous weapon. While few professional athletes have been convicted, amateur athletes in similar cases have been fined or given modest jail sentences.

Special Handling of Sport Cases

A number of cases involving athletes have resulted in interesting decisions. One of the earliest court cases involving hockey resulted from an incident on February 24, 1905, in Maxville, Ontario. During an exhibition game, a 19-year-old struck an opponent on the head, fracturing his skull and killing him instantly. Charged with murder, the player was subsequently acquitted for unknown reasons (Watson & MacLellan, 1986).

A major court case in recent years was the 1970 Chico Maki trial in Ottawa. The defendant, Maki, was cleared of an assault charge on the grounds of self-defense. Ted Green, the player who struck Maki, and thereby invoked the retaliatory blow, was known by reputation to be very aggressive. In his closing remarks the judge implied that a defense of consenting adults would have failed, and that in the future no sport league should consider players immune from criminal prosecution.

Similarly, in July 1975 the State of Minnesota indicted Dave Forbes for aggravated assault with a dangerous weapon. He was accused of assaulting Henry Boucha, who needed 25 sutures to close a stick-inflicted cut next to the eye. Boucha subsequently underwent eye surgery for continuing double-vision thought to be caused by a small fracture of the right eye socket. The trial ended in a hung jury and dismissal of the charge.

More recently, in 1988, Dino Ciccarelli of the Minnesota North Stars was charged with assault by the Toronto Police Department after he hit an opponent three times in the head and shoulder area with his stick. Warning that professional athletes are not above the law, a judge found Ciccarelli guilty and sentenced him to one day in jail, plus a $1,000 fine. The judge ruled that Ciccarelli went beyond the acceptable use of force. Personnel in other sports viewed these proceedings with interest because they may have an impact on such practices as spearing in football and the beanball and spike-high slide in baseball.

The Question of Defense

There are four possible defense arguments in these cases: Players consent to risks inherent in the specific sport when they sign contracts; the player reacts in self-defense (e.g., the Maki case); the player was provoked to retaliate for an aggressive act; or the players have agreed among themselves to enforce the informal laws of the sport (Hechter, 1977). The judge in the Forbes case, though, instructed the jury that "no one could consent to an assault either explicitly or implicitly" (Picone, 1975). There seems to be a legal limit on the degree of danger to which one is expected to consent.

The Question of Prosecution

The use of criminal law in sport settings is a new legal area, and there are few precedents. Hence, prosecutors are still somewhat reluctant to proceed to trial. As a result, athletes have remained relatively immune from criminal prosecution for acts committed during play. Kuhlman (1975) suggests that there are four possible explanations for this immunity. First, allowances are made for the structure of the subgroup. For example, fighting is a common occurrence and is viewed as normal behavior for professional hockey players, but it is atypical behavior for football players. Thus, a defense of consent in hockey may be seen as a deterrent to legal action. A second explanation is that the victim and offender will compete again in the future. A trial may only increase their hostility and that of their teammates, especially if they view the action as superseding league prosecution (i.e., the system of league fines and suspensions).

A third explanation for failing to prosecute is that there is no guarantee that a conviction, with a fine or jail sentence, will serve as a deterrent. Finally, there has been a tacit agreement that legal authority is informally delegated to the league. Kuhlman (1975) further suggests that (a) league officials know the risks assumed by the players and know what conduct is unreasonable; (b) because teams are located in different geographical regions, there may be differential treatments among jurisdictions, which would undermine the economic and moral solidarity of the league; (c) outside interference would hurt the league financially; and (d) only the league can adequately police its own employees.

Corrective Actions

The implied threat of criminal charges seems to offer little help in protecting participants or in reducing violent practices on the playing field. Sport rules, therefore, must be more severe, and league officials must enforce the internal sanctions (e.g., fines and suspensions). Otherwise, the legal system will be forced to change its laissez-faire policy toward violence in professional sport. To illustrate, in 1987 the city of Boston tried to pass a law that would permit law officers to cite players and spectators for violent acts. Similarly, as a deterrent, it has been suggested that coaches, managers, owners, or league executives be charged as conspirators or accomplices (or in lieu of the player) when an employee engages in violent behavior.

While the *criminal* cases described earlier were initiated by representatives of the law, future *civil* suits may be originated by a player (or by his or her team owner) who is attacked by another player. This action might argue that the employer (e.g., the team owner or the league) of the attacking player is responsible for the conduct of its employees. In this situation the defendant would not bear full responsibility or the social stigma of criminal prosecution. Rather, damages would be awarded to the plaintiff. These costs might be paid by the employer of the defendant or by the league, which failed to protect its players.

Some leagues continue to refuse responsibility for violent acts and enforce inconsistent or meaningless penalties. In the NHL playoffs in 1987, a goaltender, using two hands on his stick, hit an opponent on the back of the knee; the injury caused the opponent to miss the rest of the series. The goaltender was not reprimanded until the playoffs ended, when he was suspended for the first 2 weeks of the next season. The opposing team lost a star player during the playoffs. Similarly, in the 1988 playoffs a player swung his stick at the head of an opponent and hit him on the shoulder while they were waiting for a face-off. This time the league acted quickly—but it only imposed a $500 fine (no suspension) on a player who earns more than $500,000 per year!

This apparent unwillingness to accept moral and legal responsibility for sport employees may be the impetus for the legal system to intervene in the future. If sport leagues will not police themselves, criminal and civil action will be needed to bring about order.

POLITICS WITHIN SPORT

While politics and the law affect sport from the outside, some argue that **politics** within sport is also alive and well. Athletes and sport analysts have long alleged that judges at international sport events are politically biased. And some have argued that athletes themselves hold different political views than their nonathlete peers.

Political Views of Sport Organizations

Sport organizations are similar to other large organizations in that political considerations influence policy-making, the recruitment of new members, the promotion to executive positions, and the evaluation of performances. Much of the discussion concerning politics within sport is based on anecdotal information, although studies of international sport events (Ball, 1973; Colwell, 1981;

Fenwick & Chatterjee, 1981; Seppanen, 1988) have provided some evidence.

For example, a perennial question in sports such as diving, figure skating, and gymnastics is whether the decisions of judges are politically biased in international events where the outcome depends on subjective decisions. Claims and counter-claims have been made by gymnastic officials and figure skaters at recent Olympic Games, but strong research evidence for or against the presence of political bias is lacking. Highlight 4.2 describes two early studies that sought to answer whether the bias alleged in subjective scoring events has a political basis.

As in other large, voluntary organizations, there are politics within sport associations and sport federations. To illustrate, Finland's political cleavages by region are essential factors in accounting for the distribution of support among sport organizations in a specific region or community. In Finland, individuals join a particular sport organization because of the political party affiliation of that organization. Similarly, many amateur sport organizations in North America, including national Olympic Committees, recruit new members and elect officers through an "old boys" network. Who you know sometimes matters more than personal skills in determining whether you will assume leadership roles in amateur sport.

Political Views of Athletes

It has also been suggested (Norton, 1971; Rehberg & Cohen, 1976; Sage, 1974) that those involved in sport are more conservative than nonathletes on a number of issues and attitudes. There is little research to show, though, that athletes are different from nonathletes with respect to their political socialization and political views. In general, athletes as a group appear to be less interested in politics than those involved in other oc-

cupations or leisure pursuits. However, in a more recent study, Gelinas (1988) compared Canadian university athletes and nonathletes, both male and female, and found that the athletes tended to report slightly more conservative attitudes on various social and economic policy issues. There were no differences in political involvement (e.g., voting, political interest, and following political news). Gelinas also compared men and women involved in recreational sports with those not involved, in a national sample of adults. Here, too, there were few political attitude or behavior differences.

SPORT AND POLITICS

The relationship between sport and politics is one of the most enduring and pervasive examples of society's effects on sport. The governments of the city-states in ancient Greece used sport to enhance the fitness of their citizens for war and to demonstrate their superiority over other city-states. They gave large incentives to successful athletes who brought prestige to their city. During the early part of the Roman era, sport was used for military fitness; in the later years the ruling elite produced sport-like events to entertain and thereby control the masses.

Although the importance of sport has varied over time, the growth of nationalism in the late 18th and early 19th centuries revived the idea of using sport and games for promoting fitness and national integration (i.e., patriotism). Ostensibly, a main reason for reviving the Olympic Games in 1896 was to stimulate improved physical fitness among children. The Games and other international sport events soon became mechanisms for propaganda and vicarious war; today, sport and politics are inextricably intertwined and often work to demonstrate social, economic, or political supremacy over another nation.

Highlight 4.2
Is There a Political Bias in the Judging of International Sport Events?

Periodically, charges of bias are leveled against judges in subjectively evaluated sports such as figure skating, gymnastics, and diving. In these sports there are no stopwatches or tape measures to determine relative performance objectively. In effect, the charges imply that judges ignore brilliant performances by unknown athletes or penalize some performers because of hidden biases (e.g., favoritism toward past champions or toward athletes from countries that have a reputation for developing outstanding athletes in a given sport). Frequently these alleged biases are attributed to the national origins of the judges. For example, Western-bloc judges may overscore athletes from their own countries and underscore athletes from Eastern-bloc countries.

Is there any evidence for a politically based bias to judging performance in international sport events? To examine this question, two studies have computed correlations between the nationality of judges and their scoring practices at the World Figure Skating Championships from 1967 to 1971 (Ball, 1973) and at the 1980 Winter Olympics (Fenwick and Chatterjee, 1981). If the judges applied consistent judging criteria, we would expect to find a high correlation among judges. But if some type of personal or political bias were present, we would expect to find a high correlation only among judges representing politically aligned nations. The results of both studies found a high degree of agreement among the scores awarded by all judges (r = > .91), no difference between the correlations when scores by judges from socialist or nonsocialist countries were analyzed separately, and no relationship between the nationality of judges and their scores.

The only consistent bias was patriotism. That is, judges tended to rank contestants from their own nations higher than other judges did. This pattern held for Eastern, Western, and nonaligned-nation judges. Thus, contestants without a judge from their country on the panel might be penalized in close decisions. To take into account this potential patriotic bias, either the score by the judge from the competitors' country could be ignored in the averaging, or, as is already done in many competitions, the high and low scores could be deleted before computing the final composite score.

Sport as a Political Institution

Little research has been completed on the relationship between sport and politics, although there have been a number of descriptive historical, philosophical, sociological, and journalistic studies.[1] These have sought to

---

[1]For example, analyses of the relationship between sport and politics have been completed in *England* (Allison, 1986; Goodhart & Chataway, 1968; McIntosh, 1963:188-203; Natan, 1969); *France* (Bouet, 1968:575-585; Meynaud, 1966); *Finland* (Olin, 1981); the *Soviet Union* (Morton, 1963; Riordan, 1977); *Germany* (Mandell, 1971); *Canada* (Macintosh et

document the belief that sport is a political institution. Although examples cited in these sources vary, the themes tend to focus on the

- increasing nationalism in sport;
- use of sport for political propaganda (e.g., sport politics imply that success in sport can be equated with patriotism and the superiority of one political-economic system over another);
- use of sport to encourage national integration or unity;
- use of sport to foster or sustain existing social conflicts; and
- increasing politicization of the decision-making process in sport at all levels.

These themes are most prevalent at the international level, where

- political ideologies compete on the societal level and in the sport environment;
- there is public policy involvement by national governments in the organization and control of sport;
- the state uses athletes to symbolically represent national strength or character;
- sport is thought to be a visible medium for communicating national policies and ideological beliefs to the public, both at home and abroad; and
- sport is a visible and effective way to express opposition (e.g., through boycotts) to the political, economic, or social policies of other national governments.

Many aspects of sport suggest that it is *not* apolitical, nor is politics free of sport. Consider, for example, how savvy politicians use sport to enhance their political image. Sport

events are a public forum and offer politicians high visibility, either as part of the event (e.g., at the opening or award ceremonies) or as interested consumers who sit close to the action and within range of a television camera. It is no accident that politicians sit close behind the bench of the home team, and that they tend to arrive late or leave early in order to be noticed.

Being viewed as physically fit or as one who associates with athletes has become an essential aspect of the image-making of politicians, especially in North America. Political parties encourage famous athletes to endorse political candidates; successful athletes have been recruited as political candidates (e.g., Bill Bradley and Jack Kemp in the U.S.; Otto Jelinek in Canada).

Functionalist Versus Conflict Theories of Sport and Politics

In examining the relationships between sport and politics, most analyses adhere to either a *functionalist* or a *conflict* perspective. According to the functional view, sport is used to promote common values held essential to the integration and development of a society. It is further argued that all groups strive to maintain the social order, and that sport can facilitate this process.

The conflict perspective is based on the premise that the domination of particular groups, either within a country or among countries, depends on having control over economic and political resources. Conflict, then, is generated among groups vying for

al., 1987; Pooley & Webster, 1972); *New Zealand* (Thompson, 1969); *South Africa* (Archer & Bouillon, 1982; Draper, 1963; Krotee, 1988; Jarvie, 1985; Tatz, 1983); the *United States* (Edwards, 1984; Shaikin, 1988); and *Rhodesia* (Cheffers, 1972). More detailed reviews concerning the international scene have been presented by Goodhart and Chataway (1968), Petrie (1975), Guldenpfenning and Schulke (1980), Espy (1981), MacAloon (1981), Segrave and Chu (1981, 1988), Seppanen (1984), Meyer (1984), Tomlinson and Whannel (1984), Redmond (1986), Hoberman (1986), and Wilson (1988).

control of these resources and thereby acquiring power in the decision-making process. Sport replaces outright war as a way of demonstrating superiority over opposing groups. In recent years an expanding body of literature has examined the relationships among sport, politics, and the economy. This field of study is known as *sport and political economy* (Cantelon & Gruneau, 1982; Hargreaves, 1982; Hoberman, 1984; Morgan, 1985).

PUBLIC POLICY AND SPORT

In the 1980s, the responsibility for international sport is increasingly being allocated to government agencies in both socialist and democratic nations. This has occurred because politicians are using international sporting success for propaganda purposes and are seeking to host major international sport festivals for political and economic benefits. Because the world of international sport has become so politicized, amateur volunteers no longer have the skills, contacts, or resources to bid for or to host sport events at this level. As sport has become more popular, local, regional, and national government agencies have initiated public policy and legislation to govern it (Douglas, 1978; Johnson, 1982; Johnson & Frey, 1985). In this manner, many government agencies exert much **power** in the sport world.

This government involvement has implications for elite athletes and for sport consumers. Some of the policy-related issues that have evolved include

- influencing the values, beliefs, and behavior of citizens by promoting mass participation through motivational programs (e.g., *Participaction* in Canada and the *Sport for All* movement in Europe);

- building and operating public sport facilities;
- providing social and economic control for a sport by introducing and enforcing regulatory policies that pertain to safety (e.g., boxing), violence (e.g., hockey), economic competition (e.g., antitrust laws), television (e.g., antiblackout laws), international competition (e.g., financial support to amateur governing bodies), and democratization (e.g., removing ethnic, racial, class, gender, or age barriers);
- building or enhancing the image of a community or nation by hosting major sport events (e.g., the Olympic Games);
- building facilities and awarding tax incentives to attract a professional sport team (e.g., Indianapolis attracted the Colts from Baltimore) and thereby, ostensibly, promoting community or national unity, pride, and identity;
- using sport to reinforce existing social policies (e.g., apartheid in South Africa).

In some countries, government agencies provide much of the financial support for high-level amateur sport, directly or indirectly. To protect their investment and to maximize the benefits gained from supporting international sport, many federal governments now virtually control the world of amateur and Olympic sport. This has created controversy in some democratic societies, where it is seen as an example of government interference. In other countries, government involvement is deemed desirable and necessary for success in international competitions and for the construction of sport facilities.

To illustrate, since the passage in 1961 of the Fitness and Amateur Sport Act, the Canadian government has invested millions of dollars annually to support amateur and quasi-amateur sport. With considerable support from the federal government, Canada

To achieve public policy objectives in sport, private sector financing is needed to build such facilities as the Olympic velodrome in Carson, California, which was financed by the Southland Corporation.

has hosted the 1976 Summer Olympics, the 1978 Commonwealth Games, and the 1988 Winter Olympics. Canada now hopes to host the 1996 Summer Olympic Games.

In contrast, in the United States the 1984 Summer Olympic Games were financed and organized primarily by the private sector, although it should be noted that federal and state governments contributed indirectly (e.g., providing security personnel and equipment).

INTERNATIONAL POLITICS AND SPORT

Because the media increasingly view sport as both entertainment and news, international sporting events are receiving greater global coverage. Such events have become a public stage, where the weaknesses and deficiencies of ideological rivalries can be noted and debated. Some of these debates include capitalism versus socialism; developing nations versus industrialized nations; and apartheid versus nonapartheid societies. To date, we have seen sport used

- as propaganda to promote the superiority of one nation over another, by comparing relative or absolute success on the playing field (i.e., number of championships or medals won) and thereby showing the strength of one's national character and the viability of a given political and economic system;

- to protest and impose sanctions (e.g., boycotts by athletes or teams) on other nations because of national policies;
- to foster improved diplomatic relations (e.g., the exchange of Ping-Pong players, which fostered improved relations between the U.S. and China in the 1970s).

The Olympic Games have been a natural and frequent platform for the airing of political differences. Nowhere has the interaction of sport and politics been woven more tightly than in the Summer Olympic Games. There is less political controversy at the Winter Games, because fewer nations are involved and there is less television exposure. However, a new cycle for the Summer and Winter Games will begin in 1994: Instead of being held in the same year, they will be held alternately every 2 years. This will increase Olympic exposure, and perhaps increase the use of the Winter Games as an arena for propaganda wars.

Political controversy has plagued virtually every Summer Olympics since Hitler hosted the 1936 Nazi Olympics to demonstrate the superiority of the German race (Hart-Davis, 1986). It is simply naive to place much credence in the statement made by Avery Brundage, former president of the International Olympic Committee, after six nations withdrew from the 1956 Olympic Games (Natan, 1969): "By their decision these countries show that they are unaware of one of our most important principles, namely, that sport is completely free of politics" (p. 204).

The reality of the sport-politics linkage is clearly illustrated by the following recent remarks about the Olympic Games. First, Peter Ueberroth, president of the Los Angeles Olympic Organizing Committee stated (Edwards, 1984), "We now have to face the reality that the Olympics constitute not only an athletic event but a political event" (p. 177).

Even more revealing are two statements from South Korea. First, a leader of the op-position party in South Korea stated the following (Johnson, 1987):

> If the 1988 Olympics are to be a self-advertisement for this government, and if the people are to be coerced by the use of government force to participate, then our Olympics will be no more than a reenactment of the Berlin Olympics of 1936 under the Nazis. (p. 39)

More bluntly, a member of the Catholic clergy in South Korea declared (Johnson, 1987) that

> instead of achieving the status of an advanced nation through a sports event, we should attain that status by protecting human rights and eliminating injustices and corruption. . . . No event or project can constitute a reason to suppress even temporarily the people's right to a decent life. (p. 39)

These views are similar to those expressed by MacAloon in the preface to his insightful biography of Pierre de Coubertin. MacAloon (1981) wrote that, writing the book, he

> felt compelled to understand how on earth someone came to the extraordinary idea that a group of people running around in short pants every four years had something to do with international understanding and world peace. Rather, he began with the premise that the Olympic Games are a contest between nations that are intertwined with world politics. (p. xi)

International disputes among governments or political ideologies that have been carried into the sport milieu include the following:

1952—The U.S. strongly opposes the entry of a U.S.S.R. team into the 1952 Summer Olympics. The Soviets escalate the race for medals by claiming that they won more than any other country.

1956—Following the Suez invasion and the Hungarian Revolution, Arab nations boycott the Melbourne Olympics; a blood bath results when the U.S.S.R. and Hungary meet in a waterpolo match.

1964—Street riots in Tokyo before the Games demonstrate the plight of students in Japan.

1968—Black U.S. athletes revolt at home, while two athletes give the black power salute on the victory stand to show the world that racial discrimination is a problem in America. In contrast, another black athlete waves the U.S. flag following his victory.

1972—Arab terrorists assassinate Israeli athletes in the Olympic Village in Munich.

1976—Taiwan is banned from participating; 28 African nations boycott the Montreal Olympics because the IOC refuses to ban New Zealand for sending a rugby team to compete in South Africa during the Soweto uprising.

1980—The U.S. leads a boycott of the Moscow Olympics to protest the Soviet invasion of Afghanistan. Officially, the U.S. returns the formal invitation to compete and thereby declines to participate.

1984—The U.S.S.R. leads socialist nations in a boycott of the Los Angeles Olympics; but China sends 200 athletes to participate for the first time in 32 years.

1988—The Seoul Olympics provide the potential for further political battles, because South Korea experiences considerable external political tensions and threats from North Korea. As well, there is civil conflict between the ruling and opposition parties and protests by university students and the clergy for constitutional reform. The developing nation invests a large percentage of its resources to host the Games, which further increases internal tension.

Clearly most international sport events, and particularly the Olympics, promote the flaunting of national identity. This nationalism is fostered by each National Olympic Committee, which selects a team and outfits the members with a common uniform, flag, and anthem. In effect, the goal of achieving national success by a nation seems incompatible with a stated goal of the Olympics, that is, to contribute to international peace, friendship, goodwill, and understanding (Heinila, 1985; Hoberman, 1986). And yet the Games retain an essentially positive image. In 1986, for the third year in a row, the International Olympic Committee was nominated for the Nobel Peace Prize. The basis for this nomination was that the Committee is perceived to promote world harmony by providing the opportunity for nations with different political views to meet for friendly competition.

THE CASE OF APARTHEID IN SOUTH AFRICA

The Republic of South Africa offers a striking example of how politics can affect sport. The government has institutionalized certain kinds of discrimination in a political policy known as **apartheid**. The word *apartheid* means *apartness*; the policy was introduced by the white minority (which comprises about 20% of the total population) to separate and maintain the traditions and cultures of four national groups: Europeans (whites), Coloreds (part-whites), Indians, and Africans. The nation's constitution prohibits various

These demonstrators at a sport event are protesting South Africa's apartheid, a policy of discrimination that prohibits nonwhites from participating in many social settings, including sport.

forms of interracial contact. About 80% of the population is thus disenfranchised from participating in a number of social settings or institutions, including sport. Nonwhite groups are restricted to specific geographical areas, with their own educational, economic, political, and sport institutions. Interaction and contests between whites and nonwhites are largely prohibited. As a result, nonwhites may not represent South Africa in international sporting events (Archer & Bouillon, 1982; Hain, 1982; Jarvie, 1985; Krotee, 1988; Lapchick, 1975). If the best athlete in an objective event (e.g., a race against the clock) is not white he or she cannot compete for the Republic. And although blacks outnumber whites four to one, the government reportedly spends 5 times as much money on sport for whites as for blacks (Hain, 1982).

Although no specific law prohibits interracial sport teams or competition, other laws impose residential segregation, require separate toilet facilities, and prohibit whites and nonwhites from drinking together. These and other restrictions make interracial sport almost impossible. Indirectly, different laws effectively ban

- interracial teams;
- interracial competition;
- participation of nonwhites in games played in white-only areas;
- the racial mix of foreign teams or individuals traveling in South Africa; and
- interracial audiences at sport events.

Apartheid has isolated South Africa from the international community and particularly from international sport events since the early 1960s. South African athletes competing abroad tend to incite protest demonstrations; in 1976, 29 African countries boycotted the Olympics to protest New Zealand's participation in a rugby match in South Africa. This *third-party* boycott resulted when the International Olympic Committee refused to suspend New Zealand from the Montreal Olympics as punishment for its rugby teams continuing to tour South Africa. More recently sport tours to the Republic have been canceled.

External pressure, including numerous United Nations' Resolutions since 1971 against apartheid in sport, has encouraged some change. A 1971 government policy permits all international teams to be integrated and permits interracial contests at the national and club level. But continuing hostility and the many Apartheid Acts governing public behavior discourage interracial teams or contests. A recent study of the attitudes of urban South Africans suggests that citizens of all races favor open national and club competition (Scholtz & Olivier, 1984), although, as Highlight 4.3 indicates, whites are more reluctant than members of the other three groups.

For years South Africa has argued that it offers multiracial sport opportunities and that the world no longer should exclude the coun-

Highlight 4.3
South African Attitudes Toward Racially Integrated Sport

South Africa is characterized by divergent cultural, language, and racial groups (blacks, Indians, coloreds, and whites), and it is on the basis of skin color that most social life is regulated. Apartheid limits social activity by race to certain geographical areas. The effect of apartheid has been to segregate sport, a practice condemned by the leaders and citizens of most sporting nations. As a result, South Africa has been excluded from the Olympic Games since 1964 and from most other athletic and nonathletic international competitions.

Recent surveys suggest that South Africans are beginning to have more positive attitudes toward integrated sport. Most of these favorable attitudes are directed toward sport at the national level, not the club or school level. Based on the responses of 3,391 individuals from the black, Indian, colored, and white communities in 1983, Scholtz and Olivier (1984) found that a majority of urban South Africans strongly favor integrated sport at national and club competition levels (see chart). But, in 1983, among whites, the acceptance of integrated sport had actually declined since 1980-81. At the school level, 55% of the white respondents, compared with more than 87% of the other three groups, favored nonracial school sport. These results suggest that within South Africa there is still much resistance to integrated sport, especially at the levels where most respondents would likely participate.

| Race | Percentage of respondents who strongly favor integrated sport at national and club competition level | |
	1980-1981	1983
White	78	67
Indian	91	91
Colored	80	89
Black	76	82

Note. Data from Scholtz and Olivier, 1984.

try from international sport events. Indeed, some reforms introduced in 1982 have increased the opportunities for racial integration in sport. These reforms mean that a white soccer team *could* go to a black township to play, that players of different races *could* use the same locker rooms and socialize together after the game, and that teams *could* be comprised of players of different races. As yet these *possibilities* have not become realities.

WRAP-UP

This chapter has discussed how disputes in the world of sport, like other social domains, are being settled, increasingly, in the courts. As a result, sport law has become a subspeciality within the law profession, and more lawyers are earning fees for sport-related work. Cases involving sport have centered on challenges to the antitrust laws, on the search for civil rights to participate in sport (e.g., by women and members of minority groups), on incidents of violence, and on contract disputes concerning the right to bargain in a free market.

We examined what appears to be a reciprocal relationship between politics and sport. Although the relationship is not well understood at this time, we discussed many ways in which the two institutions overlap and interact.

We need to study further the process by which governments seek power within sport to achieve their goals. Specifically, many governments have increased their level of involvement from that of providing direct or indirect financial support to that of seeking increasing control of sport policy. This increased involvement and intervention, which is further amplified by the mass media, has heightened the level of nationalism within international sport. Moreover, sport has become an important diplomatic tool and is a means of protesting and reinforcing social values (such as the use of sport to oppose apartheid in South Africa).

REFERENCES

Allison, L. (Ed.) (1986). *The politics of sport.* Manchester, United Kingdom: Manchester University Press.

Archer, R., & Bouillon, A. (1982). *The South African game: Sport and racism.* London: Zed.

Ball, D.W. (1973). A politicized social psychology of sport: Some assumptions and evidence from international figure skating competition. *International Review of Sport Sociology,* 8(3/4), 63–71.

Barnes, J. (1983). *Sport and the law in Canada.* Toronto: Butterworths.

Berry, R.C., Gould, W.B., & Staudohar, P.D. (1986). *Labor relations in professional sports.* Dover, MA: Auburn.

Bouet, M.A. (1968). *Signification du sport.* Paris: Editions Universitaires.

Cantelon, H., & Gruneau, R.S. (Eds.) (1982). *Sport, culture and the modern state.* Toronto: University of Toronto Press.

Cheffers, J.T.F. (1972). *A wilderness of spite: Rhodesia denied.* New York: Vantage.

Colwell, J. (1981). *Sociocultural determinants of international sporting success: The 1976 Summer Olympic Games.* Unpublished doctoral dissertation, University of Waterloo, Waterloo, Ontario.

Douglas, S.A. (1978). Policy issues in sport and athletics. *Policy Studies Journal,* 7(1), 137–151.

Draper, M. (1963). *Sport and race in South Africa.* Johannesburg: Johannesburg Institute of Race Relations.

Edwards, H. (1969). *The revolt of the black athlete.* New York: Free Press.

Edwards, H. (1984). Sport politics: Los Angeles, 1984—The Olympic tradition continues. *Sociology of Sport Journal,* 1, 172–183.

Espy, R. (1981). *The politics of the Olympic Games: With an epilogue, 1976-1980.* Berkeley: University of California Press.

Fenwick, I., & Chatterjee, S. (1981). Perception, preference and patriotism: An exploratory analysis of the 1980 Winter Olympics. *The American Statistician*, **35**, 170–183.

Friedman, W. (1987). *Professional sports and antitrust*. Westport, CT: Quorum Books.

Gelinas, M. (1988). *The relationship between sport involvement and political attitudes and behaviours*. Unpublished master's thesis, University of Waterloo, Waterloo, Ontario.

Goodhart, P., & Chataway, C. (1968). *War without weapons: The rise of mass sport in the twentieth century and its effects on men and nations*. London: W.H. Allen.

Guldenpfenning, S., & Schulke, H. (1980). The need for politological research on sport and its relation to the sociology of sport. *International Review of Sport Sociology*, **15**(1), 127–137.

Gulland, E.D., Byrne, J.P., & Steinbach, S.E. (1984). Intercollegiate athletics and television contracts: Beyond economic justifications in antitrust analysis of agreements among colleges. *Fordham Law Review*, **52**, 717–731.

Gulotta, S.J., Jr. (1980). Torts in sports—deterring violence in professional athletics. *Fordham Law Review*, **48**, 764–793.

Hain, P. (1982). The politics of sport and apartheid. In J. Hargreaves (Ed.), *Sport, Culture and Ideology* (pp. 232–248). London: Routledge and Kegan Paul.

Hargreaves, J. (Ed.) (1982). *Sport, culture and ideology*. London: Routledge and Kegan Paul.

Hart-Davis, D. (1986). *Hitler's game: The 1936 Olympics*. New York: Harper and Row.

Hechter, W. (1977). The criminal law and violence in sports. *Criminal Law Quarterly*, **19**, 425–453.

Heinila, K. (1985). Sport and international understanding—A contradiction in terms. *Sociology of Sport Journal*, **2**, 240–247.

Hoberman, J.M. (1984). *Sport and political ideology*. Austin, TX: University of Texas Press.

Hoberman, J.M. (1986). *The Olympic crisis: Sport, politics and the moral order*. New Rochele, NY: A.D. Caratzas.

Hoch, D. (1985). What is sports law? Some introductory remarks and suggested parameters for a growing phenomenon. *Quest*, **37**, 60–70.

Jarvie, G. (1985). *Class, race and sport in South Africa's political economy*. London: Routledge and Kegan Paul.

Johnson, A.T. (1982). Government, opposition and sport: The role of domestic sports policy in generating political support. *Journal of Sport and Social Issues*, **6**(2), 22–34.

Johnson, A.T. (1983). Municipal administration and the sports franchise relocation issue. *Public Administration Review*, **43**, 519–528.

Johnson, A.T., & Frey, J. (Eds.) (1985). *Government and sport: The public policy issues*. Totowa, NJ: Rowman and Allanheld.

Johnson, W.O. (1987, June 8). A strange and resolute calm. *Sports Illustrated*, **66**, pp. 38–42.

Krotee, M. (1988). Apartheid and sport: South Africa revisited. *Sociology of Sport Journal*, **5**, 125–135.

Kuhlman, W. (1975). Violence in professional sports. *Wisconsin Law Review*, **3**, 771–790.

Lapchick, R.E. (1975). *Politics of race and international sport: The case of South Africa*. Westport, CT: Greenwood.

MacAloon, J.J. (1981). *This great symbol: Pierre de Coubertin and the origins of the modern Olympic games*. Chicago: University of Chicago Press.

Macintosh, D., Bedecki, T.G., & Frank, C.E.S. (1987). *Sport and politics in Canada: Federal government involvement since 1961*.

Kingston, ON: McGill-Queen's University Press.

Mandell, R.D. (1971). *The Nazi Olympics*. New York: MacMillan.

McIntosh, P.C. (1963). Sport, politics and internationalism. In H.M. Hart (Ed.), *Sport in the socio-cultural process* (pp. 486–500). Dubuque, IA: Wm. C. Brown.

Meyer, E.S. (1984). The Olympic games and world politics: A select annotated bibliography. *Reference Quarterly*, **23**, 297–305.

Meynaud, J. (1966). *Sport et politique*. Paris: Payot.

Michener, J. (1976). *Sports in America*. New York: Random House.

Morgan, W.J. (1985). Radical social theory of sport: A critique and conceptual emendation. *Sociology of Sport Journal*, **2**, 56–71.

Morton, H.W. (1963). *Soviet sport*. New York: Cromwell-Collier.

Natan, A. (1969). Sport and politics. In J.W. Loy & G.S. Kenyon (Eds.), *Sport, culture and society: A reader in the sociology of sport* (pp. 203–210). New York: MacMillan.

Norton, D. (1971). *A comparison of political attitudes and political participation of athletes and non-athletes*. Unpublished master's thesis, University of Oregon, Eugene.

Olin, K. (1981). Structure of sport policy in Finland. *International Review of Sport Sociology*, **16**(3), 87–95.

Ontario Hockey Council. (1982). *You and your child in hockey*. Toronto: Ontario Ministry of Tourism and Recreation.

Pacey, P.L. (1985). The courts and college football: New playing rules off the field? *American Journal of Economics and Sociology*, **44**(2), 145–154.

Petrie, B.M. (1975). Sport and politics. In D.W. Ball & J.W. Loy (Eds.), *Sport and social order: Contributions to the sociology of sport*

(pp. 187-237). Reading MA: Addison-Wesley.

Picone, L. (1975, July 19). Hung jury ends Forbes trial. *Minneapolis Tribune*, pp. 1A, 4A.

Pooley, J.C., & Webster, A.V. (1975). Sport and politics: Power play. *Canadian Association for Health, Physical Education and Recreation Journal*, **41**(3), 10–19.

Redmond, G. (Ed.) (1986). *Sport and politics*. Champaign, IL: Human Kinetics.

Rehberg, R.A., & Cohen, M. (1976). Political attitudes and participation in extracurricular activities. In D.M. Landers (Ed.), *Social problems in athletics: Essays in the sociology of sport* (pp. 201–211). Urbana, IL: University of Illinois Press.

Riordan, J. (1977). *Sport in Soviet society: Development of sport and physical education in Russia and the U.S.S.R.* London: Cambridge University Press.

Sage, G.H. (1974). Value orientations of American college coaches compared to those of male college students and businessmen. In G. Sage (Ed.), *Sport and American society: Selected readings* (pp. 207-228). Reading, MA: Addison-Wesley.

Scholtz, G.J.L., & Olivier, J.L. (1984). Attitude of urban South Africans toward non-racial sport and their expectations of future race relations—A comparative study. *International Review for the Sociology of Sport*, **19**, 129-142.

Segrave, J.O., & Chu, D.B. (1981). *Olympism*. Champaign, IL: Human Kinetics.

Segrave, J.O., & Chu, D.B. (1988). *The Olympic Games in transition*. Champaign, IL: Human Kinetics.

Seppanen, P. (1984). The Olympics: A sociological perspective. *International Review for the Sociology of Sport*, **19**, 113–127.

Seppanen, P. (1988). A revisit to social and cultural preconditions for top level sport.

International Review for the Sociology of Sport, **23**, 3–13.

Shaikin, B. (1988). *Sports and politics: The Olympics and the Los Angeles Games*. New York: Praeger.

Staudohar, P.D. (1985). Team relocation in professional sports. *Labor Law Journal*, **36**, 728–733.

Tatz, C. (1983). Sport in South Africa: The myth of integration. *The Australian Quarterly*, **55**, 405–420.

Thompson, R. (1964). *Race and sport*. New York: Oxford University Press.

Tomlinson, A., & Whannel, G. (Ed.) (1984). *Five ring circus: Money, power and politics at the Olympic games*. London: Pluto.

Watson, R.C., & MacLellan, J.C. (1986). Smitting to spitting: 80 years of ice-hockey in Canadian courts. *Canadian Journal of History of Sport*, **17**(2), 10–27.

Wilson, J. (1988). *Politics and leisure*. London: Unwin.

Yasser, R.L. (1985). *Torts and sports: Legal liability in professional and amateur athletics*. Westport, CT: Quorum.

C H A P T E R 5

Sport and the Economy

Since television became widely available in the 1960s, sport has become an increasingly profitable commodity, especially in North America. Many organizations (e.g., equipment manufacturers, retailers of sport paraphernalia, universities) gain revenue from their association with sport. Success or failure in sport can send ripples through major portions of our **economy**. Clearly the economic significance of sport affects sport practices and the people involved.

ECONOMIC ACTIVITY ASSOCIATED WITH SPORT

A shorter work week, an increase in the value we place on leisure, and the growth of the television industry have combined with other factors to usher in an era of high mass communication. These developments have helped sport become a commodity to be produced, marketed, and sold to the public. As a result, amateur and professional sport have become embedded in the local and national economies of most industrialized and developing nations. Institutionalized sport at the youth, college, professional, and Olympic level has become an economic enterprise that may be as concerned with profits and losses as with wins and losses.

The magnitude and scope of this economic enterprise for a number of sport-related industries is illustrated in this chapter. You will gain insight into the size of the revenue and expenses associated with amateur, college, professional, and Olympic sport. Selected dollar amounts, percentages, or other figures are presented to illustrate points or to indicate trends. Many of these figures can change quite quickly and dramatically. For this reason, we have not burdened the reader with numerous sources of documentation. We urge the curious student who is interested in the economics of sport to seek out similar current information in local and national newspapers and magazines.

The Sporting Goods Industry

The production of sporting goods is a rapidly growing multibillion, multinational industry that can become an important element in the local, regional, or national economy. For example, in 1989, *Sports Illustrated* reported that the sporting goods industry in the United States alone does $40 billion worth of business in a year (Ballard, 1989).

Increasingly, sporting goods are manufactured in developing countries and exported. Sport products have become an important element in the trade between countries. Much of the clothing (e.g., T-shirts and shoes) is marketed and sold as leisure wear that is never used for athletic pursuits. Expanding technology and a style-conscious marketplace create new designs annually, which further increase sales.

As an example of the size of this overall market, consider the market for athletic footwear, which sells over 246 million pairs per year in the U.S. The retail value of these sales exceeds $5 billion. One company, Reebok International, earned a $132.1 million profit on sales of $919 million in 1986. It is estimated that only about 30% of the buyers of athletic footwear actually participate in the sport for which the shoe is intended. In fact, some parents are willing to pay up to $40 for a pair of designer baby "runners," even though the infant cannot walk, let alone run!

The Construction Industry

Building and maintaining facilities for college, professional, and Olympic events and for recreational sport centers (e.g., pools, courts, fitness facilities) constitute a multibillion dollar industry that employs architects, engineers, and laborers. An estimated 1,330 to 1,610 worker *years* of labor went into the construction of facilities for the 1988 Winter Olympic Games in Calgary. The Toronto Skydome, completed in July 1989, cost an estimated $500 million.

The Souvenir and Concession Industry

To raise revenue and increase profits, teams and organizations, from youth sport to the Olympic level, sell souvenirs (with team or league logos), food, and beverages. The diversity of products and the size of profits are impressive.

- The NFL licenses the sale of more than 400 items with the NFL logo.
- College teams sell their logos to manufacturers who, in turn, produce and sell such items as toilet seats, soda pop, T-shirts, pens, and wastebaskets that display the college logo.

- The organizing committee for the 1988 Calgary Olympic Winter Games received more than $87 million by selling rights to their logo. For example, a knitting company paid $100,000 to put the Olympic logo on sweaters and sportswear for 3 years. The company predicted that the Olympic logo would increase its sales by as much as $2 million.
- More than $200 million is invested annually in baseball cards, autographs, and other baseball collectibles (Geringer, 1988). This hobby has spawned for-profit magazines such as *Baseball Cards* and *Sports Collectors Digest*.
- Concessions sold during sporting events represent a billion-dollar industry. To illustrate: If one baseball team attracted one million admissions for the season and each fan spent an average of $3 per game on concessions (e.g., one hot dog and one drink), the annual concession revenue would be $3 million. If each fan spent $6 (e.g., two beers, one hot dog, and peanuts), the revenue would be $6 million per year.
- An estimated $80 million worth of NFL franchised products were sold in England in 1986—a nation that has no NFL team and only one NFL exhibition game per year.
- It is estimated that a Super Bowl crowd spends an average of about $20 per person on food, drink, and souvenirs.

The Tourism Industry

Cities and nations actively seek to host major sport events or to acquire a professional sport franchise to attract tourists. The influx of visitors stimulates the local economy, particularly for hotels, bars and restaurants, taxis, and other retail businesses. Visitors stimulate the economy through a *multiplier effect* as well. That is, for every new dollar spent by a visitor, a certain percentage of that dollar is spent four to six times in the community by local employers and employees.

Marsh (1984) reported that a youth hockey tournament for 72 teams generated about $165,000 of new money into a town of 50,000 people, without considering the multiplier effect. An example of the multiplier effect is the yearly $4.04 million spent by visitors who attend Atlanta Falcon football games. This amount *multiplies* to an impact of approximately $13.3 million on the local economy when the original sum is spent in subsequent rounds (Schaffer & Davidson, 1975). As another example, the 1976 Summer Olympics increased tourism-generated income across Canada by an estimated $300 million and had an estimated $2.2 billion impact on the total Canadian economy. Alternatively, prolonged player strikes in professional baseball and football can have a profound effect on lost revenue for the local tourist-generated economy.

The Advertising, Entertainment, and Promotion Industry

The competition to sell sport products requires innovative and expensive marketing campaigns. Sport is also a setting to entertain clients and a medium to market nonsport products. Companies spend $20,000 to $40,000 per season to rent boxes at stadiums to entertain clients. It is estimated that $6 billion to $15 billion per year is spent in North America on advertising, marketing, and public relations related to sport or nonsport products. About $1.3 billion is spent per year in the United States for advertising on televised sport programs. Companies spent more than $30 million for television advertising ($600,000/30 seconds) during the 1987 Super Bowl. For the 1989 Super Bowl, a 60-second spot averaged $1.35 million.

For the 1988 Winter Olympic Games, Petro Canada invested about $40 million to stage the Trans-Canada Olympic Torch Relay. In return, the company expected to realize a 2% increase in market share and an additional $221 million in annual revenues. Similarly, as a result of a $13 million to $15 million investment in its Olympic program, Labatts Brewery expected to increase its market share by one percentage point, which would yield a net profit of about $10 million.

In tennis alone, five corporations spent about $25 million to sponsor events in 1985. And Martina Navratilova earns over $2 million per year by advertising products on her tennis clothes or by wearing specific brands of tennis wear. To illustrate, Computerland paid about $200,000 a year for her to wear its logo on her left shoulder.

Financial institutions have sought to recruit investment money by tying the rate of interest to the performance of sport teams. To illustrate, an Illinois savings company, in January 1986, advertised a Super Bowl Certificate of Deposit whose rate went up .01% with every point by which the Chicago Bears outscored the New England Patriots. Investors purchased $13.8 million in CDs; the final score of 46-10 for Chicago raised the rate of return to 8.61%. Similar investment plans have been linked with other sport events (Sullivan, 1986).

Sport as a Profession

Athletes in a number of team and individual sports earn base salaries, plus performance bonuses and endorsements. For some this results in incomes greater than those received by chief executive officers of major corporations, by U.S. Senators, by surgeons, or by U.S. Supreme Court justices. There is also a small but generally well-paid sport labor force of full-time or part-time employees (e.g.,

Because of the size of sport audiences at games or via television, major companies advertise their products at sport events.

managers, coaches, officials, media personnel, lawyers and agents, accountants).

Leading tennis players and golfers can earn $2 million per year in tournament prize money, plus another $3 million to $5 million for exhibition matches, endorsement of products, and public appearances. To illustrate, Sport magazine reported in June 1987 that Ivan Lendl earned $6 million in endorsements, including about $2.5 million from Adidas for wearing Adidas clothing and shoes and playing with an Adidas racquet (Pesmen, 1987).

An increasing number of professional athletes earn more than $1 million per year. Sport magazine (Levine, 1988; Pesmen, 1987) has reported that in 1977, million-dollar contracts in sport did not exist. By 1982, 23 athletes had attained millionaire status, and in 1988, 118 athletes qualified for the Sport 100 list (those who earn at least one million dollars per year). The two leading money-winners for 1987-88 were Marvin Hagler ($15 million) and Sugar Ray Leonard ($10.8 million). The list of millionaires includes baseball players, basketball players, boxers, football players, tennis players, golfers, jockeys, and an automobile racer. Only one woman, Steffi Graf, made the list in 1987–1988.

A December 17, 1988, Canadian Press story reported that the average annual salary in the four major professional sports in the 1988–89 season was $447,291 in baseball, $625,000 in basketball, $240,000 in football, and $188,000 in hockey. In baseball, the annual team player payroll for the 1987 season ranged from $5,624,500 for the Seattle Mariners to $18,569,714 for the New York Yankees ("Major League," 1987, p. 6C). The total major league payroll in 1987 was $295.8 million. Team mascots who appear at games and promotional events may earn over $200,000 per year.

In addition, a number of television sportscasters earn more than $1 million per year. A personality like John Madden may earn an additional million in endorsements, commercials, or appearance fees.

The Voluntary, Nonprofit Sector

In youth and Olympic sport, a considerable amount of time, money, and energy is donated to such activities as coaching, fund raising, and administration. It is impossible to determine the equivalent dollar value of this free labor and financial contribution, although estimates in the billions have been suggested. For example, an estimated 10% to 15% of the population in the U.S. and Canada is involved in volunteer work pertaining to sport. If volunteers averaged 9 hours a week for a year, this would be the equivalent of more than 3 million people working full time for 1 year (Malenfant, 1982).

ORGANIZATIONAL STRUCTURE OF PROFESSIONAL SPORT

Like the major oil-producing nations, each professional sport league consists of independently owned franchises that operate within a **cartel** to produce a product (i.e., sport as entertainment) and maximize profits. A cartel (e.g., a league or association) is a group of firms (e.g., teams in a league) that agrees to operate under common rules to restrict competition (e.g., revenue sharing, acquiring and hiring players, advertising, playing rules).

The net result is that the owners have a monopoly on the access to and use of players, on the right to operate a franchise in a specific geographical territory without competition, and on the control over local and national broadcast rights. Until players acquired free-agency status, the cartel had absolute control in any bargaining relationship with employees (Staudohar, 1986).

The goal of a cartel is to maximize the joint profits of all its members; the goal of each member (e.g., the team franchise) is to earn more profit and be more successful on the playing field than the other members. Neither goal is ever attained, because they conflict. In reality, a compromise is normally realized, where the teams earn enough profit so that they and the cartel remain economically viable. Different teams within a cartel can make more or less money because of variations in the size of the market (e.g., New York vs. Green Bay in the NFL), the size of the payroll, the success of the team, and the business philosophy and practices of the owners.

In a sport cartel, rules ensure that playing talent is distributed relatively equally among teams. Ideally, this should create fair competition and a high level of spectator interest. Teams acquire future players through a universal draft where teams with the weakest record pick new players first. Once drafted and signed to a team contract, the player is bound to that team by a reserve clause (in the standard players contract).

Only in recent years has **free agency** been introduced as an option for the players. This rule states that after a certain number of years in the league, players can enter an open market and try to sell their services to another team. The type of free agency varies from a very liberal policy in basketball to a highly restrictive policy in hockey. Where free agency operates, a team losing a player to another team normally is compensated in some manner (e.g., money, another player, a future draft choice). It is argued that the universal draft system and the reserve system prevent wealthier teams from buying up the contracts of outstanding players and disrupting the balance of playing strength. At the same time, the systems should ensure more equitable competition and therefore, by inference, bring greater profit for all members.

Despite cartel regulations, playing talent is distributed *unequally* among members, because each team attempts to maximize its pool of talent and win championships. Teams get better players by buying or trading player contracts within their league. An especially good player may have more market potential in a large city; small-city teams can sell or trade a single star to big-city teams in return for more players, cash, or future draft choices. Quirk & El Hodiri (1974) argue that the universal draft has little effect on equality of competition because the weaker teams function as conveyor belts. They buy talent at low prices through the draft and then trade or sell these athletes at a higher price.

Research studies indicate that these contractual arrangements do not distort the distribution of playing talent. Canes (1974) compared teams that won championships in the four major professional sports before and after each of the contractual arrangements (the reserve clause, the free-agent draft, and the intraleague draft) were instituted. He found that these restrictive league rules had no significant effect on the distribution of playing talent.

A BUSINESS MODEL FOR PROFESSIONAL SPORT

To show how economic theory can be applied to the business operations of professional sport, Quirk and El Hodiri (1974) developed a theoretical model based on two assumptions: (a) each owner wants to maximize profit and (b) an equilibrium exists within the system (i.e., the stock of playing skills for each team remains fixed, with new players replacing those whose skills depreciate).

This theory assumes that a basic unit of playing skill can be assigned to each player; the playing skill of a team is the sum of these skills. Owners must determine how many units of playing skill they need to succeed on the field and maximize their profits. In effect, they must set a wage expense per unit of playing skill and balance this with revenues (e.g., from gate receipts, broadcast rights, and the sale of players' contracts). A unique feature of the model is that each firm operates in conjunction with others. Revenue and access to units of playing skill depend on the product produced (i.e., equity of competition) and a team's degree of success (e.g., the least successful gets first choice of the new players).

Theoretically, owners strive to produce a team with more units of playing skill than the league average. But they cannot have *too* many units, or they will always win. Fans then lose interest, and the revenue from gate receipts declines. Because owners want to maximize profit, they (Quirk & El Hodiri, 1974) "add additional units of playing skills only to the point where the last unit acquired adds as much to revenue as it does to cost" (p. 37). In recent years we have seen a number of reasonably successful teams trade high-salaried players for younger, lower-salaried players to reduce expenses and increase profit.

Based on an empirical test of their model, Quirk and El Hodiri concluded that

- big-city teams tend to win more league championships than small-city teams;
- small-city franchises tend to be more mobile or disappear more frequently than big-city franchises; and
- little evidence supports the commonly held assumption that the present structural rules equalize the playing strengths of teams.

The imbalance we see results from variation in the size of the market area and in the extent to which an owner actively buys and sells player contracts. Thus, neither the draft nor the reserve system can guarantee economic balance among the teams in a league.

Rules prohibiting the sale of player contracts might guarantee convergence over time to equal playing strength among teams—if it can be demonstrated that achieving equal strength maximizes profit. Another alternative is to subsidize the weak clubs with players. Or, large cities could host more than one franchise; the increased competition in these strong market areas would reduce revenue to the level of teams in small cities.

Perhaps the simplest mechanism to equalize profit maximization would be to pool revenue from tickets and television rights, have the league pay all the players' salaries (Lock & Hoffman, 1985), and divide the profits equally. But these practices violate the principle of free enterprise for both the athlete and the owner and are unlikely to be adopted.

REVENUE AND EXPENSE IN PROFESSIONAL SPORT

In 1970, Schecter (1970) noted that "winning, losing, playing the game, all count far less than counting the money" (p. 8). More recently, millionaire businessman Peter Pocklington, owner of the Edmonton Oilers, said "sport is too much of a business for it to be just a sport" (Houston, 1987, p. D5). This comment was made as Pocklington sought league approval to sell public shares in the Oilers. Denied league approval, in July 1988 he traded his major asset, Wayne Gretzky, to another team in return for an estimated $15 million.

Almost 20 years after Schecter's insightful comments, sport clearly continues to be perceived and operated as a business enterprise (Berry & Wong, 1986; Berry, Gould, & Staudohar, 1986). This reflects the values of most industrialized nations, where such principles as the competitive spirit, the work ethic, achievement, free enterprise, the maximization of profits and economic growth, and the importance of production and consumption all have helped to include sport as an element of the economy.

As sport has become increasingly work-like and professionalized, the concepts and methods used to analyze it have become similar to those used in any other industry. In recent years the following concepts have been applied to sport: productivity, exchange of goods and services, division of labor, allocation of resources, intrinsic versus extrinsic rewards, job satisfaction, strikes, unions, franchises, monopolies, depreciation, tax concessions and subsidies, operating revenues, direct and indirect costs, maximization of profits and minimization of losses, bonuses, and marketing.

Professional sport is often perceived as big business in that it provides high salaries, large profits, and luxurious lifestyles. But many owners argue that a sport franchise is a losing proposition. A number of factors affect whether a professional sport team is a profitable investment. Profits and losses are determined by

- whether an individual or corporation owns the team;
- ownership or leasing of the playing facility;
- market strength (e.g., population size) of the franchise area;
- whether the team is a charter member of the league or an expansion team;
- whether the team has moved recently; and
- the relative economic strength of the team's area (e.g., payroll and travel costs are considerably higher for teams in Canada because of a weak exchange rate).

There is also considerable variation in the economic structure and viability of sport franchises, both within a league and across different sports.

Sources of Revenue

There are three main sources of income for professional sport teams: gate receipts, radio and television rights, and income from, for example, concessions, parking, and the sale of programs and souvenirs.

Gate Receipts. Ticket sales net more than $300 million dollars annually for teams in the major sports. Prices range from about $3 to more than $200, depending on the sport and the importance of the event. The annual revenue for hockey (in some cities) and football (in most cities) is predictable because a high percentage of sales are season tickets. This revenue is banked before the season even begins, and the owners earn interest.

Many season tickets are bought by business firms and corporations as a tax-deductible business expense for entertaining clients. It is estimated that closing this tax loophole would bring $2 billion in tax revenue per year in the United States. In sports where season tickets are not the major source of revenue, ticket sales fluctuate daily, often depending on the team's success that season, the opponents for a specific game, or the weather.

Ticket sales are an essential component of revenue, but can be unpredictable. In fact, prices may be reaching their upper limit. The Miller Lite Survey of American attitudes toward sport found that 50% of the respondents felt the price of tickets was too high (Miller Brewing Company, 1983).

With increased competition for the public's entertainment dollar and the considerable availability of sport on television, recent research has focused on factors influencing team attendance (Greenstein & Marcum, 1981; Marcum & Greenstein, 1985; Russell, 1986). Most of these studies have found that a number of factors interact to influence the size of attendance per season.

Improving the team's standing in the league, winning a championship, or fielding a popular player will influence attendance patterns. For example, Noll (1974) estimated that a baseball team that improves its position by ten games over the previous season will yearly draw an additional 180,000 fans for each million residents in the area.

A star player will increase attendance at home games by an additional 150,000 per season if there are 3.5 million residents in the area. Having a star may add approximately $450,000 in revenues. The $550,000 salary earned by Michael Jordan of the Chicago Bulls in his rookie season netted a return of 350% on the investment. Attendance increased 87% over the previous year, and ticket revenue increased about $1.8 million. The team also made the playoffs, which generated further revenue. With the addition of one star player,

Highlight 5.1
Factors Influencing Attendance at Professional Sport Events

Although many adults attend professional sport events, their attendance patterns vary from sport to sport, from team to team, from time to time in the season, and from year to year.

What are some of the factors that might explain this variation in attendance? Some commonly suggested factors include

- team performance (i.e., won-lost percentage);
- weather;
- population size and composition of the community;
- presence of competing alternatives, including other sport teams;
- cost and availability of tickets;
- accessibility and location of the stadium or arena;
- promotional efforts;
- closeness of the pennant race;
- number of star players;
- day of the week; and
- amount of violence in the game (e.g., ice hockey).

Two recent studies in different sports have examined the importance of some of these factors. The authors studied the attendance patterns for all baseball games played by two teams (Marcum & Green-stein, 1985) and for the two most violent and the two least violent games for each team in a professional hockey league (Russell, 1986).

For baseball, most of the variation in attendance was attributed to three factors: quality of the opponent, day of the week, and promotions. For a team with a losing record, the quality of the opponent and the offering of a major promotional gift were most important in determining whether an individual would attend.

In ice hockey, where it is argued that violence is promoted to sell the game, conventional wisdom suggests that attendance would increase after a particularly violent game. What Russell actually found is that a violent contest does not increase the crowd at the next home game. However, he did not control for games in which the same team was the next opponent. That is, if two teams engaged in a particularly violent game and then were scheduled to play each other in the next game, attendance might go up. Indeed, anecdotal evidence suggests that this hypothesis might be supported during the play-offs in hockey or basketball, where two teams may face each other in as many as seven consecutive games.

the team gained about $2 million over the previous season (Lidz, 1985). In Highlight 5.1 some of the important factors influencing attendance at professional sport events are examined.

Fees for Radio and Television Rights. A far more stable and major source of revenue is radio and television rights for local and national broadcasts. In recent years the rights to televise games in the four major professional sports (i.e., baseball, basketball, football, and hockey) have generated billions of dollars. To illustrate, in December of 1988, professional baseball signed a 4-year (1990 to 1994) television contract with CBS that guarantees the teams a total of $1.08 billion. In return, CBS gains exclusive rights to a network package that includes 12 regular season games, the playoff games, the World Series, and the All-Star game. Then, in January 1989, major league baseball signed a 4-year $400 million contract with ESPN, a sum that averages $14 million per team per year. In addition, each team negotiates *local* television rights; large markets may pay $1.5 million to $2.5 million per year. Similarly, the NFL signed a $1.4 billion television contract in 1987 that guarantees each team about $17 million per year.

Some sport cartels divide the revenue from national television rights equally among the firms (e.g., football); others (e.g., hockey) divide it so that teams in larger cities, or the more successful teams who appear more frequently on television, receive larger shares. This source of revenue is so critical that franchises move to more lucrative television markets (e.g., the Oakland Raiders moved to Los Angeles), and new leagues fail if they cannot sign national television contracts (e.g., the World Football Association, the United States Football League, and the World Hockey Association).

Professional sport owners strive to sign multiyear television contracts to provide a stable source of revenue. Once locked into a long-term contract, however, they have little flexibility to meet inflationary costs and increased salary demands by free agents. The amount of money negotiated for local television rights depends on, for example, the

- profit-making goals of the owner;
- size of the potential viewing audience;
- history of spectator interest in the team;
- past performance and future prospects of the team;
- number of competitive sport broadcasts;
- length of the contract; and

- bargaining skills of those involved (e.g., threatening to move a franchise to another city may increase the local rights revenue).

The price of national rights is determined mainly by the interest of advertisers and the interest (as expressed in television ratings) of fans. For example, hockey is no longer televised nationally in the United States; tennis coverage has been reduced; and soccer has yet to attain a national television contract, primarily because of projected low ratings.

Ancillary Sales. A third source of revenue is the income derived from concessions, parking lots, fees for the right to logos on products, and the sale of programs and souvenirs. By far the largest proportion of this source is the sale of food and beverages at athletic contests. It has been estimated that this is a billion-dollar industry. Money from these sales goes directly to team owners if they operate the parking lots and concessions. Some owners receive a fixed income, or an income plus a percentage, from the sale of concession rights to other entrepreneurs. For example, many of the concession rights at stadiums and arenas in North America are owned by large food and beverage corporations, which guarantee a certain income to the team owner.

Sources of Expenses

Sport teams face increasing expenses in the form of salaries, operating costs (recruiting, food, travel), equipment, taxes, and, in some situations, fees for renting facilities. These expenses are difficult to estimate because most teams are not public corporations and therefore are not required to publish an annual audit statement.

Salaries. Until the late 1960s, professional athletes received low salaries, especially in relation to the owners' profits. This situation resulted from legislative rules imposed by the cartel (e.g., the reserve system), which gave a team monopoly rights to a player for life; the lack of competing cartels (i.e., other leagues) and player associations (i.e., unions); and the practice of not using player agents (Garvey, 1984).

Since the 1960s, such factors as the emergence of competing cartels, improvements gained through collective bargaining (e.g., free-agent status), increased revenues from television, expanded leagues, and an awareness of the profits made by owners, have contributed to escalating salaries. For example, the St. Louis Cardinal baseball team won the National League Championship in 1968 and 1983. The total salary paid to the starting lineup and the best pitcher on each team rose 1,046% (from $565,000 to $5.9 million) over the 15-year period (Kirshenbaum, 1983). Minimum salaries have increased, pension and other fringe benefits have improved, and teams have awarded multiyear contracts. More recently, the 1988 six-year agreement signed by the NBA and the league's players' association is expected to raise the average annual salary from $510,000 to $900,000 by 1993.

Salaries very greatly among sports, among leagues in a given sport, and within clubs. The position played, level of ability, and popularity with fans affect individual salaries. Salaries for star performers, already high, may continue to escalate, because they improve the team's performance and increase gate receipts. This is especially true where free-agent status allows athletes' lawyers to bargain in a relatively free market. For example, athletes can negotiate contractual agreements that include

- special clauses that provide extra income via a bonus payable within one month of signing;

- investment accounts;
- bonuses for increased attendance;
- off-season jobs for the duration of the contract;
- deferred payments or annuities payable for 15 years after retirement;
- rental property or franchises;
- *no-cut* or *no-trade* clauses that pay full salaries for a number of years if they are cut from the team;
- new cars each year;
- guarantees on the contract in case of disability or death; and
- fees and service commissions for agents.

Players' salaries are discussed in greater detail in the following section.

Other Operating Costs. Owners face increased operating expenses with expanded schedules and higher travel costs, and complain that it is virtually impossible to break even or realize a profit. Because many sport teams are private corporations, and therefore are not required to publish an annual statement showing profits and losses, it is difficult to verify the total expenses. Table 5.1 illustrates the projected average expenses for a National Hockey league team. Despite these high costs new stadiums are constructed and eager entrepreneurs continue to buy new or existing franchises.

SALARIES AND ECONOMIC FREEDOM OF PROFESSIONAL ATHLETES

Even until about 1975, salaries for professional athletes were quite low in relation to the profits earned by the owners. Studies conducted in the 1970s (Medoff, 1976; Scully, 1974) suggested that baseball players were paid between 11% and 50% of their economic worth to a team in terms of attracting

Table 5.1   Estimated Annual Expenses for a National Hockey League Team, 1983

Expense	Amount ($)
NHL payroll	3,000,000
Minor league payroll	700,000
Facility rental[a]	750,000
NHL assessment fee	300,000
Nonplayer payroll	350,000
Scouting budget	350,000
Equipment	200,000
Deferred salaries	200,000
Office staff and costs	500,000
Marketing and promotion	300,000
Training camp	200,000
Travel	250,000
Miscellaneous costs	400,000
TOTAL	7,500,000

Note. Data from "The Bottom Line" by A. Strachan, 1983, December 26, *The Globe and Mail*, p. S1. Copyright 1983 by The Globe and Mail, Toronto. Reprinted by permission.

[a]Does not apply when the team owns the building or leases the facility for a nominal amount.

fans to the game or increasing broadcast revenues. Owners controlled the size of the market (i.e., the number and size of the teams), and players could only negotiate with one owner because of the reserve clause. Players did not use agents and lacked the negotiating skills of their business-oriented owners; they also had no way to compare salaries, as these were considered private matters. The lack of competing leagues meant that there was no way to bid up the value of their services.

Contemporary professional athletes are in a stronger bargaining position. Since the early 1970s, the economic freedom and salaries of players have increased for a variety of reasons, including

- the creation of competing leagues;

- the formation of players' associations and the onset of collective bargaining for minimum salaries, fringe benefits, and pensions (Dworkin & Park, 1986);
- a significant increase in the value of television rights, which the players now share for salaries and pensions;
- the use of agents, who began to publicize and compare salaries; and
- the winning of free-agent status.

Owners have awarded higher salaries because they fervently want to win a major sport championship. One or two players may make the difference between winning and losing, and an ego-involved owner is willing to pay the price. In recent years we have seen bidding wars in professional baseball, as owners try to sign free agents who will help them win the World Series. Certain linkages between a sport team and the owner's other business interests (e.g., television, a brewery) may justify raising salaries to enhance the television and radio ratings for the station or to acquire a monopoly in advertising products to a large and known audience.

Have Salary Levels Peaked?

Although free agency and escalating salaries have benefited players in recent years, the owners are beginning to tighten the purse strings. For one thing, television networks are lowering their fees for broadcast rights. As a result, annual incomes are leveling off in some sports. Professional baseball reduced by one the number of active players on a team, beginning with the 1986 season; some owners are selling high-salaried players, especially older ones, to wealthier teams and releasing aging players; long-term contracts are less likely to be offered, reducing both the security and loyalty of players; owners are limiting the playing time of players with incentive or bonus clauses; and it is alleged that owners are colluding to avoid negotiating with free agents, a practice that violates a provision in the collective-bargaining agreement.

The end result is that salary levels may fall. In addition, some players will have to choose between signing a contract at the owner's price (if they are not eligible for arbitration) and sitting out the season.

The Wage-Determination Process

A variety of methods have been proposed and used to determine wages in professional sport. Rottenberg's (1956) analysis assumed that baseball clubs only pay players according to the income expected from gate receipts. Extra sources of income were thus ignored. The Victorian Football League, in Australia, directs extra income toward ensuring that a club fields the best possible team (Dabscheck, 1975).

Another unique feature of this Australian league is that players' wages are a function of seniority, not skill level. All players, theoretically, are treated equally, no matter what club they play for, and wealthier clubs cannot buy all the best talent. In reality this rule is not enforced, and special payments and allowances are made at the discretion of the club (Dabscheck, 1975). The extra payments stem from a club's desire to recruit good players and win as many games as possible (utility-maximization) rather than from a desire to maintain equitable competition (profit-maximization).

This tendency of firms to operate as utility maximizers rather than as profit maximizers affects the supply and demand of athletes. Owners are willing to pay higher salaries to better players, retain the better players, and use income as an incentive to win.

Players demand higher salaries when they see other players' demands being met. As

you enter the labor force in a few years, you may experience this feeling of perceived injustice. Perhaps at a summer job you resented being paid a minimum wage to perform a job for which a regular employee received 2 to 3 times as much.

Dabscheck (1975) suggests that owners will pay each player only his supply price (i.e., the minimum wage necessary to induce players to give their best performance). Further, the wage structure of the firm is established to maximize winning and minimize dissatisfaction among the players. A highly skilled player on a financially weak team may thus earn less money than a moderately skilled player on a wealthier team.

Another factor affecting wage levels is the method of payment, which can be based on results from the previous year or guaranteed for an established number of years. Owners prefer the former system; most players prefer an income guaranteed over a longer period of time and that is not renegotiated, especially late in their careers when their skills or motivation may depreciate.

Although it was not accepted, the National Football League Players Association (NFLPA) suggested an interesting method for determining salaries during the negotiations following the player strike in 1982 (Lock & Hoffman, 1985). The proposed system would have guaranteed players a share of league revenues and eliminated the traditional system of each player negotiating a salary with his own team.

Under this percentage of gross proposal, the NFLPA would collect a percentage of the league's monthly revenue. Each player would receive a base salary depending on seniority. Increases in base salary would be based on *team* merit (e.g., standing in the league, league ranking on team defense) or *individual* merit (e.g., number of downs played, pro-Bowl selection). NBA owners and players introduced a version of this proposal in 1983. Faced with financial difficulties, they agreed to impose a ceiling on team salaries and to allocate no more than 53% of league revenues to players' salaries.

IS PROFESSIONAL SPORT A PROFITABLE INVESTMENT?

With the large revenue derived from television rights and the large salaries paid to some players, fans tend to believe that team owners earn large profits. But every time the players demand higher salaries, or a franchise moves, or ticket prices go up, owners lament that sport is not profitable (although they usually realize a large capital gain when the franchise is eventually sold).

Until the expansion and relocation movement of the 1970s, teams often were owned by the same person or family for many years. Today's teams are more likely to be owned by successful businessmen as an investment or by large diversified corporations that buy a franchise for advertising or tax purposes.

Are sport leagues as "big" as other industries? Are individual teams as "big" as other companies? Based on an analysis reported in *Sport* magazine (Levine, 1986), the answer is that, in comparison to other industries and single companies, sport is not as big as it is commonly portrayed. To illustrate, the combined gross revenues of the four major sports (baseball, basketball, football, and hockey) is about $1.73 billion per year. In contrast, the movie industry grosses $3.76 billion, book publishing $9 billion, hard liquor $22 billion, and the auto industry $260 billion. Compared to the $700 million in gross revenue for the NFL, an estimated 1,000 companies on the stock market have larger revenues.

On a company by sport league comparison, baseball grossed $625 million, but Walt Disney World and Disneyland, and Nike Shoes grossed $1.15 billion and $1.04 billion,

respectively (Levine, 1986). When placed in other comparative terms, a baseball franchise might gross as much as a typical department store, a football team as much as a single supermarket, and a basketball team as much as a gas station.

Highlight 5.2 illustrates that professional sport team owners are successful and well-connected businessmen in the local community or region. However, for the most part they are not the most powerful or influential people in North America, as conventional wisdom often implies.

Franchise owners realize profit in a number of ways: direct salaries; stock dividends; tax benefits charged against personal income or other enterprises; the sale of franchise rights or facilities; and sharing in the fee paid to the league when a new team enters. As an example, the four new teams admitted to the NBA for the 1988 season paid a $32.5 million entry fee. Each of the existing 23 teams received $5.6 million.

Tax Advantages

As was noted earlier, it is difficult to examine the finances of many professional teams. A team may show a loss on paper, but this loss can be used as a tax deduction against another part of the corporation's tax statement or against the owner's personal income tax. Apparent losses can thus represent indirect profit. Even where leagues (e.g., WFL, USFL, WHA, ABA) have failed, some owners realized profits, at least indirectly, through tax benefits.

Many franchises remain profitable through local and federal subsidies that provide tax concessions or low rental payments for facilities. At the local level, more than 70% of the stadiums or arenas are owned by municipalities or counties, which rent the facilities at an artificially low rate. These low rent-

---

Highlight 5.2
Sport Team Owners: Small Fish in a Big Pond?

It is frequently assumed that those who control sport at the Olympic or professional levels tend to be members of the social and economic elite of a nation. Indeed, there are often direct relationships or connections between owning a professional team and being involved as a high-level decision-maker in the economy.

The conventional wisdom in the sociology of sport is that these sport team owners are an elite group of business people who sit as members of interlocking boards and belong to important social or political organizations. They are thought to be part of a corporate elite who control the decisions and directions of several sectors of North American life. Yet when we think of the powerful elites in the United States we think of the Rockefeller, Ford, or Kennedy families. None of these families has had any direct involvement in the ownership of professional sport teams. Moreover, a sport business is not as large as a major company in other sectors of the economy. Thus, although sport team owners are successful and wealthy business persons, they are not as highly influential

in the corporate and political affairs of the nation as conventional wisdom would have us believe.

Recent evidence to refute the myth of the powerful and influential sport owner has been provided by Flint and Eitzen (1987) in a study of 141 persons who owned major league teams from 1982 to 1984. They found that owners tend to make their fortunes in business activities that do not lead them into national or international corporate linkages nor into the national level of social organizations. Most of their influence, if any, remains at the local or regional level. For the 22 wealthiest sport team owners who were listed in the *1982 Forbes Four Hundred* (a list of people with wealth greater than $100 million), it was found that they sat on boards of directors or belonged to influential social clubs only at the local or regional level. These owners were not linked to a national elite network, other than that involved in their own sport league. Sport owners are relatively small fish in a big pond—the national economy.

---

als are tolerated because it is believed that a professional sport team enhances the prestige of the community; stimulates the local economy; generates employment at the sport facility; and improves the morale of the citizens. Similarly, indirect local subsidies are available to the owners through artificially low property taxes.

At the federal level, professional sport teams or communities receive tax exemptions

on bonds sold to finance the construction of new facilities. Owners can depreciate player contracts up to about 50% of their value on income tax returns for a period of 5 years and are exempt from capital gains tax on the sale of players, franchises, or equipment (Ambrose, 1985). For example, if a professional sport team sells its star player for $700,000 to offset an expected deficit, a capital gains tax is not assessed. The sport owner acquires

$700,000 in tax-free revenue. A manufacturer in another industry who sold a piece of machinery or a building for $700,000 would have to pay a capital gains tax.

Buying and Selling Franchises

One way to realize a profit in professional sport is to acquire a franchise and sell the team later at a profit. This is possible because there are many wealthy individuals or corporations who seek to acquire a franchise for intrinsic reasons, for the monopoly they gain in advertising on sport broadcasts, for the special tax advantages, or for the advertising value it can bring to other business interests. For example, when a new owner acquires a franchise he or she negotiates with federal tax personnel about what percentage of the purchase price can be allocated to player contracts. These contracts can then be depreciated over a 5-year period so that they offset the tax payable on income. This tax advantage immediately increases the value of the franchise to the owner.

The estimated purchase prices of three sport franchises sold in recent years were

1983—Dallas Cowboys, $86 million

1984—Denver Broncos, $70 million

1986—New York Mets, $80 million

1989—Dallas Cowboys, $140 million

In most cases, the selling price of a franchise is influenced by the size of the local television market and the success of the team. For example, when the Cleveland Indians became a pennant contender in 1986, the perceived value of the franchise went up, even though the local television market remained relatively small.

Most sport franchises appear to be a good long-term investment, even when consider-ing inflation. For example, the Dallas Cowboys franchise cost about $140 million in 1989 and about $600,000 in 1960. Similarly, the Toronto Blue Jays, sold in 1976 for $7.2 million, increased in value to $45 million by 1986. In hockey, the Montreal Canadien franchise in the NHL was purchased by the Molson family in 1957 for an estimated $2.7 million. Over the next 14 years, the franchise paid annual dividends of about $3 million to the owners. In 1971, they sold 58% of the shares for an estimated $15 million.

Consider also the case of Maple Leaf Gardens, Ltd., owners of the Toronto Maple Leafs in the NHL. One person controls 79% of the shares. During 1987 the value of each share went from $60 to about $140—an increase for that owner of about $50 million. In the previous fiscal year the company reported a profit of $2.6 million. The major assets of the company are the team and the building, which have been carried since 1931 as a declared asset in the company's books at $100,000 and $358,811, respectively. In today's market, it is estimated that *each* asset could be sold for about $50 million.

Some franchises are now selling stock. In December 1986 the Boston Celtics offered shares at $18.32 on the New York Stock Exchange. The entire lot (2.6 million shares) was sold in one day, increasing the team's total value to about $120 million.

Like other speculative stocks, the value of a sport franchise can fluctuate. By June 15, 1987, a Celtic share was trading at $13.12. This loss of about $5 a share resulted in the team's total worth falling to about $85 million. Yet, this still represents a sizeable profit from the 1983 purchase price of $15 million. Thus, despite public statements by some owners that sport franchises are a losing proposition, most teams in the four major sports consistently realize a profit. This occurs even in the National Hockey League, which still lacks a national television contract in the United States.

Lately we have seen franchises being bought by corporations with existing media enterprises and by breweries—especially in the Canadian market, where three major brewing companies compete vigorously for the total market share. In the United States the Turner Broadcasting Company owns the Atlanta Braves and Hawks; Gulf and Western Industries owns the New York Knicks and Rangers. These companies acquire exclusive local rights to the television broadcasts of their teams and charge high advertising fees. In Canada, when a brewing company owns a specific team it gains monopoly rights to advertise its products on the telecasts, in game programs, and on signs in the home facility. And the company prohibits the sale of competitors' products at the games. This brewery sporting war is most heated in Quebec, where two rival breweries own the Quebec Nordiques and the Montreal Canadiens. The intense fight for beer sales has spilled over into an intense, and often bloody, rivalry on the ice. The third major brewery in Canada, which does not own an NHL team in Quebec, has seen declining sales in the province since the hockey war escalated.

Franchise Location and Relocation

Even the early days of baseball saw a considerable number of team mergers, failures, or relocations to more desirable locations. For example, Ingham, Howell, and Schilperoort (1987) report that 850 baseball clubs were formed between 1869 and 1900. Of these, 650 lasted 2 years or less; only 50 survived 6 years or more. Seeking added stability through a monopoly and a cartel, the teams formed the National Baseball League in 1876. For the first time a professional sport established rules that governed the location and relocation of each franchise in the league.

Like a local fast-food outlet, location is a prime element in the profitability of a sport franchise. Thus, when professional sport leagues expanded in the 1960s and 1970s, owners and leagues sought large metropolitan areas that would generate both gate receipts and a large television market (Johnson, 1985). Cities and regions tried to win sport franchises to their area by enticing teams to relocate or by hosting a new franchise created when leagues expanded or new leagues were created.

To acquire a team, eager communities offer subsidies such as low rent for facilities, tax concessions, or stadium improvements. Politicians and business entrepreneurs support these incentives, arguing that having a team boosts urban renewal and tourism. Are these arguments valid? Does the acquisition of a sport franchise represent a profitable enterprise for the city or region? Johnson (1986) analyzed the revenue and expenditures for baseball and football in Baltimore and found that in 1983 the estimated expenditures by the city for the stadium and police were about $2.4 million; revenue from rent, concession sales, parking, and admissions tax was about $3.3 million. He concluded that cities can profit if the team is successful, especially in postseason play, but only if they are not supporting a new stadium with a heavy construction debt. In this latter case, the city experiences a loss, although merchants in the food, beverage, hotel, and transportation areas may earn related profits.

To relocate, a team must, by league rules, receive the approval of most of the other teams in the league. Until recently, this approval was normally granted. About 68 franchises in the major professional sports moved between 1950 and 1983, with 37 occurring after 1970 (Johnson, 1984). One outcome has been the alienation of fans from the team and the sport.

Recognizing that the fans and city do not want a team to leave, owners have used the implied threat of relocation to gain increased subsidies from the city. Between 1981 and 1983, 13 of the 42 cities in the United States with professional sport teams faced demands from owners for new or increased subsidies—tax breaks, stadium improvements, or a new stadium (Johnson, 1984).

Most recently, two franchises in the NFL moved without the permission of the league or the cooperation of the original city. The Raiders moved from Oakland to Los Angeles to tap a larger television and cable TV market. The Baltimore Colts rented trucks and drove out of town in the middle of the night, moving to Indianapolis when the Baltimore city government would not renovate the existing stadium or build a new one.

One outcome of these overt or covert relocation plans has been an attempt by cities (e.g., Oakland) to seek legislation to restrict franchise relocations, thereby protecting their investment and meeting their perceived need for a franchise in the city. Basically, cities are competing for a scarce resource. They are willing to offer public-funded incentives to owners, much as they try to attract industries that will hire local workers. The major difference between sport and other industries, however, is the magnitude and duration of the financial commitment.

COLLEGE SPORT AS BIG BUSINESS

In most countries, university or college sport programs began as clubs. Players organized their schedule, appointed a coach, and paid all or most of their expenses. In North America, as sport became more professionalized, athletics departments were created and given more administrative and financial responsibility for intercollegiate sport. Today, differences in the structure of college athletics in different countries are based on value differences and economic demands. For example, intercollegiate sport in the United States, and to a lesser extent in Canada, is considered an essential part of the social life of the student body. It is important for the prestige and economic health of the institution. As a result, athletic departments have become separate economic entities within the institution, administered by an athletic director who may be responsible for a multimillion dollar budget. Some of these budgets include salaries for football and basketball coaches that exceed that of the university's president (Lawrence, 1987). Tables 5.2 and 5.3 illustrate the budgets for a large athletic program and for the NCAA.

The present structure of college sport in North America reflects an emphasis on excellence, increasing specialization, the desire of the student body and alumni to consume sport, and the belief that a successful college athletic program enhances the prestige of the institution and thereby helps to recruit students. As a result, college sport has become a separate business enterprise that depends on gate receipts, television and radio rights, alumni assistance, and, in the case of football, guarantees for playing in Bowl games. The estimated bonus paid to colleges in 1989 for participating in 17 postseason football Bowl games was nearly $50 million, with the revenue per team ranging from $180,000 for the California Bowl to $6 million for the Rose Bowl (The Lineups and Money, 1988).

Of course, larger gate receipts and television fees result from winning on the playing field. And winning requires recruiting highly skilled players and employing a large coaching and scouting staff.

In contrast, university sport in Great Britain, Australia, the German Federal Republic, Japan, and many other countries is organized by a council of university sports clubs. Each

Table 5.2   A "Big-Time" Athletic Program Budget: University of Michigan, 1986

Revenue (in millions $)		Expenditures (in millions $)	
Ticket sales		Gate guarantees to visiting teams	
Football	8.6	Football	2.2
Basketball	1.3	Other sports	0.1
Other Sports	0.2		
Postseason games	1.5	Postseason games	0.7
Publications and advertising	0.3	Publications and advertising	0.4
TV and radio	1.4	Facilities	1.5
Stadium and facilities rental	0.6	Administration	0.7
Camps and clinics	0.4	Camps and clinics	0.3
Investment income	0.5	Salaries, wages, fringe benefits	4.0
Other	1.4	Capital expenses & debt service	0.3
		Team and game expenses	
		Football	1.1
		Other sports	1.4
		Grants-in-aid[a]	
		Football	1.0
		Other sports	1.4
		Other	0.7
Total revenues	16.2	Total expenditures	15.8

Note. Reprinted from October 27, 1986 issue of *Business Week* by special permission, copyright © 1986 by McGraw-Hill, Inc.

[a]Excludes $850,00 in the Athletic Scholarship Fund.

sport club sends a representative to the governing council, which arranges competitions with other universities or community sport clubs. There are no athletics departments, no full-time athletic administrators. There are other differences in sport in other countries as well.

- Where the club structure predominates, coaches are normally volunteers.
- Spectators pay no admission fee for games.
- Athletes do not view their participation as preprofessional socialization.
- Competition is available at up to four or five levels of ability.
- Players do not receive athletic scholarships.

- Games are not televised.

Economics of College Sport

Like professional sport, college sport depends on gate receipts and television revenues from the major sports (primarily football and basketball) to survive. Like other enterprises, college sport programs must face inflation, reduce costs, and increase revenue. But lowering salaries or offering fewer scholarships could reduce the quality of a team (i.e., success on the field) and thereby reduce revenues. And because most stadiums have a fixed seating capacity (which would be extremely expensive to expand) the only way to make more money is to raise ticket prices.

Table 5.3   The 1987–88 NCAA Budget

Revenue (in millions $)		Expenditures (in millions $)	
Division I men's basketball championship	$64.5	Division I men's basketball championship	$32.1
Other Division I championships	5.6	Grant to National Collegiate Foundation	6.8
Communications department	2.4	Championships—transportation guarantees	4.7
Football television assessments	1.5	Championships—game and administrative expense	4.0
Investments	1.3	Block grants to Divisions II and III reserves	3.1
Corporate sponsorships	1.0	Championships—per diem allowances	3.0
Membership dues	0.9	Communications department	2.8
Division II championships	0.6	Other championships distributions	2.2
General	0.4	Drug testing and education	2.0
Division III championships	0.3	Compliance and enforcement department	2.0
Total revenue	$79.4	Publishing department	1.9
		Legal services	1.5
		Administration department	1.5
		General	1.4
		Committees	1.2
		Championships department	1.0
		Funded operating reserve	1.0
		Insurance—catastrophic	1.0
		National Forum	1.0
		Insurance—general and liability	0.7
		Legislative services department	0.7
		Rent	0.7
		Contingency	0.7
		Business department	0.6
		Postgraduate scholarships	0.6
		Royalties to members	0.7
		Development—clinics and competition	0.5
		Total expenditures	$79.4

Note. Reprinted by permission of the National Collegiate Athletic Association. Data are accurate only for the years indicated.

Institutions then run the risk of pricing themselves out of the entertainment market. Athletics departments thus find themselves in something of a bind.

This has been compounded by the Title IX Educational Amendment of 1972, which requires that women's athletic programs at institutions that receive federal funds have an equal opportunity to operate as full athletic programs. This translates into reducing the cost of men's athletic programs or expanding the total budget considerably. Probably only donations from alumni watching the games on television will help colleges avoid major deficits in their athletic budgets. Another choice is to abandon the most intense levels of competition.

Organizational Structure: The NCAA

Major college athletic programs in the United States are organized and regulated by a cartel, the NCAA. This association was created to

- establish a ceiling on grants to student-athletes;
- define and enforce rules pertaining to years of eligibility and recruiting;
- establish the rules of the game and limit the number of games;
- pool and divide cartel profits;
- inform cartel members about transactions, market conditions, and business procedures; and
- monitor cartel rules (e.g., Proposition 48) and impose sanctions (e.g., probation; the death penalty, a forfeited season, no television exposure, and no accompanying revenue) (Koch, 1983).

The NCAA has an annual operating budget of more than $79 million. Regional conferences (e.g., Big Ten) may also impose rules and regulations on their members.

Basically the NCAA strives to promote equal competition. College athletes also have a contract in the form of a letter of intent, which binds them to one university for at least one year. If they transfer, they cannot compete for one year. Mobility among teams thus is discouraged, partly to prevent the wealthier teams from raiding less successful ones.

Despite the equalizing effect of the NCAA, universities increasingly are forced to choose between two tiers of competition: *major* colleges and the *others*. To illustrate the advantages of competing at the major level, each of the final four teams in the 1989 NCAA basketball tournament received over $1 million from television revenues. In addition, they received funds to cover their expenses and an indeterminate amount of free publicity that may help recruit students and solicit alumni donations.

Tiers Within the NCAA

There are unique and commonly accepted economic, philosophical, and structural differences among the institutions affiliated with the NCAA. Raiborn (1970) classified NCAA membership ". . . into five homogeneous groups based upon the criteria of dominance of particular sports within the program and apparent strength of programs as determined by the nature of the scheduled opposition (p. 2). His fivefold classification is as follows.[1]

Class A. These institutions sponsor football teams that the NCAA defines as *major* on the strength of their football schedules. A *major* football team plays most of its regularly scheduled games against other *major* institutions during each consecutive two-year period.

Class B. These institutions may occasionally compete against others in the Class A

[1]*Note.* Reprinted by permission of the National Collegiate Athletic Association. Data are accurate only for the year indicated.

Division, but schedule most of their football games against institutions in their own division.

Class C. These institutions rarely play football against a Class A institution and only periodically compete against a Class B institution.

Class D. This category includes institutions that did not sponsor an intercollegiate football team but did sponsor a *major* intercollegiate basketball team.

Class E. These institutions did not sponsor an intercollegiate football team or a *major* intercollegiate basketball team.

The classes can be grouped according to their economic commitment to athletics. Class A institutions stress the concept of *athletics for entertainment*. Classes C and E, and to some extent Class D, stress *athletics for education*. Class B tries to blend *athletics for pay* and *athletics for play*. In brief, some institutions have elected not to enter the economic race of intercollegiate athletics. Some are trying to compete in the race with limited resources, which can result in a financial squeeze and elimination of some nonrevenue athletic programs.

In recent years the NCAA has started to lose control over the firms within the cartel, mainly for three reasons. First, the cartel has become so large it cannot enforce the multitude of regulations and not all actions by the various institutions are known to the other members. Second, the athletic and academic interests and policies of the members vary greatly (e.g., Division 1A vs. Division III; men's versus women's athletics; independent schools vs. large conferences).

Third, the NCAA lost control of a large source of revenue following a 1984 Supreme Court decision. This ruling stated that the NCAA violated the Sherman Antitrust law by controlling the sale of broadcast rights for all NCAA football games (Pacey, 1985). The court ruled that each institution had the right to sell the broadcast rights for its football team. Large football schools thus have gained increased revenues and increased exposure to potential recruits and to alumni donors. Football fans have gained a wider choice of viewing options.

Alumni Boosterism and Control of Intercollegiate Athletics

One way athletic departments have tried to solve their economic woes is by launching extensive fund-raising programs among alumni and local boosters. Institutions encourage this fund-raising, believing that successful athletic teams generate general alumni donations and increase student enrollment. Recent evidence suggests that there is not a strong correlation between winning in football and basketball and the amount alumni contribute to the university (Sigelman & Bookheimer, 1983). However, Sigelman and Bookheimer did find a strong relationship between football success and the amount of donations contributed directly to the athletics department. There also appears to be a strong correlation between success and attendance at the games, and attendance at games may be a better predictor of alumni contributions than the percentage of wins (Coughlin & Erekson, 1985).

Faced with an increasing economic crisis over the past 20 years, athletics departments have courted wealthy alumni and local businessmen through booster clubs. These clubs were created to attract fans and help recruit athletes. Over time, however, they have become highly influential in the operation and economic stability of the athletics department. Some booster clubs virtually control the policies and practices of the athletics department, which has become so financially dependent it is no longer under the control of the central university administration (Frey, 1985). Booster club members often are responsible for the illegal recruitment and support of athletes—violations that members of the athletics department claim to know nothing about.

ECONOMICS AND SPORT FOR WOMEN

Since passage in the United States of Title IX of the Higher Education Act in 1972 and because of the women's movement and civil rights legislation, the number of female participants at all levels of competition has increased. Sport and fitness activities have become more socially acceptable and available for women of all ages. These increasing opportunities have created financial problems for sport organizations, especially the cost of operating facilities and programs and paying salaries.

A shift in philosophy in women's sport toward professionalism, commercialism, and an emphasis on spectator-oriented sports to generate revenue has led to inflated budgets for voluntary associations, community recreation programs and Olympic programs. Boutilier and SanGiovanni (1983) argue that the financial woes in women's intercollegiate sport programs have increased because the number of competitors has doubled or tripled since the early 1970s. Demand has increased for larger coaching staffs, more games per season, and expanded travel and recruiting budgets. Revenues have not increased at the same rate as expenses, despite increased gate receipts and television exposure. The increased costs for women's programs have been offset by transferring funds from male intercollegiate programs—notably from the revenue-producing sports of football and basketball.

For women's intercollegiate sport, revenues have not increased at the same rate as expenses, despite increased visibility and a higher level of competitive play.

The greatest cost increases have occurred in Division I colleges, which incur more travel expenses and offer more full scholarships. There are considerably fewer full scholarships and less disparity between male and female programs in the lower divisions, where sport is less highly valued (Boutilier & SanGiovanni, 1983; Coakley & Pacey, 1984).

This increased emphasis on women's competition has brought abuses in recruiting, a lower quality of education for female athletes, increased aggression by players and coaches, and the appearance of coaching behaviors once seen only in the men's intercollegiate program (e.g., verbal and physical abuse of opposing players and of officials; searching for new coaching positions with higher salaries; false or unfulfilled promises to recruited athletes).

At the community recreation level, increased participation by girls has strained the availability of facilities (e.g., soccer fields, tennis courts), increased the demand for coaches, led to further demands on the private sector for financial support, and encouraged the formation of private clubs (e.g., swimming, track, tennis, gymnastics) with salaried full-time coaches and rental costs for facilities. Often only affluent parents can pay these costs, and girls from low-income families are denied equal opportunity to become involved in sport. Another outcome has been increased tension between volunteer groups representing boys' and girls' sports. In Canada, minor hockey executives (i.e., boys' hockey) now find themselves competing for ice-time in community-owned arenas and for local sponsors against representatives of girls' ringette, broomball, and hockey.

ECONOMICS OF INTERNATIONAL SPORT

Although amateur sport at the international level is theoretically organized for the competitor, increasingly this level of sport competition has become an integral part of the marketplace, particularly with respect to the Olympics, the World Cups of soccer and skiing, and most recently, the America's Cup Challenge for 12-meter sailing yachts.

Cost of Hosting an Event

Auf der Maur (1976) has called the Olympic Games "The Billion-Dollar Game"; indeed, the Olympic Games have ceased to be a festival associated with religion and become big business (Seifart, 1984). In 1972, the cost to host the Munich Olympics was estimated at $4 million to $6 million—about $30,000 per *minute* for the privilege of hosting the 2-week

event. One justification for this investment was that the city gained an excellent sport facility and additional housing when the Olympic Village was converted to apartments. Unfortunately, in Mexico City, Munich, and Montreal, the Olympic Village apartments have proven costly investments. And the sport facilities are so expensive to operate that few organizations can afford to pay the rental fee to host events at the site. To illustrate the cost of hosting the Olympics, Highlight 5.3 explains how the cost for the 1976 Summer Olympics escalated from $10 million to $1.4 billion.

In contrast to Montreal (see Highlight 5.3), where there was considerable financial investment by the city, provincial, and federal governments, the 1984 Summer Olympics in Los Angeles were funded primarily by the private sector. Construction of facilities and donations by private corporations, a large unpaid volunteer labor force, and indirect government subsidies that provided security personnel contributed to $150 million in profit on revenue of about $619 million. Among the expenses were $5 million for the opening and closing ceremonies, $98 million for facilities, $98 million for administration, and $70 million for housing and medical services. The major sources of revenue were about $95 million from sponsors and licensee royalties, $280 million from worldwide radio and television rights, $123 million from ticket sales, and $18 million from the sale of commemorative coins. The Los Angeles organizing committee brought in a new era in the economic funding of the Olympics: private sector funding and management rather than government involvement.

Cost to Athletes

The cost of winning a medal has increased significantly. To be competitive, athletes must

---

Highlight 5.3
The High Cost of Hosting the Olympics

In 1970, despite a debt of $12.3 million to the Canadian federal government for assistance in hosting Expo 67 (the 1967 World's Fair), the city of Montreal won the right to host the 1976 Summer Olympic Games. It was predicted in 1968 that the cost would range from $10 to $15 million; in 1973 a revised, but balanced, budget of $310 million was struck. The revised budget included $250 million for facilities (not including the Olympic Village, which was to be constructed by a private developer) and $32.5 million in operating expenses. Revenue was expected from the sale of Olympic coins and stamps, rights to the Olympic symbol, television rights, gate receipts, and a national lottery.

By May 1976 the revenue included $5 million from the sale of stamps, $100 million from coins, $170 million from lottery tickets, $20.4 million from tickets, $34.4 million from television rights, and $30 million from endorsement rights. This represented a total revenue of $359.8 million 2 months before the Games opened. But the estimated expenses, because of inflation, labor problems, corruption, and mismanagement, had risen to $1.4 billion or $726 for each Montreal taxpayer. Following the Games, the best final estimate of revenue was approximately $400 million, with a projected deficit of somewhere between $.5 million to $1 million dollars. By comparison, Auf der Maur (1976) noted that the St. Lawrence Seaway was completed in 1959 at a cost of $470 million ($1.23 billion in 1975 dollars) and that the 220-mile Trans-Canada gas pipeline would have cost $970 million dollars in 1975. Moreover, he noted that a billion-dollar investment in the city of Montreal in 1976 would have provided either low-rental housing for 120,000 citizens, free public transportation for 10 years, or 400 community arenas. Although these figures are only estimates, they reflect the inflationary and escalating cost of producing international sport events.

---

now train year-round. Athletes *do* receive bursaries, scholarships, jobs, or per diems to compensate for losses in income, living expenses, training costs, and travel. But depending on the athlete, the sport, and the country, the percentage of expenses recovered by the athlete varies widely. For example, one speed skater in North America, who did not win a medal in 1976, estimated that training expenses for his family were $20,000 over a 20-year period. Even more costly are some minor hockey programs in the United States, where parents reportedly spend $5,000 to $10,000 per year. In other cases, athletes cannot hold a job full- or part-time in an Olympic year and must be subsidized by their families or some outside organization.

Financial Benefits of Hosting an Event

For the 1988 Winter Olympics in Calgary, based on projected expenses of $516 million and income of $556 million, the Organizing Committee reported a profit of $40 million. This profit is allotted for developing athletes for future Olympics and operating the facilities as training sites for international athletes. Revenue came from private-sector donations; subsidies from the federal, provincial, and city governments; television rights ($326 million); ticket sales ($42 million); and fees ($87 million) for using the official game logo. The federal government, which invested about $200 million, received about $240 million in taxes on everything from gasoline to construction materials.

The Olympics has also been profitable for television networks, especially when the Games are held in Europe or North America. Since the 1960 Olympic Games, the fees paid by U.S. networks for broadcast rights have escalated from $50,000 to $309 million for the 1988 Winter Games and from $394,000 to $320 million for the 1988 Summer Games. In May of 1988, CBS obtained the rights to the 1992 Winter Olympic Games in Albertville, France for $243 million. A new rights record was established in late 1988 when NBC agreed to pay $401 million for the 1992 Summer Olympic Games in Barcelona, Spain. In turn, the network sells advertising time for as much as $330,000 for a 30-second spot. It is estimated that ABC received about $650 million from advertisers for the 1984 Olympics, earning the network an estimated $300 million profit after production and promotion costs (Seifart, 1984). ABC also benefited indirectly by promoting its forthcoming schedule of fall television programs to a large and diverse audience. For the 1988 Seoul Summer Olympics, NBC charged $325,000 for a 30-second commercial.

Benefits to Athletes

At the amateur level, some successful athletes now earn high incomes for competing and making public appearances. This income involves cash prizes or gifts for winning, appearance fees for entering certain events, and money for endorsing or promoting products. Depending on the rules for a sport, the income either goes into a trust fund until the athlete retires or is viewed as salary. To illustrate the magnitude of these amateur earnings, the winner of the 1987 Los Angeles Marathon won an expensive European car, a camera set, and $15,000.

GAMBLING AND SPORT

One indirect consequence of increased spectator involvement in sport has been the development of a nationwide and worldwide gambling business. Gambling, which can become addictive, is a pervasive element of modern sport. It involves avid sport consumers as well as those who seldom consume sport and is pursued by both sexes and by members of all social classes, ethnic groups, nationalities, and age groups. Excluding horse racing, most gambling is on the traditional spectator sports of football, baseball, basketball, and hockey; but any sport event, including Little League games and tennis matches among friends, provides the opportunity for a wager.

Some betting action is legal, such as at race tracks or off-track betting offices for football (i.e., soccer) in Great Britain and sport-betting shops in Las Vegas. Increasingly, legalized gambling events (e.g., casinos, raffles, lotteries) are held to raise money to build sport facilities or operate youth sport programs. This, of course, becomes a public policy issue when the event is operated by a local, state, or federal government.

What We Know About Gambling and Sport

Much of the gambling associated with sport events is illegal, although few people are

Even a game among friends presents an opportunity for gambling.

charged with offenses. Because the behavior is illegal, it is impossible to determine who or how many people are involved (Ignatin, 1984); how much money changes hands; and how much profit is made. Various sources (Abt, McGurrin, & Smith, 1984; Frey, 1984, 1985; Kaplan, 1983; Smith, 1986; Straw, 1983; Underwood, 1963) have estimated that

- the amount wagered in the United States alone may range from $17 billion to $70 billion per year;
- Americans lose $220 million on sport bets in a year;
- more than 25 million Americans have placed a bet on an intercollegiate game at least once;
- about two thirds of North Americans gamble at least once per year, with only about .005% ever becoming compulsive gamblers; and

- as much as $40 million may be bet on the Super Bowl with Nevada sports books.

The pervasiveness of gambling is reflected further in the relatively recent appearance of

- an increase in the number of office pools, usually operated on a nonprofit basis at work;
- an increase in the number of illegal bookmakers;
- television experts who provide inside information, opinions, and point spreads for upcoming games;
- the publication of injury lists, betting lines, and point spreads in daily newspapers;
- commercialized publications, telephone services, or online computer sources to provide up-to-the minute information for sport bets;
- on-site casual betting on specific events during a game;
- players being offered money, favors, or gifts in exchange for inside information about strategy, injuries, impending trades, or retirements; and
- betting shops in Las Vegas exclusively devoted to sport wagers.

Again, because most of this sport gambling is illegal and is perceived as a harmless activity, we do not know much about those who gamble regularly. It appears, though, that most of the action involves males, many of whom have enough money to attend games. In fact, betting may increase the interest and emotional involvement in games and compensate for the games' becoming less exciting (e.g., more frequent games, more teams, and more televised games). In recent years, an increasing number of women seem to be gambling on sport events. As Highlight 5.4 shows, gambling can become a self-destructive addiction.

Highlight 5.4
The Addicted Sport Gambler

Legal or illegal betting on football, basketball, baseball, and hockey games has become a multibillion dollar per year industry and a major leisure pursuit in North America. Yet gambling can become a compulsive, pathological disease that can destroy an individual and her or his family. To combat the disease and to help the addicted, Gamblers Anonymous offers group therapy, and some hospitals provide gambling treatment programs.

Who are these compulsive sport gamblers, and how did they become addicted? Many begin gambling in their teens in a social setting with friends or participating in a football pool, often because of a genuine interest in the sport. Many people never go beyond this stage. The next stage often involves a big win, which encourages some gamblers to bet more and to bet more often, especially if they are bored at work or with life in general. If they begin to lose, they may be forced to lie about financial matters and to beg, borrow, or steal money to cover the debts. The final stage involves irrational, illogical betting. By this stage, compulsive gamblers have lost most or all of their intrinsic interest in sport. Sometimes this stage is accompanied by alcohol or drug addiction, loss of job, marital breakup, and perhaps suicide—a high price to an activity that may have begun simply as a genuine and deep interest in sport.

Questions Raised by Gambling

As a result of the emerging epidemic of sport gambling, scholars, journalists, and sport executives have begun to consider how they can maintain the integrity of sport. For example, should sport betting be legalized, and therefore, taxed? Legalization might encourage more people to become involved, more *fixing* of games, and more pressure on coaches and athletes. Alternatively, it would provide a significant source of revenue for the government and perhaps for the sport industry. Legalized sport betting might also lessen the influence of organized crime, although most evidence seems to indicate that bookies do not fix games or use their profits to fund other illegal activities.

Should point spreads be published? Most would argue no, to avoid the implication that gambling is encouraged or permitted and to remove the temptation to "fix" games.

Do professional team owners and college presidents support gambling? Despite a public antigambling stance, many quietly support legalized gambling because they believe it contributes to the popularity and profitability of the sport. That is, even in a contest that is clearly decided by half-time, people who have wagered on the game will continue to watch until the final point spread is confirmed. This continued interest increases the sale of refreshments at the game and maintains television ratings to the end of the show.

Is gambling, as a form of risk-taking behavior, a healthy and educational experience and a part of the psychology of modern life? Participating in an office pool provides sociability, status (if successful), decision-making experience, and a sense of excitement. Some argue that this form of leisure behavior should be encouraged.

Another consideration is the recent scandals associated with "fixing" games. This is especially worrying when athletes have been convicted of gambling on sport events in which they were a participant.

WRAP-UP

Since the advent of television in the early 1960s, sport has become a highly profitable commodity to be produced and marketed, especially in North America. Sport has also become an important element of the food and beverage, media, marketing, tourism, construction, manufacturing, and gambling industries.

At the professional and college level, sport leagues operate as a cartel, where the goal is equal competition within a monopoly. In reality, however, each team or college strives to maximize individual profits. Sport team ownership has been profitable for owners, often because they receive large media fees and tax or rental subsidies for facilities. Profitability may vary by location and by the success of the team.

For the few who attain the highest level of competition, a sport career, at least for a few years, can provide lucrative earnings. For those with the most talent and charisma, earnings from sport and endorsements can create instant millionaires.

In the United States, college sport has become a major business enterprise, especially if the football or basketball team plays in the major leagues, which generate national media coverage and considerable interest among alumni and local fans. The search for success and profits by some universities has led to illegal practices. These goals have also led to a de-emphasis or elimination of minor sports

and, until recent legislation, to a suppression of the growth of women's sport.

Like college sport, international sport has become transformed by economic considerations. Amateur athletes must now have costly year-round training and a level of individual financial support that only the wealthy or government-subsidized can afford.

Clearly, the evidence indicates that in modern sport financial statements are as important as the number of wins and losses.

REFERENCES

Abt, V., McGurrin, M.C., & Smith, J.F. (1984). Gambling: The misunderstood sport: A problem in social definition. *Leisure Sciences*, **6**, 205–220.

Ambrose, J.F. (1985). The impact of tax policy on sports. In A.T. Johnson & J.H. Frey (Eds.), *Government and sport: The public policy issues* (pp. 171–186). Totowa, NJ: Rowman and Allanheld.

Auf der Maur, N. (1976). *The billion-dollar game: Jean Drapeau and the 1976 Olympics.* Toronto, ON: James Lorimer.

Ballard, S. (1989, February 20). A show that has the goods. *Sports Illustrated*, p. 38.

Berry, R.C., & Wong, G.M. (1986). *Law and business of the sports industries. Volume I. Professional sports leagues.* Dover, MA: Auburn House.

Berry, R.C., Gould, W.B., & Staudohar, P.D. (1986). *Labor relations in professional sports.* Dover MA: Auburn.

Boutilier, M.A., & SanGiovanni, L. (1983). *The sporting woman.* Champaign, IL: Human Kinetics.

Canes, M.E. (1974). The social benefits of restrictions on team quality. In R.C. Noll (Ed.), *Government and the sports business: Studies in the regulation of economic ac-*

tivity (pp. 81–114). Washington, DC: Brookings Institution.

Coakley, J.J., & Pacey, P.L. (1984). The distribution of athletic scholarships among women in intercollegiate sport. In N. Theberge & P. Donnelly (Eds.), *Sport and the sociological imagination* (pp. 228–241). Fort Worth: Texas Christian University Press.

Coughlin, C.C., & Erekson, O.A. (1985). Contributions to intercollegiate athletic programs: Further evidence. *Social Science Quarterly*, **66**(1), 194–202.

Dabscheck, B. (1975). The wage determination process for sportsmen. *The Economic Record*, **51**(133), 52–64.

Dworkin, J.B., & Park, J. (1986). Collective bargaining in professional basketball: An empirical investigation. *Journal of Sport Behavior*, **9**(3), 131–140.

Flint, W.C., & Eitzen, D.S. (1987). Professional sports team ownership and entrepreneurial capitalism. *Sociology of Sport Journal*, **4**, 17–27.

Frey, J.H. (1984). Gambling and college sports: Views of coaches and athletic directors. *Sociology of Sport Journal*, **1**, 36–45.

Frey, J.H. (1985). Gambling, sports, and public policy. In A.T. Johnson & J.H. Frey (Eds.), *Government and sport: The public policy issues* (pp. 189–218). Totowa, NJ: Rowman and Allanheld.

Garvey, E. (1984). *The agent game: Selling players short*. Washington, DC: Federation of Professional Athletes.

Geringer, D. (1988, July 4). Mr. Mint. *Sports Illustrated*, pp. 78–88.

Greenstein, T.N., & Marcum, J.P. (1981). Factors affecting attendance of major league baseball: Team performance. *Review of Sport and Leisure*, **6**(2), 21–34.

Houston, W. (1987, March 18). Taking stock of NHL Oilers. *The Globe and Mail*, p. D5.

Ignatin, G. (1984). Sports betting. *Annals of the American Academy of Political and Social Science*, **474**, 168–177.

Ingham, A., Howell, J.W., & Schilperoort, T.S. (1987). Professional sports and community: A review and exegesis. In K. Pandolf (Ed.), *Exercise and sport sciences reviews. Volume 15* (pp. 427–465). New York: Macmillan.

Johnson, A.T. (1984). The uneasy partnership of cities and professional sport: Public policy considerations. In N. Theberge & P. Donnelly (Eds.) *Sport and the sociological imagination* (pp. 210–227). Fort Worth: Texas Christian University Press.

Johnson, A.T. (1985). The sports franchise relocation issue and public policy responses. In A.T. Johnson & J.M. Frey (Eds.), *Government and sport: The public policy issues* (pp. 219–247). Totowa, NJ: Rowman and Allanheld.

Johnson, A.T. (1986). Economic and policy implications of hosting sports franchises: Lessons from Baltimore. *Urban Affairs Quarterly*, **21**, 411–433.

Kaplan, H.R. (1983). Sport, gambling and television: The emerging alliance. *Arena Review*, **7**(1), 1–11.

Kirshenbaum, J. (Ed.) (1983, March 14). Keeping ahead of inflation [In *Scorecard*]. *Sports Illustrated*, p. 13.

Koch, J.W. (1983). Intercollegiate athletics: An economic explanation. *Social Science Quarterly*, **64**, 360–374.

Lawrence, P. (1987). *Unsportsmanlike conduct: The National Collegiate Athletic Association and the business of college football*. Westport, CT: Greenwood.

Levine, D. (Ed.) (1986, June). The Fourth Annual Sport 100 Salary Survey. *Sport*, pp. 21–31.

Levine, D. (Ed.) (1988, June). The Sport 100 Salary Report. *Sport*, pp. 23–39.

Lidz, F. (Ed.) (1985, May 13). Bully for Jordan [In *Scorecard*]. *Sports Illustrated*, p. 19.

The lineups and money for this season's bowl games. (1988, December 7). *The Chronicle of Higher Education*, p. A40.

Lock, E., & Hoffman, J. (1985). The national football league players associations' proposed alternative to individual player-team salary negotiations. *Journal of Sport and Social Issues*, **9**(2), 34–43.

Major league payroll comparisons. (1987, November 5). *USA Today*, p. 6C.

Malenfant, C. (1982). The economics of sport in France. *International Social Science Journal*, **34**, 233–246.

Marcum, J.P., & Greenstein, T. (1985). Factors affecting attendance of major league baseball: II. A within-season analysis. *Sociology of Sport Journal*, **2**, 314–322.

Marsh, J. (1984). The economic impact of a small city annual sporting event: An initial case study of the Peterborough church league atom hockey tournament. *Recreation Research Review*, **11**(1), 48–55.

Medoff, M.H. (1976). On monopsonistic exploitation in professional baseball. *Quarterly Review of Economics and Business*, **16**(2), 113–121.

Miller Brewing Co. (1983). *Miller Lite report on American attitudes towards sports*. Milwaukee: Author.

Noll, R.G. (1974). Attendance and price setting. In R.G. Noll (Ed.), *Government and sports business: Studies in the regulation of economic activity* (pp. 115-158). Washington, DC: Brookings Institution.

Pacey, P.L. (1985). The courts and college football: New playing rules off the field? *American Journal of Economics and Sociology*, **44**(2), 145–154.

Pesmen, C. (Ed.) (1987, June). 5th Annual Sport 100 Salary Survey. *Sport*, pp. 23–38.

Quirk, J., & El Hodiri, M. (1974). The economic theory of a professional sports league. In R.G. Noll (Ed.), *Government and the sports business: Studies in the regulation of economic activity* (pp. 33–80). Washington, DC: Brookings Institution.

Raiborn, M.H. (1970). *Financial analysis of intercollegiate athletics*. Kansas City, MO: The National Collegiate Athletic Association.

Rottenberg, S. (1956). The baseball players' labour market. *Journal of Political Economy*, **64**, 242–258.

Russell, G.W. (1986). Does sports violence increase box office receipts. *International Journal of Sport Psychology*, **17**, 173–182.

Schaffer, W.A., & Davidson, L.S. (1975). The economic impact of professional football on Atlanta. In S.P. Ladany (Ed.), *Management science applications to leisure-time operations* (pp. 276–296). Amsterdam: North-Holland.

Schecter, L. (1970). *The jocks*. New York: Paperback Library.

Scully, G.W. (1974). Player salaries. In G. Burman (Ed.), *Conference on the economics of professional sport* (pp. 33–37). Washington, DC: National Football League Player Association.

Seifart, H. (1984). Sport and economy: The commercialization of Olympic sport by the media. *International Review for the Sociology of Sport*, **19**, 305–316.

Sigelman, L., & Bookheimer, S. (1983). Is it whether you win or lose? Monetary contributions to big-time college athletic programs. *Social Science Quarterly*, **64**, 347–359.

Smith, G. (1986). *Gambling and sport: The Canadian experience*. Paper presented at the Annual Meeting of the North American Society for the Sociology of Sport, Boston.

Staudohar, P.D. (1986). *The sports industry and collective bargaining*. Ithaca, NY: Cornell University Press.

Strachan, A. (1983, December 26). The bottom line. *The Globe and Mail*, Section S, p. 1.

Straw, P. (1983). Pointspreads and journalistic ethics. *Arena Review*, **7**(1), 43–48.

Sullivan, R. (Ed.) (1986, June 2). Boosting Fan Interest [In *Scorecard*]. *Sports Illustrated*, pp. 15–16.

Underwood, J. (1963, May 20). The true crisis. *Sports Illustrated*, pp. 16–19, 83.

CHAPTER 6

Sport and the Mass Media

The first sport story in an American newspaper appeared on May 5, 1733, in the *Boston Gazette*; it was reprinted from a report on a boxing match held in England (Greendorfer, 1981). In the 1700s and 1800s, newspapers occasionally published news about prize fights, horse races, and boat races. But it was not until 1819 that the first American periodical on sport, *The American Farmer*, began to publish the results of hunting, fishing, shooting, and bicycling matches. A particularly interesting feature of this periodical was that it included articles on the philosophy of sport. By the 1850s items on sport appeared regularly in newspapers, and in the 1890s a sport department and sport section were created (Kozlik, 1985; Lever & Wheeler, 1984). At about the same time, daily newspapers devoted exclusively to sport came into being in Europe.

By the 1850s, the electronic media were beginning to be used for sport communication. The telegraph reported results of horse races, yachting races, and boxing matches. In the late 1800s, the Atlantic cable carried sport news from England; in the 1920s, radio stations broadcast sport events live, at first locally and then nationally; and in the 1930s, sport events were telecast experimentally. For example, a baseball game was telecast between New York and Philadelphia in the 1920s, and the 1936 Olympic Games were televised, although the only viewers were on the Games site. It was not until the 1950s that sport events became part of the regular program format of television networks. Table 6.1 shows when and how sport has appeared in the mass media.

Today *Sports Illustrated* prints an average of more than 3 million copies each week; an estimated 2.5 billion people watched the opening and closing ceremonies of the 1984 Summer Olympic Games on television; and an estimated 12.8 billion people (including multiple viewings) watched the 52 games of the 1986 World Cup soccer tournament. These three statistics clearly illustrate that the print and broadcast media have become a significant factor in the promotion and transmission of sport as a social product. Just as sport has become an influential part of the entertainment industry, the mass media (particularly television) have become intimately involved in the growth, production, and control of modern sport (Betts, 1953; Birrell & Loy, 1979; Greendorfer, 1981, 1983; Powers, 1984; Rader, 1984; Whannel, 1984).

This chapter examines the relation between sport and the mass media. Specifically, we are interested in how and why this "marriage" arrangement evolved, whether the partners have equal shares in the marriage in terms of influence and economic gain, and whether the marriage will last in the future.

WHAT DO WE MEAN BY *MASS MEDIA*?

The term **mass media** describes a process that allows a relatively small number of people to communicate rapidly and simultaneously with a large percentage of a population. The effect of mass media is to narrow physical, temporal, and social distances. The media consist of printed communication such as newspapers, magazines, and books; and electronic communication such as radio, television, and the movies.

The media reach a large and diverse population and can serve a variety of purposes. They can provide information, produce an aesthetic experience, provide vicarious thrills and excitement, and fill our leisure hours. The mass media also reflect and sometimes help create cultural values, beliefs, and norms. Advances in communication technology have helped the mass media create a mass culture.

Sport has become a major component of our new mass culture, along with popular music, movies, and television shows. It has been associated with the dominant forms of media for some time, as we described earlier. And a mutually beneficial relationship has evolved. For example, the marriage of sport and the mass media has contributed greatly to the economic growth of the sport industry in several countries (McKay & Rowe, 1987; Thompson, 1986). The media provide an essential source of revenue for college and professional sports in North America and a primary source of funding for the Olympic Games.

In the following sections we discuss how this symbiotic relationship developed between sport and the media and consider its consequences. But first we must understand some of the relevant sociological theories of mass communication.

THEORIES OF MASS COMMUNICATION

Sociology commonly uses four theories to describe how mass communication operates. The theories focus on individual differences, social categories, social relationships, and cultural norms.

Table 6.1   The Coverage of Sport by the Mass Media

Year	Event
1733	(May 5) First sport story in an American newspaper. The *Boston Gazette* carries the prizefight between John Faulconer and Bob Russel on the "Bowling Green at Harrow on the Hill." It was copied directly from a London daily.
1796	The *Charleston City Gazette* carries notices for the Charleston Golf Club.
1801	The *Sports and Pastimes of People in England* is published—a first for England.
1819	Colonel John Stuart Skinner, postmaster of Baltimore, publishes the first American periodical on sport, *The American Farmer*. It featured the results of hunting, fishing, shooting, and bicycling matches as well as essays on the philosophy of sport.
1823	The *New York Evening Post* carries the full-scale account of a boxing match.
1831	The *Spirit of the Times*, the first weekly on sport, is started.
1850s	The only member of a newspaper staff who in any way resembles the modern sports editor is the turf man. Horse racing and cricket are the most popular sports of the day, and only the *New York Anglo-American* and the *Albion* cover cricket. Henry Chadwick begins to cover (without pay) cricket matches between the United States and Canadian teams for the *New York Times*. The visit of a British cricket team in 1859 causes so much interest that the *Herald* finally hires Chadwick.
1862	Chadwick becomes the first sport reporter, covering baseball in New York.
1866	The Atlantic cable opens.
1870	Middie Morgan becomes the first female sportswriter. She covers races and cattle shows for the *New York Times*.
1883	Joseph Pulitzer purchases the *World* and sets up the first sport department. (By 1892, all good papers have them.) Reports of baseball, horse racing, pedestrian tournaments, and other events are combined into a single article. They are less concerned with personalities than with final scores.
1886	The *Sporting News*, a St. Louis weekly, begins. It is devoted to baseball and becomes the bible of the diamond.
1889	Joe Villa, sports editor of the *New York Sun*, uses the play-by-play technique for the first time in covering the Harvard-Princeton football game. The *Sun* devotes three columns to the game.
1895	Hearst begins the first sport section in a newspaper.
1899	The wireless is used for news reporting in connection with international yacht races.
1921	Baseball games and fights are reported on KDKA. Florent Gibson becomes the first sport broadcaster. The Dempsey-Carpentier fight becomes the first million-dollar gate.
1923	The first televised broadcast between New York and Philadelphia occurs.
1925	The first play-by-play broadcast of major league baseball and football occurs.
1940	Sport cartoons emerge.
1945	The AP sports wire is established for the opening day of major league baseball.
1950s	Regular broadcasts of major league baseball and NFL football begin on the major television networks.
1960s	Telstar, a communications satellite is launched, facilitating live international telecasts.
1963	The first instant replay is broadcast on television.

(Cont.)

Table 6.1   (Continued)

Year	Event
1970s	Cable and satellite television increase the number and frequency of sport broadcasts available to the viewing public.
1973	Congress enacts Public Law 93-107, which amends the Communication Act of 1934. This is the anti-blackout ruling: If a home game is sold out 72 hours before the game, the game cannot be blacked out in the home viewing area.
1980s	ESPN and TSN, 24-hour all-sport networks begin in the U.S.A. and Canada, respectively.
1984	The opening and closing ceremonies of the Los Angeles Olympic Games attract the largest live viewing audience for a sport event—2.5 billion people throughout the world.

Note. From "Sport and the Mass Media" by S.L. Greendorfer. In *Handbook of Social Science of Sport* (pp. 162–165) by G.R.F. Luschen and G.H. Sage (Eds.), 1981, Urbana, IL: Stipes. Copyright 1981 by Stipes. Adapted by permission.

Individual Differences Theory

This theory argues that the mass media present images that appeal to the personality characteristics of viewers. Individuals' specific psychological needs predispose them to use the mass media to satisfy their needs. For example, Katz, Gurevitch, and Haas (1973) identified four categories of needs the media fulfill: cognitive (strengthening information, knowledge, and understanding); affective (providing an aesthetic, pleasurable, emotional experience); integrative (providing credibility, confidence, status, contact with family and friends); and escapist (providing tension release and escape from one's normal social roles).

With regard to sport in particular, Birrell and Loy (1979) proposed that the media bring about four consequences:

- the *information* function provides knowledge of the game, game results, and statistics on players and teams;
- the *integrative* function offers affiliation with a social group and a social experience shared with other spectators;
- the *arousal* or *affective* function provides excitement; and
- the *escape* function helps release pent-up emotions.

Birrell and Loy also suggest that cognitive needs in sport are best met by newspapers and magazines, followed in order by television and radio; that integrative needs are best met by attending an event, followed in order by television, radio, and newspapers; that affective needs are best met by direct attendance or via television; and that escapist needs probably are gratified by every form of the media, but especially by television.

Social Categories Theory

This theory argues (De Fleur, 1970) that "there are broad collectivities, aggregates or social categories in urban industrial societies whose behavior in the face of a given set of stimuli is more or less uniform" (pp. 122–123). In other words, there are broad subgroups that react differently to the mass media. This theory is supported by our knowledge that there are age, sex, social class, education, and marital-status differences in patterns of sport consumption.

One limitation of this approach is that the social categories tend to be considered in isolation, and the pattern of a lower-class, poorly educated, 50-year-old black female is not usually identified. That is, the lifestyles of specific subgroups are often overlooked. This approach reminds us that the contact and influence of the mass media, although significant, do not uniformly affect members of different subgroups.

Social Relationships Theory

This theory suggests (De Fleur, 1970) that "informal social relationships play a significant role in modifying the manner in which individuals will act upon a message which comes to their attention via the mass media" (p. 127). Some support for this theory is found in a study of the process by which adolescents are socialized into the role of sport consumer (McPherson, 1976a, 1976b). Whether an adolescent is socialized into the role of sport consumer is related to the

- number of significant others who consume sport;
- frequency of sport consumption by significant others;
- amount of interaction with significant others who consume sport;
- number of sanctions to consume sport received from others in the family who are ego-involved in sport;
- importance of sport in the hierarchy of parents' leisure pursuits;
- amount of primary sport involvement of the adolescent; and
- opportunity to participate in sport in the adolescent's social environment.

Thus, an individual's pattern of mass media sport consumption is influenced in many ways by the values and behaviors of significant others in his or her social world (Guttman, 1986).

Cultural Norms Theory

The final approach argues that the mass media selectively presents and emphasizes certain contemporary ideas or values. Three recent examples are (a) sport consumption is a valued leisure activity; (b) aging need not mean diminished involvement in physical and social activity; and (c) only young adult males drink beer after a workout or game. De Fleur (1970) notes that the mass media influences normative perceptions of individuals in three ways: (a) "existing norms and patterns are reinforced"; (b) "new ideas or norms are created"; and (c) "existing norms can be changed, thereby leading to new forms of behavior" (p. 13).

Although the evidence has yet to be amassed, the way the mass media in North America has presented sport probably has helped change attitudes and behaviors in a number of sport domains. To illustrate, as a result of media consumption, members of the general population have probably changed their negative stereotypes of black and female athletes; attitudes toward amateurism, professionalism, and Olympic ideals; and beliefs on the merit of both primary and secondary sport involvement across the life cycle. Consider "The Golden Girls," a television show featuring four older women. Each character has a physically and socially active lifestyle. The cultural norm theory would argue that by presenting an active lifestyle for older women in the media, the attitudes of older people and those with whom they interact will change in this direction.

The media also provide a retrospective look at how our lives have changed over a period of time. Newspapers, in particular, have always been an excellent direct or indirect source of facts, opinions, values, beliefs, and norms inherent in the social life of a particular era. By examining newspapers over a period of time we can document changes in particular facets of our lives and in some of our most important social institutions. Highlight 6.1 illustrates how sport has changed over a 75-year period in North America.

TELEVISION AND SPORT: A MARRIAGE OF CONVENIENCE

It is estimated that in North America the major commercial television networks produce more than 1,100 sport events annually. In addition, some smaller networks and stations devote most or all of their schedule to sport events, some on a 24-hour basis to satisfy the most devout sport fan and accommodate fans who work at night. Sport telecasts, particularly the Super Bowl, the final game of the World Series, and the Olympics, consistently draw the largest viewing audience of all television shows produced. At the same time, radio stations in North America broadcast an estimated 400,000 hours of sport annually, devoting a large portion of this time to professional baseball and college sport events. Also, sport events are transmitted regularly throughout the world, especially during an Olympic year or when significant international championships are held (e.g., the World Cup of soccer).

Why have radio and television shown so much interest in the world of sport? First, they need to fill air-time with a product that will attract both advertisers and consumers. Sport meets these criteria well. Even better, sport attracts a known and specialized audience (i.e., primarily males who are more likely to purchase specific products). Advertisers thereby gain direct access to many potential consumers of their products.

Compared with other popular programs on television (e.g., drama, comedy, or adventure series) sport programs cost less to produce and generate more revenue from advertising. For example, even though a 30-second commercial cost $650,000 for the January 31, 1988, Super Bowl, the size of the viewing audience reduced the advertising cost to about 42 cents per viewer. This is about one-half to two-thirds the cost per viewer for nonsport shows. Although the newspaper and radio media are heavily involved in sport, it is television that has virtually gained control of major professional, college, and international sport events.

Sport is a form of mass entertainment (Hughes & Coakley, 1984), but it is also a vehicle of public education or socialization. The mass media reflect society and have the potential to shape the images we receive of people, values, and attitudes. Specifically, the media select, construct, and present information that reproduces and legitimates underlying values and assumptions in a region or society. To illustrate, McKay and Rowe (1987) found that the Australian media perpetuate traditional masculine, chauvinistic, corporate, and nationalistic images of sport.

Sometimes the media manipulate visual images of sport and make us believe something that is not real or not fully accurate. For example, only the most articulate players may be interviewed after the game, which perpetuates the image of well-educated athletes. As another example, visual images in magazines often show women participating passively as spectators or in more socially acceptable sports. And given their actual involvement in sport, women are highly underrepresented in the coverage allocated to sport in newspapers and on television (Cronk, 1985). When television fails to broadcast women's sport events, it implies that these are trivial or second-class events of little or no consequence, and therefore of little inter-

Highlight 6.1
Changes in Sport as Reflected in the Newspaper: 1900-1975

To better understand the changing role of sport in American society, Lever and Wheeler (1984) analyzed the contents of the sport pages of the *Chicago Tribune* for 1900, 1925, 1950, and 1975. They argued that if changes had occurred, they would be reflected in the contents of the sport pages. To collect their data, they read all stories one inch or more in length for the first seven days of February, May, August, and November. The authors found that as a percentage of the total newspaper content (minus advertisements) the sport section had almost doubled in size, from 9% in 1900 to 17% in 1975; that it constituted, as of 1975, about half the coverage allocated to local, national, or international news; and that the mean length of sport stories had increased from 7.0 inches in 1900 to 8.7 inches in 1975.

Analyzing the content of the sport stories revealed these significant changes:

- a considerable shift in the coverage from local, amateur individual sport to nationwide, professional team sport;
- a dramatic decrease in the coverage of horse racing and a considerable increase in the coverage of basketball;
- a consistent coverage of baseball across the 75 years;
- a consistent focus on events pertaining to the playing field and on the personalities of the athletes;
- a reduction from 25% to 10% in pregame promotional stories, with the focus shifting to reports of game outcomes; and

- only a 2.9% increase in stories devoted exclusively to women athletes, despite the women's movement and legislation that has increased the sport participation opportunities for women.

In this case the newspaper does not accurately reflect the growth of women's sport, but rather reinforces women's second-class status in the world of sport. The following figure illustrates the changing coverage of major sports from 1900 to 1975.

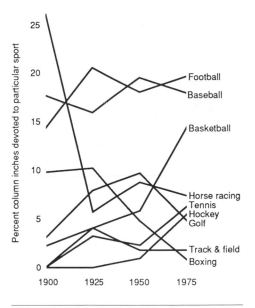

The changing coverage of major sports, 1900-1975. *Note.* From "The Chicago Tribune Sports Page, 1900-1975" by J. Lever and S. Wheeler, 1984, *Sociology of Sport Journal*, **1**, p. 304. Copyright 1984 by Human Kinetics. Reprinted by permission.

(Cont.)

Highlight 6.1 Continued

Have these trends continued in the 1980s? Does the coverage of women's sport reflect the increased participation rates by women? Are popular individual sports like tennis, running, and cycling receiving increased coverage? These are questions you might consider as you read the daily newspaper.

The media frequently show women participating in sports considered socially acceptable.

est to the general population (Duncan & Hasbrook, 1988).

Production of Sport Images

Our values, beliefs, and knowledge about sport and athletes are shaped by how the mass media present the games and the sport news. What appears or does not appear, what is said or not said, and what is highlighted (e.g., in replays or slow-motion) can define and shape public perceptions of the sport event, issue, or personality. Frequently coverage of some events is expanded because they are thought more newsworthy or more capable of attracting readers or viewers (i.e., paying customers).

Examples of Sport Images. To illustrate, the story of an elderly woman robbed of $5 or $10 may be front-page news and imply that crime among the elderly is more serious than actual statistics would support. Another example is Eddie "The Eagle" Edwards, a ski jumper from England. He became an instant international hero during and following the 1988 Winter Olympic Games—not for his athletic prowess, but because of the attention he received from the mass media.

Similarly, fights in hockey or baseball often receive more prominent media attention (e.g., photographs, sensational headlines, repeated replays on subsequent news and sport shows long after the event has occurred) than skillful plays or sportsmanlike acts. Aggressive acts provoke more interest among the general public, and the incidents sell more newspapers and attract more viewers than typical behavior. To illustrate further how images are molded to suit the consumer, Highlight 6.2 gives two contrasting views of the same violent incident in a hockey game.

Guidelines for Sport Reporting. The practice of producing news that attracts readers or viewers began early in the history of sport reporting. As early as 1906, American reporters were provided with an instructional

Highlight 6.2
Two Contrasting Perceptions of a Sport Incident

In October 1987, according to Houston (1987), television viewers in Canada and the United States watched numerous replays, on both news broadcasts and sport shows, of a vicious cross-check to the face of Tomas Sandstrom (of the New York Rangers) by Dave Brown (of the Philadelphia Flyers) during a pro hockey game. Sandstrom suffered a mild concussion, and Brown was suspended for 12 games. As you might expect, the attack, which many hockey experts claimed was the worst they had ever seen, was reported quite differently by the respective team broadcast crews. A Rangers' commentator stated:*

> There he goes again. There's a cross-check to the face. You really wonder what makes this person tick. This is beyond belief. What a senseless, idiotic play, again by Brown. You tell me he deserves to play in this league? They (the Flyers) are out of their minds. Send him to another league some place. . . . Get a doctor out to help this guy. . . . This is a sick individual. They should put this guy in jail.

In the Flyer booth, two commentators expressed a different view:*

> Sandstrom is playing dead, because he doesn't want to get up and retaliate.

> He wants the Flyers to pick up another five-minute major, as he did in the game in Philadelphia last year.

> He . . . took a slash at Hextall [the Flyer goalie]. . . . He's going to make sure he doesn't get up, because he might have to answer to it. Acting school.

Similarly, newspapers from the two cities stressed different views of the game. A Philadelphia paper read:*

> Regular-season hockey doesn't get any better than this, even though the finger-waggers and moralists were heard claiming that the high stick in the third period had spoiled everything.

A New York newspaper read:*

> The NHL is nuts to be sleeping in the same bed with a thug who cashes a paycheque only because he (1) strikes fear into talented players (2) has memorized the Flyer's bully manual (3) obeys coach Mike Keenan.

Clearly, where you live influences what you see, read, and hear about sport and shapes the sport reality to which you are exposed through the media.

---

*Note. From "A Vicious Hockey Act, or Not" by W. Houston, 1987, November 12. *The Globe and Mail*, p. C12. Copyright 1987 by The Globe and Mail, Toronto. Reprinted by permission.

manual that told them what should be included in a story. MacCarthy (1906) offered specific guidelines for sport reporting.

> The majority of sporting events are the result of challenges. Give full name and standing of the challenger and the challenged; the time and place they or their representatives met to arrange details; note disputed points and arguments on both sides; terms and conditions; day, hour, and place decided upon for the contest; list of officials; programme of events, entries, prizes and size of the bets. (p. 39)

> When the event has taken place, your report would include these points—time and place; winners and time made; weather; size, character and deportment of crowd; society women and their gowns, automobiles and carriages; excitement and betting; methods and manner of contestants; officials of the day; scores; summaries; exact official time; accidents and police; statements from both sides; will loser challenge again? (pp. 39–40)

A thesaurus-like list of selected words and phrases accompanied these directives and were intended to help inexperienced reporters add color to their stories. Note in MacCarthy's guidelines that even early in this century there was interest in reporting betting at sport contests.

Today, detailed guidelines are prepared for television announcers who broadcast North American sport events. Along with their responsibility to entertain, report, and inform, broadcast crews must promote the sport and keep viewers or listeners tuned to the game. Mainly to improve the programs' ratings, sport announcers are expected to be public relations employees of the sport, league, and team. Like the athletes, they have play books. To illustrate, included in the guidelines for television broadcasts in one major male professional sport are directives to

- refrain from derogatory remarks about the officials;
- call players on the visiting team by their last name but use both names or first names for players on the home team;
- create enthusiasm and excitement by emphasizing the first word of each sentence;
- avoid using old-fashioned expressions;
- attribute negative statements to someone else (e.g., "that is what John Smith would call a stupid foul");
- rephrase the question as a response if you don't have an answer to a question from a broadcast partner;
- use the following terms often: momentum, great team effort, an important game, second effort, a game of emotion, a game of inches, all-star, hard-working, promising rookie, underrated player;
- never refer to the personal lives of a player; and
- comment on a player's poor performance only by discussing an injury, how hard he is working when he plays, or how unlucky he has been in recent games.

Perception of Sport Images

Broadcast crews are required to embellish the drama of the game to create suspense, sustain tension, and attract and retain viewers or listeners. This embellishment has an impact on both the perception and the enjoyment of the game by viewers. To explore this, Comisky, Bryant, and Zillman (1977) asked volunteer viewers to watch segments of hockey games with and without verbal comments. Those who listened to the verbal commentary thought the action was rougher and more entertaining than those who watched the same segments without commentary.

In another study, Bryant, Comisky, and Zillman (1977) analyzed the content of sentences used by broadcasters in six NFL games. They classified sentences as descriptive (72%), dramatic (27%), or humorous (1%). The most frequently used dramatic sentences commented on the general ability of the players or the team; the expenditure of effort or the "old college try"; the gamesmanship of a player or team; and comparisons of a player or team with other players or teams, with league averages, or with past performances of the player or team.

In short, a sizeable proportion of the audio portion of the telecast is devoted to the broadcast crew embellishing the action to increase or maintain the drama of sport. These dramatizations often reflect prevailing values and beliefs found in the society. Because there is competition to attract viewers with different tastes, there seem to be network differences in the extent to which drama or humor are used in the broadcast presentations.

Race Discrimination and Sport Images.

It has been suggested that, consciously or unconsciously, announcers present racially prejudiced impressions of players' performances. In a content analysis of 16 NFL broadcasts, Rainville and McCormick (1977) found that white players received significantly more positive performance-related statements about being aggressive. In contrast, black players received more references about low levels of performance in the past and more negative comments about their levels of play. At the same time, white players received more attention in replays and more excuses for mistakes (e.g., he is playing with an injury). The amount of coverage in daily newspapers and magazines that is allocated to black athletes versus white athletes appears to vary by city, by sport, and by the race of the majority of readers (Condor & Anderson, 1984; Pearman, 1978).

Gender Discrimination and Sport Images.

Another obvious example of how the media can distort reality is in the portrayal of gender roles. If women are portrayed less frequently than their participation merits and if stereotypical or negative themes are stressed when women are included, this may have an impact on the socialization of young girls' and boys' views of women's sport (Bryant, 1980). To illustrate, Boutilier and San-Giovanni (1983) report that there is little coverage (text or photos) of women's sport events in daily newspapers; and that in the first 25 years of publication (1,250 covers), *Sports Illustrated* featured only 115 women on the cover. Of these 115 women, only 55 were athletes.

Another illustration of how the media influences and reflects images and beliefs can be found in a detailed analysis of 115 articles on leading male and female tennis players. Hilliard (1984) found that articles tended to trivialize the performance of female athletes. Major themes in articles about women tennis players suggested that the tour is not glamorous; that these highly successful athletes still depend on a parent, coach, or agent; that they constantly seek to legitimate or apologize for being a tennis player; and that their marriage and family life is adversely affected by their sport activity. In short, female tennis players were often portrayed as flawed heroines with problems rather than as highly skilled and successful athletes engaged in a demanding career.

In the larger sport context, the news media generally imply that sport is for males. In fact, compared to total sport news space, the space allocated to women's sport is about 15% in newspapers and 10% in magazines in North America (Rintala & Birrell, 1984) and about 1.3% in newspapers in Australia (McKay and Rowe, 1987). This limited coverage of female athletes extends even to articles about recreational physical activity. In a recent study of two newspapers, one each from English and French Canada, where gender was specified in an article, females were much less likely to be mentioned as being involved in a recreational sport activity (Gelinas & Theberge, 1986). Table 6.2 illustrates the limited coverage of women's sport in the print media by analyzing a magazine published for teenage athletes.

As Highlight 6.3 indicates, this underrepresentation of women is not due simply to journalists' bias against women's sport. It re-sults partly from how news is uncovered and produced and from traditional beliefs about what sport news merits reporting.

INFLUENCE OF THE MEDIA ON SPORT

Both the print and electronic media increasingly regulate sport to varying degrees, largely because of the economic dependence of sport on the media. Increasingly a small number of firms control a large percentage of the media. They thus acquire a monopoly over the content, form, and meaning of the images and news items disseminated to the public.

Table 6.2   Representation of Females in *Young Athlete* Magazine, 1975–1982

	Females (%)	Males (%)	Both (%)	N
Prominence of photographs				
Cover—primary figure	19	72	9	43
Cover—secondary figure	22	78	0	9
Centerfold	13	84	3	38
Full-page color photo	24	71	5	99
Other photographs	31	63	6	3,014
Type of written material				
Articles	20	78	2	422
Guest editorials	20	80	0	10
Reader responses	40	60	0	965
Sport-related careers portrayed				
Coach/leader	17	83	0	142
Official	53	47	0	15
Athlete	32	62	6	2,910
Sport activity depicted				
Demonstration of strength; overpowering opponent	9	89	1	438
High-risk activities	17	82	1	102
Neutral activities	32	61	6	1,847
Aesthetic activities	64	27	9	290

Note. From "Fair Treatment for the Active Female: A Content Analysis of Young Athletes Magazine" by J. Rintala and S. Birrell, 1984, *Sociology of Sport Journal*, 1, pp. 238–240. Copyright 1984 by Human Kinetics. Adapted by permission.

Highlight 6.3
The Production of Sport News: Sport Is Men's Sport

Women's sport gets less coverage in both print and electronic media than men's sport, thereby perpetuating the image of sport as a man's world. A common explanation for this underrepresentation is that most media personnel are males who are biased against the coverage of women's sport events or personalities. An alternative explanation is that, given limited time or space, the media will cover activities and personalities that attract the most readers and viewers.

To better understand why women's sport is underrepresented in newspapers, Cronk (Cronk, 1985; Theberge & Cronk, 1986) spent over a year as a copyeditor for the sport section of a daily paper in a southern U.S. city. During this period of participant observation he studied the production process, where among the many local, national, and global sport events on a given day only some events are selected as news to be reported and analyzed in the sport section.

Cronk found that the following factors affected whether a sport event or personality becomes news:

- having public and media relations departments to produce press releases (there are more in professional sport and men's college sport);
- perceiving major commercial elements (e.g., the Olympics) or spectator appeal (e.g., college football or basketball), or being a professional sport;
- having a reporter assigned to a "beat" to provide regular and continuing coverage of a team, athlete, or university;
- needing to allocate limited space to statistics, standings, and league results;
- relying on national wire services, which provide newspapers with daily nonlocal news.

Professional sport and men's college sport have advantages in all of these areas, so women's sport is often neglected, especially in local newspapers.

Merely increasing the number of females in sport journalism may not substantially change the coverage of women's sport. Nor will eliminating chauvinistic male reporters necessarily increase the coverage. Rather, the buying and viewing public must convince sport executives and publishers that women's sport is important and interesting.

To illustrate, four Australian conglomerates control the Australia Broadcasting Corporation, the newspapers in every major city and in most suburban areas, 8 of the 15 commercial television stations, almost all of the national magazines, and many of the radio stations (McKay & Rowe, 1987).

How the Media Control Sport

Before the dominance of television, changes in the rules, structure, and schedules were introduced to improve the sport or increase attendance at games. Since the economic control has shifted to television, changes are introduced to appeal to the television audience or to generate more revenue from advertising. Some examples include

- using *sudden death* for tie games in football, hockey, and basketball;
- converting the scoring in golf matches from match to medal play;
- scheduling more evening games to increase prime-time ratings and advertising revenue;
- expanding schedules to include more exhibition games, more league games, and more teams being eligible for the play-offs;
- starting the World Series on a Saturday instead of the traditional Wednesday to increase the likelihood that the Series will span two weekends and capture a larger television audience;
- creating new sports or pseudosports to satiate the public's desire (e.g., indoor soccer, arena football, Battle of the Network Stars, the Super Stars competition);
- producing local amateur sport events as major media attractions (e.g., the Boston and New York Marathons, the Hawaii "Iron Man" triathlon, the Old-Timer's Baseball Classic);
- shifting starting times of games on the West Coast to 5:00 p.m. to coincide with the evening viewing patterns of the larger East Coast television market;
- adding the 24-second clock and the 3-point shot and eliminating some foul shots to increase the action and excitement in basketball;

- hiring sport broadcasters as entertainers and television personalities rather than as news reporters;
- hosting gambling experts on televised sport shows to comment on point spreads, odds, and injuries, because the viewer is thought to want or need this type of information; and
- scheduling time-outs for commercials (e.g., the television director beeps an official when an officials' time-out is needed to air a commercial).

Based on a content analysis of championship games in baseball, football, basketball, and hockey in the 1982-83 season, Meier (1984) found an inverse relationship between the amount of live play and the popularity of the championship event as measured by viewer ratings. Specifically, only 3.7% of the broadcast for the Super Bowl involved live play, compared with 21.2% of the time allocated to advertising. Yet this event annually draws the highest viewer ratings for any televised show. Ironically, soccer, with the fewest time-outs of any sport and 90 minutes of continuous play, has not been able to attract a television contract. Table 6.3 shows the mean time allocated to live play for the four major sports, and compares the amount of time allocated to live play and to commercials for the 1982-1983 championship game in four sports.

Nowhere is the media influence more evident than in the Summer Olympic Games, where more housing must be reserved for media representatives than for competitors. Whannel (1984) refers to the Olympics as a global *media* festival, which subsidizes and supports the Olympic movement. With an estimated 2.5 billion viewers (more than 50% of the world's population) for the 1984 Summer Olympics' opening and closing ceremonies, the games have become the largest international media event. As a result of this

Table 6.3   Coverage of Live Play Versus Advertising Time During Televised Professional Championship Games, 1982–1983

Sport	Live-play time % (minutes:seconds)		Advertising time % (minutes:seconds)	
Football	3.7	(13:35)	21.2	(76:35)
Baseball	6.6	(14:38)	21.7	(48:25)
Basketball	27.4	(48:00)	18.0	(31:35)
Hockey	30.9	(60:00)	17.0	(30:30)

Note. From "Much Ado About Nothing: The Television Broadcast Packaging of Team Sport Championship Games" by K. Meier, 1984, *Sociology of Sport Journal*, **1**, pp. 263–279. Copyright 1984 by Human Kinetics. Adapted by permission.

large audience, some athletes have become instant celebrities with large subsequent economic pay-offs through endorsements or new media-related careers (e.g., Mark Spitz, Elizabeth Manley).

The Media Sponsor Sport

Since the 1960s, televised sport programs have become an increasingly important source of low-cost entertainment for the public and the major source of fixed revenue for sport organizations. In effect, the media serve as a middleman in this three-way relationship. The networks or local stations collect revenues from commercial sponsors and deduct their expenses (including fees for broadcast rights, which are paid to sport organizations) and pocket the profit. But the process actually works in reverse, because the league or owners control the sale of national and local broadcast rights.

At the local level, owners can package and present the games themselves; they can sell the rights directly to a sponsor, who then negotiates a radio or television contract; or

they can sell the rights to a station or network, which packages the games and sells commercial time to sponsors. This latter arrangement is most prevalent at both the local (i.e., team) and the national (i.e., league) level. Because of the insatiable demand for televised sport in the past 20 years, owners have been able to raise the fees for broadcast rights whenever a new contract is negotiated. Owners and leagues have created something of a bidding war among the networks. However, in the process they have become almost totally dependent on this source of revenue.

Although some network executives claim that sport is a bad investment and is produced as a public service, most televised sport events make a profit. To illustrate, ABC incurred expenses of about $500 million (rights' fees and production costs) producing the 1984 Summer and Winter Olympic Games. These expenses were offset by about $615 million in advertising revenue, for an estimated $115 million or 23% profit. In addition, ABC promoted its nonsport shows during coverage of the Games. A further indirect benefit was that advertisers found this network a better investment for their advertising dollars in nonsport productions. Most recently, the network televising the 1988 Winter Olympic Games suffered a multimillion dollar loss, primarily because it paid too much for rights' fee and because the U.S. hockey team left the medal round early, which dramatically lowered ratings and the number of telecasts.

The sponsor (ultimately the consumer) pays for the sport events that appear on television. In effect, sponsors gain a monopoly on the consumer's attention and can direct their advertising to a known audience that purchases specific products. Sponsors of sport events knowledgeably sell products that appeal to adult males below 50 years of age (e.g., beer, automobiles, tires, petroleum products, shaving products, and insurance). Although the cost of sponsoring sport events is increasing, the cost per household is considerably lower than that for other television shows, because of the size of the audience and because the composition of the sport audience is highly predictable (i.e., males 20 to 50 years of age). Nevertheless, the escalating cost of advertising on prime-time network shows means that only the largest industries, and the largest firms within each industry, can afford to sponsor shows. These firms thus acquire a monopoly on the advertising market. Furthermore, through long-term contracts they erect a barrier that prevents competitors from entering this advertising market.

One concern over increased television coverage has been the fear that the exposure results in decreased attendance at games. The prime examples are boxing matches and minor league baseball, which experienced considerable declines in attendance when television began broadcasting major league sport events in the 1960s. Yet with blackout laws and restricted coverage, recent evidence suggests that television generates an interest in sport and attracts new fans, especially women, who want to attend games. A recent study by Kaempfer and Pacey (1986) found that even though there was a 40 percent increase in college football telecasts in 1978, attendance at the games increased 2.6 percent. Thus, it is possible that increased television exposure leads to increased attendance, especially among the nonmajor college football powers.

INFLUENCE OF SPORT ON THE MEDIA

As sport has become a larger part of the programming of network and cable television and the coverage of daily newspapers and numerous periodicals, the media have become increasingly dependent on sport. The media need to fill air-time and column inches.

To illustrate, Lever and Wheeler (1984) found that, based on a content analysis of the *Chicago Tribune*, the amount of sport coverage increased from 9% to 17% from 1900 to 1975. The amount of sport news compared with local, national, and international news increased from 14% to 52%. Similarly, in North America, network or cable television stations broadcast between 10,000 and 15,000 hours per year of sport. In some European countries there are daily newspapers devoted exclusively to sport, and in North America the cable television networks that exclusively or primarily produce sport events are gaining a larger share of the viewing audience.

Sport is also needed by the media to help sell advertising and to maintain or increase their ratings. They charge more for advertising on sport pages and sport broadcasts because they know that many people buy newspapers or watch television primarily or solely to consume sport. For example, newspapers sell better to the more affluent readers in suburbia; thus large metropolitan newspapers allocate more coverage to suburban high school sport than to central urban high school sport.

How Sport Controls the Media

Professional sport has some control over the media, although most of the power is clearly in the media's hands. To illustrate how sport controls the media, in recent years television stations have been showing baseball highlights on the late evening news. Professional baseball sends out these highlights free, via satellite, to every station in North America. A condition of broadcasting the highlights is that bloopers (e.g., errors, collisions) be deleted. Many stations have violated this condition. Major league baseball views these bloopers as detrimental to the game's image. So, as of June 1, 1988, every local television station must obtain a descrambler from major league baseball if they want to receive the highlights for later rebroadcast. If a station shows blooper segments or shows highlights of any one game for more than 2 minutes, it must forfeit the descrambler. In this way, major league baseball can force television to cover baseball the way it wants the game covered. Because stations need these highlights to fill late evening sport shows, they tend to comply with these regulations.

At the local level, newspapers, radio, and television have become indirectly responsible for promoting local sport events as entertainment rather than news. As we learned earlier, the role of sport reporter or broadcaster involves public relations, advertising, and entertainment as well as objective reporting of news items. This generally results in favorable images about a sport being presented. There is little incisive reporting on the business side of sport, and seamy events that might be considered unfavorable advertising by the owners and officials of the sport tend to be suppressed. Sport news usually presents scores and strategies and seldom, if ever, levels criticism. Only recently, and because of increased media competition for readers or viewers, have negative stories been pursued. But to maximize profits, the media often accentuate aggressiveness, unfairness, and spectator violence to the point that these occurrences appear normal (Weis, 1986; Young, 1986).

How Sport Controls the Individual Reporter

The generally favorable approach to sport reporting is part of a club-like environment within sport and media organizations. Sport teams either hire or approve the hiring of the local radio and television play-by-play announcers who broadcast their games. Team executives may monitor the broadcasts to ensure that a favorable image is being presented. For example, the announcer Whitfield (1983) reports how his on-air performance was influenced by the owner of the Washington Senators. Whitfield claims he was discouraged from making negative comments about the weather or the attendance, and was instructed not to announce the scores of rival teams.

Newspaper reporters often have greater obligations to please because they are more likely to travel with one team. In this situation, reporters may experience role conflict as to whether they should objectively report the news (i.e., say the team played poorly) or try to sell the sport, the team, and newspapers (i.e., say the team had bad luck). In this respect they face difficulties similar to journalists covering a specific political candidate's election campaign.

In reality, sportwriters depend on the personnel of the team for both information and financial assistance. They generally receive regular team statistics, and news about trades, promotions, and demotions arrives in time to meet their press deadlines. But reporters who fall out of favor may receive news releases too late for that day's newspaper. Additionally, they may not be notified of press conferences, they may be banned from the press box or locker room, and they may not be invited to travel on the team's bus or plane with other media personnel.

Cooperative reporters may receive direct gratuities, such as expenses while traveling with the team or honorariums for writing press releases or feature stories for the program sold at the game. They may receive valuable complimentary tickets, which they can sell or give to friends. Thus, an economic interdependence between media personnel and club executives can be created. This ensures an element of social control over the media by sport organizations, at least at the local level (Koppett, 1981; McFarlane, 1955; Smith & Valeriote, 1983).

The shared views that have arisen around media sports help reporters handle any feelings of role conflict. The prevailing view is that everyone behaves the same way and that noncritical reporting is in the interest of the game and necessary for the team's financial success. It is also, of course, necessary for a reporter's career advancement. In this way, sport promoters (i.e., the owners) create a monopoly that allows them to shape the news and public opinion to meet their needs.

The public, at least until the recent emergence of independent critical columnists, thus often receives a biased view of sport. There is more censorship of sport stories and sport broadcasts than of nonsport news items. To date, these practices continue because of economics and tradition, and because the practices have seldom been challenged on a legal or moral basis.

THE MASS MEDIA AND SPORT IN CONFLICT

In the 1960s, with increased competition from television and a new era of critical thinking and investigative journalism, sport writers and authors began to take a hard look inside sport and "tell it like it is." Writers of popular sport books (e.g., Bouton, 1970; Edwards, 1969; Merchant, 1971; Scott, 1971) attacked the world of sport and demystified the life and values of athletes. Although these authors were severely criticized for opening the door to sport's back regions, they did sensitize the public to the business and professional side of sport. More importantly, they made it possible for daily columnists and feature writers to take a more critical and realistic view of their subject matter and to provide more complete reports to their audiences. As a result, readers increasingly are de-

Critical and investigative journalism is the current trend in sport reporting.

manding more objectivity and criticism and fewer "fairy tales" (Telander, 1984).

One outcome of more critical writing about sport has been increasing conflict between the press and the athletes and management. Today, reporters write columns about the inadequacies of athletes, coaches, general managers, or owners. Reporters see themselves as representatives of the paying public, who have a right to demand that competent athletes perform to their potential. Often these stories are written to hasten the departure (i.e., firing) of an athlete, coach, or general manager; sometimes the strategy is successful. They may also be written to increase newspaper sales in cities or regions where the newspaper is competing with one or two other daily papers.

This more critical approach to sport journalism has led to banning some reporters from the locker room and sport representatives' (e.g., players, coaches, general managers) refusing to communicate with the press. Some athletes refuse to speak to some or all reporters because they do not trust them and do not understand the role and responsibilities of the press. They may also have been misquoted or misinterpreted in the past, been criticized, or had aspects of their private lives made public. Telander (1984) reports that sportswriters sometimes cause conflict because they envy athletes or do not respect those who earn large salaries and do not perform to their perceived potential. Also, most reporters are white and there is an alleged cultural gap between the white reporters and the black athletes in some sports. This may inhibit communication. More recently, female sport reporters in some *male* team sports have encountered negative reactions ranging from lack of respect to outright discrimination in access to news stories (e.g., they are banned from the press box or not allowed to enter the locker room until players are dressed and therefore ready to leave).

Another outcome of this conflict has been an increasing concern with the ethics of sport journalism (Smith & Valeriote, 1983; Telander, 1984; Wulfemeyer, 1984). As public figures in an entertainment business where salaries are paid indirectly by the public, athletes have a responsibility to cooperate with the press. They also have a professional responsibility to promote and maintain the integrity of the game. At the same time, journalists have a responsibility to report accurately and fairly, and to criticize where it is warranted and supported by hard evidence. They should resist, as well, pressure from their superiors to engage in muckraking or vendettas to increase sales. Finally, reporters are the gatekeepers of information that could flow between the back regions of sport and the public. They have a social responsibility to judge what is appropriate and necessary news and what is smut or irrelevant information.

THE FUTURE OF TELEVISION AND SPORT

As we have seen, sport has become increasingly dependent on the support of the mass media's audience. In effect, the size of the live audience attending games counts far less than in the past, as teams and leagues derive an increasingly large proportion of their revenue from the sale of broadcast rights. For example, the 28 teams in the NFL depend on network television for 60% of their revenue. If the rights' fees decline, players' salaries and owners' profits will decrease—and ticket prices will increase.

The marriage between the media and sport has endured comfortably for about 35 years but is now beginning to experience strain and conflict. Not unlike the stress in many marriages, this tension is related to money. In 1985, for the first time in many years, the three major television networks lost an estimated $45 million on the production of NFL games, and two of the three networks experienced a loss in the millions on all sport telecasts. In 1986, the networks lost a combined $75 million on the NFL alone. Meanwhile, rights' fees have continued to escalate over a 10-year period (1976–1986): $50 million to $500 million for the NFL; $9 million to $43 million for the NBA; and $21 million to $160 million for baseball.

The Ratings Game

During the 1980s, after almost two decades of growth, television ratings for some sport events have declined quite dramatically. To illustrate the decline in ratings, consider the Belmont Stakes. This event experienced a 58% decrease in viewers from 1981 to 1986 and was consequently dropped by all three major networks in 1987. Lower ratings have been recorded for other major horse races, auto races, college and professional football, and some college Bowl games. Despite this trend, an estimated 120 million home viewers watched the January 1988 Super Bowl. This was the largest national audience in the United States for any television program in history. Some owners argue that this figure is grossly underestimated, because the normal procedure for estimating the size of viewing audiences only considers the home as the viewing location. The viewers who consume this event in public bars and restaurants are thus ignored.

In contrast, nonsport television shows are receiving higher ratings, especially when in direct competition with some specific sport events. Recognizing that more women are buying cars, automobile manufacturers are opting to advertise on nonsport shows, at a cheaper rate.

As a result of these trends, some formerly high-rated sport shows are no longer televised, and advertisers are refusing to pay a premium price to advertise on sport shows.

At the same time, sport leagues are facing reduced rights fees from the networks. The 5-year, $2.1 billion contract between the three major networks and the NFL expired at the end of the 1986 season. The renewed package was for 3 years at $1.43 billion and included a contribution by ESPN for eight prime-time Sunday games in the second half of the season. This was the first time pay-TV was included. The net result of the shorter and smaller contract is that each NFL team will receive $17 million a year, or 3.3% less than the previous year. Indeed, even the rights fees for the Olympic Games, which have escalated constantly since the 1960s, are peaking. NBC purchased the rights to the 1988 Summer Olympics in Seoul for $309 million, a figure considerably lower than the predicted $1 billion. Similarly, CBS will pay $243 million for the U.S. broadcast rights to the 1992 Winter Olympics at Albertville, France.

Surprisingly, ABC, which has broadcast 10 of the previous 13 Olympics, withdrew from the Albertville bidding. If this trend continues, the fiscal picture of future Olympiads may be in jeopardy (Alaszkiewicz & McPhail, 1986).

Recently, ratings for sport events have declined. There are three basic reasons for this. First, sport has been overexposed on television, especially with the advent of 24-hour sport networks, independent local stations, and satellite superstations that broadcast sport events. In effect, sport is no longer a unique viewing experience, and the three major networks no longer have a monopoly on sport telecasts.

Second, fans have become disillusioned and lost interest because of strikes by players or officials; large salaries and a lack of player loyalty to a team; franchises relocating; diluted quality of play because of expansion; drug and recruiting scandals; and the number of commercials, the lack of new gimmicks, and the poor efforts of some players in some games. Are they also bored by the length of the schedule?

Third, there are many alternatives competing for the viewers' leisure time, such as the fitness movement, the use of VCRs for home movie viewing, and dual-career families with greater discretionary incomes for leisure pursuits outside the home and perhaps, less discretionary time for television viewing.

Marriage Prospects

The marriage between television and sport will survive, but perhaps in an altered form. By the early 1990s most of the potential television market in North America will be equipped with either cable television or satellite antennas. The three major networks, superstations, specialty channels, and local independent stations will all, theoretically, be available in every household. Thus, there will be more competition among television stations to acquire the rights for major sport events. These events may become more costly for the media producer, but will still likely be available on network television. But minor events may be offered only on pay-television to those who can afford to buy the broadcast.

For major sport events that are extremely costly (e.g., the Olympics), the various television companies may pool their resources. In this scenario, each network might telecast specific sports—especially if the Olympics ever opts to create a multisite event, which has been suggested as a way of reducing costs and making the Games a truly global event. Finally, as viewer interests fluctuate, the availability of specific sports on television will ebb and flow in a pattern similar to that of nonsport shows. We will see fewer long-term television/sport contracts, and sport shows may be dropped in midseason if they perform poorly in the ratings games. The salaries of players and media broadcasters will decline as the owners and the media earn lower profits.

WRAP-UP

The mass media are processes that communicate with a large proportion of the population rapidly and at a relatively low cost per viewer, listener, or reader. These media, and their sport contents, are consumed differently by different segments of the general population.

In addition to supplying information, the mass media teach norms and values to consumers, and they may shape or distort our views of a sport, a team, or an athlete. For example, with respect to sport, the media present news on sporting events (e.g., game scores) but also teach the values (e.g., ag-gressive acts are normative) of sport consumption and competition, and they tend to trivialize women's sport by giving it little coverage. Through their presentation of sport, the media socialize people as well as entertain them.

Over the past century or so, as a mutually beneficial marriage between mass media and sport has evolved, sport content has become a major message category communicated through the mass media.

Through the development of the media-sport-advertiser relationship, the content of the mass media has changed dramatically, and much more sport material is now presented. But the content of sport has also been affected by the media. Media influences have changed the rules and procedures of games (e.g., to suit the timetable of the media); increased the financial success of sport organizations; made possible increases in athletes' salaries; and led to both professionalization and glamorization of sport. Most importantly, though, the economic dependence of sport on the mass media has increased profoundly.

The future, in North America, probably holds continued economic dependence of sport on the mass media, but there are reasons to believe that the link cannot grow stronger and may weaken somewhat.

REFERENCES

Alaszkiewicz, R., & McPhail, T.L. (1986). Olympic television rights. *International Review for the Sociology of Sport*, **21**, 211–266.

Betts, J.R. (1953). The technological revolution and the rise of sport, 1850–1900. *Mississippi Valley Historical Review*, **40**, 231–256.

Birrell, S., & Loy, J.W. (1979). Media sport: Hot and cool. *International Review of Sport Sociology*, **14**(1), 5–19.

Boutilier, M.A., & SanGiovanni, L. (1983). *The sporting woman*. Champaign, IL: Human Kinetics.

Bouton, J. (1970). *Ball four*. New York: Dell.

Bryant, J., Comisky, P., & Zillman, D. (1977). Drama in sports commentary. *Journal of Communications*, **27**(3), 140–149.

Bryant, J. (1980). A two year selective investigation of the female in sport as reported in the paper media. *Arena Review*, **4**(2), 32–44.

Comisky, P., Bryant, J., & Zillman, D. (1977). Commentary as a substitute for action. *Journal of Communication*, **27**(3), 150–153.

Condor, R., & Anderson, D.F. (1984). Longitudinal analysis of coverage accorded black and white athletes in feature articles of *Sports Illustrated* (1960–1980). *Journal of Sport Behavior*, **7**(1), 39–43.

Cronk, A. (1985). *Behind the press box: The social construction of the working desk in a newspaper's sports department*. Unpublished master's thesis, University of Waterloo, Ontario, Canada.

De Fleur, M.L. (1970). *Theories of mass communication* (2nd ed.). New York: McKay.

Duncan, M.C., & Hasbrook, C.A. (1988). Denial of power in televised women's sport. *Sociology of Sport Journal*, **5**, 1–21.

Edwards, H. (1969). *The revolt of the black athlete*. New York: Free Press.

Gelinas, M., & Theberge, N. (1986). Analysis of the coverage of physical activity in two Canadian newspapers. *International Review for the Sociology of Sport*, **21**, 141–149.

Greendorfer, S.L. (1981). Sport and the mass media. In G.R.F. Luschen & G.H. Sage (Eds.), *Handbook of social science of sport* (pp. 160–180). Urbana, IL: Stipes.

Greendorfer, S.L. (1983). Sport and the mass media: General overview. *Arena Review*, **7**(2), 1–6.

Guttman, A. (1986). *Sports spectators*. New York: Columbia University Press.

Hilliard, D.C. (1984). Media images of male and female professional athletes: An interpretive analysis of magazine articles. *Sociology of Sport Journal*, **1**, 251–262.

Houston, W. (1987, November 12). A vicious hockey act, or not. *The Globe and Mail*, Section C, p. 12.

Hughes, R.H., & Coakley, J.J. (1984). Mass society and the commercialization of sport. *Sociology of Sport Journal*, **1**, 57–63.

Kaempfer, W.H., & Pacey, P.L. (1986). Televising college football: The complementarity of attendance and viewing. *Social Science Quarterly*, **67**(1), 176–185.

Katz, E., Gurevitch, M., & Haas, H. (1973). On the use of the mass media for important things. *American Sociological Review*, **38**, 164–181.

Koppett, L. (1981). *Sport illusion, sport reality*. Boston: Houghton Mifflin.

Kozlik, C.A. (1985). *Baseball in the New York sporting press, 1870-1900: A conceptual and methodological approach to the study of the social meanings of sport*. Unpublished master's thesis, University of Waterloo, Ontario, Canada.

Lever, J., & Wheeler, S. (1984). The Chicago Tribune sports page, 1900–1975. *Sociology of Sport Journal*, **1**, 299–313.

MacCarthy, J. (1906). *The newspaper worker*. New York: Press Guild.

McFarlane, B. (1955). *The sociology of sports promotion*. Unpublished master's thesis, McGill University, Montreal.

McKay, J., & Rowe, D. (1987). Ideology, the media and Australian sport. *Sociology of Sport Journal*, **4**, 258–273.

McPherson, B.D. (1976a). Socialization into the role of sport consumer: A theory and causal model. *Canadian Review of Sociology and Anthropology*, **13**, 165–177.

McPherson, B.D. (1976b). Consumer role socialization: A within system model. *Sportwissenschaft*, **6**, 144–154.

Meier, K. (1984). Much ado about nothing: The television broadcast packaging of team sport championship games. *Sociology of Sport Journal*, **1**, 263–279.

Merchant, L. (1971). *Everyday you take another bite*. New York: Doubleday.

Pearman, W.A. (1978). Race on the sports page. *Review of Sport and Leisure*, **3**(2), 54–68.

Powers, R. (1984). *Supertube: The rise of television sport*. New York: Coward-McCann.

Rader, B.G. (1984). *In its own image: How television has transformed sports*. New York: Free Press.

Rainville, R.E. & McCormick, E. (1977). Extent of covert racial prejudice in pro football announcers' speech. *Journalism Quarterly*, **54**(1), 20–26.

Rintala, J., & Birrell, S. (1984). Fair treatment for the active female: A content analysis of Young Athletes magazine. *Sociology of Sport Journal*, **1**, 231–250.

Scott, J. (1971). *The athletic revolution*. New York: Free Press.

Smith, G.J., & Valeriote, T.A. (1983). Ethics in sports journalism. *Arena Review*, **7**(2), 7–14.

Telander, R. (1984). The written word: Player-press relationships in American sports. *Sociology of Sport Journal*, **1**, 3–14.

Theberge, N., & Cronk, A.R. (1986). Work routines in newspaper sports departments and the coverage of women's sports. *Sociology of Sport Journal*, **3**, 195–203.

Thompson, L.A. (1986). Professional wrestling in Japan: Media and message. *International Review for the Sociology of Sport*, **21**, 65–80.

Weis, K. (1986). How the print media affect sports and violence: The problems of sport journalism. *International Review for the Sociology of Sport*, **21**, 239–250.

Whannel, G. (1984). The television spectacular. In A. Tomlinson & G. Whannel (Eds.), *Five ring circus: Money, power and politics at the Olympic Games* (pp. 30–43). London: Pluto.

Whitfield, S. (1983). *Kiss it goodbye*. New York: Abelard-Schuman.

Wulfemeyer, K.T. (1984, July). *Out of bounds: Ethics in sports journalism*. Paper presented at the Sport Literature Association annual conference, University of California, San Diego.

Young, K. (1986). "The killing field": Themes in mass media responses to the Heysel Stadium riot. *International Review for the Sociology of Sport*, **21**, 253–264.

P A R T II

SPORT REINFORCES SOCIAL INEQUALITIES

As we continue our sociological journey into the world of sport, we now consider five aspects of people's social backgrounds that influence life chances and lifestyles in sport: social class, race, ethnicity, gender, and age.

Until sport sociologists began to ask questions about the backgrounds and opportunities of those who participate or spectate, conventional wisdom held that sport was a unique institution where everyone had an equal opportunity. Sport was portrayed as an egalitarian activity where only talent and desire were needed—whether you wanted to be an athlete, spectator, coach, official, or sport executive. Our parents, teachers, and the media placed sport on a pedestal as a model of social equality.

As you will learn in the next three chapters, *ascribed* (race, ethnicity, gender, age) and *achieved* (social class) social attributes *do* matter in the world of sport. Not all of us have the same chance to become an Olympic gymnast, boxer, professional golfer or tennis player, coach, or member of a minor sport executive board. Even with innate ability, it matters whether we are black or white, male or female, of high or low social standing, or members of minority or mainstream groups. In short, some of the same social inequalities that we find in the wider society are present and reinforced in sport.

Chapter 7 shows how social class is a source of inequality in sport; chapter 8 considers the disadvantages introduced by membership in a minority racial or ethnic group; and chapter 9 addresses sport opportunities as they relate to gender. Chapter 9 also introduces some recent evidence on ageism in sport.

Social Class, Socioeconomic Status, and Sport

In North America, as Tumin (1967) notes, "One is generally considered better, superior, or more worthy if one is:

- White-collar rather than blue-collar
- Educated rather than uneducated
- White rather than black
- Native-born rather than of foreign descent
- Young rather than old
- Male rather than female" (p. 27).

One has greater access to the valued scarce resources of income, wealth, and power if one has the superior statuses in this list. This differential ranking and rewarding of people is called **social stratification**.

In these cases, differential evaluation and rewarding is based on social or biological characteristics rather than individual ability. Thus, individuals may be denied access to specific opportunities or roles because of, for example, their social class background, race,

171

ethnicity, gender, or age. Sometimes several characteristics combine to further disadvantage the individual (e.g., an older black female or a recently arrived Vietnamese male with the equivalent of a grade 10 education).

There are many consequences, for both the individual and society, of a social structure with widespread inequalities. Within a society, depending on the degree and type of stratification, we can see the emergence of such processes as

- conflict (e.g., blacks vs. whites), segregation, and discrimination (e.g., against blacks, women, and lower-class members);
- social mobility (e.g., moving from lower-middle class to upper class);
- democratization (e.g., participation changing from a few elite members to large numbers, as in golf over the past 50 years);
- collective behavior (e.g., a group of lower-class youth, known as *hooligans*, rioting in and around soccer stadiums in Great Britain); and
- social change (e.g., the civil rights and women's liberation movements).

Social backgrounds influence life chances, particularly with respect to mental and physical health, the selection of a marital partner, access to education and occupations, and opportunities for social or geographical mobility. Social backgrounds also determine individual lifestyles, including our manner of speech and dress, our type and style of residence, our preference for the type and frequency of leisure activities, the type of friends and social relations we have, and the material and symbolic rewards we seek and achieve.

Sport mirrors society to some extent, and we find in sport some of the inequalities prevailing in the wider society. Indeed, social inequalities have been a significant influence in the structure of sport and on the sporting behavior of participants, leaders, and spectators. Social inequalities have become important issues in society, and in the world of sport as well.

DEFINING SOCIAL CLASS AND SOCIOECONOMIC STATUS

Social class refers to persistent social inequalities. Two distinct types of social inequality have been identified by researchers, who have been guided in their thinking by two different sociological theories. One theory is derived from the work of Karl Marx (1859/1970); the other from writings by Max Weber (1958). The latter approach, which is somewhat critical of Marx's work, is sometimes called the functionalist approach.

Under the Marxian approach, social classes are defined by who owns the means of production and labor power, and they exist in all societies based on **capitalism**. *Means of production* includes the machines, buildings, land, and materials used in the production of goods and services. *Labor power* is the physical and mental capacity of people to work; it is bought and sold for wages (or salary) by those who own the means of production.

Marxists identify three main classes: the **proletariat** or working class, who do not own the means of production and who sell their labor power for wages; the **petite bourgeoisie**, who own businesses (the means of production), work for themselves, and do not employ others; and the **bourgeoisie** or capitalist class, who own the means of production and accumulate wealth from surplus value provided through workers' labor. An example of the bourgeoisie in professional team sport is team owners. The players in their employ are members of the proletariat.

Marxian social class distinctions do not refer to types of occupation or levels of income.

For example, a plumber could be a member of the working class (if he sells labor power and does not own a business), a member of the petite bourgeoisie (if he owns a plumbing business but does not have employees) or a capitalist (if he owns a company and purchases the labor of several plumbers). Also, members of different classes may have similar incomes. An owner of a small engineering firm with a few employees may earn less than a worker (e.g., a successful engineer employed by a large firm or a highly paid sport star). But capitalists generally have more power than workers to determine the distribution of wealth. This occurs because capitalists own and control the means of production and because the working class is not fully organized in opposition (e.g., in unions or political organizations).

Marxists believe that a conflict of interest (e.g., wage disputes and opposition by capitalists to the formation of unions) between capitalists and the working class is an inherent feature of capitalism. Capitalists try to keep wages low and productivity high to maximize their wealth. Workers try to increase their wages and improve their working conditions. A Marxist might point to labor-management conflicts in North American professional team sports such as baseball, football, basketball, and hockey; labor (players) try to better their lot and capitalists (owners) conspire to limit the strength of the players' organizations and keep wages low.

On the other hand, the Weberians or *functionalists* claim that social classes can be defined through inequalities in income, educational attainment, and occupational prestige. These forms of inequalities are called **socioeconomic status** or **social status** differences. Categorizing people in this way creates a difficulty, however, in that the same people may fall into different ranks. For example, the rich, the middle class, and the poor can be easily distinguished from one another

by using standards of income and wealth. But those in the middle-income category (i.e., white-collar and blue-collar workers) will be accorded different degrees of prestige for their different jobs. By the same token, white-collar jobs do not always carry more income. The same is true of differences in educational levels. Those with secondary-school diplomas more often have white-collar jobs and higher incomes than those with less education. But skilled blue-collar workers, such as electricians, earn comparatively high wages without college training. Or, professional athletes may be low on formal education but high on occupational prestige and income.

Functionalists emphasize the distribution patterns of scarce rewards (i.e., the numbers and social backgrounds of people who acquire a university education or a high-prestige job); Marxists emphasize the social interactions of the classes (e.g., who purchases labor power from whom and the rate of exploitation of one class by another). Functionalists are concerned with explaining patterns of social inequality; Marxists study the way class relations explain social change. Because of its attention to change, Marxist research generally has a historical dimension. You will see both of these perspectives reflected when we consider patterns of social inequality in this chapter, and resistance and social conflict in Part III.

WHY ARE THERE SOCIAL INEQUALITIES?

There have been two basic approaches to examining why and how social inequality emerges and persists. The **functionalist perspective on social inequality** argues that social inequality is necessary for any society, or for any small or large social organization, to survive. There must be a division of labor (e.g., not everyone can be the quarterback or head coach), and to attract people to both the more important (e.g., head coach) and less important (e.g., trainer) roles, there must be variation in the rewards (i.e., income) and prestige involved. This variation motivates individuals to make the necessary effort and sacrifices to train for the top positions. People will also perform better in the positions if they are rewarded well and accorded prestige.

Supporters of this view argue that there is consensus among the members of a society or group concerning which positions have higher status and rewards—and that this consensus is necessary to preserve the social order. This means that the haves and have-nots accept that some people should be subordinate to others.

The **conflict perspective on social inequality**, which includes the Marxist approach, argues that inequality is unjust and that the existing social structure should be changed to eliminate or minimize inequality. According to this view, the inequalities persist because the dominant class seeks greater economic gain by exploiting those who are less advantaged. Perhaps the best recent illustration of class relations within sport is the conflict between owners and athletes in some North American professional team sports. This conflict has resulted in the creation of unions, strikes, higher salary demands, and legal arbitration. It has arisen between a group of dissatisfied, often underpaid athletes and a group of powerful, profit-seeking owners.

The conflict perspective is illustrated, as well, in the social movements for civil rights, women's liberation, gay liberation, and improved status of senior citizens (e.g., Grey Panthers). These movements, each of which involves **social conflict**, seek to change the social order by creating either orderly or disorderly redistribution of power among competing groups.

These perspectives offer sharply contrasting explanations of social inequalities. But a more realistic view is that both conflict and shared views are present to varying degrees within societies and within sport. We must consider both perspectives as we seek an understanding of inequality in sport.

SOCIAL CLASS AND PRIMARY SPORT INVOLVEMENT

Athletes have had varying levels of prestige at different times. In ancient Greece and Rome, as in Eastern European countries today, an athlete was accorded high status and prestige. In contrast, in the post-Roman period in Europe and during the early part of this century in China, an athlete had low status. Similarly, the opportunity to participate in sport, or in particular sports, has varied by social class background. In the Middle Ages only the nobles and landowners competed in many sports; they often abandoned a sport when the lower strata began to participate. In fact, when a sport became dominated by the lower strata, it often became a professional sport.

During the Victorian era, sport became institutionalized in the elite "public schools" (these are really private schools) of England's dominant economic class. Later, the graduates of Oxford and Cambridge established sport governing bodies. Furthermore, sport competition among the lower classes or among ethnic groups was traditionally discouraged or prohibited. It was not until the 1880s that working-class soccer clubs in England began to compete on an equal basis with clubs of middle- and upper-social status opponents.

Elitism

Elitism in sport has been maintained through the formation of private clubs, which restrict

---

Highlight 7.1
The Social Class of Members of Amateur Sport Clubs
in North America at the Turn of the Century

In the late 1800s and early 1900s private amateur sport clubs in Canada and the United States maintained elitism by restricting membership to those from the middle or upper class. To illustrate, the New York Athletic Club and the University Athletic Club in New York City were controlled by an elite group of business owners, stockbrokers, lawyers, corporation officers, and bankers (Wettan & Willis, 1976). Similarly, in Canada, the Montreal Racquet Club and the Toronto Cricket Club were founded by high-ranking British army officers who restricted membership to those of acceptable social and financial standing (Metcalfe, 1976, 1987). Thus, the economic and political elite had access to fa-

cilities that they built and controlled, thereby inhibiting the democratization of sport.

These patterns continue today in that most communities have private clubs with large initiation fees, annual dues, and entry by sponsorship only. However, since about 1970, more sporting opportunities have become more widely available for lower classes. These range from less restrictive private clubs to pay-as-you-play facilities with nominal membership fees, to public facilities provided by the local community. But there is still considerable variation in the opportunity to succeed and in the quality of the sport environment.

---

membership to those with specific ascribed or achieved characteristics. For example, the first governing bodies of sport in Victorian England consisted of members of the aristocracy. In Canada, the founding members of metropolitan cricket and racquet clubs also belonged to the military elite, who restricted membership to those of acceptable social and financial standing (Metcalfe, 1976). In the United States, the formation and early development of influential athletic clubs was controlled by a social elite comprised mainly of business owners, stock brokers, lawyers, corporate officers, and bankers (Wettan & Willis, 1976). At the other end of the social scale, a small number of working-class clubs

were formed in the period after 1860. Highlight 7.1 illustrates the restricted access to membership in sport clubs at the turn of the century and the slow changes occurring now. Clearly, members were admitted on the basis of social characteristics and not athletic ability.

As a result of elitism, different sports have come to be associated with dominant or subordinate classes and social statuses. For example, certain sport artifacts have become symbolic status indicators (e.g., carrying a tennis racket rather than a baseball bat in public). Also, certain sports have become integral parts of particular class or racial subcultures (e.g., basketball is often viewed as the "city game" unique to the inner core ghettoes of large cities in the Eastern United States).

Types of Research Studies

To date, four types of research studies have sought to examine and understand class-based and status-based inequality in sport settings. First, social historians have examined historical documents to describe and explain the social origins of the earliest participants in organized sports (see Highlight 7.1). The second type of study—by far the largest number—has surveyed child, adolescent, or adult participants or spectators in particular sports at a specific time (see Highlight 7.2). These studies have collected information on the social status background (i.e., occupation, education, income) of the respondents and the respondents' fathers and mothers. Most of these studies have focused on males rather than females.

The third type of study has surveyed successful athletes (e.g., college, Olympic, or professional) to determine their social class background as children. The fathers' class position, occupation, education, or income are identified to assess differences in access to sport or in opportunities for social mobility following the sport career. The final type of study has involved surveys to determine the backgrounds of those who hold varying levels of power in sport settings (e.g., volunteer and salaried executives in amateur sport associations; referees and umpires; professional sport owners).

In many of these studies females have not been included, and most do not include a national sample. They represent the situation in one location at one time and therefore lack generalizability. Nor do many of them deal with social class as opposed to social status backgrounds. Nevertheless, because there

have been so many studies of the social status background of athletes, we can place some faith in the conclusion that access to certain types and levels of sport involvement is strongly influenced by the background of one's parents.

Mass Participation

During childhood and adolescence, certain sport opportunities are available in the community and through intramural or interscholastic teams within the school. Ideally, the school system provides equality of opportunity so that a number of sports are generally available to interested youth. Even given this situation, as the study by Macintosh (1982) reveals (Highlight 7.2), youth from the middle class and above tend to participate on interschool teams to a much greater extent. One notable exception is that many lower-class youth participate in school soccer, especially if they are members of an ethnic group with a long history of playing soccer. Similarly, there tend to be fewer participants from the lower socioeconomic strata in intramural sport programs. These patterns are even more prevalent for girls and for older students (grade 11 and beyond).

This effect of social status suggests that the cost of some sports discourages less affluent people, but cost is not the only factor. Part of the explanation may be that there are variations in the subcultural values and lifestyles of different social classes. Those from a middle-class and higher status family background are more likely to have parents who are actively involved in sport or who encourage sport participation. They are also more likely to adhere to a healthier lifestyle that involves physical activity. On the other hand, lower-status adolescents who do not participate in sport are more likely to smoke, to hold part-time jobs, and to devalue athletic involvement (Macintosh, 1982).

Highlight 7.2
The Class Backgrounds of Canadian High School Athletes

It is often argued that class differences in sport participation result from variation in the ability to pay for coaching, equipment, and facilities. For school sport, however, every student theoretically has an equal opportunity to participate because schools provide these necessities to all students. We might expect that high school interscholastic sport would reflect a process of democratization by drawing team members equally from a variety of social class backgrounds.

Based on a questionnaire survey of 4,700 students selected randomly from 60 high schools, Macintosh (1982) recorded the occupations of the parents of 1,582 students who were on interschool and community teams (see chart).

These patterns held for both male and female athletes. Thus, the higher classes were markedly overrepresented on interschool teams compared with their frequency in the wider community. Lower-class youth seem to be more involved in community sport teams than on school teams.

Does this pattern result because lower-class children do not identify with middle-class values of the school? Or do they perceive school sport as a potential source of failure? Or are they not encouraged to participate by teachers and peers to the same extent as youth from the middle class and above? Or do more students from clerical and labor backgrounds have jobs that interfere with after-school practices and games?

Parental occupational category	Interschool athlete (%)	Community team athlete (%)
Professional	57	49
Clerical	11	13
Labor	32	38

Note. From "Socio-Economic, Educational, and Status Characteristics of Ontario Interschool Athletes" by D. Macintosh, 1982, *Canadian Journal of Applied Sport Sciences*, *7*, p. 275. Copyright 1975 by the Canadian Association of Sport Sciences. Adapted by permission.

Cost is a greater factor for sport involvement in the wider community, because the user-pay principle tends to prevail. Thus, it is not surprising to find that sports such as golf, gymnastics, skiing, and competitive swimming are more likely to involve youth from middle-class and higher status families. To illustrate, a survey of 336 junior tennis players competing in a prestigious tournament in Miami found that over 61% of the players were from families who made a minimum of $60,000 a year. Moreover, 71% of these competitive junior players reported that their tennis-related expenses were at least $5,000 annually; almost one third said their expenses totalled $10,000 or more (Neff, 1987).

Traditional team sports such as basketball, football and baseball tend to have more variation in the socioeconomic backgrounds of the participants. Interestingly, competitive youth hockey at the all-star level in Canada tends to involve lower- and middle-class boys; U.S. youth hockey attracts more middle- and upper-class youth. This contrast is partly related to the fact that communities subsidize the cost of arenas and teams in Canada; many U.S. arenas are privately owned, and parents must pay a much larger share of the cost. As a result, fewer total children are involved, and participation is limited to families with high incomes.

Among adults in the general population, those classified as middle or upper class participate more in sport, although there tend to be specific sport differences related to class-based values, lifestyles, and occupations. Most studies find a strong positive association between higher levels of education or professional occupations and participation in individual sports. This is especially true for those that can be enjoyed in private settings such as tennis, squash, golf, and ski clubs. Highlight 7.3 illustrates the different educational and occupational characteristics of active versus sedentary adults.

A final piece of evidence for the lack of egalitarianism in sport at the level of mass participation can be found by analyzing how much money different strata spend on sport equipment. For example, downhill and cross-country skiers in Canada tend to be well-educated professionals with household in-

comes greater than $40,000 (Williams, 1986). As expected, there is a linear relationship between income and the purchase of sport equipment. Similar examples can be found in a variety of other sports, ranging from boxing and bowling to polo and other equestrian events.

Elite Athletes

At the intercollegiate or professional level of sport, studies have found class differences in the backgrounds of male athletes. A higher percentage of college and professional athletes in the traditional team sports of football, baseball, hockey, and basketball tend to come from lower- to middle-class backgrounds. Among individual sports, those involved in boxing, wrestling, and track are primarily from the lower strata; those participating in tennis, skiing, golf, and crew are from the upper strata (Loy, 1972). It must be stressed again that in most sports, participants come from a range of backgrounds (though the middle classes tend to be overrepresented in most sports). Among Winter Olympic events, such as skating and skiing, the upper-middle and upper strata are generally overrepresented. This pattern emerges because the high costs of training, travel, and coaching are usually provided by the athlete and his or her family.

Among female elite athletes, there is some evidence to suggest that most are from a middle-class or higher background, particularly in sports that traditionally have involved women. Again, this probably results from differences by stratum in values concerning the appropriate behavior for women. Hasbrook (1986) found that among high school students and youth soccer players, girls from the lower social classes participate less than girls from the upper social classes. In contrast, boys from all social classes ap-

Highlight 7.3
Social Status Characteristics of Active and Sedentary Adults in Canada

A 1981 national survey (Stephens, Furrie, & Craig, 1983) asked 22,000 Canadians 15 years and older to indicate which activities they had participated in, and with what frequency, during the previous 12 months. Based on their responses, members of the sample were classified as *active* (averaged 3 or more hours per week of physical activity for 9 months or more), *moderately active*, and *sedentary* (less than 3 hours per week for less than 9 months per year). As the data below indicate, involvement in physical activity during leisure time is related to social status; namely, as education increases so does the likelihood of participating in sport and exercise. Similarly, those employed in a profession or in managerial positions are more likely to spend their leisure time being physically active than are those in other occupational groups, especially blue-collar workers (60% vs. 48%).

Social characteristic	Level of activity	
	Active (%)	Sedentary (%)
Education		
Elementary	41	25
Some secondary	53	12
Secondary or more	56	8
Certificate or diploma	58	7
University degree	63	5
Occupation		
Manager/professional	60	6
Other white collar	53	8
Blue collar	48	10

Note. From Stephens, T., Furrie, A. and Craig, C.L. Fitness and Lifestyle in Canada: A Canada Fitness Survey Report. Canadian Fitness and Lifestyle Research Institute and Fitness Canada, 1983. Reprinted by permission.

peared to participate to an equal degree. It may be that class and gender interact to restrict sport opportunities for girls. In a subsequent study, Hasbrook (1987) reported that lack of economic opportunity influenced lower participation rates more than parental values, beliefs, and practices.

SOCIAL CLASS AND SECONDARY SPORT INVOLVEMENT

How and to what extent individuals consume sport is closely related to their social characteristics. Although economically there is little to prevent most individuals from consuming sport on radio or television, some class-based differences seem to affect which types of media sport events are consumed. For example, college graduates are more likely to consume football and basketball; baseball attracts viewers from across the social spectrum (Loy, 1972).

With respect to attending sport events, those in the lower strata are less likely to attend the more popular team sport events—especially football, which has roots in the college environment. Members of the lower strata are the major consumers of car racing, horse racing, and boxing (Loy, 1972).

Those who organize, administer, and control sport tend to come from the upper social strata and capitalist class. At the professional level in the United States, Clark (1977) has reported that there are close corporate ties between owners of professional football, baseball, and basketball teams and membership on the boards of directors of large financial, political, media, or educational institutions. Specifically, he found that 56 of the 67 presidents of professional sport teams had 216 business links (e.g., automobile, oil, transportation, real estate, construction, insurance, banking), 72 government links (e.g., public officials, government committees, or commissions), 40 educational links, and 41 media links (e.g., television, radio, newspaper, book publishing, movies, theater).

In a detailed examination of who controls sport, Gruneau (1978) found that many owners of professional team sports serve as directors of large corporations. Through interviews and analyses of library sources, he

discovered that the executive officers and directors of the Canadian Football League and the National Hockey League teams are linked with similar positions in the financial, trade, transportation, and communication sectors of the economy. Similarly, in Finland, commercial leaders tend to dominate the higher executive positions of sport organizations (Kiviaho & Simola, 1974). Similar high social standing characterizes members on the national and international Olympic committees. Finally, and following the sex structure of the corporate world, most professional and Olympic sport executives are male, although a few women now hold senior management or ownership positions in professional football and baseball.

The amateur level also shows differences in the backgrounds of volunteer leaders (coaches, executives). Coaches may represent a wider variety of social status backgrounds, but those who sit on local, regional, or national executive committees tend to be employed in professional occupations. This is partly due to interpersonal skills and experience in directing people, flexible and discretionary hours, and higher income. Having discretionary hours and income are important factors, because volunteer work can consume a large amount of money and leisure time. Some sports, such as hockey (in Canada only), soccer, volleyball, and boxing have coaches and executive members who are more likely to come from blue-collar backgrounds. This pattern is especially likely where there are strong ethnic (e.g., soccer) or racial (e.g., boxing) subcultures associated with the sport.

Across sports the prevailing pattern tends to be reproduced, with new leaders usually coming from the same social, ethnic, or racial stratum. Women, people from particular ethnic groups, and those from low socioeconomic backgrounds are likely to continue being underrepresented in local or national sport organizations in the foreseeable future (Macintosh & Beamish, 1988).

SOME COMPARATIVE PERSPECTIVES

Researchers have examined class influence in other societies, which vary in culture, degree of industrialization, political structure, or ideology.

Belgium. Among adults in Belgium, Renson (1976) noted that sport involvement is related to the country's class structure. Specifically, participants in skiing, golf, tennis, and fencing are overrepresented by those in the higher social strata. In contrast, gymnastics, calisthenics, track and field, judo, boxing, soccer, and team handball are more popular among the lower strata.

Japan. Takenoshita (1967) noted that before World War II all national and international champion athletes in Japan were college students or college graduates. This reflects the privileged status accorded students before the war. With the rise of industrialization after the war, the students' privileged position was lost, and many industries began to sponsor sport activities. As a result, most male and female champion athletes since World War II have been industrial workers sponsored by their place of employment.

Poland. Although not considered in the purest sense a social class difference, both Starosta (1967) and Nowak (1969) found that successful Polish athletes had differential sport opportunities. For example, most of the students admitted to the Warsaw Figure Skating School were children of parents who belonged to the *intelligentsia*, which are people who have a university education or who hold a high political or military office (Starosta, 1967). In a comparative analysis of fig-

ure skaters from other countries, it was found that figure skaters of international calibre were generally children of well-to-do people who could pay the expenses incurred in pursuing success in this sport. Similarly, although the recruitment process is reversed, Nowak (1969) found that over 70% of the elite Polish boxers were from a working-class family environment, rather than from a peasant or intelligentsia background.

Australia. Pavia (1973) analyzed the social class background of 174 male and female members of the 1972 Australian Olympic team. He found that 60% of these athletes belonged to the upper three social classes. In a more detailed study of a variety of other sports, Pavia and Jacques (1976) noted that, as a group, athletes from the upper class are overrepresented and that a large percentage of the females were of upper-class origin.

Most recently, McKay and Pearson (1986) examined the class backgrounds of 219 Australian athletes who participated in the 1982 Commonwealth Games. Most of the athletes were from the higher socioeconomic strata and most were male. There was a double jeopardy effect for female athletes from a low socioeconomic background, in that they were more underrepresented than any other background in the study. This latter finding suggests that there may be greater social obstacles within sport for females from a lower-class background than for males (Gruneau, 1975; Luschen, 1969). Part of this gender differentiation is no doubt due to the greater availability of jobs in professional sport for males.

Across cultures. Studies of elite athletes in Australia, Great Britain, and New Zealand suggest that children from professional and high-status families are overrepresented in athletics. Again, reality does not support the conventional wisdom that sport is an egalitarian and meritocratic institution. For example, on the basis of a study of British male athletes at the Mexico Olympic Games, Collins (1972) derived the following four categories of sport: *egalitarian* (e.g., swimming, cycling, canoeing); *independent* (e.g., gymnastics and the modern pentathlon, which are not firmly enough established in the British culture to have become class-based); *working-class* (e.g., boxing, weight lifting, and wrestling); and *middle-class* (e.g., track and field, rowing, fencing, field hockey, equestrian).

Eggleston (1965) found that males attending a grammar school (a public school) in England, compared with ex-public (private) school students, were at a disadvantage in competing in cricket and rugby at Oxford and Cambridge. This study was replicated in the United States by Berryman and Loy (1976), who reported that with the exception of basketball those who attended private high schools were overrepresented on Harvard and Yale athletic teams. Similarly, Ulrich (1976) found that

> The lower classes, which after all constitute half of the inhabitants of the FRG (Federal Republic of Germany), do not participate in high-level sport. The failure of many talented athletes to cope with the demands and to overcome the class barriers of today's competitive sport is par excellence a social inequality regarding chances. (p. 148)

Research in a number of countries has demonstrated that class background, race, ethnic background, and gender interact to produce varying degrees of unequal access to and control of amateur and professional sport. As Berry (1977) aptly noted:

> By analogy, a meritocracy is like a fairly contested race in which all

competitors start together and run over the same track, with victory and the spoils going to the quickest. The Australian situation, in contrast, more closely resembles the case where a few competitors start one metre from the finishing line, a few more fifty metres back up the track, a larger group are further back hammering in their starting blocks, others are still changing in a crowded dressing room, while the remainder are at home under the impression that the race starts tomorrow. (p. 43)

Finally, there can be cross-national differences in the prestige ranking of a given sport. Compared to other sports within the country, gymnastics is accorded low status in Belgium (Renson, 1976), middle status in West Germany (Luschen, 1969), and upper-middle status in the United States (Loy, 1972). To explain why this is the case requires an understanding of the historical development of the specific sport, and of sport involvement in general, within each country. Within a given country the status accorded a given sport, and thereby the class background of the participants, can vary over time as a result of social change in the class values and norms in the larger society. The process by which a sport becomes more accessible to and popular among the middle and lower stratum of society is known as *democratization*.

ARE SOCIAL CLASS DIFFERENCES IN SPORT INVOLVEMENT DIMINISHING?

In recent years, North American journalists have noted a trend toward egalitarianism and enhanced democratization within all social institutions. Sport has been cited as one of the systems promoting and facilitating this process of democratization. That is, merit is more important than ascribed attributes in gaining access to sport and achieving success. Similarly, researchers have tried to analyze movement from a situation where sport involvement is elitist and restrictive to a situation where it is more open and equal (i.e., democratization).

Although sports increasingly draw participants from all social backgrounds, some sports are still dominated by those from specific social strata. Similarly, even where a sport (e.g., golf or tennis) represents all class backgrounds, participants tend to play with those of a similar class background (e.g., at private vs. public facilities). Ascriptive criteria seem to control access to certain sport opportunities and sport facilities. Thus, although participation in sport is no longer solely the prerogative of the elite, differential patterns of involvement suggest that unequal opportunities persist.

Gruneau (1975) suggests that modern sport actually contributes to the reinforcement of class distinctions. He illustrates this point by describing membership in Canada's Olympic Trust Committee, a fund-raising arm of the Canadian Olympic Association. Of the 43 members, 30 were members of Canada's corporate elite. And these 30 individuals occupied 85 dominant directorships in 113 major corporations in Canada. Gruneau suggests that this reflects the social closure that remains so much a part of the Canadian class structure. For the task of fund raising, however, these people are needed if the Committee is to succeed. The functionalist would conclude that because this type of person is necessary for this task, the recruitment of new members must be restricted to the business and corporate elite.

The lack of complete democratization is also clearly revealed by an analysis of sport organized on a club basis. Here, rigid mem-

Strict membership criteria at elite sport clubs place limits on the type of people who can belong.

bership criteria (social or economic) effectively eliminate many potential members. To illustrate, Davis (1973) analyzed how many officers and members of the board of directors of two riding associations (the American Horse Shows Association and the United States Equestrian Team, Inc.) were listed in the *Social Register* from 1917 to 1973. The *Social Register* lists only .04% to .05% of the total population of the United States; but Davis found that between 71% and 83% of the executives of these two associations were listed. The organizations were dominated and controlled by socially prominent individuals. Clearly democratization has not affected all sports at all levels.

SOCIAL MOBILITY AND SPORT

The process by which individuals move from one social stratum to another is known as

social mobility. Where there is social inequality in a society, many individuals try to improve their life chances and lifestyle, usually through upward occupational mobility. At the outset, we must recognize that social movement can be cyclical (up and down). Upward mobility may occur when a son or daughter acquires a higher social status (i.e., income and wealth) and lifestyle than the parents or during the life cycle of a specific individual (e.g., from stable boy to jockey to owner).

Is Sport an Avenue of Social Mobility?

Any social movement that takes place can be the result of either *contest* or *sponsored* mobility (Turner, 1960). **Contest mobility**, which is more prevalent in North America, involves earning higher status through personal motivation and ability. That is, an individual competes against others in an open contest. Usually this requires attaining a high level of education and then using the acquired skills in an employment setting.

Sponsored mobility is more likely to be a norm in class-oriented England, where high status is granted to elites on the basis of birth. In contemporary society, however, *sponsored mobility* refers to acquiring status or opportunities through the efforts or assistance of others (e.g., a former professional athlete obtains a highly visible media job for which he has no formal training or experience).

For former athletes, depending on the specific role and situation, both types of mobility may operate. But sponsored mobility seems to be the norm, given the low levels of education generally attained by athletes. This is especially true for members of a minority racial or ethnic group, who may be less likely to have the opportunity or motivation to achieve through education. Early in child-

hood and adolescence they may begin to view sport as a way of improving their position in life. This represents the functional model of sport and mobility.

Given recent evidence, members of some racial and ethnic groups are arguing that sport is dysfunctional for youth as a mobility mechanism. Thus, many black leaders have argued that too much emphasis and time is allocated to sport involvement and the unrealistic dream of its possible riches. Focusing only on sport may lead to a neglected education; after the playing career ends, lack of education can contribute to downward mobility. Unless athletes acquire unique skills or experiences during their sport careers, success may end with sport involvement.

Few black or white athletes (less than 1% of all who ever participate) ever make a team beyond high school, let alone achieve a career in professional sport or the Olympics. Even for the few who become professional athletes, most (except the superstars) have a sport career that only lasts for 5 to 8 years. At the age of 25 to 30, the ex-athlete must be prepared to find other employment. The world of sport absorbs (usually via sponsorship) only a small percentage of former athletes, as coaches, managers, scouts, or officials (Massengale, 1982). Most are left to seek employment in the world outside sport. Lacking the experience and education of their age-peers, they often lose whatever mobility they have achieved and sink to a lower lifestyle or income.

Research studies of former boxers (Weinberg & Arond, 1952), soccer players (Houlston, 1982; Lever, 1969; Semyonov, 1984, 1986), and hockey players (Smith & Diamond, 1976) have shown that any social or economic gains made during the playing career are often lost soon after retirement. Usually only a few star athletes, with very high salary and endorsement earnings, or average athletes with college degrees and off-season

Highlight 7.4
Examples of the Downward Mobility of Former Professional Athletes

Two studies illustrate the lack of upward social mobility experienced by professional athletes. A study by Smith and Diamond (1976) of former professional hockey players in Canada found that 70% of the players ended their careers in the minor leagues, or in a state of downward mobility with less prestige and income. Many continued this downward slide when they entered the labor force.

In Britain professional soccer players, like Canadian hockey players, are recruited primarily from lower socioeconomic backgrounds. Houlston (1982) found that, as expected, ex-soccer players had lower prestige and income than they had during their playing career. The following graph illustrates this pattern of downward mobility by showing the mean occupational earnings at four stages in the athletes' adult lives. Even with inflation in recent years, the present annual salary is considerably less than the highest salary earned during the professional soccer career.

British professional football (soccer) players' pre- and postcareer earnings. *Note.* From "The Occupational Mobility of Professional Athletes" by D.R. Houlston, 1982, *International Review of Sport Sociology*, **17**(2), pp. 15-16. Copyright 1982 by the International Review of Sport Sociology. Adapted by permission.

work experience are able to transfer from a sport career into permanent upward mobility (Kramer & Schapp, 1985). Highlight 7.4 illustrates the extent to which many former professional athletes experience downward social mobility.

It has been stated that there is a relationship between high school and college participation in sport and social mobility. The evidence is conflicting because longitudinal studies are lacking and athletes at these levels have not been compared with nonathletes in the same age group. Moreover, studies that

have shown that athletes experience intergenerational mobility (compared to their fathers) have not been able to fully explain this finding. The outcome could be the result of inflation, enhanced employment opportunities at a specific period in history, or all members of the generation (athletes and nonathletes, males and females, blacks and whites) experiencing mobility due to a higher-quality education.

Recent research has involved panel studies that follow former high school or college athletes into their work years (Howell, Miracle,

---

Highlight 7.5
Do High School Athletics Pay Later Life Dividends?

A recent U.S. study has suggested that athletic participation in high school affects economic achievement, even 11 years after graduation. Based on 964 questionnaires completed by 366 white males, 258 white females, 159 black males, and 181 black females, Picou, McCarter, and Howell (1985) found that the payoffs in terms of greater income and higher occupational attainment varied by subgroup. Specifically, athletic participation was found to be an important predictor of adult achievement for white males only; black females suffered negative consequences from participation. Compared with white nonathletes in the study, white male former athletes averaged $252 per month more in earnings; black male former athletes earned $116 more than black nonathletes.

Why are white males able to cash in on their participation in high school sport? Definitive answers are not yet available. Perhaps they learn skills and values that are useful in other domains, acquire an enhanced self-image, or establish networks that help them later in life. But why can't black males and females capitalize on this early life experience in the same way? Is it that women's sports are devalued and that blacks, regardless of their success in athletics, still face discrimination and unequal opportunities in the labor force? Is it that the positive effects of sport cannot counteract the effects of discrimination? Longitudinal studies with control groups and in-depth interviews concerning career patterns are needed to more fully answer these questions.

& Rees, 1984; Picou, McCarter, & Howell, 1985; Sack & Thiel, 1979). These studies show that involvement in high school and college sport may not have an immediate impact on earnings or social mobility. But athletes who graduated from college may have higher earnings and occupational prestige in midlife than members of their peer group who did not participate in sport, as is described in Highlight 7.5. We do not yet know whether this apparent social mobility is the outcome of sponsorship related to participation in sport, of an open contest based on ability, or of a combination of ability and sponsorship.

Factors Contributing to Upward Mobility

At least four hypotheses exist that describe how active sport participation may facilitate upward social mobility. First, high school athletes must achieve at least a minimal academic level to remain athletically eligible. If they can remain in high school, this increases their chances of being awarded an athletic scholarship (in the United States), which enhances the possibility of their completing a college degree. Thus, athletic scholarships should provide opportunities for many who might not otherwise acquire a college degree. However, as we saw earlier in chapter 3, many athletes never graduate, either because of a lack of ability or interest or because they enter a professional sport career and never return to the classroom.

A second way sport involvement may enhance mobility is that ability in some sports (e.g., tennis, figure skating) may lead directly into a preprofessional training program. Those who survive this path and become successful may have little formal education but high earnings for a number of years. With good financial management, this early success may persist throughout the life cycle. However, in some sports the high cost of early coaching and training may restrict participation to those from the higher social strata, who have little room for upward mobility in any case. Also, high incomes go to the higher visibility positions (e.g., quarterbacks, pitchers) in team sports and to athletes who remain successful in professional sport for at least 10 years.

The third mechanism by which upward mobility may occur is the possibility of making contacts with influential people within or outside sport. These contacts may subsequently sponsor an ex-athlete for preferential treatment in hiring or promotion. Most who acquire sponsorship are highly visible athletes with charisma (e.g., John Madden).

A final hypothesized mechanism of upward mobility results from the possible learning of middle-class attitudes, behaviors, and social skills. Through exposure to coaches, the media, or teammates from a higher social standing, lower-class youth may learn to aspire to higher levels of educational and occupational attainment. They also may acquire the values and skills needed for success in higher prestige occupations. To date, there is little research evidence that socialization via sport can precipitate upward mobility on the social scale.

SOCIAL CLASS, CONFLICT, AND SPORT

A class stratification system raises the possibility of class conflict. The appearance of consensus or conflict is related to the process of social integration. In sport teams, a number of diverse individuals or groups unite into one common group and largely eliminate former social and cultural group differences and previous group identities. The new group has a new identity, which may or may not lead to conflict with other groups that hold different values or goals. This section examines the role of sport in facilitating social integration, in transferring within-group consensus in sport groups to other social issues, in stimulating intergroup conflict, and in controlling the public.

Wohl (1966) argued that within-group integration of social classes during national crises has been facilitated by sport groups. As an example, he described the 1929 to 1934 period of class struggle for power in Poland. Here, the workers' sport organizations unified the working class, which drew most of its leaders from the leaders of sport clubs. Through sport clubs, individuals interacted with those of the same social class. This, in turn, facilitated the learning of common norms and values and the raising of class consciousness.

A similar phenomenon exists in other countries, where class background may explain a large part of the recruitment to membership in sport organizations. To illustrate, Kiviaho (1974a) reported that in Finland the middle and upper strata are overrepresented in the leadership of the Central Sports Federation. In contrast, leaders of the Worker's Sports Federation are from the working class. Kiviaho noted a close link between the political ideologies of the members and the clubs with which they affiliate. In this type of structure there is potential for intergroup conflict arising from underlying differences in political beliefs. Furthermore, Kiviaho (1974b) found that the selection of a favorite Finnish baseball team, in a game where the teams represent different sport organizations, is based more on class division and political opinion than whatever geographical region the team represents. This method of selecting one's favorite team is certainly different from that reported in Great Britain or North America.

In contrast, Dunning and Sheard (1976) describe the process associated with the division of rugby into two different forms: Rugby Union and Rugby League. Although having a common origin, the bifurcation resulted from the growth in power of the working classes in the late 1800s. This led to increasing class consciousness and class conflict, which was partly manifested in the split in the Rugby game along class, regional, and amateur-professional lines. Rugby Union is now played throughout Britain by middle-class amateurs; Rugby League is played by working-class amateurs and professionals in Northern England.

The appearance of class conflict in a sport milieu is further illustrated by the rise of *hooliganism* during and after soccer games in Great Britain. It has been suggested that this type of youth behavior expresses value differences that have arisen because the structure and ethos of the game are no longer working-class. To express their displeasure at the increasing professionalism and middle-class domination of soccer, some working-class youth engage in disruptive and destructive behavior. In this context, soccer serves to increase the conflict among social classes in Great Britain. More is said about this phenomenon in chapter 11.

Sport may also be used by the dominant social class to control the public. Few have attempted to analyze or study this phenomenon, although many claim that sport is the

Rugby leagues have been divided along class lines in Great Britain.

opiate of the masses. One exception is the study by Taylor (1971), which examined the use of football (soccer) by the ruling political party to control the citizens of Mexico. He argued that football is an example of the solidarity of the Mexican people. Thus, public demonstrations associated with football are acceptable; similar demonstrations of a political nature are quelled immediately, often violently. Similarly, city officials sometimes allow sport celebrations to go beyond the normal boundaries of acceptable social behavior to provide participants a time-out from their real lives and to foster community cohesion (see chapter 11).

WRAP-UP

In this chapter we have described ways in which social inequality, as reflected in social class and socioeconomic status differences, can influence life chances and lifestyles in the world of sport and beyond. Social status background does affect access to sport opportunities. Social background can also influence our values and beliefs concerning the importance of sport involvement in leisure time.

We also discussed the meanings of social class and social status and showed that involvement in a variety of sport roles is related to social background. That is, social inequality operates in all societies to open or block access to specific sports and to elite status within sport teams or organizations.

Contrary to conventional wisdom, upward social mobility is not guaranteed to those who successfully compete in college, professional, or Olympic sport in North America. Although athletes may acquire some temporary social mobility during their college or professional careers, unless they graduate from college this mobility falters beyond the playing career. Finally, we saw that where social inequalities are present, there is the potential for conflict to occur within a sport setting.

REFERENCES

Berry, M. (1977). Inequality. In A.F. Davies, S. Encel, & M.J. Berry (Eds.), *Australian society: A sociological introduction* (pp. 18–54). Melbourne: Longman.

Berryman, J., & Loy, J. (1976). Secondary schools and Ivy League letters: A comparative replication of Eggleston's "Oxbridge Blues." *The British Journal of Sociology*, **27**, 61–77.

Clark, M. (1977, March). *Power elites and American sport*. Paper presented at the American Alliance for Health, Physical Education and Recreation National Conference, Seattle.

Collins, L.J. (1972). Social class and the Olympic athletes. *British Journal of Physical Education*, **3**(4), 25–27.

Davis, S.P. (1973). A study of social class and the sport of riding. Unpublished manuscript, University of Massachusetts, Department of Sport Studies, Amherst.

Dunning, E., & Sheard, K. (1976). The bifurcation of Rugby Union and Rugby League: A case study of organizational conflict and change. *International Review of Sport Sociology*, **11**(2), 31–72.

Eggleston, J. (1965). Secondary schools and Oxbridge blues. *British Journal of Sociology*, **16**, 232–242.

Gruneau, R.S. (1975). Sport, social differentiation and social inequality. In D.W. Ball & J.W. Loy (Eds.), *Sport and social order: Contributions to the sociology of sport* (pp. 117–184). Reading, MA: Addison-Wesley.

Gruneau, R.S. (1978). Elites, class and corporate power in Canadian sport: Some preliminary findings. In F. Landry & W.A.R. Orban (Eds.), *Sociology of sport: Sociological studies and administrative, economic and legal aspects of sports and leisure* (pp. 201–242). Miami: Symposia Specialists.

Hasbrook, C.A. (1986). The sport participation—social class relationship: Some recent youth sport participation data. *Sociology of Sport Journal*, **3**, 154–159.

Hasbrook, C.A. (1987). The sport participation—social class relationship among a selected sample of female adolescents. *Sociology of Sport Journal*, **4**, 37–47.

Houlston, D.R. (1982). The occupational mobility of professional athletes. *International Review of Sport Sociology*, **17**(2), 15–26.

Howell, F.M., Miracle, A.W., & Rees, C.R. (1984). Do high school athletics pay? The effects of varsity participation on socioeconomic attainment. *Sociology of Sport Journal*, **1**, 15–25.

Kiviaho, P. (1974a). The regional distribution of sport organizations as a function of political cleavages. *Sportwissenschaft*, **4**(1), 72–81.

Kiviaho, P. (1974b, August). Sport and class conflict in Finland. Paper presented at the 8th World Congress of Sociology, Toronto.

Kiviaho, P., & Simola, M. (1974). Who leads sport in Finland. *Sociologica*, **11**, 267–274.

Kramer, J., & Schapp, D. (1985). *Distant replay*. New York: G.P. Putnam's Sons.

Lever, J. (1969). Soccer: Opium of the Brazilian people. *Transaction*, **7**(2), 36–43.

Loy, J.W. (1972). Social origins and occupational mobility of a selected sample of American athletes. *International Review of Sport Sociology*, **7**, 5–23.

Luschen, G. (1969). Social stratification and social mobility among young sportsmen. In J.W. Loy & G.S. Kenyon (Eds.), *Sport culture and society: A reader on the sociology of sport* (pp. 258–276). Toronto: Macmillan.

Macintosh, D. (1982). Socio-economic, educational, and status characteristics of Ontario interschool athletes. *Canadian Journal of Applied Sport Sciences*, **7**, 272–283.

Macintosh, D., & Beamish, R. (1988). Socioeconomic and demographic characteristics of national sport administrators. *Canadian Journal of Sport Sciences*, **13**(1), 66–72.

Marx, K. (1970). *A contribution to the critique of political economy*. Progress: Moscow. (Original work published 1859)

Massengale, J.D. (1982). The prestigious football university coaching staff: An analysis of sponsored and contest career mobility. In A.G. Ingham & E.F. Broom (Eds.), *Career patterns and career contingencies in sport* (pp. 400–412). Vancouver: University of British Columbia.

McKay, J.P., & Pearson, K. (1986). Sociodemographic characteristics of elite Australian athletes: An exploratory case study. In J. Mangan & R. Small (Eds.), *Sport, culture and society* (pp. 298–305). New York: E. and F.N. Spon.

Metcalfe, A. (1976). Organized sport and social stratification in Montreal: 1840-1901. In R.S. Gruneau & J.G. Albinson (Eds.), *Canadian sport: Sociological perspectives* (pp. 77–101). Don Mills, ON: Addison-Wesley.

Metcalfe, A. (1987). *Canada learns to play: The emergence of organized sport: 1807–1914*. Toronto: McClelland and Stewart.

Neff, C. (Ed.) (1987, April 20). Socioeconomics II [In *Scorecard*]. *Sports Illustrated*, p. 34.

Nowak, W. (1969). Social aspects of Polish boxers and their environment in the light of questionnaires and surveys. *International Review of Sport Sociology*, **4**, 137–150.

Pavia, G.R. (1973). An analysis of the social class of the 1972 Australian Olympic team. *Australian Journal of Physical Education*, **61**, 14–19.

Pavia, G.R., & Jacques, T.D. (1978). The socioeconomic origin, academic attainment, occupational mobility, and parental background of selected Australian athletes. In F. Landry & W.A.R. Orban (Eds.), *Sociology of sport: Sociological studies and administrative, economic and legal aspects of sports and leisure* (pp. 87–95). Miami: Symposia Specialists.

Picou, J.S., McCarter, V., & Howell, F.M. (1985). Do high school athletics pay? Some further evidence. *Sociology of Sport Journal*, **2**, 72–76.

Renson, R. (1976). Social status symbolism of sport stratification. *Hermes*, **10**, 433–443.

Sack, A.L., & Thiel, R. (1979). College football and social mobility: A case study of Notre Dame football players. *Sociology of Education*, **52**(1), 60–66.

Semyonov, M. (1984). Sport and beyond: Ethnic inequalities in attainment. *Sociology of Sport Journal*, **1**, 358–365.

Smith, M.D., & Diamond, F. (1976). Career mobility in professional hockey. In R.S. Gruneau & J.G. Albinson (Eds.), *Canadian sport: Sociological perspectives*. Don Mills, ON: Addison-Wesley.

Starosta, W. (1967). Some data concerning social characteristics of figure skaters. *International Review of Sport Sociology*, **2**, 165–178.

Stephens, T., Furrie, A., and Craig, C.L. (1983). *Fitness and lifestyle in Canada: A Canadian fitness survey report*. Ottawa: Canada Fitness Survey.

Takenoshita, K. (1967). The social structure of the sport population in Japan. *International Review of Sport Sociology*, **2**, 5–18.

Taylor, I.R. (1971). *Social control through sport: Football in Mexico*. Paper presented at the Annual Conference of the British Sociological Association, London.

Tumin, M.M. (1967). *Social stratification*. Englewood Cliffs, NJ: Prentice-Hall.

Turner, R.H. (1960). Sponsored and contest mobility in the school system. *American Sociological Review*, **25**, 855–867.

Ulrich, H. (1976). The social structure of high-level sport. *International Review of Sport Sociology*, **11**(2), 139–149.

Weinberg, S.K., & Arond, H. (1952). The occupational culture of the boxer. *American Journal of Sociology*, **57**, 460–469.

Weber, M. (1958). *From Max Weber; Essays in sociology* (H.H. Gerth & C.W. Mills, Trans.). New York: Oxford University Press.

Wettan, R., & Willis, J. (1976). Social stratification in the New York athletic club: A preliminary analysis of the impact of the club on amateur sport in late nineteenth century America. *Canadian Journal of History of Sport and Physical Education*, **7**(1), 41–53.

Williams, P. (1986). *Where do the trails lead; A focus on the Canadian ski market*. Toronto: Ryerson Polytechnical Institute.

Wohl, A. (1966). Social aspects of the development of rural sport in Poland according to research. *International Review of Sport Sociology*, **1**, 109–135.

C H A P T E R 8

Race, Ethnicity, and Sport

Just as "amateur gentlemen" at one time would not lower themselves to compete with "professionals" of lesser moral character, so too have whites sometimes sought to avoid competing with people of other races in sport. Where whites constitute the numerical majority in a society, they tend to impose their rules on blacks and other **minority groups**. As a result of prejudices and stereotypes, **institutional discrimination** on the basis of skin color occurs in some societies and within sport. This **discrimination** involves differential treatment and opportunities among individuals who are identical in all relevant characteristics—except race.

Race (like gender, ethnic background, nationality, or age) should be an irrelevant characteristic in interpersonal relations, but the attribute often becomes subject to value judgments. That is, people with certain attributes are assigned less value and receive less favorable treatment from others. In the United States, blacks may be excluded or discouraged from participating in some sport settings. To illustrate, blacks were excluded from major league baseball until 1947 and were forced to establish their own segregated leagues (Peterson, 1970). In the early years of professional baseball, spectators were often segregated by race. Similarly, in Australia,

193

the native aborigines receive little encouragement to participate at the national or international level unless they can demonstrate an exceptionally high level of proficiency or success.

The casual observer of professional sport in North America might claim that black athletes are highly visible and successful in the more popular team sports, and in boxing and track and field. Indeed, people in the United States have argued that sport

- is a model of the extent to which racial equality can be attained in a society;
- facilitates the integration of blacks into the dominant society;
- provides a viable avenue for the upward mobility of blacks; and
- is devoid of the racial segregation and discrimination found in other areas of social life.

Some journalists have glorified sport as an ideal model of race relations. Boyle (1963) and Olsen (1968), respectively, stated the following:

> Sport has often served minority groups as the first rung on the social ladder. As such, it has helped further their assimilation into American life. (p. 100)

> Every morning the world of sport wakes up and congratulates itself on its contribution to race relations. (p. 7)

In reality, however, racism was common in the sport press from the 1920s until well into the late 1960s (Mead, 1985; Tygiel, 1983). In the late 1980s, as you recall from chapter 6, racist attitudes are still periodically expressed, directly or indirectly, especially on television sport shows.

The questionable validity of the claim made in the 1960s that sport is a model of race relations has resulted in much research, debate, and civil action in recent decades. Most of this discussion has centered on males rather than females, and on the extent to which sport involvement facilitates or inhibits the integration of blacks into all facets of American society. In the following sections we describe the extent to which blacks and ethnic minorities are involved in sport and discuss the sources and consequences of racial and ethnic inequalities.

HISTORY OF BLACK INVOLVEMENT IN SPORT

Discrimination has been present in most societies where, usually because of historical events, one group acquires a superordinate position over one or more other groups. Social class, wealth, and education can generate subtle forms of discrimination. However, discrimination is more likely to occur and to become institutionalized on the basis of race or ethnicity, because these attributes are inherited and visible and cannot be changed or removed. Institutionalized discrimination has evolved in North America through the social evaluation of groups and individuals on the basis of their racial or ethnic origins. Members of many racial and ethnic groups have been involved in North American sport since late in the 19th century, although none has been as involved or successful as blacks. As a result, most of the literature that focuses on discrimination in the sociology of sport has been concerned with black athletes in professional, college, or Olympic sport.

A detailed historical account of black involvement in sport is beyond the scope of this chapter (see Wiggins, 1986). Some evidence suggests that many of the professional athletes in Ancient Greece were black. Since that time, blacks' involvement in institutionalized sport has been characterized by cycles of segregation and integration, depending on the value and role of sport in a particular society.

In North America, black slaves often boxed for the entertainment of other slaves and their master. They also fought against other blacks in contests sponsored by owners, who frequently bet large sums of money on the match. Successful black boxers gained preferential treatment and status; occasionally they and their families were freed. In this way social mobility and increased opportunities through boxing were available for a few blacks in early American society.

Throughout the 1800s and early 1900s, black athletes were highly involved in individual sports such as boxing and racing. For example, 14 of the 15 riders in the first Kentucky Derby in 1875 were black; a black jockey named Isaac Murphy was the first to win three Kentucky Derby races; and a black boxer, Thomas Molineaux, gained fame in England and the United States in 1800 as the first heavyweight boxing champion.

There were black baseball teams as early as 1880. However, a few black baseball stars were able to play in the National or American leagues. Increasing discrimination in the late 1800s forced blacks out of horse racing, and by 1898 the last black was eliminated from professional baseball of that era (Peterson, 1970). Only in boxing were they allowed to continue competing, and even here they often had to agree to lose before they could obtain a match (Boyle, 1963). Faced with institutionalized discrimination, blacks formed their own baseball (Peterson, 1970) and basketball leagues in the 1920s.

Since 1947, when Jackie Robinson became a member of the Brooklyn Dodgers (Dodson, 1954; Tygiel, 1983), black representation in professional and college sport has increased, especially following the 1954 Supreme Court ruling that made racial segregation illegal. The civil rights movement of the 1960s, and the revolt of U.S. black athletes before and at the 1968 Mexico Summer Olympics also drew attention to the problem, and indirectly led to greater representation in some sports (Edwards, 1969). Members of the white sport establishment began to realize, as well, that black athletes could significantly contribute to the athletic success of a team and thus increase revenues. It was not until well into the 1970s, however, before some athletic teams at southern colleges were desegregated, before a black quarterback started in the NFL, before a black manager was appointed in baseball, and before a black golfer could compete in the Master's Golf Tournament. Some of you may recall the media attention in January 1988 that focused on Doug Williams, the first black to start at quarterback in the Super Bowl. Similarly, the first black was appointed to work as a head referee in the 1988-89 NFL season.

RACE AND PRIMARY SPORT INVOLVEMENT

Blacks comprise approximately 13% of the U.S. population. According to recent newspaper and magazine reports, the representation of blacks is approximately 75% in the NBA; 55% in the NFL; and 20% in the American and National baseball leagues. Berghorn, Yetman, and Hanna (1988) report that blacks comprise 61% of the male and 30% of the female players in Division I of NCAA basketball. In each sport the percentage varies from team to team (i.e., there are differences among cities and regions). In professional baseball, the percentage of blacks has decreased in recent years, perhaps because more Hispanic players are recruited. This decrease may also be due to the fact that more blacks are attracted to track, basketball, and

Table 8.1   The Relationship Between the Racial Composition of a City and Its NBA Team

Percentage of blacks in the city	Racial composition of team (1980–1981)	
	Black (%)	White (%)
Less than 10%	63.6	36.4
10% to 20%	72.7	27.3
More than 20%	87.3	12.7
Total for the league	72.7	27.3

Note. From "Color on the Court" by J. Karabel and D. Karen, 1982, February 10–16, *In These Times*, pp. 23, 24. Copyright 1982 by Jerome Karabel and David Karen. Adapted by permission.

Table 8.2   The Percentage of Black Players in the NCAA by Region (1985)

Region	Men (%)	Women (%)
Northeast	38	16
Midwest	44	16
West	49	20
South	61	40

Note. Data from "Racial Participation and Integration in Men's and Women's Intercollegiate Basketball: Continuity and Change, 1958–1985" by F.J. Berghorn, N.R. Yetman, and W.E. Hanna, 1988, *Sociology of Sport Journal,* 5, pp. 107–124. Copyright 1988 by Human Kinetics. Adapted by permission.

other sports where opportunities have increased.

The pattern of city differences is most evident in professional basketball, where there appears to be a relationship between the racial composition of the city and the racial composition of the basketball team. Table 8.1 suggests that there may be a conscious attempt to match the proportion of blacks on a team to the proportion of blacks living in the city. Indirectly, this relationship implies that owners adjust the number of blacks or whites on a team to attract black or white fans to the game. Similarly, in NCAA basketball, the percentage of black men and women during the 1985 season varied regionally as shown in Table 8.2.

Blacks are also heavily involved in boxing and in track and field, but much less involved in most other spectator sports (e.g., hockey, tennis, golf, and many Olympic events). Highlight 8.1 shows the disproportionate representation of black male and female athletes on U.S. Olympic teams over a 44-year period.

An increasing number of blacks are involved in college and professional sport and

it is important to realize that many of them are highly successful (Samson & Yerles, 1988). They are often high draft choices, all-stars, and recipients of league (e.g., Heisman Trophy) and championship (e.g., MVP) awards for their outstanding levels of performance. The explanation for this increasing number of highly successful black athletes is probably more rooted in the social structure of society than in the hypothesized biological superiority of blacks. Nevertheless, there are still only about 2,400 blacks employed in all professional sports in North America (Edwards, 1984).

RACE AND SECONDARY SPORT INVOLVEMENT

As consumers and producers of sport, black spectators have moved from sitting in segregated sections to integrated seating and from not being involved to positions as officials, both on and off the playing field. Differences in the extent to which blacks are involved as fans now result from black subcultural values (Rudman, 1986) and historical

Highlight 8.1
The Racial Composition of U.S. Olympic Teams

In order to document the degree of integration of black athletes into Olympic teams over time, Kjeldsen (1984) analyzed individual and team photographs in books published by the United States Olympic Committee following the 1936, 1960, and 1980 Summer and Winter Olympic Games.

When Summer and Winter Olympic teams were combined, the results showed that, compared with the U.S. Census estimate of blacks in the U.S. population, representation increased slightly during these years (see accompanying chart). In all three Olympiads black women were highly underrepresented on teams where both men or women could compete (e.g., archery, fencing, judo, yachting). However, on women's teams they increased their representation from 2.6% in 1936 to 21.8% in 1980.

Compared with the general population, blacks moved from a position of underrepresentation in 1936, to near parity in 1960, to a slight overrepresentation in 1980. There were also important differences by sport. Blacks have always at least attained parity, and have usually been overrepresented, in track, basketball, and boxing. In contrast, they have been highly underrepresented on winter teams, on many summer teams, and as coaches. There has been a growth in representation, but the increase has certainly not paralleled that achieved in the professional team sports of basketball, football, and baseball.

Black athletes were represented on 15.4% of the U.S. Olympic teams in 1956, 23% in 1960, and 35.3% in 1980. Most of the sports in which they were underrepresented or not represented were those associated with the upper social classes (e.g., rowing, swimming, yachting, equestrian). In a few specific sports, black male and female athletes now comprise the majority of the team (e.g., basketball, boxing, and track).

The pattern of increased access by blacks to involvement in mainstream society seems to be reflected in greater opportunities to represent their country in the Olympic Games, although parity or an equal opportunity has certainly not been achieved.

Year	Combined representation of blacks on Summer and Winter Olympic teams (%)	Representation of blacks in U.S. population (%)
1936	3.7	11.1
1960	11.2	11.5
1980	14.6	12.1

Note. Data from Kjeldsen, 1984.

patterns rather than from overt **prejudice** or segregation.

Few blacks have been appointed to sport leadership positions (e.g., coaches, managers, officials, executives, and owners) except in basketball. To illustrate, 55% of the players in the NFL in 1986 were black. Black athletes scored 81% of the touchdowns, and all starting cornerbacks on the 10 playoff teams were black. Yet there were no black head coaches and only 34 assistant coaches—about 1 per 10-man staff. In professional baseball, where about 20% of the players are black, only 2% of the top administrative positions are held by blacks. Only three blacks have ever been a manager in the major leagues. It is interesting that following the racist comments of Al Campanis in 1987, Peter Ueberroth, the commissioner of baseball, hired Harry Edwards (as a sign of affirmative action) to help create more management positions for blacks.

Where blacks do gain coaching opportunities, it is mainly as an assistant coach or in the minor leagues (Fabianic, 1984). In Division I of the NCAA in 1987, blacks occupied only 3 of 105 head football coaching positions; 2 of 105 athletic directorships; and 29 of 283 head basketball coaching positions (Lederman, 1987). Similarly, although the number has increased in recent years, blacks are underrepresented among the journalists and announcers who report the games in which so many blacks participate (Chu & Segrave, 1981). To illustrate, a USA Today survey (Shuster, 1987) found that in baseball there were only 4 blacks among the 254 writers who cover the major leagues on a full-time basis, 5 blacks among 141 television broadcasters (excluding national broadcast networks' employees), and no black play-by-play announcers or analysts on local English-language radio.

UNEQUAL OPPORTUNITIES FOR EQUAL ABILITY?

In trying to explain why blacks have not gained greater access to college and professional sport teams, some have suggested that there is unequal opportunity for equal ability (Yetman & Eitzen, 1972). That is, a black player must demonstrate greater skill than a white player in order to have an equal chance of being recruited or drafted. This may also apply to remaining on a team or being designated a starter. This pattern is more likely to occur if performance is judged subjectively by a coach or manager (e.g., football linemen) than if the performance is judged by more objective measures of time, distance, or face-to-face competition (e.g., tennis, track and field events). It may also vary by sport, city, and league and may vary over time, depending on prevailing civil rights legislation and on personal media-generated attitudes, values, or beliefs (e.g., stereotypes).

The argument of unequal opportunity for equal ability was frequently proposed in the 1960s and 1970s. To illustrate, Pascal and Rapping (1972) reported that on the average black players in professional baseball must perform at higher levels in batting and fielding if they are to have an equal chance of moving into the major leagues. Scully (1974) concluded that black baseball players must outperform whites throughout their careers if they want to remain in the major leagues. Similarly, Yetman and Eitzen (1971) found that blacks on college basketball teams were overrepresented in the star category in all regions of the country, perhaps because only sure black starters were likely to be recruited. Some anecdotal evidence for this latter practice is revealed by Al McGuire, who stated:[1]

---

[1]*Note.* From "Al McGuire Was in Town Last Week" by R. Lipsyte, 1971, March 1, *The New York Times*, p. 37. Copyright © 1971 by The New York Times Company. Reprinted by permission.

Unequal opportunity for equal ability means that a black player must demonstrate greater skill than a white player in order to have an equal chance of being recruited or drafted.

... the ghetto environment of the black demands that he be a star. . . . He could never justify an understudy's role to himself or to [those] . . . left behind . . . there is no point recruiting blacks who will not start (Lipsyte, 1971).

Today, this "be better" argument is seldom made, and evidence for it is lacking (Hill & Spellman, 1984; Mogull, 1981). However, some NBA players still claim that marginal white players get more playing time than marginal or average black players. They refer to this phenomenon as *stealing*; that is, whites steal positions on a team that could be occupied by higher-ability black players (Karabel & Karen, 1982).

The "be better" pattern also has implications for explaining hypothesized income differentials by race. In the 1960s it was argued that there was unequal pay for equal ability, in both salaries and endorsement opportunities for professional black athletes. Quite likely, in the absence of player agents and players' associations, black athletes did not complain about lower salaries because they were satisfied just to have the opportunity to participate. Then, with the civil rights movement and resulting revolt of black athletes in the late 1960s and early '70s (Edwards, 1969), blacks began to complain of salary discrimination when compared with whites of perceived equal ability.

A number of well-designed studies in the 1970s and 1980s (Christiano, 1986, 1988; Hill

& Spellman, 1984; Mogull, 1981; Pascal & Rapping, 1972; Raimondo, 1983) indicated that there is little wage discrimination by race in major league baseball. Indeed, it has been reported (Hill & Spellman, 1984; Pascal & Rapping, 1972; Scully, 1974) that the average salaries of black players are, for some playing positions, higher than those of white players. To illustrate, Christiano (1988) found that, based on the reported 1987 salaries for 356 veteran major league hitters (pitchers and rookies were not included in the analyses), the mean salary was $488,137 for blacks and $425,210 for whites. This represents a 15% difference in favor of black players, which may reflect the generally higher average level of performance by black players. Christiano (1988) concluded, after a comprehensive series of analyses, that there is no longer any reliable evidence of economic discrimination by race in professional baseball.

Other economic areas in which blacks may experience discrimination are the size of bonuses received for signing initial contracts and opportunities to make money from commercial endorsements. Pascal and Rapping (1972) reported that although blacks received smaller bonuses when they were first permitted to play major league baseball (in 1947), by the mid-1960s the difference between the races was minimal or nonexistent. They did find, however, that black athletes were underrepresented in television commercials. Even before the steroid scandal, much was written about the inability of Ben Johnson (the "World's Fastest Human" in 1988) to sign endorsement contracts, although this probably had more to do with his Canadian citizenship and his difficulty speaking in public than with his being black.

A Quota System?

A factor that has limited the entry of blacks to professional teams is an alleged informal quota system. According to this argument, only a certain number of blacks are permitted on the team or in the starting line-up. Journalists, based on interviews with black athletes, have suggested that such a system operates in college and professional sport. One reason for a possible quota system is the need to attract more affluent white fans to the game. It is difficult to substantiate through research evidence the existence of a quota system, other than to note anecdotal media statements. One such statement was made in 1982 by the new owner of the Cleveland Cavaliers in the NBA (Karabel & Karen, 1982). He stated:

> This is not to sound prejudiced, but half the squad would be white. . . . I think the Cavs have too many blacks, 10 of 11. You need a blend of black and white. (p. 22)

Not unexpectedly, one year after he bought this predominantly black team, there were six whites and five blacks on the payroll.

Although claims of a quota system continue, they occur less frequently than in the 1970s (Lapchick, 1984). Indeed many starting line-ups in basketball consist almost entirely of black players.

Stacking by Player Position

Related to the alleged quota system is the phenomenon of **stacking** (Curtis & Loy, 1978, 1979). Here, blacks must compete among themselves for a limited number of specific positions that have been designated *black positions* (e.g., cornerback or fullback in football, forward in basketball, outfield in baseball). Often, black positions are the noncentral positions on a team. Central positions are closer to most of the action (e.g., second base, quarterback, nose tackle). They involve

Table 8.3   Positional Segregation of Blacks in Professional Baseball

Position	Representation of blacks (%) 1970	Representation of blacks (%) 1984
Infield (central)	33	34
Outfield (noncentral)	48	44
Pitcher (nonclassified)	19	23

Note. From "Positional Segregation and the Economic Hypothesis" by M.H. Medoff, 1986, *Sociology of Sport Journal*, **3**, p. 301. Copyright 1986 by Human Kinetics. Adapted by permission.

greater interaction with other players and offer higher visibility. Some empirical evidence indicates that blacks are more likely to be found in noncentral positions in specific sports.

A common explanation for stacking is that it evolves from stereotypes held by coaches and the public that blacks have more physical ability and less mental ability and, thus, fit better in some positions. A second explanation is that once the practice becomes institutionalized, black youth target these noncentral positions early in their sport career. That is, they see these positions as the only viable opportunity for a black player. It is often argued that stacking contributes to team cohesion and inhibits racial conflict, because direct interracial competition for a position is avoided. Stacking also ensures a balance of black and white players on a team.

The classic study by Loy and McElvogue (1970) noted that blacks are overrepresented in baseball in the outfield positions, and in football on defense (especially as defensive back) and in the offensive backfield. Table 8.3 shows that although there has been a slight decline in black representation in noncentral (outfield) positions in baseball, blacks still predominantly occupy outfield positions.

We should note that these data only pertain to stacking according to defensive alignment. Studies have not considered baseball's offensive alignment, represented by the batting order. Here the skill and power positions (numbers 3, 4, and 5 in the order) are often held by black athletes, who, incidentally, also are often outfielders.

Similar patterns seem to occur in other sports as well. For example, blacks were at one time more likely to play the two forward positions in basketball. But the game has changed since the 1970s, and black players are now as likely as whites to play the guard and forward positions. However, as of 1985 there remained a substantial racial imbalance at the center position in men's college basketball: blacks 35%, whites 65% (Berghorn, Yetman, & Hanna, 1988). These same authors also reported a tendency for black female basketball players in the NCAA to be stacked at the forward (27%) or guard (23%) positions, with only 19% of the centers being black.

Now that blacks seem to be *over*represented in sport, compared with their numbers in the general population, they are more readily gaining access to all playing positions. However, Curtis and Loy (1979), in the most detailed analysis of this phenomenon, conclude that there is still stacking of black players in noncentral positions in professional baseball and professional and college football. Furthermore, black players seem likely to be shifted from infield to outfield positions between their first and fifth years in baseball (Guppy, 1983). The degree of stacking seems to have declined in basketball, particularly at the center position (Leonard, 1987); but the practice continues, although to a lesser degree than 20 years ago, in football (Best, 1987) and baseball (Curtis & Loy, 1979).

Alternative Explanations of Stacking

Journalists, sociologists, and advocates of equal rights have argued that blacks play noncentral positions because of discrimination and segregation by the majority group. Indeed, numerous explanations for positional segregation have been proposed (Berghorn, Yetman, & Hanna, 1988; Chu & Griffey, 1982; Curtis & Loy, 1979; Guppy, 1983; Loy, McPherson, & Kenyon, 1978; Medoff, 1986; Yetman, 1987). The competing explanations focus on biological, psychological, economic, and cultural factors.

Biological Explanations. Biological studies have found significant anatomical and physiological differences between blacks and whites. Some have inferred that blacks have certain genetic advantages that make them more suitable or superior for the requirements of specific sport positions. These inferential studies are based on mean differences for the general population and ignore the wide individual differences within each racial group. Moreover, these studies have not compared top-level athletes in the major sports to determine whether there are significant biological differences between those who occupy the position and those who do not.

Psychological Explanations. Worthy and Markle (1970) proposed that whites tend to excel at self-paced activities. They described a *self-paced* activity as "one in which the individual responds, when he chooses, to a relatively static or unchanging stimulus" (p. 439). A *reactive* activity "is one in which the individual must respond appropriately and at the right time to changes in the stimulus situation" (p. 439).

To test their thesis, Worthy and Markle examined racial variations in professional baseball and basketball. First, they hypothesized that because pitching is a self-paced activity and hitting a reactive activity, whites would excel as pitchers and blacks would excel at other positions. In support of this hypothesis, they found that in major league baseball 7%

of the pitchers were black and 24% of the nonpitchers were black. Second, they hypothesized that free-throw shooting is self-paced and field-goal shooting is reactive. They argued that difference scores derived by subtracting the percentage of successful field-goal attempts from the percentage of successful free-throw attempts would be higher for whites than blacks. In support of their hypothesis, they found that whites had significantly higher difference scores than blacks.

The evidence supporting Worthy and Markle's hypothesis is inconclusive. But the hypothesis may account for why blacks are overrepresented in reactive playing positions such as the outfield, running back, wide receiver, and cornerback and underrepresented in self-paced sports such as bowling, golf, and swimming. It does not explain why blacks are underrepresented in such reactive sports as autoracing, fencing, skiing, squash, and tennis.

Social Psychological Explanations. Some have argued that it is the early self-imposed socialization and personality development of blacks that leads to their occupying specific positions. For example, Jones and Hochner (1973) suggested that black athletes, in contrast to white athletes, emphasize individual rather than team orientation and stress style or expressive performance rather than success or technical performance. Although Jones and Hochner only cite examples from basketball, their observations could be extended to the performance of black athletes in outfield positions in baseball, and in the running back, wide receiver, and defensive back positions in football.

Another social psychological model hypothesizes that because success increases visibility, those occupying a given position will be imitated by novices (McPherson, 1975). This *minority group socialization hypothesis* argues that black youth seek to play the specific sport roles they see blacks playing in professional sport. There is little direct empirical support for this hypothesis. However, there appear to be some differences in the early socialization experiences of black and white athletes. To illustrate, Brower (1972), based on interviews with 23 white and 20 black high school athletes, found that 90% of the black athletes reported having one or more black athlete role models. On the other hand, white athletes had a high and almost equal number of black (70%) and white (78%) athlete role models. A majority of the black football players in the sample aspired to play traditionally black positions, whereas the white players aspired to play positions open to blacks and whites.

In a direct empirical test, Castine and Roberts (1974) concluded that there was some support for the modeling hypothesis. They found that 57% of the black college athletes in their sample who had a black idol played the same position as the idol when they were in high school. Further, 48% of these athletes played the same position as their idol while in college. Thus, blacks may learn and subsequently occupy specific roles held by those who have attained success. Eitzen and Tessendorf (1975) note that "although the role model hypothesis does not explain the initial discrimination that caused early entry blacks to take non-central positions, it helps explain why . . . the pattern of discrimination by player position tends to be maintained" (p. 325).

Economic Explanations. The social psychological explanations described earlier imply that positional segregation in sport is self-initiated. That is, they suggest that blacks, because of particular personality orientations and unique socialization experiences, seek out specific sports and particular playing positions. Thus, their marked overrepresentation in given sports and playing positions does not result from discriminatory practices.

One type of economic explanation also endorses the self-selection thesis. In brief, this explanation argues that black athletes are predisposed to select playing positions that offer the greatest opportunity for individual achievement, prestige, popularity, and monetary rewards. For example, outfield positions in baseball and running back, wide receiver, and cornerback positions in football typically involve independent tasks, have a great deal of visibility, receive more publicity, and generally are associated with higher average salaries than other playing positions. This type of economic explanation does *not* explain the underrepresentation of blacks among catchers, pitchers, and quarterbacks. Nor does it explain the absence of blacks in the lucrative sports of professional golf or tennis. It may partially explain black involvement in boxing.

Another economic explanation is based on the work of Medoff (1977). He argued that blacks may be stacked in noncentral positions because it costs less to train and coach blacks to play these positions. However, as the general economic status of blacks has improved, they have been more likely to gain access to positions that in the past may have been beyond their reach financially. Specifically, Medoff (1986) suggests that, because blacks are now more likely to attend integrated schools and have more equal access to better facilities, coaching, and equipment, the cost to develop their skills has gone down significantly. He argues that we have seen the disappearance of stacking in basketball and that more blacks are playing central positions in baseball (i.e., the infield) and football (e.g., quarterback). Considerable debate has arisen concerning the economic hypothesis. Some evidence suggests that the assumptions and data used for this argument are not valid (Phillips, 1988; Yetman, 1987).

Sociocultural Explanations. These explanations of positional segregation argue that there are discriminatory processes within sport. One explanation at this level suggests that there is social stereotyping by coaches, managers, and owners. For example, Williams and Youssef (1972, 1975) have shown in the context of college football that coaches stereotype football positions. That is, they judge some personal characteristics to be more important for success in some football positions than in others. Coaches also stereotype players according to race.

Findings similar to those of Williams and Youssef have been reported by Brower (1972) in the context of professional football. He reported that black athletes are overrepresented at playing positions believed to require strength, quickness, emotion, instinct, and speed. They are underrepresented at those positions believed to require intellect, leadership, poise under pressure, finesse, technique, and control. Another explanation, alluded to earlier, is that white coaches and players prefer not to interact with blacks and encourage or force blacks to occupy noncentral positions. However, given the recent evidence that blacks are successful in a number of sport positions, typical arguments that black players lack the intelligence or leadership skills for certain positions are simply unacceptable.

RACE, SPORT, AND EDUCATIONAL ATTAINMENT

College coaches and administrators argue that participation in sport improves blacks' opportunities to receive an education and thereby improves their social opportunities. A close analysis, however, suggests that although athletic ability may permit some athletes to receive grants-in-aid from colleges, there is no guarantee they will acquire a quality education (Leonard, 1986). Indeed, numerous scholarly and journalistic articles, especially in the last few years, have reported that many athletes, black and white, often fail to graduate because they lack sufficient credits or required courses. And because of questionable admission standards, many lack the academic preparation they need to succeed in the college classroom.

Edwards (1984) reports that an estimated 25% to 35% of black high school athletes cannot accept an athletic scholarship offer because of academic deficiencies at the high school level. More recently, an NCAA survey found that at least 600 athletes who failed to meet the minimum academic standards to compete in college sport were enrolled in Division I schools in September 1987. More than 60% of these nonqualifiers were black (Lederman, 1988).

The pattern of low graduation rates is even more pronounced for those who become professional athletes. For example, between 70% and 80% of all players in the NFL or NBA have not graduated from a college or university. As Highlight 8.2 illustrates, studies show that black athletes are less likely than white athletes to graduate. It is not surprising that concern over the exploitation of black student athletes is increasing (Leonard, 1986).

Propositions 48 and 42

To introduce more control over the academic qualifications of athletes admitted to college, the NCAA introduced Proposition 48 on August 1, 1986. The rule applies only to Division I athletics and requires that entering freshmen have a minimum 2.0 cumulative grade point average based on six, seven, or eight semesters in a core curriculum of at least 11 academic courses. This curriculum must include at least three courses in English, two in mathematics, two in the social sciences, and two in the natural or physical sciences,

---

Highlight 8.2
U.S. College Graduation Rates of Athletes by Race

Since the 1970s Americans have been increasingly concerned about both the quality of education received by college athletes and their graduation rates.

In 1981, the NCAA completed a study of 46, primarily Division I, institutions and found that of the athletes who entered college as freshmen in the fall of 1975, 43% of the football players, 42% of the basketball players, and 49% of the baseball players had graduated 5 years later ("Athletes' Graduation Rates," 1981). Unfortunately, graduation rates were not reported for black and white athletes separately, even though many scholars and civil rights advocates have argued that blacks are less well prepared for the college classroom and may be exploited to a greater extent by college coaches.

Two small studies (Kiger & Lorentzen, 1986; Shapiro, 1984) at specific institutions have found that across all sports, but particularly in the major revenue sports, black athletes have higher attrition rates, lower grade point averages, and lower graduation rates than their white counterparts. To illustrate, Shapiro (1984) reported that the graduation rate over a 25-year period was 74% for white athletes and 57% for black athletes. Clearly there is a need for more extensive national surveys to compare the graduation rates for black and white athletes at all types of universities and in all sports.

---

and completion must be certified on the high school transcript or by official correspondence. In addition, the student must have a combined score of at least 700 on the verbal and math sections of the Scholastic Aptitude Test (SAT) or a composite score of at least 15 on the American College Test (ACT). Previously, the NCAA only required an entering athlete to have an overall 2.0 average in high school, however it was attained. The average must now be attained in a mandatory core curriculum. This regulation attempts to raise the minimum academic standards for incoming athletes. It also offers greater assurance that those admitted can read and write and have a reasonable chance of graduating with their class, or at least soon thereafter.

In 1989, Division I schools strengthened Proposition 48 by passing Proposition 42, which becomes effective in 1990. This ruling states that student-athletes must obtain at least a 2.0 GPA in the core curriculum and a minimum score on the SAT or ACT test to be eligible for financial aid while sitting out their freshman year.

Reactions to and Results of Proposition 48

This legislation has generated two opposing reactions from blacks. Those who support the legislation claim it is long overdue. They believe the rule will reduce the exploitation of blacks who are recruited primarily to enhance gate receipts and television revenues.

Those opposed to the rule argue that

- it is unconstitutional, because it creates a double standard for admission (one for athletes, another for nonathletes);
- it will severely penalize black colleges who need and want to remain competitive at the highest level of competition (Division I);
- the scores of 700 (SAT) and 15 (ACT) as cut-off points were selected arbitrarily; and
- the rule discriminates against blacks, who are not prepared for standardized tests (SAT, ACT) that may be biased toward the belief, knowledge, and value systems of white America (Williams, 1983).

In support of the latter argument, Edwards (1984) reported that of the students taking the SAT test in 1981, 51% of black males, 26% of males in other minority groups, and 9% of white males failed to achieve a combined score of at least 700.

It is argued that the net outcome of Proposition 48 will be twofold. First, there will be fewer black athletes on Division I football and basketball teams. Second, blacks will lose an opportunity to achieve a college education. Colleges can still recruit and support freshman athletes who do not meet the Proposition 48 criteria. But the athletes cannot practice or play until they are eligible.

In short, Proposition 48 calls for a greater emphasis on academic performance among high school athletes aspiring to a college sport career. With this greater emphasis on academic achievement, athletes will have a much better chance of completing a quality educational program. And if they do graduate, they will be better prepared to compete in society when they retire from sport.

RACE RELATIONS AND SPORT

Does participation on interracial sport teams promote intergroup cohesion and reduce prejudices? Scholars have proposed that exposure to other racial groups, in a situation where there is a common group goal and equal status, should lead to positive changes in intergroup attitudes and behaviors. This is known as the *contact hypothesis*, which suggests basically that close contact reduces prejudices. However, increased contact could have little or no effect on existing prejudices. Or it could lead to an increase in prejudice and conflict, if previous beliefs are confirmed or enhanced by closer interaction.

With the integration of blacks into college and professional sport, it has been argued that black athletes have been totally integrated into American society. But despite integration on the playing field and in the locker room, black athletes claim that they are still subjected to the same prejudices and discrimination as other blacks, often by their own teammates. This feeling may be compounded by black and white athletes who, like others in society, prefer to spend their leisure time with those of similar class, age, and racial backgrounds.

At the recreational and amateur sport level, a number of studies have examined the effect on attitudes and interaction of involvement on interracial teams. The evidence to date suggests that little, if any, permanent change in attitudes or prejudices occurs from participating on an interracial team (Chu & Griffey, 1982, 1985; Rees & Miracle, 1984).

Competing against a team comprised exclusively of members of another race may actually increase racial hostility. This situation may result in violent game or postgame behavior by players and spectators, respectively. Sport thus may provide yet another social setting where deep-rooted inequality and discrimination are reinforced. In fact, sport may visibly demonstrate that race relations are still strained in America (Edwards, 1969; Lapchick, 1984).

Competition between blacks and whites in sport may increase racial hostility when underlying prejudicial attitudes already exist.

ETHNICITY AND SPORT

Multicultural or multinational societies such as the United States and Canada have relatively liberal immigration policies. The social structure is likely to be stratified along ethnic characteristics, across the society and within specific social strata (Yinger, 1985). This results when minority groups are differentiated on the basis of language, national origin, or culture. Generally, the closer members of a given **ethnic group** are to the perceived average member of a society (e.g., white and middle class in North America), the more likely they are to be viewed as normal and nonthreatening. In this way they earn a higher relative ranking in the social structure. The relative standing of a particular group is often a function of

- how recently it arrived in the host society;

- its degree of residential concentration in urban areas;
- its size;
- the type of occupations its members tend to pursue; and
- the extent to which its members are perceived as remaining isolated from mainstream society.

It is assumed that members of ethnic groups, through contact with the majority group, eventually assimilate into the dominant society by adopting the values, norms, beliefs, behaviors, customs, and language of the host society. This process has been referred to as a *melting pot*. However, some ethnic groups or individuals remain isolated within the physical and social environment of their own ethnic community (e.g., Chinatown). As Greeley (1971) suggests:

Ethnic groups . . . even if they are not subcultures (and I suspect they are)—are at least substructures of the larger society, and in some cities, comprehensive substructures. The Polish community in Chicago, for example; the Jewish community in New York; the Irish community in Boston; the black community of Harlem all represent a pool of preferred associates so vast and so variegated that it is possible, if one chooses, to live almost entirely within the bounds of the community. (p. 47)

Most ethnic groups go through a four-stage process of integration into the host society. This involves contact, competition, accommodation, and assimilation. However, there is an important difference between cultural and structural assimilation, both of which must occur before the ethnic group is no longer part of the stratification system. In most instances, there is little structural assimilation, and ethnic groups do not gain completely equal access to the major associations and institutions of the dominant group. Thus, even where interethnic group contact is frequent, some ethnic groups retain elements of culturally specific behaviors and values. As a result, some degree of ethnic diversity is maintained in a society. This same ethnic diversity can be found in sport (Allison, 1979).

Ethnic Group Involvement in Sport

During some periods of history, members of specific ethnic groups have tended to dominate particular sports. At other times, members of certain ethnic groups have experienced discrimination within sport settings. Riesman and Denney's (1951) study of football in America shows that there is a close

Sport involvement of ethnic groups in the United States corresponds to the history of immigration patterns.

correspondence between the history of major immigration patterns to the United States and the recruitment of members of ethnic groups to intercollegiate football. For example, most of the earliest non-Anglo-Saxon collegiate football players were of German, Irish, and Jewish backgrounds. This corresponds to the large number of immigrants from these groups, who came to America between 1790 and 1880. The next ethnic wave into collegiate football circles came largely from eastern and southern Europe, between 1880 and 1930. Similarly, where Jews once dominated basketball in the early 1900s (when it was associated with the Ys) and the Irish prevailed in boxing, these sports are now dominated primarily by blacks.

The involvement of ethnic group members in sport often parallels or follows shifts in migration or immigration waves. For example, before World War II professional sport teams in New York City hired ballplayers of

Jewish and Italian descent to attract a particular type of immigrant audience to the games. After World War II, there was a mass migration of rural southern blacks to northern cities. This was followed by increasing primary and secondary involvement by blacks in professional sport (Harney, 1985).

The presence of an ethnic stratification system within sport in another culture is described by Semyonov and his colleague (Semyonov, 1984, 1986; Semyonov & Yuchtman-Yaar, 1981). They illustrate how ethnicity is a central dimension in the Israeli stratification system. The two major ethnic groups are Jews of European or American origin and Jews of Asian or African origin. While the two groups are about equal in size, the former were the original settlers and hold the higher status positions. Consequently, Jews of European or American origin living in Israel have had more favorable opportunities for achievement in education, at work, and in sport.

For Canadian or American Indians, there is involvement in both traditional native games and in more modern sports, especially by those on reservations. In many instances, North American Indians use indigenous sporting contexts to express and maintain identity, thereby resisting assimilation into mainstream society (Cheska, 1987). In Canada, lacrosse was originally an Indian game. The game was taken over by whites in the 1850s and became, ironically, an example of discrimination and segregation between cultural groups. Once professional lacrosse became popular, Indians were recruited to play on white teams but experienced segregation and discrimination away from the playing field.

In the United States, there is extensive involvement by some Navajo Indians in basketball (Allison, 1980) and by some Choctaw Indians in baseball (Blanchard, 1980). Another recent example in North America is the increased involvement of the Inuit in cross-country skiing. For the most part, however, Native Americans and Native Canadians seldom compete at the college, professional, or Olympic level. Is this because of discrimination, lack of opportunity, or a cultural system that devalues sport involvement in order to resist assimilation?

For recent immigrant groups, participation in competitive sport is likely to be minimal in the early years. Most of their time is devoted to making a living. However, there may be some recreational involvement in sport that is closely related to their cultural roots (e.g., soccer). Members of the second generation, born and educated in the host society, begin to assimilate the adolescent and adult value system of the dominant society. They may view sport as an avenue of assimilation and mobility and become involved in traditional team sports. Some may aspire to compete at the professional or Olympic level. By the third generation, some degree of social mobility and assimilation has likely occurred. The members of this generation often become involved in individual sports that are more characteristic of the lifestyles of the middle class and beyond (e.g., racket sports, golf, jogging). At the same time, this generation may place less emphasis on a sport career and more on success through educational and occupational attainment.

The Case of French-Canadians

The French were an early ethnic group to settle and develop North America. Today, they are most visible in the province of Quebec, in Canada. Cultural differences persist in Quebec, with a dominant English culture (Anglophones) and a minority French culture (Francophones), which defies assimilation. From the earliest contact between the French and English there were segregated social and sport clubs, although there were contests between the two groups. Recent evidence suggests that this segregation has continued and has led to an underrepresentation of French-Canadians at national and international sport events. That is, structural barriers impede equal opportunities for participation and success in sport in the larger societal context.

French-Canadians, who mostly live in the province of Quebec, comprise about 31% of the Canadian population. Relative to their proportion of the general population, they are underrepresented in sport. This underrepresentation has been documented for professional hockey and for Canada's Olympic teams. To illustrate, French-Canadian representation in the 1936, 1960, and 1980 Olympic Games only increased from 6.4% to 10.2% to 15.6%, respectively (Boileau, Landry, & Trempe, 1976; Kjeldsen, 1984). In 1980, the following Canadian Olympic teams had two or fewer French-Canadians on the team: boxing, canoeing, basketball, judo, men's track and field, rowing, shooting, alpine skiing, luge, bobsled, nordic skiing, yachting, figure skating, equestrian, and wrestling. Moreover, for these 15 sports, 6 did not have a single French-Canadian on the team.

In the National Hockey League, French-Canadians account for only 12% of the Canadian players. Moreover, the number of French-Canadian players has declined by 37% in the past 10 years (from 78 of 478 players to 49 of 532 players). Some of this decline can be attributed to the changing demands of the game. Size and defensive skills are perceived as more important than flashy offensive skills—a traditional characteristic of the Quebecois style of hockey. Some of the attrition could result from English-Canadian Scouts ignoring French-Canadian players, who are thus not drafted (Lavoie, 1989). More recently, younger players state that they are quitting hockey because they do not want to leave their cultural roots and language to play for a team in the United States or Western Canada (Coulombe & Lavoie, 1985).

Although the explanation for underrepresentation by French-Canadians on Canadian teams is frequently assumed to be discrimination, some alternative explanations focus on

- a disadvantaged opportunity set in the sport milieu in Quebec for the necessary early socialization into sport roles;
- the underdevelopment, until the 1980s, of the organization of sport in Quebec;
- a deemphasis of sport in what has traditionally been a rural and parish social life;
- language difficulties with Anglophone coaches; and
- a lack of physical education and interscholastic sport programs in many parts of the province.

Recent changes in Quebec have led to sport being more highly valued by politicians and the general population. French-Canadians have assumed the leadership of a large number of sport associations within the province, and the provincial team finished first in the 1987 Canada Winter Games. With changing values and increased economic resources dedicated to sport, the number of French-Canadians at the professional and Olympic levels should increase, assuming there is little or no institutional discrimination.

ETHNICITY, SPORT, AND SOCIAL CONFLICT

Social integration of minority groups occurs through the process of acculturation and structural assimilation. Thus, sport organizations provide one medium where individuals might realize full participation in the social institutions of the host or dominant group (McKay, 1975; Pooley, 1981; Wohl, 1966). For example, Wohl describes how the introduction of volleyball into a Polish peasant community led to group identification and subsequent sport competitions with neighboring villages. Sport competitions came to replace the intervillage fights that were previously taken quite seriously by those involved, although the fights had never attained the status of attracting spectators. The volleyball competitions served as a mechanism that more fully integrated all segments of the village—young and old, male and female, wealthy and poor. Similarly, baseball has been used in Pueblo Indian society to enable youth to act out aggressive and competitive tendencies in an essentially noncompetitive social system (Fox, 1961).

Assimilation or Diversity?

There is a continuing debate as to whether society should encourage ethnic groups to assimilate into the host society (the *melting pot theory*) or maintain their ethnic identity and diversity (the *cultural mosaic theory*). In reality, the process of assimilation represents a continuum and not a dichotomy (all or none). The degree of assimilation experienced by an ethnic group can range from total isolation or segregation to complete structural and cultural assimilation, thereby losing all former ethnic identity.

A few studies (McKay, 1975; Pooley, 1981) have examined whether sport teams sponsored by ethnic clubs facilitate or inhibit the assimilation of these athletes into mainstream society. It has been found, based on surveys of soccer teams at the community level, that assimilation may occur where the members of the team come from diverse ethnic backgrounds. If a club is exclusively comprised of team members from the same ethnic group, assimilation is less likely to occur. This greater integration into the ethnic community occurs primarily because the ethnic language and customs are used on the playing field, at team meetings, and at all social events.

Further evidence for this lack of assimilation is available for the ethnic groups in two different cultures. First, in a recent study that compared athletes and nonathletes among Turkish migrant workers in West Germany, the athletes were no more likely to be integrated into German society than the nonparticipants (Frogner, 1985). Similarly, participation in a Japanese-American youth basketball league did not promote assimilation into the mainstream American culture. Instead, participation in the ethnic sport club tended to promote ethnic solidarity and structural pluralism among the Japanese-American males. Highlight 8.3 describes this phenomenon.

It must also be recognized that acculturation and assimilation are not unidirectional processes, as is so often assumed (Allison, 1982). That is, ethnic groups may adopt the game or sport of the host society but maintain culturally specific behaviors and values with respect to the game. To illustrate, the Navajo Indians do not play the traditional aggressive style of American basketball, yet they are highly skilled players (Allison, 1980). Similarly, French-Canadian and European hockey players emphasize skating and scoring (offense) rather than bodychecking and fighting.

In short, ethnic groups may develop their own definitions of achievement or style of play that best fit their cultural roots. Eventually the style or strategy of the game in the host society may change as elements of the ethnic playing style are assimilated by members of the dominant society. Some recent examples of this are the European style of hockey in North America and black cultural

---

Highlight 8.3
Japanese-American Basketball Leagues:
A Source of Ethnic Solidarity or Cultural Assimilation?

Japanese-Americans are often perceived as one of the most mobile, adaptive, and Westernized immigrant groups in the United States. Most members of this group appear to actively seek upward economic mobility and to experience rapid acculturation.

In order to determine whether participation in an ethnic basketball league in Japanese-American communities accelerates or retards the rate of assimilation into American society, Nogawa and Suttie (1984) studied 50 basketball players and 36 nonplayers who were 15 to 18 years old. The study was conducted over a season and measured six different dimensions of assimilation: cultural, structural, marital, identificational, attitude-receptional, and behavior-receptional.

Significant differences were found between the two groups in the structural,

marital, and identificational dimensions of assimilation. This suggests that participation in the ethnic basketball league retarded the rate of assimilation in these three areas. For the other three dimensions of assimilation, the lack of significant differences indicated that participation in an ethnic league did not inhibit assimilation and may have facilitated the establishment and maintenance of ethnic solidarity.

Studies of other ethnic groups and other sports have yielded equally equivocal findings concerning the role of sport in cultural and structural assimilation. Whether sport inhibits or facilitates assimilation probably depends on the ethnic group involved, the meaning of the sport to the ethnic group, and the degree to which the host society values the sport.

---

elements (high five, slam dunk, run and shoot) in college and professional basketball.

Social Mobility

Similar to the situation for black athletes in the United States, members of some ethnic groups have sought to achieve social mobility through sport involvement. However, not all ethnic groups see sport as a viable avenue to improve their life chances. Rather, the cultural and educational values of a particular ethnic group may influence first-generation

parents to strongly discourage sport involvement by their children. Similarly, some ethnic groups may encounter discrimination and discouragement in their attempts to participate in sport settings, especially if they are recent arrivals and comprise large numbers. That is, they may be perceived as a threat to the majority group.

The sport many immigrants of European or Third World origin are most likely to pursue is soccer. But soccer is not a viable avenue to large salaries, endorsements, or stable employment in North America. Thus, few ethnic group members, at least until the second or third generation have experienced social mobility through sport in North America.

WRAP-UP

Given the evidence of the proportion of blacks involved in various primary and secondary sport roles, one could easily conclude that there is little or no racial discrimination in sport. Indeed, because blacks are overrepresented in many professional team sports, one might conclude that democratization has occurred within sport in America.

But black females remain underrepresented and there appears to be underrepresentation of blacks in the positions of coach, executive, manager, owner, official, and media personnel. Moreover, various types of differential treatment by race are hypothesized to exist within sport, including a restricted opportunity to occupy specific positions (e.g., stacking and quota systems); unequal opportunity for equal ability; exclusion from promotion to the role of manager or executive after retiring from play; lower bonuses, salaries, and endorsements; and inequity in the quality of college education acquired. The amount of evidence to support or refute these varying forms of differential treatment by race is inconclusive and seems to vary depending on the time and location of a given research study.

Similar patterns and outcomes can be found for members of ethnic groups who become involved in sport. Moreover, sport involvement has been proposed as a social activity that can either facilitate assimilation into the host society or strengthen ethnic solidarity and ethnic identity. To date, the evidence for both of these views is equivocal. Perhaps this occurs because the processes vary by sport, community, ethnic group, economic climate, and length of time the ethnic group has lived in the host society.

We must conclude from the evidence that there still exist differential opportunities in the sport system, which vary by race and ethnicity. Although much of this evidence pertains to professional sport, similar patterns exist in elite amateur sport and among the many who participate in amateur sport. There is little evidence that sport is a democratic institution with respect to the involvement of minorities or members of ethnic groups, although the opportunity for more equal involvement has increased in recent years.

REFERENCES

Allison, M.T. (1979). On the ethnicity of ethnic minorities in sport. *International Review of Sport Sociology*, **14**(1), 89–95.

Allison, M.T. (1980). *A structural analysis of Navajo basketball*. Unpublished doctoral dissertation, University of Illinois, Urbana-Champaign.

Allison, M.T. (1982). Sport, ethnicity and assimilation. *Quest*, **34**, 83–91.

Athletes' graduation rates surpass nonathletes'. (1981, April 30). *NCAA News*, p. 1.

Berghorn, F.J., Yetman, N.R., & Hanna, W.E. (1988). Racial participation and integration in men's and women's intercollegiate basketball: Continuity and change, 1958–1985. *Sociology of Sport Journal*, **5**, 107–124.

Best, C. (1987). Experience and career length in professional football: The effect of positional segregation. *Sociology of Sport Journal*, **4**, 410–420.

Blanchard, K. (1980). Sport and ritual in Choctaw society: Structure and perspective. In H. Schwartzman (Ed.), *Play and culture* (pp. 83–91). Champaign, IL: Leisure Press.

Boileau, R., Landry, F., & Trempe, Y. (1976). Les Canadiens-francais et les grands jeux internationaux (1908–1974) [French-Canadian participation in international sport events (1908–1974)]. In R.S. Gruneau & J.G. Albinson (Eds.), *Canadian sport: Sociological perspectives* (pp. 141–169). Don Mills, ON: Addison-Wesley.

Boyle, R.H. (1963). A minority group: The Negro baseball player. In R.H. Boyle (Ed.), *Sport: Mirror of American life* (pp. 100–134). Boston: Little, Brown.

Brower, J.J. (1972, April). *The racial basis of the division of labor among players in the National Football League as a function of racial stereotypes.* Paper presented at the Pacific Sociological Association annual meeting, Portland, OR.

Castine, S.C., & Roberts, G.C. (1974). Modeling in the socialization process of the black athlete. *International Review of Sport Sociology, 9*(3/4), 59–74.

Cheska, A. (1987). Ethnicity, identity and sport: The persistence of power. *International Review for the Sociology of Sport, 22,* 99–108.

Christiano, K.J. (1986). Salary discrimination in major league baseball: The effect of race. *Sociology of Sport Journal, 3,* 144–153.

Christiano, K.J. (1988). Salaries and race in professional baseball: Discrimination 10 years later. *Sociology of Sport Journal, 5,* 136–149.

Chu, D.B., & Segrave, J.C. (1981). Leadership recruitment and ethnic stratification in basketball. *Journal of Sport and Social Issues, 5*(1), 15–22.

Chu, D.B., & Griffey, D.C. (1982). Sport and racial integration: The relationship of personal contact, attitudes and behavior. In A.D. Dunleavy, A.W. Miracle, & C.R. Rees (Eds.), *Studies of the sociology of sport* (pp. 271–282). Fort Worth: Texas Christian University Press.

Chu, D.B., & Griffey, D.C. (1985). The contact theory of racial integration: The case of sport. *Sociology of Sport Journal, 2,* 323–333.

Coulombe, S., & Lavoie, M. (1985). Les francophones dans la ligue nationale de hockey: Une analyse economique de la discrimination [Francophones in the National Hockey Leagues: An economic analysis of discrimination]. *L'Actualité Économique. Revue d'Analyse Économique, 61*(1), 63–72.

Curtis, J.E., & Loy, J.W. (1978). Positional segregation in professional baseball: Replications, trend data and critical observation. *International Review of Sport Sociology, 13*(4), 5–21.

Curtis, J.E., & Loy, J.W. (1979). Race/ethnicity and relative centrality of playing positions in team sports. In R.S. Hutton (Ed.), *Exercise and sport sciences reviews.* (Vol. 6, pp. 285–313). Philadelphia: Franklin Institute.

Dodson, D.W. (1954). The integration of Negroes in baseball. *Journal of Educational Sociology, 28*(October), 73–82.

Edwards, H. (1969). *The revolt of the black athlete.* New York: Free Press.

Edwards, H. (1984). The collegiate athletic arms race: Origins and implications of the Rule 48 controversy. *Journal of Sport and Social Issues, 8*(1), 4–22.

Eitzen, D.S., & Tessendorf, I. (1975). Racial segregation by position in sports: The special case of basketball. In D.M. Landers, D.V. Harris, & R.W. Christina (Eds.), *Proceedings of the 2nd Conference of the North American Society for the Psychology of Sport and Physical Activity* (pp. 321–332). University Park: Pennsylvania State University Press.

Fabianic, D. (1984). Minority managers in professional baseball. *Sociology of Sport Journal, 1,* 163–171.

Fox, J.R. (1961). Pueblo baseball: A new use for old witchcraft. *Journal of American Folklore, 74,* 9–15.

Frogner, E. (1985). On ethnic sport among Turkish migrants in the Federal Republic of Germany. *International Review for the Sociology of Sport*, **20**, 75–85.

Greeley, A. (1971). *Why can't they all be like us? America's white ethnic groups*. New York: E.P. Dutton.

Guppy, N. (1983). Positional centrality and racial segregation in professional baseball. *International Review of Sport Sociology*, **18**(4), 95–108.

Harney, R.F. (Ed.) (1985). Sports and ethnicity [Special issue]. *Polyphony: The Bulletin of the Multicultural History Society of Ontario*, **7**(1).

Hill, J.R., & Spellman, W. (1984). Pay discrimination in baseball: Data from the seventies. *Industrial Relations*, **23**(1), 103–112.

Jones, J.M., & Hochner, A.R. (1973). Racial differences in sport activities: A look at the self-paced versus reactive hypothesis. *Journal of Personality and Social Psychology*, **27**(1), 86–95.

Karabel, J., & Karen, D. (1982, February). Color on the court. *In These Times*, pp. 23, 24.

Kiger, G., & Lorentzen, D. (1986). The relative effects of gender, race and sport on university academic performance. *Sociology of Sport Journal*, **3**, 160–167.

Kjeldsen, E.K. (1984). Integration of minorities into Olympic sport in Canada and the USA. *Journal of Sport and Social Issues*, **8**(2), 29–44.

Lapchick, R. (1984). *Broken promises: Racism in American sports*. New York: St. Martins/Marek.

Lavoie, M. (1989). Stacking, performance differentials, and salary discrimination in professional ice hockey: A survey of evidence. *Sociology of Sport Journal*, **6**(1), 17–35.

Lederman, D. (1987, November 11). Organizer of protest at 1968 Olympics hints at boycott of big games by black players. *The Chronicle of Higher Education*, p. A40.

Lederman, D. (1988, May 4). 600 enrolled but failed to meet NCAA academic standards, study finds. *The Chronicle of Higher Education*, p. A44.

Leonard, W.M. (1986). The sports experience of the black college athletes: Exploitation in the academy. *International Review for the Sociology of Sport*, **21**, 35–49.

Leonard, W.M. (1987). Stacking in college basketball: A neglected analysis. *Sociology of Sport Journal*, **4**, 403–409.

Lipsyte, R. (1971, March 1). Al McGuire was in town last week. *The New York Times*, p. 37.

Loy, J.W., & McElvogue, J.F. (1970). Racial segregation in American sport. *International Review of Sport Sociology*, **5**, 5–24.

Loy, J., McPherson, B.D., & Kenyon, G.S. (1978). *Sport and social systems*. Don Mills, ON: Addison-Wesley.

McKay, J.P. (1975). *Sport and ethnicity: Acculturation, structural assimilation, and voluntary association involvement among Italian immigrants in metropolitan Toronto*. Unpublished master's thesis, University of Waterloo, Ontario, Canada.

McPherson, B.D. (1975). The segregation of playing position hypothesis in sport: An alternative explanation. *Social Science Quarterly*, **55**, 960–966.

Mead, C. (1985). *Champion: Joe Louis, black hero in white America*. New York: Scribner.

Medoff, M.H. (1977). Positional segregation and professional baseball. *International Review of Sport Sociology*, **12**(1), 49–54.

Medoff, M.H. (1986). Positional segregation and the economic hypothesis. *Sociology of Sport Journal*, **3**, 297–304.

Mogull, R.G. (1981). Racial discrimination in professional sports. *Arena Review*, **5**(2), 12–15.

Nogawa, H., & Suttie, S.J. (1984). A Japanese-American basketball league and the assimilation of its members into the mainstream of United States society. *International Review for the Sociology of Sport*, **19**, 259–271.

Olsen, J. (1968). *The black athlete: A shameful story; The myth of integration in American sport*. New York: Time-Life.

Pascal, A.H., & Rapping, L.A. (1972). The economics of racial discrimination in organized baseball. In A.H. Pascal (Ed.), *Racial discrimination in economic life*. Lexington, MA: Lexington Books.

Peterson, R. (1970). *Only the ball was white*. Englewood Cliffs, NJ: Prentice-Hall.

Phillips, J.C. (1988). A further comment on the "economic hypothesis" of positional segregation in baseball. *Sociology of Sport Journal*, **5**, 63–65.

Pooley, J.C. (1981). Ethnic soccer clubs in Milwaukee: A study of assimilation. In M. Hart & S. Birrell (Ed.), *Sport in the socio-cultural process* (3rd ed., pp. 430–447). Dubuque, IA: Wm. C. Brown.

Raimondo, H. (1983). Free agents' impact on the labor market for baseball players. *Journal of Labor Research*, **4**(Spring), 183–193.

Rees, C.R., & Miracle, A.W. (1984). Participation in sport and the reduction of racial prejudices: Contact theory, superordinate goals hypothesis or wishful thinking? In N. Theberge & P. Donnelly (Eds.), *Sport and the sociological imagination* (pp. 140–152). Fort Worth: Texas Christian University Press.

Riesman, D., & Denney, R. (1951). Football in America: A study of culture diffusion. *American Quarterly*, **3**, 309–319.

Rudman, W.J. (1986). The sport mystique in black culture. *Sociology of Sport Journal*, **3**, 305–319.

Samson, J., & Yerles, M. (1988). Racial differences in sports performance. *Canadian Journal of Sport Sciences*, **13**(2), 109–116.

Scully, G. (1974). Discrimination: The case of baseball. In R. Noll (Ed.), *Government and the sports business: Studies in the regulation of economic activities* (pp. 221–275). Washington, DC: Brookings Institution.

Semyonov, M. (1984). Sport and beyond: Ethnic inequalities in attainment. *Sociology of Sport Journal*, **1**, 358–365.

Semyonov, M. (1986). Occupational mobility through sport: The case of Israeli soccer. *International Review for the Sociology of Sport*, **21**, 23–31.

Semyonov, M., & Yuchtman-Yaar, E. (1981). Professional sports as an alternative channel of social mobility. *Sociological Inquiry*, **51**(1), 47–53.

Shapiro, B.J. (1984). Intercollegiate athletic participation and academic achievement: A case study of Michigan State University student-athletes, 1950–1980. *Sociology of Sport Journal*, **1**, 46–51.

Shuster, R. (1987, June 26). Black baseball writers rare, too. *USA Today*, p. 8C.

Tygiel, J. (1983). *Baseball's great experiment: Jackie Robinson and his legacy*. New York: Oxford University Press.

Wiggins, D.K. (1986). From plantation to playing field: Historical writings on the black athlete in American sport. *Research Quarterly for Exercise and Sport*, **57**(2), 101–116.

Williams, A. (1983). The impact of Rule 48 upon the black student athletes: A comment. *Journal of Negro Education*, **52**, 362–373.

Williams, R.L., & Youssef, Z.I. (1972). Consistency of football coaches in stereotyping for personality of each position's player. *International Journal of Sport Psychology*, **3**(1), 3–11.

Williams, R.L., & Youssef, Z.I. (1975). Division of labor in college football along racial lines. *International Journal of Sport Psychology*, **6**(1), 3–13.

Wohl, A. (1966). Social aspects of the development of rural sport in Poland according to research. *International Review of Sport Sociology*, **1**, 109–135.

Worthy, M., & Markle, A. (1970). Racial differences in reactive versus self-paced sports activities. *Journal of Personality and Social Psychology*, **16**, 439–443.

Yetman, N.R. (1987). Positional segregation and the economic hypothesis: A critique. *Sociology of Sport Journal*, **4**, 274–277.

Yetman, N.R., & Eitzen, S. (1971). Black athletes on intercollegiate basketball teams: An empirical test of discrimination. In N.R. Yetman (Ed.), *Majority and minority: The dynamics of racial and ethnic relations* (pp. 509–517). Boston: Allyn and Bacon.

Yetman, N.R., & Eitzen, D.S. (1972). Black Americans in sports: Unequal opportunity for equal ability. *Civil Rights Digest*, **5**(1), 20–34.

Yinger, M. (1985). Ethnicity. *Annual Review of Sociology*, **11**, 151–180.

Yuchtman-Yaar, E., & Semyonov, M. (1979). Ethnic inequality in Israeli schools and sports: An expectation-states approach. *American Journal of Sociology*, **85**, 576–590.

C H A P T E R 9

Gender, Age, and Sport

Throughout much of history, women have been perceived as inferior to men and have been denied access to equal opportunities in most social institutions, including sport. Research evidence has shown that women are not biologically or intellectually inferior to men; rather, they have somewhat lower limits of physical potential. To illustrate, with increased opportunity to participate and train, the percentage difference between males and females in the time for the marathon decreased from 37.2% in 1963 to 11.7% in 1980 (Ferris, 1981). Similarly, the percentage difference in the 100-meter sprint decreased from 18.8% in 1927 to 8.0% in 1984 (Dyer, 1986).

Research has also shown that simply being female influences social status, life chances, and lifestyles. These differences persist to varying degrees across societies and within the various institutions in a given society. In most cultures, male roles have been valued more than female roles. This differentiation results in the **social problem** of a dominant-subordinate relationship between the genders (Messner, 1988). Questioning this relationship has sometimes generated social conflict, as with the women's movement in the 1960s and the suffragette movements in the early 1900s in the United States and Canada.

Within the primarily male-oriented and male-dominated world of sport, a number of myths have evolved concerning the extent to which females should be involved. Many of these myths have been initiated and perpetuated by the medical and teaching professions and by journalists. These unfounded beliefs suggest, for example, that female participation in sport at any level

- is harmful to the female reproductive system and a threat to childbearing;
- masculinizes a female, particularly her facial and upper-body appearance:
- threatens the development of male masculinity if girls out-perform adolescent boys in sport;
- wastes human and economic resources because females' performance levels are lower than males'; and
- is not important for their social development, because they do not need or value achievement, aggressiveness, competitiveness, independence, or productivity.

Although scientific evidence refutes these beliefs, many males and females in the general population cling to them tenaciously. The net result is that many females, despite recent advances, still encounter barriers to involvement in sport. And these beliefs are perpetuated in the sex-role socialization of succeeding generations.

GENDER DEFINED

Gender refers to a cultural or social definition of what it is psychologically to be male and female; **sex** refers to the dichotomous phys-

iological differences between males and females. The term *gender* is used when referring to the process of learning the roles of man and woman, boy and girl. *Gender relations* concern the social relations between males and females. In most social contexts, males have more power then females. **Sexism** is a term that refers to those values, beliefs, and norms that support the definition of one gender as less worthy and capable.

Because gender is a socially defined concept, it is possible to change gender relations and make them more equal. We simply need to find ways of persuading males and females to accept definitions of equal worth for the two genders.

HISTORY OF WOMEN'S INVOLVEMENT IN SPORT

The study of female involvement in sport reveals an interesting example of social change, both within and across cultures. This social change has involved cultural definitions of femininity; the normative behavior expected of males and females in all social institutions; the number and kind of sport opportunities provided to women, compared with men; and varying rates of cultural change across societies (e.g., Eastern Europe vs. North America vs. China vs. India).

Attitudes Toward Women's Sport Involvement

Although many goddesses in Ancient Greece exhibited physical prowess and many mythic stories (e.g., Atlantis, the Amazons) stressed the superiority of women, only males competed in the famous athletic festivals that were the precursors of the Olympic Games. Moreover, women were prohibited from attending the contests as spectators. The Greeks later

Defying the attitudes of the era, these women played basketball on a 1911 university team.

established the Hera Games to provide opportunities for women to compete. By the Medieval era, women—especially those in the upper class—were encouraged to attend jousting and other selected events as spectators, because these were viewed as social events.

In general, women did not publicly participate in physical activities to any great extent until the late 19th century. Even then, only "functional" activities such as riding horses (side-saddle only), skating (on the arm of a gentleman at first), and cycling (at first as passengers only) were considered appropriate activities for "ladies" (Gerber, Berlin, Felshin, & Wyrick, 1974; Lucas & Smith, 1978; Spears, 1978; Boutilier & SanGiovanni, 1983).

Despite women's strides in the late 19th century, many thought female athletes were contrary to the Victorian concept of an ideal woman. Participation and competition re-

mained restricted, and debate continued through the 1950s as to whether women should compete at all. Highly competitive athletic events such as the Olympic Games sparked particularly heated debate. To some extent this debate continues over distance, strength, and endurance events, although current record times of women in some swimming and track events exceed those of men who competed in the same events before World War II. Also, the differential between male and female records in the same event has decreased considerably in the past 50 years. Surprisingly, the 1984 Olympic Games introduced the marathon for women and still closed competition in the 5,000- and 10,000-meter races.

Biases Against Female Competition

The arguments against female participation in sport are often based on a set of beliefs left over from the Victoria era. Victorians believed that the ideal woman should perform her patriotic duties of attracting a mate, bearing and rearing children, and serving her husband. Any social activity that might restrict or interfere with these responsibilities was discouraged or prevented. Medical and journalistic opinions perpetuated the myth of the frail female, and early feminists argued that to sweat and strain was unfeminine.

The arguments were primarily based on two unfounded sets of beliefs. First, people drew on physiological, biological, and medical opinions (usually expressed by males) that sport was harmful to women. Second, people sought to perpetuate culturally based definitions of ideal "feminine" dress and behavior. Women often sanctioned these definitions.

These beliefs resulted in stereotypes that became part of the informal gender-role socialization process of succeeding generations.

These stereotypes governed women's involvement in sport. Sometimes these beliefs were institutionalized as bizarre local laws. For example, it is illegal, according to local law, for women in Nacogdoches, Texas, to wink at men at a track meet. In Colby, Kansas, a woman cannot wear a hat while playing golf. In Joplin, Missouri, it is against the law to knit at football games.

Highlight 9.1 illustrates medical and journalistic opinions as well as cultural beliefs regarding women's sport participation. While most of these are opinions from the past, it is clear that they have affected present-day beliefs.

GENDER AND INVOLVEMENT IN SPORT

During World War II, women played major roles in the military and civilian labor force, thus shattering myths of the fragile female. For a number of reasons, women now participate in greater numbers, in a greater variety of sport events, and at higher levels of performance: medical and physiological research that refutes earlier opinions about the lower ability and capacity of females; the women's movement in the 1960s, combined with the fitness boom of the 1970s; and greater numbers of visible female role models (e.g., Babe Didrickson, Billy Jean King, Althea Gibson). Despite these advances, equality of opportunity has not yet been achieved or offered and progress is painfully slow.

Primary Involvement

It is difficult to estimate the extent to which women, compared with men, are involved in recreational sport and physical activity. Some recent cross-sectional national surveys in North America suggest that participation has increased in a limited set of activities. Females are still much less involved than men at all ages. In one of the largest surveys, people in almost 12,000 households (22,000 persons in total; 12,200 females) responded to the 1981 Canada Fitness Survey (1984). Female respondents reported an increase in *sport* activity from 46% participating in 1976 to 72% participating in 1981. The percentage of females engaged in *exercise* activities increased from 58% to 71%. Thus, women were more likely to be involved in exercise than in sport as a form of physical activity in 1976. Since then, the difference in the two types of activity has disappeared, perhaps suggesting that sport has become more socially acceptable and that more sport opportunities are available. Clearly, more women are jogging, entering marathon and triathlon races, and playing racket sports.

It must be recognized that activity levels (and likely opportunity) are highest among women who are young, single, or well educated. Moreover, women who are full-time students or employed full time are more likely to be active than housewives, regardless of age. In short, married women appear to have less leisure time. They may also have less freedom to plan when, where, and how to use their leisure time, which may be more interrupted and less predictable (Fasting & Sisjord, 1985; Shaw, 1985).

A serious concern raised by available data is that there appears to be little difference in the activity levels of active girls and boys up to about age 12. At about age 12 or 13, among those girls who have been active we begin to see a steady decrease in the percentage who remain active throughout the middle and later adolescent years. This decline does not begin for boys until age 16 or 17, with the greatest decline at age 18 or 19 after they leave high school. Highlight 9.2 describes a longitudinal analysis of this declining sport involvement by adolescent girls and intro-

Highlight 9.1
Past Medical, Journalistic, and Cultural Opinions
About Women's Sport Participation

Medical Beliefs

Early medical practitioners thought sport posed hazards for the "weaker" gender. Lenskyj (1984) cites this turn-of-the-century opinion:

Kenealy, a female doctor, commented in 1899 on: the passing of a dainty, elusive quality in the face of the athletic woman, whose "bicycle face" was characterized by muscular tension where formerly there had been sympathy and tenderness.

In the early 1900s, concern was shown for women's priorities, in which reproducing perforce came first. Parry, 1912, had this opinion: "The reproductive system is often dwarfed by the force going to overdeveloped arms and legs" (p. 347).

This concern for women's reproductive systems was further reinforced by Westman (1939):

The male organism is used by nature to produce, while the female is made to reproduce. . . . Too much activity in sports of a masculine character causes the female body to become more like that of a man. This holds good not only in regard to the outward appearance, but in regard to the genital organs, for they tend to decay. The monthly preparations for proliferation, which was previously normal, is disturbed, and may even cease altogether; the power to proliferate may be lost (pp. 648).

Westman also felt sport was "useless as well as harmful in relation to the primary tasks of woman's life, maternity" (p. ix).

Twin (1979) helps to summarize these opinions, noting that doctors ascribed all kinds of fashionable female disorders to overactivity:

Physicians warned that too much activity unnerved females, creating everything from hysteria to dyspepsia. Since the uterus, they thought, was connected to the nervous system, nervous shocks induced by overexertion threatened reproduction and might lead to weak and degenerate offspring. Women were to conserve the little energy they had (p. xviii).

Journalistic Opinions

Similar beliefs were printed and reinforced by the news media. Consider this opinion printed in *The Mail* in 1890:

The [female] sex should avoid any pursuit or diversion which necessarily involves violent running. She can do it after a fashion . . . but the movement is . . . a kind of precipitate waddle with neither grace, fitness, nor dignity.

(Cont.)

Highlight 9.1 Continued

In the early 1900s it was de Coubertin who most vocally protested women's sport involvement:

In public competitions, [women's] participation must be absolutely prohibited. It is indecent that the spectators should be exposed to the risk of seeing the body of a woman being smashed before their eyes. Besides, . . . her organism is not cut out to sustain certain shocks. Her nerves rule her muscles, nature wanted it that way. (cited in Gerber et al., 1974, p. 137)

And Lenskyj (1984) cites this belief as another reason female sport participation was discouraged:

The men want the girls to stay beautiful, graceful and sightly. . . . Runners were usually flat-chested, leather-limbed, horselike . . . and had as much sex appeal as grandmother's old sewing machine. (p. 158)

Cultural Norms

Clearly, as Lenskyj (1984) states when commenting on the myth of the frail female in the late 19th and early 20th centuries:

There were three mutually reinforcing dimensions to the argument against running: the medical rationales, the aesthetic and the social considerations . . . the economic security offered by marriage was conditional upon their "femininity" being beyond reproach. With femininity defined . . . as the capacity to bear children and to please men, running, clearly, was not a "feminine" pursuit. (p. 160.)

The cycle of reinforcement was completed by established cultural norms concerning women. These norms governed more than appearance or *excessive* physical activity. Indeed, they limited women's involvement in virtually every sphere outside the home (Cushman, 1940):

Every girl should have some business experience . . . but no girl should remain in business for more than five years. . . . The whole purpose of a relatively short business career should be to make the girl a better homemaker. . . . A business career was acceptable for those women with glandular deficiencies, or who honestly did not desire children, or who could never find warmth on a glowing hearthstone. (pp. 356-357)

duces some of the reasons adolescent girls drop out of sport.

In the United States, the Miller Brewing Company (1983) and a 1980 Gallup Poll (Loy & Rudman, 1983) have reported that men participate in a greater variety and number of sports, although women are catching up. The Miller Lite study of 1,139 adults in October 1982 found that 58% of the men and 37% of the women reported participating in

Highlight 9.2
Why Do Adolescent Girls Withdraw From Sport and Physical Activity?

Numerous studies have documented the pattern where girls dramatically decrease their level of involvement in sport and physical activity during adolescence, often before they reach their peak learning or performance potential. Most of these studies have compared different age groups at one point in time rather than studying the same girls from preadolescence into the adolescent years. However, a study by Butcher (1985) is an exception. She examined the activity patterns of girls from Grade 6 (age 11) through Grade 10 (age 15) to identify factors related to their continued participation in sport. In the end, 140 girls were studied across all 5 years. She found a consistent decrease in the average number of hours per day spent in physical activity from Grades 6 to 10 and an increase in secondary involvement. She also found a dramatic decrease in participation on both interscholastic and intramural teams in Grade 10.

The factors most strongly related to continued participation were

- satisfaction with movement activities, especially one's own sport ability;
- a preference for active versus sedentary activities;
- independent, self-assertive descriptions of the self;
- participation by and encouragement from significant others, especially parents; and
- availability of sport equipment.

A related study by Brown (1985) addressed this withdrawal problem more directly by studying factors influencing girls to drop out of age-group swimming. The responses of 211 former and 193 current age-group swimmers showed that continued participation, contrary to conventional wisdom, is not solely a function of the degree of success attained, nor is withdrawal solely a function of lack of success or of negative sport experiences. Rather, withdrawal from intense involvement during adolescence is gradual and involves increased participation in other activities that are endorsed and encouraged by significant others. Other salient factors in the process of withdrawal for adolescent swimmers, according to Brown, include a decreasing importance of the athlete role in one's self-identity; a perceived increase in the cost-benefit ratio of competitive swimming; and a gradual detachment from the subculture of the swim club through increased social interaction with friends outside the swim world.

In short, withdrawal from sport during adolescence is not solely related to failure or declining success, although these factors hasten the process. Rather, adolescent girls over time divest themselves from the sport role as they become oriented to other interests that are valued and encouraged by the peer group and significant others.

five or more different sports at least once or twice a month. Among the five most popular sports, four activities (swimming, jogging, bicycling, and calisthenics) were reported by both males and females.

High School, Community, and College Sport Teams.
Since the middle 1970s, many more girls and young women have begun participating in competitive sport. To illustrate, the Miller Lite Report (Miller Brewing Company, 1983) cited statistics from the Women's Sports Foundation, which showed that the percentage of female high school athletes increased from 7% to 35% from 1972 to 1984. Similarly, from 1972 to 1986 the number of high school girls in interscholastic sport increased from 300,000 to 1,800,000; and at the college level, from 32,000 to 150,000. There has also been an increase from 5.6 to 6.9 sports per college available to women between 1977 and 1984. In contrast, the increase for males was from 7.3 to 7.4 teams (Acosta & Carpenter, 1985).

At the community level, this rapid increase in women's involvement is illustrated by the growth in girls' soccer. The number of female teams registered with the United States Soccer Association increased from 245 in 1971 to 2,448 in 1981 ("More Women," 1982). Clearly at the formal, competitive level of sport, more women are involved than in the past. It is not known whether this trend will continue, peak, or decline in the future. One determining factor will be the economic resources available for competitive sport.

The Olympic Games.
Although ostensibly a model of international freedom and equal rights, the Olympic Games have provided a relatively accurate international mirror of the minimal opportunities for women in sport. Women were not included in the ancient Olympic Games, and female athletes did not participate in the first modern Olympic Games in 1896. This was partly due to Pierre de Coubertin, the founder and first president of the modern Olympics. Highlight 9.3 outlines de Coubertin's views.

Despite the views of de Coubertin, the Paris Olympic Organizing Committee introduced competition for women in the socially accepted games of tennis and golf, and 12 participants competed in 1904. Since 1904 there has been a steady, slow increase in both the number of events for women and the number of female entrants (Krotee, 1988).

Great variation still exists in the number of women sent by each nation. Semyonov (1981) found that the participation rates of women increase as the fertility rate in a country decreases and as the percentage of women in the labor force increases. In effect, these indices reflect social change with respect to women's rights and the increasing opportunities for women in a given society. Semyonov noted that in societies where women tend to be segregated in traditional female occupations, they tend to participate in traditional female sports. Both Semyonov (1981) and Riordan (1985) have noted interesting political and cultural differences in the participation rates of women in eastern and western bloc countries. Highlight 9.4 focuses on some of these differences.

Secondary Involvement

In addition to participating directly in sport, women have increasingly become involved as spectators and leaders. The actual number of women who attend sport events is unknown, but it is clearly increasing as women become more involved as participants. For example, in the Miller Lite study (Miller Brewing Company, 1983) 55% of the men and 49% of the women reported that they were interested in watching five or more different sports. The patterns of attendance were highly sport specific, with women preferring

---

Highlight 9.3
Views of de Coubertin: 1901 to 1935

Pierre de Coubertin was influential in perpetuating the norm that women be excluded from competitive sport. In fairness to de Coubertin, his views were strongly influenced by the social period in which he lived. In France and many other countries at the time, the Catholic and Protestant churches opposed women's participation. Even the Pope spoke against women's participation in some competitive sport events. But de Coubertin held a high position in the sport world, and he frequently spoke out against women's sport participation. Some of his views (cited from Simri, 1980, pp. 188-189) include the following:

- in 1901, "the role of women was to applaud the male victor as a means of reward"
- in 1902, women's sport "could well be contrary to the Laws of Nature"
- in 1908, women's tobogganing is "the most unaesthetic sight human eyes could contemplate"

- in 1912, "the Olympic Games should be reserved for men," and he expressed horror at the thought of seeing women run, row, or play soccer at the Games.
- in 1924, twenty years after they had begun to compete, he recommended to the I.O.C. that they be expelled from the 1924 Games
- in 1925, he claimed their participation was illegal
- in 1934, he warned male athletes that "contact with female athletes would be bad for them"; and,
- in 1935, speaking on the "Philosophical Basis of Modern Olympism," he stated, "I personally am against the participation of women in public competitions. . . . They should not do so in public. . . . At the Olympic Games their primary role should be, as in the ancient tournaments, to crown the (male) victors with laurels."

---

tennis, gymnastics, figure skating, horse racing, professional wrestling, and baseball. More women watch sport on television than attend sport events.

As sport leaders in both women's sport and sex-integrated sport organizations, women continue to be underrepresented (Carpenter & Acosta, 1985; Grant, 1984; Holmen & Parkhouse, 1981; Pacey, 1982; Simri, 1981; Theberge, 1984; White & Brackenridge, 1985). Whether this represents direct or indirect discrimination by males or the lack of qualified

female personnel remains to be explained. Nevertheless, studies indicate that at the high school, college, national, and international level, women are not well represented in a variety of leadership positions.

To illustrate, Acosta and Carpenter (1985) note that in Iowa, where high school girls' basketball attracts as many (or more) spectators as boys' basketball and a large number of participants, women coach only 12% of the teams. They also report that in 1984 women coached only 53.8% of U.S. college

---

Highlight 9.4
Cultural Variations in the Participation Rates of Women in Olympic Games

The precedent of excluding women from the Olympics began in ancient Greece and was perpetuated by de Coubertin following the rebirth of the modern Games. Today, despite the influence of the women's movement, women are prohibited from participating in certain events (e.g., distance events in swimming, contact sports). Some countries discourage or prohibit women from representing them, often because of cultural attitudes about a woman's role in society.

Women in North America, the Soviet Union, and Eastern Europe have attained levels of athletic excellence beyond scientific predictions. They have become national and international role models for the levels of performance women can attain if given an opportunity to train and participate. However, progress toward equality in sport participation has been slow in many societies because success in sport is still equated with masculinity.

The conditions that foster changes in women's participation in the female labor force seem to encourage social change in sport. For instance, there has been considerably greater participation by women from socialist, centrally planned economies. In contrast, in countries where the church is a dominant influence in social and cultural life (especially the Catholic and Moslem churches), opportunities for women in sport have not increased as much or as rapidly.

These cross-national differences in the participation and success rates of women are shown by Riordan (1985). He notes that at the last Summer Olympic Games in which all major capitalist and communist countries participated (Montreal, 1976), women comprised 35% of the Soviet team and they won 30% of the Soviet medals; 40% of the German Democratic Republic team and over 50% of the team medals; 28% of the Cuban team; 26% of the United States team; and 21% of the British and West German teams. In contrast, many teams from Latin America, South America, and developing countries did not send any women. In short, women's participation and accomplishments in the world of sport seem to reflect the status of women in the countries involved.

---

women's teams across 12 sports. This represents a *decline* from a reported 92% in 1973, despite the increased number of participants and teams.

Moreover, as the level of college competition increases, the percentage of male coaches increases. Thus, in 1984, males occupied 50.1% of the coaching positions for women's teams in Division I; 47.8% in Division II; and 41.2% in Division III. Male athletic directors supervise 86.5% of the NCAA college or university programs; and 38% of the programs do not have a female involved at the administrative level.

These data suggest that males tend to dominate the higher echelons within sport (Ab-

Many leadership positions within women's sport are held by males.

bott & Smith, 1984). This dominance was compounded when the NCAA, long an exclusively male organization, gained complete control of women's intercollegiate athletic programs. Similarly, before passage of Title IX about 2% of college athletic budgets were spent on women. By 1986, that figure had increased only to 16%.

Similar patterns prevail at the national and international level. In the international and national sport federations throughout the world and on the International Olympic Committee, men hold virtually all of the key positions (Grant, 1984; Simri, 1981; Theberge, 1984; White & Brackenridge, 1985). Currently there are only 5 females on the 86-member International Olympic Committee. Highlight 9.5 illustrates similar patterns at lower levels of involvement.

Explaining Patterns of Female Involvement in Sport

What explains patterns of women being underrepresented in sport? Brown (1982) sug-

gests the explanations are complex and involve historical factors, outright discrimination, and events occurring in other societal institutions. Some of the hypothesized contributing factors are

- continuing prejudices, taboos, and stereotypes that lead to sport being viewed as a male "preserve" (Theberge, 1985);
- the lack of power in gender relations (Messner, 1988) and the strength of "old boys" networks and the lack of or weakness of "old girls" networks;
- a lack of qualified female personnel to coach and administer athletics;
- unconscious or unintended discrimination by males;
- failure of women to apply for job vacancies in athletics;
- time constraints imposed on married or divorced females by family responsibilities;
- a lack of female role models as participants and leaders; and
- a continuation, in some societies and some segments of society, of long-standing gender-role socialization processes that discourage females from sport.

On the positive side, different factors have encouraged participation, including

- the women's movement, which sought to enhance the status of women in all social institutions;
- the fitness movement, which stressed fitness for appearance and performance rather than just enjoyment;
- legislation, such as Title IX in the United States and the Charter of Rights in Canada, which led to increased resources being allocated to women's sport and helped institutionalize norms against discrimination;

Highlight 9.5
Is There a Gender-Based Double Standard
in Access to Sport Leadership Positions?

Most studies pertaining to the disadvantaged status of women in sport have focused on the lower participation rates and opportunities for women as athletes. Even more alarming is the lack of representation at the coaching and administrative levels.

Studies in Canada, the United States, and Great Britain have all documented that even where there has been an increase in the number of female athletes the involvement of women as coaches, officials, and administrators has not kept pace. Indeed, despite the rise in women's participation rates in sport in the United States and the merger of women's sport organizations with men's organizations (e.g., the AIAW with the NCAA at the college level; the international women's field hockey association with the men's), women's access to leadership positions has actually declined (Grant, 1984).

In Great Britain, where there has been an increase from 18% to 32% in the number of female competitors on Olympic teams from 1960 to 1980, the percentage of female executives has increased from 12% to 14% (White & Brackenridge, 1985). Thus, an increasing proportion of women athletes and women's sport events are being ruled and controlled by men. Women have not acquired representative power and influence in setting the policies, values, and priorities for their sport.

One outcome has been the appearance in women's sport of some problems of men's sport—excessive or illegal recruiting at the college level, a win-at-all costs phi-losophy, and an increasing rate of confrontation with game officials at all levels.

Why does this gender stratification persist and worsen at the leadership levels? Is there a gender-based double standard in the requirements for leadership positions? Some in the women's movement have argued that, "in order for a woman to achieve equality with a man she must be twice as good." This belief is a variation of the "unequal opportunity for equal ability" thesis with respect to blacks.

To test this idea, Theberge (1984) examined whether women have to be better than men to achieve the same status in sport organizations. She studied five organizations that administer sport for female participants and found that women hold only about 30% of the voluntary board positions. One sport, women's field hockey, was administered exclusively by women. Theberge found more similarities than differences between men and women on a variety of factors. The major difference between males and females in sport leadership positions was in social status. Men were more often employed full time in the labor force, they were in higher status jobs, and they had attained higher levels of education. As a result of these findings, Theberge concluded that at the provincial level of leadership involvement there is little evidence of a gender-based double standard in requirements for mobility to leadership positions.

At the national and international level of sports administration (e.g., national

(Cont.)

Highlight 9.5 Continued

Olympic committees, national sport federations), there may be more evidence of gender discrimination. At these levels, women may be required to demonstrate higher levels of playing and coaching experience, along with better coaching credentials, before they are appointed coach of a college, national, or international team. That is, a double standard in the promotion to leadership positions may be more likely to occur where there are fewer positions available and where high prestige and power accrue to the position.

- an increase in the number and visibility of active and successful female role models;
- research evidence refuting many of the medical and physiological myths that inhibited participation; and
- changing gender-role socialization in some societies and among some social classes.

But women still participate in fewer activities, less frequently, and, for the most part, at a lower level of competition.

INSTITUTIONALIZED DISCRIMINATION AGAINST WOMEN

Throughout the struggle to become more involved in sport, the situation of females has paralleled that of blacks (Lumpkin, 1981). Both groups were

- prohibited from participating because of cultural norms or written restrictions;
- forced to sponsor their own competitions and leagues; and
- benefactors of federal legislation guaranteeing equal rights.

Thus, some of the following points are variations of themes introduced earlier concerning racial stratification.

Sexism has led to double standards within sport. Women have received less than favorable or less than equal treatment in a number of ways, including

- lower budgets;
- fewer hours allocated to facilities;
- shorter schedules;
- fewer athletic scholarships (Coakley & Pacey, 1984);
- fewer events or types of sport available;
- fewer women in leadership positions in sport organizations;
- submission to sex-identity tests at international competitions;
- differential (i.e., lower) prize structures (e.g., in golf and tennis);
- less media coverage;
- delayed or restricted opportunities for marriage among elite athletes (Foldesi, 1984);
- different orientations to games at lower levels of involvement (Theberge, Curtis, & Brown, 1982);
- being encouraged (i.e., socialized) to restrict participation to such socially acceptable sports as tennis, swimming, or gymnastics (Snyder & Spreitzer, 1983);

- less encouragement from parents to participate in sport, especially in less-educated or blue-collar families;
- differential play experiences for young children (Lever, 1976, 1978), which tend to perpetuate the system of gender stratification;
- less access to commercial endorsements (only about 2% of all endorsements go to female athletes); and
- higher status attached to the role of cheerleader than to that of athlete (Feltz, 1979).

Highlight 9.6 looks at one of these factors—the issue of differential media coverage.

GENDER ROLE CONFLICT

Contemporary arguments suggest that the female who competes ultimately must decide whether to fulfill her socially sanctioned, ascribed role of *female* or ignore these norms and achieve her full potential in sport. The female athlete who persists may be labeled *deviant* and stigmatized as unfeminine or masculine. She may be called a Tomboy or other epithets, depending on her age.

In reality, a female athlete is not in a dichotomous *either/or* situation. Most play many different roles in different situations at different times. Many successful female athletes succeed in school, date, marry, raise children, and work full-time or part-time.

In some anecdotal evidence of female adolescents, both athletes and nonathletes report a stigma attached to womens' participating in sport—especially if it emphasizes strength, endurance, or body contact. But studies of high school, college, and elite athletes (Allison & Butler, 1984; Anthrop & Allison, 1983; Sage & Loudermilk, 1979) have found that athletes report little role conflict. Women competing in less socially sanctioned

sports (e.g., softball, volleyball, field hockey, track and field, basketball) *do* report more conflict than those in the more socially approved sports (e.g., tennis, golf, swimming, gymnastics). Possibly, the athletes report different levels of role conflict because others behave differently toward them depending on the type of sport.

It seems that contrary to conventional wisdom, female athletes are not internalizing negative stereotypes to the extent they experience role conflict. Indeed, Theberge (1985) argues convincingly that sport can liberate women instead of oppressing them. Sport ideally helps free women from male domination. The limited participation by women in sport appears to be more a problem of limited opportunities and less a problem of women's attitudes toward getting involved.

There is one possible exception to this finding. Married women, especially those with young children, increasingly report a conflict between heavy personal involvement in sport and their perceived responsibilities to be good mothers, wives, and, sometimes, workers outside the home. This conflict may arise because of scarce time or economic resources and the lack of a supportive spouse. Unfortunately, there is little research on this kind of family-induced conflict. However, female runners and their male spouses have reported in running magazines that the activity interferes with family responsibilities and sometimes contributes to marital breakdowns (Brown & Curtis, 1984; Fasting & Sisjord, 1985).

TOWARD GENDER EQUALITY

Gender equality in sport did not advance significantly in North America until the 1970s. The deciding factors were civil rights legislation and the famous Title IX amendment to the United States Education Act. The amend-

---

Highlight 9.6
The Differential Treatment of Women's Sport in the Mass Media

Even the most casual observer has noticed that women receive less media coverage from the press, radio, or television for their sport involvement (Hilliard, 1984; Klein, 1988; Messner, 1988; Rintala & Birrell, 1984). In North America women's sport represents about 15% of all newspaper sport articles, 3% to 7% of the content of sport magazines, and 1% to 3% of the articles in women's magazines (Boutilier & SanGiovanni, 1983; Hilliard, 1984; Rintala & Birrell, 1984). This marginal coverage occurs at all levels of sport competition, from local youth sport to Olympic events. Even where women are featured, much of the coverage is allocated to sports that confirm a feminine image of sport or trivialize women's sport (Messner, 1988). There is little coverage of women's team sports, and the women featured are often cast in a negative light— as flawed heroines, emotionally troubled, lonely, torn by conflict, and as unusual people. Because the media tend to ignore the female athlete or depict her as less than ideal, few positive role models of female athletes are available for young girls.

Two studies have provided compelling evidence of how the media skew the image of women's sport. Hilliard (1984) completed a content analysis of 115 articles on leading male and female tennis players over a 4-year period. Rintala and Birrell (1984) examined all issues of *Young Athlete*, a sport magazine for adolescents. They found that the articles gave more coverage to men than to women. More text was devoted to men's matches; the titles of the articles referred to men; photographs and text about the men appeared first; and men were more often depicted in action shots or poses. Moreover, all of the articles on major championships were written by men. The dominant themes surrounding the character portraits of women included their failings and flaws concerning performance, personality, and relations with others. Women athletes were often portrayed as having an almost childlike dependency on parents, coaches, and agents. These descriptions suggest the incompatibility of the athlete and traditional female roles.

If the treatment of women in the mass media is to improve and better reflect reality, media personnel must become more responsive to women's roles in sport, and they must consciously eliminate stereotypical representations of female athletes. Future generations of female athletes could use viable role models.

---

ment was passed in 1972 and became law on July 21, 1975, a day some women refer to as *Independence Day*. It prohibits sex discrimination in educational programs or activities, including competitive sport teams, that receive federal funds. The direct impact of this legislation was that increased funds went to operate and expand competitive sport programs for women. The indirect effect was an increase in the number of competitive teams

Despite the possibility of gender role conflict, many females are pursuing sport-related goals.

and athletes. Another subtle effect was that the legal and economic threat of Title IX enabled women to acquire more power and to raise issues of inequality that challenged the existing systems.

This legislated change escalated the underlying conflict between males and females for what are perceived to be scarce sport resources—money for school teams and access to practice and game facilities. This conflict has been most pronounced where male intercollegiate sport programs have experienced budget cuts in sports that produce little or no revenue (e.g., baseball, tennis) and in court battles concerning the civil rights of girls or women to play on boys' or men's teams (Jennings, 1981). Highlight 9.7 describes the legal process pursued by one preadolescent girl so she could play in a league compatible with her ability. Unfortunately, her best opportunity was in a boys' league, and it took almost 2-1/2 years for a decision to be rendered in her favor. By then her skill level

relative to her male age-peers had plateaued or declined because of the lost opportunity to compete with those of equal ability.

Despite the legal opportunity to participate on boys' teams, few teams have been integrated because of subtle and overt forms of discrimination. More recently women have sought separate but equal sport programs (Birrell, 1984a). In reality, some of these programs have been perceived as second class and have not been supported by spectators, the press, or funding agencies. As a result subtle barriers persist, and women's sport opportunities remain unequal to those of men—especially for women with the most athletic potential and the greatest desire to achieve in sport.

Until recently there was little attempt to explain why women were or were not involved in physical activity and sport. To help rectify this gap in our knowledge, the feminist perspective has recently been applied to the analysis of sport (Birrell, 1984b; Blinde, 1989; Hall, 1984; Theberge, 1985). This perspective emphasizes that women are oppressed by males, who hold the power in gender relations; that the male view of the world should not be the norm; and that the situation of women can best be understood by an examination of female social experiences, by female researchers.

In the study of sport, feminists begin with analyses that demonstrate how sport is a sexist institution that is male-dominated. They also argue that a world that views female involvement in the range of sports as inappropriate is unacceptable. Feminist scholars argue that equality will only be attained through analysis, theory, and political action based on a unique understanding of the female sport world—by females.

PARALLELS IN AGE AND SPORT

Every society has an age structure that is based on both chronological age and the so-

---

**Highlight 9.7
A Girl's Plea for Sport Equality**

Prevented from playing hockey on a boys' team, yet by most accounts more than qualified to play (in fact she had been selected by the coach to play on the team until the league required her to quit), a 12-year-old girl wrote the following letter to the editor of *The Globe and Mail* in May 1985.*

Dear Sir or Madam:

I can play! But may I?

MTHL try-out time is here again, and I'm going to hear the same words again, "Yes, you're good enough. We wish we could use you. But you're a girl."

The Canadian Charter of Rights says I can't be discriminated against, but Ontario's Human Rights Code allows sexual discrimination in amateur sports. This means it bars girls from the top levels of amateur competition.

Is there an individual or group that can help me? Is there a lawyer willing to donate his or her time to fight this unfairness? I want to be judged on my ability alone.

Justine Blainey
Hockey Player, Age 12

Through a separate set of circumstances, Miss Blainey acquired a lawyer. One year later the Ontario Court of Appeal ruled that it was not proper for the Human Rights Code to contain a provision of discrimination on the basis of sex in sport. This provision, according to the courts, violates the Canadian Charter of Rights. The issue was referred to the Ontario Human Rights Commission for a decision as to whether girls should have the right to play on boys' teams.

On December 3, 1987, the Commission tribunal ruled (a) that the Ontario Hockey Association (OHA) was guilty of discriminating against Miss Blainey on the basis of sex and (b) that if a girl has the interest and ability, she has the right to play on a boy's team. The OHA was ordered to pay Miss Blainey $3,000 plus the cost of attending a summer hockey school to upgrade her skills. More importantly for future generations, the OHA was told that it must include in its literature and public notices that all positions are open to males and females.

---

*Note. Reprinted by permission of Caroline Blainey.

---

cial meaning attached to various stages of the life cycle. In earlier periods of history the age structure generally consisted of a three-tiered system: infancy and childhood, adulthood, and old age. Today modernized societies may include as many as seven stages: infancy, childhood, adolescence, young adulthood, middle age, the young-old, and the old-old (McPherson, 1983).

An age structure influences our social behavior in many ways, including

- when we gain access to certain social positions;
- at what stage in life we gain or relinquish certain social roles;
- how and when different age cohorts interact with each other;
- what opportunities and age-role expectations are available for persons of a certain chronological age; and
- what status and power are attached to those of a specific chronological age.

Age serves as an important criterion for entering and leaving positions, interacting with others, and gaining access to some aspects of social participation. To illustrate, codified laws based on chronological age determine when we enter and leave the educational system and the labor force, when we are eligible for social benefits (e.g., pensions), and when we can vote, drive a car, consume alcohol, attend certain movies, and join certain sport teams or enter specific sport events. Chronological age, and the accompanying age stratification system, also has a significant impact on our lifestyle and life chances within the world of sport. In effect, age, like gender, reflects and reinforces the inequalities of society within a sport setting.

Often the perceived social meaning or norms attached to a particular chronological age or stage in life has more bearing on the individual than the age itself. These meanings change and vary across cultures and at different periods in history. In the previous century, those over 40 were considered *elderly*; today those over 65 or 75 are viewed as *old*. Even many pensioners in their late 60s do not consider themselves old, primarily

because more people are now living into their 80s and 90s.

Location in a particular age strata (e.g., over 60) often influences a person's behavior, attitudes, and values in a number of domains. We tend to have certain behavioral expectations of others in different age groups. Unfortunately, some of these expectations become institutionalized and lead to stereotypes, which solidify and magnify differences among age strata. Age norms also serve as a form of social control by defining socially appropriate behavior for different ages, encouraging social interaction mainly with one's age-peers, and influencing when and in what order life events should occur (e.g., complete your education, get a job, and get married). Many of these norms are proscriptive. Hence, avoiding sex after 60 and physical activity after 40 have been stereotypical age norms, at least until scientific evidence showed they are invalid beliefs.

Until recently, sport was not perceived or promoted as an adult activity. At some points in history, all forms of adult leisure were considered inappropriate and a waste of time. Our society now has more older people with more leisure than previous generations. And scientific studies have found that adults can be physically active into their later years, that exercise and fitness are important aspects of health in the middle and later years, and that older adults can compete in a variety of sport events with their age-peers (Canada Fitness Survey, 1982; McPherson, 1983, 1984, 1986; Ostrow, 1981; Rudman, 1986; Smith & Serfass, 1981).

Differences in Primary and Secondary Involvement

Scientific evidence now indicates that persons of all ages can engage in physical activity and sport (Harootyan, 1982; McPherson,

1983). Nevertheless, members of the younger age strata are still the most heavily involved.

People at different stages of life often exhibit not only different physical traits but different patterns of behavior in a number of social domains, including sport. These differences may be attributed to

- changes as the individual matures (*aging effects*);
- changes in behavior that may be unique to most or all members of a particular generation because of the impact of specific events (*cohort effects*); and
- the influence of a major historical event (e.g., the Depression, World War II) that had a more profound effect on some generations than others (*period effects*).

Thus, if variations among age groups are found in participation rates (usually in cross-sectional studies), investigators must still discover which variations are due to aging effects, cohort effects, or period effects.

To date, almost all studies investigating involvement in sport by age have been cross-sectional, comparing subjects from different age groups at the same time. The **cross-sectional design** can only indicate *differences* among age groups at a specific point in time. It alerts us to patterns of behavior that *may* vary by age or cohort. It cannot explain changes with age.

To examine age-related changes, we must use a **longitudinal design**, where people are studied over time. Many longitudinal designs depend on volunteers, who may introduce bias into the sample (e.g., volunteers may have a higher-than-average level of health, physical activity, or intelligence). Another limitation of most longitudinal designs is that they only study one age cohort. The cohort's activity involvement may be affected by some unique historical or cohort effect (e.g., their age when the fitness movement began).

People of all ages can safely participate in physical activity.

To illustrate, those who are now middle-aged have experienced the social values and opportunities resulting from the fitness boom. As a result, they will differ as an age group from middle-aged subjects studied 15 years ago. Similarly, when those now in their 40s reach their 60s and 70s, they may be considerably more active than the senior citizens of the late 1980s (McPherson, 1986).

Primary Involvement. Participation in sport is a leisure activity for many during childhood and adolescence. But during adolescence there begins a universal pattern of declining involvement in both formal sport competition and informal physical activity. The decline for participation in team sports is more frequent and rapid than for participation in individual sports. Tables 9.1 and 9.2, using cross-sectional data, illustrate this pattern in Canada and the United States, respectively. Table 9.1 indicates that levels of activity reported by active adults (an average of at least 3 hours per week for at least 9 months a year) surveyed in the 1981 Canada

Table 9.1   Age and Involvement in Physical Activity by Active Adults in Canada, 1981

	% active	
Age	Male	Female
14-19	73.2	70.9
20-24	62.8	57.0
25-34	54.5	53.0
35-44	49.9	50.3
45-54	46.1	49.9
55-64	49.4	53.6
65-74	56.4	51.9
75+	52.1	49.5

Note. Data from Canada Fitness Survey, 1982, as cited in "Age Patterns in Leisure Participation: The Canadian Case" by B.D. McPherson and C. Kozlik. In *Aging in Canada: Social Perspectives* (2nd ed., pp. 211–227) by V. Marshall (Ed.), 1987, Pickering, ON: Fitzhenry and Whiteside. Copyright 1987 by Fitzhenry and Whiteside. Reprinted by permission.

Fitness Survey (Canada Fitness Survey, 1982) decline for the first 5 age cohorts, for both males and females. Interestingly, those 55 and over report as much or more involvement as some younger age groups. These cross-sectional data do *not* imply that older adults are becoming more physically active in their later years. Similarly, Table 9.2 shows that according to a 1980 Gallup Poll in the United States, the average number of sports participated in by American adults declines by age. Moreover, the effect of age on sport involvement is independent of race, sex, occupation, education, and income.

Cross-sectional studies in a large number of countries have indicated that only a small portion of adults regularly participate in any type of sport or physical activity. These patterns also indicate that particularly sharp decreases in participation rates are observed at two stages in life: when individuals leave the formal school setting to enter the labor force and when they leave the labor force. This pattern of less involvement by successively older age cohorts is more likely to occur among

• the less educated;

Table 9.2   Average Number of Sports Participated in by Adults in the U.S. in 1980

Group	19-29	30-39	40-49	50-59	60-69	70+
White	7.6	6.3	4.7	3.1	2.4	1.5
Black	5.3	4.9	2.6	2.2	1.2	1.1
Male	8.1	7.0	5.4	4.1	2.7	1.7
Female	6.6	5.3	3.5	2.8	1.8	1.3
College education	7.8	7.1	5.7	4.3	3.2	1.7
Less than high school	5.6	3.7	2.4	2.2	1.6	1.2

Note. Data from Gallup Poll, 1980, as cited in Loy, J.W., & Rudman, W.J. (1983). Social physics and sport involvement: An analysis of sport consumption and production patterns by means of three empirical laws. *South African Journal for Research in Sport, Physical Education and Recreation*, **6**(2), 31–48. Reprinted by permission.

- those with lower incomes;
- those who live in rural areas and small towns;
- females (especially if they are married and have preschool children);
- blue-collar workers; and
- those who live in countries where sport and physical activity are not highly valued or promoted.

A definitive explanation of this pattern is lacking, partly because of the reliance on cross-sectional studies. But several studies suggest this pattern of declining involvement by age is related to

- individual disengagement;
- inadequate socialization experiences early in life, where some individuals never acquire interest or experience in sport;
- early lifestyles that continue through the life cycle;
- age-based normative beliefs about how one should behave concerning sport;
- a lack of role models, which could show that sport involvement in the middle and later years is socially acceptable and possible; and
- the presence of ageism, which restricts opportunity and encouragement for those who wish to participate during the middle and later years (McPherson, 1983, 1984).

A longitudinal study of high school sophomores, interviewed in 1955 and again 15 years later, offers some support for the idea that early-life socialization experiences in sport have some long-term effects on patterns of involvement (Howell & McKenzie, 1987). The researchers found that participation in high school varsity or nonvarsity sport programs is positively related to physical activity involvement later in adulthood. Having participated in varsity athletics as an adolescent had the most impact on playing team

sports in adulthood for men. In contrast, having participated in nonvarsity sports had a greater effect on team sport involvement in adulthood for women.

Among older active adults, there is some evidence of a decrease in the variety of sports and a tendency toward increased specialization in one or two activities (Curtis and White, 1984). To illustrate, at the North Shore Park in Tampa Bay, the Three-Quarter Century Softball Club, Inc., organizes the Kids and Kubs teams for male players over 75. Some players are in their 90s, and the club's history records reveal the eventful day in February 1967 when the Kubs executed two triple plays in one game. The combined ages of the players involved was 543 years. Similarly, newspaper stories periodically recount tales of jogging grandmothers in their 80s, ultramarathoners in their 60s, hockey players entering "old-timer" tournaments in their 70s, and a 72-year-old sophomore on a college tennis team. Increased opportunities for competitive sport experiences have been provided by the First World Masters Games held in Toronto in 1985 and by the Senior Games and Senior Olympic movements in the U.S.

Secondary Involvement. Similar to the pursuit of other leisure interests (e.g., movie attendance), involvement in sport as a spectator tends to be higher among those under 30 and declines thereafter. This decline often parallels an increase in work and family responsibilities. Television consumption of sport also shows differences in viewing patterns that vary by age and sex, although these differences tend to reflect leisure preferences rather than overt discrimination by age. For example, young males in the 1980s prefer to watch basketball; young males of about the same age in the 1960s and early 1970s preferred to watch baseball.

Until recent years, leadership positions in sport (managers, coaches, and executives)

It is only recently that people have remained or become participants in the sport world during the middle and later years of life.

were generally given to individuals considerably older than the participants. This was probably the result of a normative belief that chronological age is equivalent to experience, wisdom, and leadership ability. Since the 1970s, however, there has been a greater emphasis on a youth culture, a general loss of power by the elderly in society, and a shift away from the normative belief that authoritarian figures are needed as sport leaders. Thus, an increasing number of coaches and executives at all levels are under 40 or 45 years of age. Indeed, sometimes a college or professional coach is fired because he or she is *too old* to understand the needs of young athletes.

Age Norms and Ageism

One outcome of the system of age stratification is that normative criteria evolve as to when one can enter and when one should leave specific sport roles. For example, most youth sport organizations offer competition according to chronological age, without regard for the individual's unique physical or emotional readiness for that level of competition. It has been found that players born in the early months of the year are highly overrepresented on all-star youth hockey teams (Barnsley, Thompson, & Barnsley, 1985). This *calendar effect* is also found in the National Hockey League and in the national hockey leagues in Sweden and the Soviet Union. In fact, in the Soviet Union more than 70% of the players were born in the first 6 months.

This same pattern may occur in other sports where physical size is of primary importance. This regulation may cause some children to fail and drop out. Or because they cannot compete against others of their chronological age, they may stop participating in that particular sport. Some of these children may leave sport altogether because of the failure or rejection they experience at an early age. Physical activity may thus never become an integral facet of their lifestyle. Similarly, many professional sport organizations use age as a criterion to establish benchmarks for career progress. Many aspiring professional or Olympic athletes feel they must achieve a certain standard or level of competition by a specific age to achieve access to the elite levels.

Another outcome of age stratification is the appearance of **ageism**, where individuals of a particular chronological age are discriminated against in their lifestyles and life chances. For example, after individuals leave school there is little opportunity or encouragement to use sport facilities unless they join a private club. This is more characteristic of North America than Europe, where a sport club provides facilities for people of all ages. That is, it is more socially acceptable in Europe to continue active sport involvement throughout the life cycle.

The phenomenon of ageism is more likely to be prevalent in an age-integrated than in an age-segregated environment. In the former setting there may be conflict or competition among age levels for the use of facilities. Furthermore, in an age-segregated environment (e.g., a retirement community), the reference groups are from a similar generation, and there may be less pressure to *act your age* within a sport context.

Age and Social Change in Sport

With increased research by gerontologists and other scientists (McPherson, 1986), the myth of the sedentary older adult spending the later years in a rocking chair has been shattered.

This evidence, combined with the fitness movement, the women's movement, and a changing leisure philosophy, has encouraged increased participation in physical activity and sport among all age groups. As a result, the leisure lifestyle of middle-aged and older adults has undergone dramatic change.

Much of this increased participation in sport and physical activity has occurred because the social meanings or norms associated with chronological age strata have been altered. Today there is a considerably wider spectrum of socially approved sports for aging adults. Moreover, there are now visible role models of active older athletes and specific organizations (e.g., Masters, Veterans) for encouraging and providing participation and competition.

As the "gray power" movement expands with an aging population and as younger adults remain involved throughout the early and middle years of adulthood, future elderly persons will receive more encouragement and opportunities to be involved in sport. Thus, while the pattern of declining involvement with age will likely continue, the proportion of people who remain sedentary during the middle and later years of adulthood should decline significantly.

WRAP-UP

This chapter has shown the effects of gender stratification on the opportunities for and achievements of women in sport. Historically, the involvement of women in sport has grown from total uninvolvement to passive involvement as spectators to increasing involvement as participants, spectators, and leaders; but it has *not* reached equal gender involvement. This limited involvement by females has not occurred because of limited physical ability or threats to personal health and safety. Rather, it has come about through unfounded beliefs, sexist norms, and institutionalized discrimination against a less powerful group.

Since the onset of the women's movement and the introduction of civil rights legislation, opportunities for involvement in a number of sport roles have increased. But women still have not achieved anything near full equality in the sport domain, particularly in traditional male-dominated sports or organizations and particularly in access to leadership positions.

Contrary to the oft-repeated myth that female athletes, especially in early adolescence, experience traumatic gender role conflict, there is no evidence that this conflict is widespread. Moreover, this alleged conflict is not a valid reason to discourage or exclude young women from the pursuit of sporting interests.

Like gender, age has been a factor in determining who gains access to sport opportunities. There is a pattern of declining competitive and recreational involvement in sport with age. The decline has not been as pronounced in recent years, because of changing norms concerning age-appropriate behavior, scientific evidence that middle-aged and older adults can learn and be trained to high levels, and the onset and adoption of the fitness and wellness movements by middle-aged and elderly persons. Whether the community at large will ever be populated by large numbers of active older women and men in sweatsuits remains to be seen, but this scenario is at least possible given recent social changes.

REFERENCES

Abbott, A., & Smith, D.R. (1984). Governmental constraints and labor market mobility: Turnover among college athletic personnel. *Work and Occupations*, **11**(1), 29–53.

Acosta, R.V., & Carpenter, L.J. (1985). Women in athletics: A status report. *Journal of Physical Education, Recreation and Dance*, **56**(6), 30–34.

Allison, M.T., & Butler, B. (1984). Role conflict and the elite female athlete: Empirical findings and conceptual dilemmas. *International Review for the Sociology of Sport*, **19**, 157–166.

Anthrop, J., & Allison, M.T. (1983). Role conflict and high school female athletes. *Research Quarterly for Exercise and Sport*, **54**(2), 104–111.

Barnsley, R.H., Thompson, A.H., & Barnsley, P.E. (1985). Hockey success and birthdate: The relative age effect. *CAHPER Journal*, **51**(November/December), 23–28.

Birrell, S. (1984a). Separatism as an issue in women's sport. *Arena Review*, **8**(2), 21–29.

Birrell, S. (1984b). Studying gender in sport: A feminist perspective. In N. Theberge & P. Donnelly (Eds.), *Sport and the sociological imagination* (pp. 125–135). Fort Worth: Texas Christian University Press.

Blinde, E. (1989). Participation in a male sport model and the value alienation of female intercollegiate athletes. *Sociology of Sport Journal*, **6**(1), 36–49.

Boutilier, M.A., & SanGiovanni, L. (1983). *The sporting woman*. Champaign, IL: Human Kinetics.

Brown, B.A. (1982). Female sport involvement: A preliminary conceptualization. In A.O. Dunleavy, A.W. Miracle, & C.R. Rees (Eds.), *Studies in the sociology of sport* (pp. 121–138). Fort Worth: Texas Christian University Press.

Brown, B.A., & Curtis, J.E. (1984). Does running go against the family grain? National survey results on marital status and running. In N. Theberge & P. Donnelly (Eds.), *Sport and sociological imagination* (pp. 352–367). Fort Worth: Texas Christian University Press.

Brown, B.A. (1985). Factors influencing the process of withdrawal by female adolescents from the role of competitive age group swimmer. *Sociology of Sport Journal*, **2**, 111–129.

Butcher, J. (1985). Longitudinal analysis of adolescent girls' participation in physical activity. *Sociology of Sport Journal*, **2**, 130–143.

Canada Fitness Survey (1982). *Fitness and aging*. Ottawa: Government of Canada, Fitness and Amateur Sport Directorate.

Canada Fitness Survey (1984). *Changing times: Women and physical activity*. Ottawa: Government of Canada, Fitness and Amateur Sport Directorate.

Carpenter, L.J., & Acosta, R.V. (1985). The status of women in intercollegiate athletics: A five year national study. In D. Chu, J.O. Segrave, & B.J. Becker (Eds.), *Sport and higher education* (pp. 327–334). Champaign, IL: Human Kinetics.

Coakley, J.J., & Pacey, P.L. (1984). The distribution of athletic scholarships among women in intercollegiate sport. In N. Theberge & P. Donnelly (Eds.), *Sport and the sociological imagination* (pp. 228–241). Fort Worth: Texas Christian University Press.

Curtis, J.E., & White, P.G. (1984). Age and sport participation: Decline in participation or increased specialization with age? In N. Theberge & P. Donnelly (Eds.), *Sport and the sociological imagination* (pp. 273–293). Fort Worth: Texas Christian University Press.

Cushman, E. (1940). Office women and sex antagonism. *Harper's Magazine*, **180**, 356–363.

Dyer, K.F. (1986). The trend of the male-female differential in various speed sports, 1936–84. *Journal of Biosocial Science*, **18**, 169–177.

Fasting, K., & Sisjord, M. (1985). Gender roles and barriers to participation in sports. *Sociology of Sport Journal*, **2**, 345–351.

Feltz, D.L. (1979). Athletics in the status system of female adolescents. *Review of Sport and Leisure*, **4**(1), 110–118.

Ferris, E.A. (1981). Attitudes to women in sport: Preface towards a sociological theory. In J. Borms, M. Hebbelinck, & A. Venerando (Eds.), *The female athlete: A socio-psychological and kinanthropometric approach* (pp. 12–29). Basel, Switzerland: Karger.

Foldesi, T. (1984). Marriage chances and social status of top female athletes in Hungary. *International Review for the Sociology of Sport*, **19**, 47–61.

Gerber, E.W., Berlin, P., Felshin, J., & Wyrick, W. (1974). *The American woman in sport*. Reading, MA: Addison-Wesley.

Grant, C.H.B. (1984). The gender gap in sport: From Olympic to intercollegiate level. *Arena Review*, **8**(2), 31–47.

Hall, M.A. (1984). Towards a feminist analysis of gender inequality in sport. In N. Theberge & P. Donnelly (Eds.), *Sport and the sociological imagination* (pp. 82–103). Fort Worth: Texas Christian University Press.

Harootyan, R.A. (1982). The participation of older people in sports. In R. Pankin (Ed.), *Social approaches to sport* (pp. 122–147). East Brunswick, NJ: Associated University Presses.

Hilliard, D.C. (1984). Media images of male and female professional athletes: An interpretative analysis of magazine articles. *Sociology of Sport Journal*, **1**, 251–262.

Holmen, M.G., & Parkhouse, B.L. (1981). Trends in the selection of coaches for female athletes: A demographic inquiry. *Research Quarterly for Exercise and Sport*, **52**(1), 9–18.

Howell, F.M., & McKenzie, J.A. (1987). High school athletics and adult sport-leisure activity: Gender variations across the life cycle. *Sociology of Sport Journal*, **4**, 329–346.

Jennings, S.E. (1981). As American as hot dogs, apple pie and Chevrolet: The desegregation of Little League baseball. *Journal of American Culture*, **4**, 81–91.

Klein, M.L. (1988). Women in the discourse of sport reports. *International Review for the Sociology of Sport*, **23**, 139–151.

Krotee, M.L. (1981). Sociological perspectives of the Olympic Games. In J. Segrave & D. Chu (Eds.), *Olympism* (pp. 207–226). Champaign, IL: Human Kinetics.

Lenskyj, H. (1984). A kind of precipitate waddle: Early opposition to women running. In N. Theberge & P. Donnelly (Eds.), *Sport and the sociological imagination* (pp. 153–161). Fort Worth: Texas Christian University Press.

Lever, J. (1976). Sex differences in the games children play. *Social Problems*, **23**, 479–487.

Lever, J. (1978). Sex differences in the complexity of children's play and games. *American Sociological Review*, **43**, 471–483.

Loy, J.W., & Rudman, W.J. (1983). Social physics and sport involvement: An analysis of sport consumption and production patterns by means of three empirical laws. *South African Journal for Research in Sport, Physical Education and Recreation*, **6**(2), 31–48.

Lucas, J., & Smith, R. (1978). *Saga of American Sport*. Philadelphia: Lea and Febiger.

Lumpkin, A. (1981, May). *Blacks and females striving for athletic acceptance*. Paper presented at the Ninth Annual Convention of the North American Society for Sport History, Hamilton, ON.

McPherson, B.D. (1983). *Aging as a social process: An introduction to individual and population aging*. Toronto: Butterworths.

McPherson, B.D. (1984). Sport participation across the life cycle: A review of the literature and suggestions for future research. *Sociology of Sport Journal*, **1**, 213–230.

McPherson, B.D. (Ed.) (1986). *Sport and aging*. Champaign, IL: Human Kinetics.

McPherson, B.D. & Kozlik, C. (1987). Age patterns in leisure participation: The Canadian case. In V. Marshall (Ed.), *Aging in Canada: Social perspectives* (2nd ed., pp. 211–227). Pickering, ON: Fitzhenry and Whiteside.

Messner, M.A. (1988). Sports and male domination: The female athlete as contested ideological terrain. *Sociology of Sport Journal*, **5**, 197–211.

Miller Brewing Company. (1983). The Miller Lite report on American attitudes toward sports. Milwaukee: Author.

More women playing organized soccer. (1982, May 19). *The New York Times*, p. B12.

Ostrow, A.C. (1981). Age role expectations and sex role expectations for selected sport activities. *Research Quarterly for Exercise and Sport*, **52**, 216–227.

Pacey, P.L. (1982). Equal opportunity for women in intercollegiate sports: Financial and family background as major influences on female participation in competitive programs. *American Journal of Economics and Sociology*, **41**, 257–268.

Parry, A. (1912). The relation of athletics to the reproductive life of women. *American Journal of Obstetrics*, **66**, 341–357.

Rintala, J., & Birrell, S. (1984). Fair treatment for the active female: A content analysis of Young Athlete magazine. *Sociology of Sport Journal*, **1**, 231–250.

Riordan, J. (1985). Some comparisons of women's sport in east and west. *Inter-*

national *Review for the Sociology of Sport*, **20**, 117–125.

Rudman, W.J. (1986). Sport as part of successful aging. *American Behavioral Scientist*, **29**, 453–470.

Sage, G.H., & Loudermilk, S. (1979). The female athlete and role conflict. *Research Quarterly*, **50**(1), 88–96.

Semyonov, M. (1981). Changing roles of women: Participation in Olympic Games. *Social Science Quarterly*, **62**, 735–743.

Shaw, S.M. (1985). Gender and leisure: Inequality in the distribution of leisure time. *Journal of Leisure Research*, **17**, 266–282.

Simri, U. (1980). The development of female participation in the modern Olympic Games. *Stadion*, **6**, 187–216.

Simri, U. (1981). The state of women's sports: The Olympic, international and national scenes. In J. Segrave & D. Chu (Eds.), *Olympism* (pp. 89–97). Champaign, IL: Human Kinetics.

Smith, E.L., & Serfass, R.C. (Eds.) (1981). *Exercise and aging: The scientific basis*. Hillside, NJ: Enslow.

Snyder, E.E., & Spreitzer, E.A. (1983). Change and variation in the social acceptance of female participation in sports. *Journal of Sport Behaviour*, **6**(1), 3–8.

Spears, B. (1978). Prologue: The myth. In C.A. Oglesby (Ed.), *Women and sport: From myth to reality* (pp. 3–15). Philadelphia: Lea and Febiger.

Theberge, N. (1984). Some evidence on the existence of a sexual double standard in mobility to leadership positions in sport. *International Review for the Sociology of Sport*, **19**, 185–195.

Theberge, N. (1985). Toward a feminist alternative to sport as a male preserve. *Quest*, **37**, 193–202.

Theberge, N., Curtis, J.E., & Brown, B.A. (1982). Sex differences in orientations toward games: Tests of the sport involvement hypothesis. In A.O. Dunleavy, A.W. Miracle, & R.C. Rees (Eds.) *Studies in the sociology of sport* (pp. 285–308). Fort Worth: Texas Christian University Press.

Twin, S.L. (Ed.) (1979). *Out of the bleachers: Writings on women and sport*. Old Westbury, NY: Feminist Press.

Westman, S.K. (1939). *Sport, physical training and womanhood*. Baltimore: Williams and Wilkins.

White, A., & Brackenridge, C. (1985). Who rules sport? Gender divisions in the power structure of British sports organizations from 1960. *International Review for the Sociology of Sport*, **20**, 95–106.

P A R T   III

SPORT IS AN ARENA OF RESISTANCE AND CONFLICT

So far, this book has explored how sport is part of the wider society. We have seen how sport reflects the society and culture, both of which are replete with social inequality. And we have emphasized how sport reinforces the beliefs, norms, and values of the wider society.

Where we have discussed the influences of sport on society these have been instances, mostly, where sport takes up trends already under way in the wider society. The marriage of convenience of television and sport is such a case. To this point, the way in which people in sport resist social trends, the degree to which sport has some autonomy from the wider society and culture, and the question of whether sport is a prime instigator of sociocultural change have not been addressed. These issues are considered in Part III.

In chapter 10 we see how subcultures within sport may reflect, deviate from, or oppose trends in the wider society and culture. We emphasize that sport is a potential agent of sociocultural change, and that it has occasionally helped to initiate or foster significant change.

Chapter 11 shows that collective behavior in sport can be the basis for social movements of resistance. Only a few social movements have emanated from sport settings and influenced social change. But there is further potential for this in sport, especially with respect to changing definitions of gender and gender roles. Considerable attention is directed as well to describing where, when, and why riots occur in sport settings. In some cases the collective behavior becomes ritualized and repetitive, as in the case of soccer hooliganism. This form of behavior has led to policies and programs to control fan behavior.

Sport and Subcultures

Even the most casual consumer of the news media has observed differences in the beliefs, values, and lifestyles of people from different societies. These differences show variations in culture. Cultural variations are social products that originate in the differing experiences, values, and histories of different groups of people. This chapter examines how cultural aspects of sport compare with the wider society. It also discusses whether sport groups resist and shape the culture of a society.

Within the dominant culture or way of life in any particular society there exist a variety of subcultures. Some commonly observed subcultures are the youth culture and the culture of crime. Subcultures may evolve in opposition to the dominant culture or around a unique lifestyle considered different or deviant by members of the mainstream society. A variety of subcultures have been evident within sport.

CULTURE AND SUBCULTURES

As we noted in chapter 1, culture involves the meanings that people learn from and share with others. Culture encompasses descriptive and normative beliefs; values, which are general criteria by which we judge others' behaviors; ideologies, which are emotionally charged sets of beliefs that explain and justify how society should be organized; and norms, which include rules, regulations, laws, and informal understandings. To illustrate, informal and formal dress codes emerge and change in sports such as tennis, golf, skiing, and cycling. The colors and styles change over time, according to changing cultural beliefs and tastes.

Culture and society are different sides of the same coin. Society is made up of sets of social relationships. Culture comprises the ideas that are taught and learned through social relationships. Culture also helps determine how social relationships take place, because these relationships are guided by norms, values, beliefs, and ideologies.

Within the culture are groups that share some of the common culture but not all of it. Each of these groups is called a **subculture**. Without *some* shared culture there would be no society, because there would not exist the requisite social relationships. And without social relationships and society, there can be no culture.

The meanings of culture and subculture become clearer when we look at a few phrases. For example, *high culture* refers to classical music, ballet, theater, poetry, and the fine arts. It traditionally has been considered the domain of the upper-class or well-educated social elite, particularly in Western countries. High culture is part of the larger culture but involves only a relatively small segment of the population. It is fully known only by those who comprise a subculture.

In contrast, *mass culture* represents the aspects of culture that are transmitted to many in the society through the print and electronic media or other forms of mass communication. Similarly, *popular culture* refers to the cultural and recreational activities of many people in the society. Sport is one element of popular culture, especially because it has the potential to appeal to all segments of society in one or more of its forms. At the same time, sport is an element of mass culture, because it can be produced, reshaped, and transmitted through mass-communication networks (see chapter 6).

Subcultures as Class Statements

Gans (1974) rejects the distinction between high and popular culture as too invidious, too judgmental. He suggests we consider the concept of *taste cultures*, where membership is determined by "class, age, religion, ethnic and racial background, regional origin, and place of residence, as well as personality factors which translate themselves into wants for specific types of cultural content . . . although age and class seem to be the major factors in American society" (p. 70). Gans defines taste culture as

> values, the cultural forms which express these values: music, art, design, literature, drama, comedy, poetry, criticism, news, and the media in which these are expressed—books, magazines, newspapers, records, films, television programs, paintings and sculpture, architecture, and insofar as ordinary consumer goods also express aesthetic values or functions, furnishings, clothes, appliances and automobiles as well. (pp. 10–11)

Employing this approach, Gans identifies five taste cultures, or subcultures: high culture, upper-middle culture, lower-middle culture, low culture, and quasifolk low culture. Although the consumption of a particular cultural product, such as music, may be common to several taste groups, the form and complexity of this product could vary from opera to rock to country music. In the case of sport, preference for particular games and activities would depend on the taste culture with which one is identified. For example, one can observe distinct social groups that prefer polo and fox-hunting and distinct social groups that prefer boxing, stock-car racing, and powerboat racing. To illustrate, Renson (1976, 1978) performed a symbolic analysis of sport participation by Belgian adults and concluded that ". . . sports are social symbolic actions and they symbolize, actualize and dramatize a formulated code of social values and social canons of style and taste . . ." (p. 440). More specifically, he argued that upper-class sports were characterized by the use of "status sticks" (e.g., clubs, rackets, ski poles), which symbolize the values of "distance" and "finesse"; lower-class sports involved close contact in martial arts or in rough team games, thereby expressing toughness, asceticism, and hard manual labor.

Subcultures as Forms of Resistance

Sport can also be a way to express dissatisfaction with the existing culture. Donnelly (1984) suggests that subordinate groups can use sport to express opposition to the dominant culture through three types of resistance: political, ethnic, and subcultural.

Political Resistance. This form of political behavior is really rooted in situations outside sport that a minority finds intolerable. The behavior may occur around sport events or be expressed by players or spectators within or beyond the event itself. Boycotts and riots within sport, for example, are often politically based statements about life in the wider society.

Ethnic Resistance. Native peoples have rebelled, for example, against the efforts of a colonizing nation to eliminate or discourage their traditional folk games or sporting activities and impose new forms of sport. In some instances, the natives continue the earlier sport activity, even though it may be declared illegal. They may also adopt the new game but change its structure to fit their needs, values, and beliefs.

Subcultural Resistance. A third form of resistance to the dominant culture can occur when subcultures are created. In sport, this situation either creates a new sport (e.g., freestyle skiing, two-person surfing, beach-volleyball) or changes existing sports considerably (e.g., stickball, slow-pitch baseball). Some of these new or adapted forms may be incorporated into the dominant culture, where they cease to be a form of resistance.

ISSUES IN THE STUDY OF SUBCULTURES

Subcultures have a significant impact on the participating individual, because of the unique values, beliefs, or norms associated with the distinct groups. Central to the idea of subculture are values, beliefs, identities (Donnelly & Young, 1988), and lifestyles that arise out of social interaction within a unique social situation (Donnelly, 1981a; Pearson, 1980; Williams & Donnelly, 1985). In effect, subcultures create new aspects of culture. Once these new aspects gain acceptance by a number of individuals, they begin to influence lifestyles.

Lifestyles are influenced by one's degree of identity and involvement with a particular subculture. As a general principle, the more the subculture has special meanings, symbols, dress, values, norms, beliefs, attitudes, language, or rituals for those involved, the greater the social and physical distance from outsiders.

The Creation of Sport Subcultures

In recent years, social scientists have tried to determine how subcultures are created and how individuals come to be members. Arnold (1970) has concluded that subcultures arise (a) in response to some problem, deprivation, or opportunity common to a group of people or to a specific environment (e.g., poverty); (b) as a result of interaction that creates social distance, social conflict, or the awareness of lifestyle differences (e.g., sailors vs. powerboaters); and (c) when a shared frame of reference and group action emerge (e.g., professional women's tennis tour).

Shibutani (1955) emphasizes that an essential part of a unique social world is a formal communication network. This network serves as a reference point for the unique social world, because of the special meanings and symbols it disseminates. Furthermore, this communication system may accentuate differences and increase social distance from outsiders. For example, the social worlds of skiing, surfing, and pool rooms all have unique language and communication networks for acquiring and disseminating information among *insiders*. In the 1960s, for instance, one member of the skiing subculture could have said to another, "She was wedeling a headwall loaded with bathtubs, but caught an edge, helicoptered down the fall line and wound up with a spiral in the tibia." Translated, this passage recounts how the woman, while downhill skiing, was making a series of tight parallel turns (wedeling) on a steep incline (headwall) full of depressions (bathtubs) made by skiers who had fallen. She caught an edge of the ski and fell head over heels straight down the hill, suffering a spiral fracture of the tibia.

Pearson (1979) developed a model to describe the process of subcultural emergence and development. First, individuals with an interest in X (e.g., X = windsurfing) find themselves in a common social situation (e.g., they have joined a club or use the same setting or facilities). As a result, those not involved in X are excluded. Shared attitudes, beliefs, and behaviors unique to the group become more immediate; facets of the dominant culture are selectively (consciously or unconsciously) set aside. Individual and group beliefs, attitudes, and behavior solidify, and a new group emerges. The more this cycle is repeated, the greater the likelihood that channels of communication will expand beyond the original group. This attracts new recruits to the subculture. Even if individuals do not formally join the original group, they may become part of the subculture if they adhere to some of the attitudes, beliefs, norms, and values communicated to them. For example, the surfing subculture has diffused throughout the world, and different variants such as surfboard riders and surf lifesavers in Australia and New Zealand have evolved (Pearson, 1979, 1980).

Characteristics of Sport Subcultures

Donnelly (1981a, 1985) suggests there are eight distinguishing characteristics of subcultures:

- an identifiable group that may transcend national boundaries (e.g., surfers around the world);
- a group (or groups) of interacting members who possess common cultural characteristics;
- the creation and change in a set of unique cultural components such as beliefs, customs, values, norms, language, and dress;
- distinct and unique qualities different from those in the parent or dominant culture;

- varying degrees of commitment to the lifestyle and varying amounts of information possessed by members;
- variations in the scope and potential of the activity, interest, or belief so that there is room for personal growth (i.e., the common interest will not become simply a fad or craze and thereby disappear);
- fulfillment of participants' psychological, social, or material needs through rewards such as an identity, status, friendship, knowledge, or money; and
- a means of communication to share and disseminate information and thereby maintain the subculture.

It has been suggested that close social interaction is not always required for a subculture. For example, Pearson (1979) notes that surfboard riders in Australia comprise a subculture, because they share common values and a way of life; yet members seldom if ever interact with each other. In short, subcultures may be independent of any set of individuals and represent a pattern, with many scattered people sharing a universe of meanings.

Changes and Conflict Within Subcultures

Using surfing as an example, Irwin (1973) described how subcultures evolve. The subcultural lifestyle is facilitated by being free of other commitments, by developing new patterns of behavior and language, and by focusing leisure time and interest around one activity (e.g., surfing, skiing, skydiving). When the lifestyle comes to the attention of *outsiders*, these outsiders, in turn, may become insiders in a different locale. If the activity becomes popular, which is often facilitated by movies or television (e.g., *The Endless Summer* and songs by the Beach Boys were catalysts for surfing), a mass of outsiders dis-

cover the scene and want *in*. The influx of new members can change the scene in a variety of ways. Changes may include introduction of competition, creation of social organization(s), influx of conspicuous displays (e.g., clothing and equipment), introduction of bizarre or deviant behavior, and redefinition of the activity's meaning. The end result may be so different that the original members must create a new subculture. In effect, subcultures are dynamic social entities that constantly undergo change in membership, structure, and meaning.

Conflict sometimes arises between members of the subculture and outsiders because of different values and lifestyles. To illustrate, conflict has arisen between rock climbers and park administrators and between the public and members of the climbing subcultures over rights to the natural environment. Conflict can also occur within a subculture when contrasting meanings of the activity evolve. For example, some rock climbers view the activity as a mystical or expressive experience; others see it as a competitive experience. Similarly, some skiers identify with racing, others with the aesthetic element.

Conflict in meaning or style seldom occurs in the martial arts. This subculture tends to have a rigid social organization and demands strict adherence to certain norms and beliefs. For example, the master of the club is the peer group leader, father-figure, and folk hero, who functions as a benevolent dictator. Many individuals become interested in the martial arts as a means of self-defense (e.g., judo, karate). Those who become fully socialized accept the ritual, mystique, and discipline and accept the challenge of progressing through clearly defined levels of skill (i.e., from the novice *white belt* to several stages within the *black belt*).

This subculture is also unique in that physical and social interaction is dictated by status (i.e., the color of one's belt). In this status hierarchy, the composition of a level will change as individuals improve their skills at different rates. When they earn the right to wear different belts, they interact with those on a higher level.

Identifying Subcultures

How do we tell subcultures from each other and from the dominant culture? Some investigators conclude that a subculture can only be identified and understood when components of the culture and subculture are measured and compared to note differences, similarities, and possibilities for conflict.

And how do we determine a person's degree of involvement in one or more subcultures? For example, an individual may visit a ski area for one week a year or may migrate to the area, establish roots, and become an informal or formal leader in the community. Similarly, individuals may enter related subcultures sequentially (e.g., from skier to hang-glider to glider pilot to balloonist). Or, because of similar physical or lifestyle components, they may have multiple involvements in a variety of social worlds at the same time or during different seasons of the year (e.g., surfing, diving, and skiing; dune-buggy riding, moto-cross racing, and snowmobiling).

AVOCATIONAL SPORT SUBCULTURES

An **avocational sport subculture** is created when a leisure activity offers a substantial contribution to ordinary life (i.e., work and family). For some, an avocational pursuit represents an *ephemeral role*—one that satisfies social or psychological needs not met completely by the more dominant and lasting daily work and family roles (Steele & Zurcher

1973). The activities may enhance a person's sense of identity or provide thrills in ways not available to the person otherwise. Thus, a Little League coach acquires power and the status of a decision-making leader. Similarly, Jacobs (1976) describes the karate dojo as a "place where some aspect of their many-sided selves can become rooted, a place where a uniform and a colored belt become the criteria of who they are and what they do, in this time, in that place" (p. 142).

Today, some of the more popular mass participation avocational subcultures are fitness-related and include such activities as bodybuilding (Featherston & Hepworth, 1984; Klein, 1986), cycling (Albert, 1984), and running (Brown & Curtis, 1984; McTeer & Curtis, 1984).

Types of Avocational Subcultures

Some avocational subcultures are unique adaptations of popular spectator sports, with different rules and structure, a different style, a special language, and a freedom to experiment and have fun in a nonthreatening environment. Some recent examples include the inner-city (playground) game of basketball; ball hockey or roller-skate hockey instead of ice hockey; and stickball or *pitching-in* instead of baseball. People in these subcultures may dislike or oppose the existing sport opportunities.

Nonspectator, high-risk subcultures exist, where involvement is voluntary, challenging, vigorous, and escapist. Some examples include skiing, surfing, parachuting, rock climbing, mountain climbing, the martial arts, and such technologically based sports as windsurfing, hang gliding, sailplaning (soaring), bobsledding, scuba diving, dragracing, hot rodding, dune-buggy riding, snowmobiling, powerboat racing, or moto-cross racing. Many of these subcultures have been

The martial arts is one example of a nonspectator, high-risk subculture.

studied in depth, because they are perceived to represent unique lifestyles, often with values and norms that are distinct from, and sometimes in opposition to, the dominant culture. Indeed, sometimes the behavior of these groups may be perceived as deviant in the eyes of mainstream society.

Avocational Versus Occupational Subcultures

Within an avocational subculture, not everyone is involved to the same degree or at the same time. For some, involvement is cyclical; for others it is regular and well integrated into their lifestyle; still others become totally immersed in the activity. Participation in a subculture may become a full-time commitment—an occupational subculture. To illustrate, the recreational skier may become

a ski instructor; the surfer may open a surf shop at a favorite beach.

Similarly, what is ostensibly an avocational subculture can become a preoccupational subculture when a leisure activity is fashioned after the professional world. For example, youth sport programs have increasingly become training environments for high school, college, or professional sport. Youth sport teaches the appropriate norms, values, attitudes, and skills needed to succeed at a higher level of competition.

To illustrate, youth sport participants learn about occupational patterns of behavior (e.g., only the highly skilled play and get rewarded); values (e.g., winning is all that counts; be aggressive; deviate from the rules if necessary); beliefs (e.g., an elite career must begin early in life and include extensive competition, perhaps more games per year than some professional teams); and symbols (e.g., trophies, uniforms, jackets, bonuses for playing for a specific team). Highlight 10.1 shows the importance coaches assign to aggressiveness among young hockey players and the ways they encourage young athletes to model the behavior of professional athletes.

Similar practices and views are reported by Ralbovsky (1974a, 1974b) and Voigt (1974) in their analyses of Little League baseball. Voigt wrote the following based on his experience as a Little League baseball manager:[1]

> . . . a new league ruling changed to our advantage the months of a boy's age eligibility. It was a ruling Fred and I helped to push through. . . . Given this diplomatic coup, I planned to . . . lure one of the star players from the Updyke Boy's

Highlight 10.1
The Introduction of Professional Sport Behavior Into Minor Hockey

Coaches of minor hockey frequently expect their team members to behave like professional hockey players. Nowhere is this better illustrated than in pregame speeches where young players are urged to play aggressively. Some believe that the demonstration of aggressiveness has become more highly rewarded than the demonstration of fundamental skills. The following quotes from a participant observation study of minor hockey (Vaz and Thomas, 1974) illustrate this preprofessional training and the concern with aggressiveness.

Be ready tonight. . . . You're going to get mad at them right now, and we are going to hit them. (p. 4)

As long as they are playing competitive hockey, there's nothing wrong with playing it tough, and that's the way kids should be taught. . . . Otherwise they should go to the park with a puck and stick and go for a skate. That's the game. . . . You take Gordie Howe. . . . You try to out-muscle him in the corner with the puck and you'll get 17 elbows in the face. . . . If you want to play the game, play it tough, don't play it like a sissy. (p. 9)

League into our camp. If this new strategy worked we had a darned good shot at the championship. . . . (p. 13)

We had to make the most of a recruiting campaign. (p. 15)

With only eleven good players on hand we had no problem identifying the six "plumbers" whose fate would be to ride the bench and work to develop their skills for shots at starting posts in 1974. (p. 13)

Being a plumber meant spending hours standing in the field waiting to get in somewhat fewer licks. It was a clear caste system. (p. 23)

Vic's best asset was a father who worked him daily and saw to it that he moonlighted in another league with kids his own age. (p. 19)

Although it has many of the same characteristics as an occupational subculture, an avocational subculture is unique in that

- the meaning of the activity is normally more expressive than instrumental;
- there is normally less time commitment, at least in the initial stages;
- the recruitment and socialization processes are less formalized;
- the social organization is less bureaucratic;
- withdrawal from the sport is normally voluntary and less traumatic;
- there is less status differentiation and mobility within the sport, although pres-

tige rankings based on skill do evolve; and

- the activity is more likely to occur without an audience.

Rewards for Involvement in Avocational Subcultures

Through avocational subcultures, participants escape the dominant culture and engage in social interaction with others who have similar interests, knowledge, norms, and experiences. For some, involvement in the subculture may be sporadic or limited only to weekends and holidays; for others it may comprise their central life interest and activity (e.g., the surfer or ski bum). Regardless of the degree of commitment, those involved share common meanings of the activity. These include a desire to escape from daily routine or to search for and experience freedom; a desire to challenge the self; and a desire to escape an urban setting and enjoy a more natural environment.

To illustrate, Pearson (1979) contrasts the surfboard-riding and surf-lifesaving subcultures. Each group has developed a different meaning of surfing and contrasting value orientations. The surfboard riders are hedonistic and mobile. The surf lifesavers are achievement-oriented and stable. The latter simply wish to compete as a member of their club and to save lives. Table 10.1 illustrates a number of differences between these two surfing subcultures.

OCCUPATIONAL SPORT SUBCULTURES

Sport has mirrored the social trend toward specialization and greater time commitment. This has led to some sport roles becoming an *occupation* rather than an *avocation*. Sport now

requires full-time occupations such as athlete, coach, owner, trainer, league or game official, and various media roles. In order to recruit and socialize personnel, an **occupational sport subculture** has evolved for each of these roles, particularly that of athlete.

Because there are different lifestyles within and among sports, a number of studies have examined various career contingencies and ways of life in specific sport occupations. Some of these include the worlds of boxing (Weinberg & Arond, 1952); wrestling (Rosenberg & Turowetz, 1975); baseball (Brandmeyer & Alexander, 1982); horseracing (Scott, 1968); football (Stebbins, 1987); hockey (Gallmeier, 1987; Vaz, 1982); the women's professional golf tour (Theberge, 1977); game officials (Rains, 1984; Snyder & Purdy, 1987); and college football (Brislin, 1982). These analyses have been based on the autobiographies of former athletes or officials or on the work of journalists or scholars who have explored sport from the inside.

Through observing participants or using survey-research technique, these studies have described (and to varying degrees explained)

- anticipatory socialization and the acquisition of prerequisite technical and social skills;
- recruitment patterns;
- informal and formal occupational socialization processes;
- norms, values, and expectations concerning interaction with those inside (e.g., the team) and outside (e.g., owners, media, fans, officials) the subculture;
- the learning and diffusion of the subculture's argot (language);
- social organization, social status, and social mobility within the sport; and
- mechanisms of coping with failure, demotion, dismissal, and retirement and subsequent adjustment to the dominant culture.

Table 10.1   Two Contrasting Avocational Subcultures: Surf Lifesavers Versus Surfboard Riders

Surf lifesavers	Surfboard riders
Surf weekends and on holidays in the summer.	Surf all year at every opportunity, not just weekends and holidays. More likely to surf full time in the summer or winter.
Surf after work.	Surf before, after, or during work hours.
Can't drop work to surf (typically).	Can drop work to surf.
More likely to live in one place most of the year.	Less likely to live in one place for most of the year (though a majority do).
Surf close to home at a few spots.	Travel further to more spots to surf.
Prefer to surf well-known beaches or surf spots.	Perfer to surf lesser-known spots.
Definitely favor surf lifesaving competition.	Less likely to favor surf lifesaving competition.
In favor of competitive boardriding.	Less in favor of competitive boardriding.
Belong to clubs and associations.	Typically do not belong to clubs or associations.
Highly likely to own regular (sedan type) car.	More likely to own a panel van, or similar vehicle, which may be used for sleeping.
Sleep in a vehicle only on occasional weekends or holidays.	Likely to sleep in a vehicle frequently or even to live in it for weeks or months at a time.
Perceive authorities' attitude as unthreatening.	Perceive authorities' attitude as threatening or hostile.
More likely to feel that drugs play no part or a small part in surfing.	Likely to consider drugs a part of surfing.
Believe work should be more important than leisure.	Believe leisure should be more important than work.

Note. Reprinted with permission from: PEARSON K. The Concept Subculture: A Basic Tool in Defining and Understanding Sports Phenomena. (in) LANDRY F, ORBAN WAR (Eds). Physical Activity and Human Well-Being. Volume 2, Miami: Symposia Specialists, 1978, p. 566.

In short, professional sport teams, as occupational subcultures, must recruit and socialize new members, develop and maintain stability in the organization, and require or permit members to leave when their skill declines.

Recruitment and Socialization Into Occupational Sport Subcultures

The process of recruiting and socializing potential members into some professional sport roles actually begins in early childhood. It continues during the high school and college years via a preprofessional training program (Brislin, 1982; Vaz, 1982). The process begins, indirectly, when youths identify early in life with role models in professional sport. For some this may involve a face-to-face interaction (e.g., with boxers in a neighborhood gym or club); it may be vicarious interaction, through watching or following sports in the mass media. Whether an individual becomes socialized into a specific type of sport subculture (e.g., boxing rather than tennis) is often related to the social class or ethnic or racial background of the family and neighborhood.

Youth Sport Programs.

A youth interested in sport can become involved in organized youth sport programs, which are modeled after professional sport, including such facets as rules, rankings, uniforms, practices, norms, attitudes, values, language, rituals, and symbols.

To illustrate, Vaz (1972) reports that the values and institutionalized aggressive behavior (e.g., fighting) characteristic of professional hockey is encouraged, taught, and learned in minor hockey programs. Here aspiring professionals acquire definitions, meanings, and skills associated with that sport and begin to construct an identity similar to the professionals. They begin to exhibit the attitudes, mannerisms, dress, speech, and behavior (on and off the playing field) of those they admire in the profession. As a result some are labeled, and label themselves, as particular types of role players early in the occupational socialization process (e.g., a goon in hockey, a relief pitcher in baseball, a defensive specialist).

Preprofessional Athletics.

Having demonstrated some potential in a youth sport subculture, athletes are recruited to the more formal preprofessional stages, which may or may not be conducted in a school setting. For example, professional football and basketball depend on colleges and universities for training new members; baseball, hockey, and tennis depend on the private, voluntary sector and minor league affiliates.

Professional wrestling promoters recruit former football players or college wrestlers for their potential skill; they also recruit others for some unique physical, social, or personality characteristic (e.g., the heavyweight, the midget, the aggressive female, or the ethnic stereotype). The recruits are trained first to acquire the physical skills and then to work up a social identity that fits their physical image (e.g., Hulk Hogan, the good guy; King Kong Bundy, the heaviest wrestler, at 490 pounds; Big John Stud or Andre the Giant, the tallest at over 7 feet), which will appeal to the wrestling audience (Birrell & Turowetz, 1979; Stone 1972).

Although much of the general skills socialization is complete by the time an athlete enters a professional sport subculture, further socialization into the subculture of a specific team is usually necessary. That is, an *integrated unit* must be developed that understands and shares the values, behaviors, and attitudes deemed essential for the team's success.

Maintenance of Occupational Sport Subcultures

The continued existence of any professional or occupational subculture depends on the presence of a clearly identified social structure. Generally this consists of *insiders*, such as athletes, coaches, owners, scouts, managers, and trainers; and *outsiders*, such as league officials, media personnel, and the fans. Both categories place varying demands on the individual, and role conflicts often arise. Conflicts can be resolved by quitting or by being consistent and successful at impression management or identity make-up. For example, fans value baseball as a game, which conflicts with the players' view that it is work and the owners' view that it is a business. Athletes must thus play different roles for insiders and outsiders.

Assigning Levels.

Within subcultures there are varying degrees of prestige attached to various roles, depending on skill, the level of competition, or the ability to work up a marketable identity. For example, in most team sports and in some individual sports there are major and minor leagues, each with different values, norms, and lifestyles. Major league teams travel by air, assign players single rooms in luxury hotels, and give players trainers to look after their equipment. Minor league teams usually travel on buses, assign three or four players to a room in motels that vary in quality, and expect players to pack and carry their own equipment.

Most sports have a system of rankings or ratings that place individuals somewhere on a vertical ladder, either within an organization (e.g., baseball players are assigned to teams designated as major league, Triple A, Double A, etc.) or across the sport (e.g., tennis players and boxers are ranked within their countries and throughout the world; there are 33 different belt rankings in the martial arts). These rankings provide incentive and encourage mobility. But they also encourage age-grading, that is, individuals recognize that they must attain a certain level of competition by a specific age if they are to be successful in their chosen sport. Often this opportunity is as much related to chance as ability, especially if a player is drafted by a successful organization, where competition for positions at the highest level is more demanding.

Learning Identities. Once an athlete enters the subculture at the highest professional level, his or her socialization continues. By this stage the learning is more informal and more concerned with developing a professional identity. Athletes learn and internalize certain values and coping styles. This involves learning occupational norms and the art of impression management in order to establish respect, avoid conflict, and become a marketable performer. Each athlete must learn the tolerable range of behavior in order to gain and retain the approval of teammates, opponents, management, and fans. To illustrate, Faulkner (1974) stresses the importance

of hockey players *making respect* or establishing a reputation in a new league and team by demonstrating physical toughness and a willingness to fight when challenged. This also involves putting on a game face by staging emotions (Gallmeier, 1987).

Similarly, professional wrestlers are expected to play their agreed-upon roles and not attempt to *shoot* a match (i.e., not go against the prescribed outcome and try to win on skill). Wrestling novices must work to develop and maintain an identity for outsiders, whether it be hero or villain. This involves learning cues, learning how to display and dramatize identity characteristics (e.g., behave like a madman), and learning how to generate responses from the audience.

In professional wrestling, performers sometimes must present contradictory images on succeeding nights in different towns. This process is risky, because wrestlers may come to believe that they are truly invincible or truly evil. They can go beyond the dramatized identity and adopt the characteristics in their everyday lives. Stone (1972) cites examples of former wrestlers whose careers ended abruptly when their wrestling identities became considered *real* by themselves or others, resulting in personal attacks by fans or bizarre personal behaviors.

Professional athletes become adept at impression management or identity work in the public region of their social world (Goffman, 1959). These images are mentioned rigorously and systematically to please the fans. Charnofsky (1968) discusses how baseball players have traditionally accepted public criticism, signed autographs by the thousands, avoided fraternization away from the field with opponents who are friends, and presented themselves as All-American males in order to sell tickets and thereby earn a salary. These behaviors may be violated in the private region of the locker or hotel room, where players often speak of adult fans as naive, uninformed, and fickle (Bouton, 1970).

The role of the audience in maintaining these images varies from having no influence (e.g., jai-alai), to some influence (e.g., demands made of athletes on professional team sports), to a great deal (e.g., in professional wrestling, where they are part of the scene). Many professional wrestling fans accept that the match is staged and demand only that it be done well and that *good* win out over *evil*. It does not matter whether the contest represents conflict between social classes, ethnic groups, racial groups, good guys and bad guys, or beauty and ugliness. Stone (1972) suggests that the primarily lower-class status of wrestling fans, with their predisposition to not question the concrete world, makes them more susceptible to staging—as long as it is done well and represents a conflict with which they can identify.

Rituals and Argots.

An occupational subculture also needs, for its continuation, a link with its history, a continuing development of an argot (language), and the presence of rituals, superstitions, and taboos unique to itself. For example, most subcultures search for and draw comparisons between new recruits and past heroes to promote both continuity and interest among the fans (e.g., the *next* Michael Jordan, Wayne Gretzky, Martina Navratilova). Similarly, development of a new argot reflects innovation and increasing sophistication. A unique language can isolate athletes from fans, or it can stimulate greater cognitive and emotional involvement among fans. The latter is illustrated by the evolution of basketball terminology (e.g., lay-up, reverse lay-up, slam dunk, run-and-gun, sky hook, tomahawk slam, 360 thunder dunk, and finger-rolls).

Withdrawal From Occupational Sport Subcultures

Retirement comes early in sport for most athletes (often before 30 years of age) and is usually involuntary. Athletes, many of whom have little experience outside the world of sport, must either leave the subculture or remain in a different capacity. Often the new capacity involves less prestige and less money.

Boxers, for example, may retire with serious and lasting physical or mental impairments. With few job skills and often little money, many boxers experience a rapid descent in economic and social status. Often this is accompanied by severe emotional problems as they try to adjust to life outside the boxing subculture. Many return to the boxing world and attempt to fight past their prime or occupy low-status positions in local boxing clubs as trainers or *gophers*. Some simply cannot leave or escape the subculture.

Sources of Difficulty.

How athletes leave the subculture is partially related to how they entered it. For example, athletes generally enter male professional team sports via college or after high school. The noncollege player appears to be more involved in the occupation and signs a professional contract much earlier in life. He spends more time in professional sport, is more likely to postpone planning for the retirement years, and, if possible, resists retirement and plays into his 30s at some level of competition. He often spends years at the end of the career in lesser leagues before leaving the subculture.

These individuals have limited career options once their playing career is ended. Withdrawal may be traumatic, because the players have lived within the subculture their entire adult lives. Indeed, many never leave and find lesser-status roles as scouts, coaches, or trainers. Faced with an identity crisis and having few marketable skills, they retreat to other employment within the sport subculture.

A different career profile is represented by the college-educated player, who begins a professional career later and usually ends it much earlier. Sport may serve these individuals as a mobility path, where they acquire a prestigious postplaying position outside the subculture before they are forced to retire. Often they have a university degree and marketable skills, and use their qualifications to retire from sport at an early age. Moreover, these individuals are usually less committed to the subcultural life of professional sport.

Coping Mechanisms. Marginal players, who are unlikely to move up to the major leagues or get a chance at the big money, may use face-saving techniques to maintain an image of success. For example, Faulkner (1975) found that players used various mechanisms to sustain their motivation in the minor leagues. Players might redefine their self-images to rationalize lack of mobility or demotions, stressing the benefits of their present positions (e.g., the kids are in a good school; it is a nice community; the money is good here). Other arguments used by career minor league players to rationalize their permanent status include: (a) there is a price to be paid in moving up the career ladder (e.g., more pressure; instability for the family; loss of good friends); (b) average recognition or esteem is better than being out of the public eye (e.g., I am well known here); and (c) the position provides time to develop other interests outside sport (e.g., family; leisure pursuits in a smaller community; off-season career possibilities).

DEVIANT SPORT SUBCULTURES

Most avocational and occupational subcultures involve acceptable patterns of social behavior. A sport subculture may differ sufficiently from the mainstream society to be labeled a **deviant sport subculture**. Some examples include sport environments where hustling, cheating, gambling, institutionalized violence, or deviant social acts take place.

Until about the early 1970s, athletes and sport were perceived as models of normative social behavior. We placed athletes on pedestals and encouraged youth to emulate them. Sport once seemed to be a social institution that was immune to deviant behavior; this is no longer true, for a variety of reasons. The incidence of deviant behavior is increasing, and so is the reporting of deviant acts and the study of deviant behavior by scholars and journalists. At one time deviant acts by athletes may have been covered up, ignored, or denied; modern journalists and scholars report and study the phenomenon.

Sport sociologists in particular have been interested in three questions.

- Are athletes less likely to engage in deviant behavior than nonathletes?
- To what extent, and why, are the formal and informal rules of sport violated?
- To what extent, and why, are athletes engaging in nonsport-related deviance?

Although some sport subcultures are labeled as deviant per se (e.g., rugby), some form of deviant behavior is often present in most sport subcultures.

Sources of Deviance

Deviant behavior is a product of numerous interacting social and cultural forces. These include an inadequate socialization process; lack of, or failure of, social controls; perceived inequities in a situation; the individual's definition of the situation; and the labeling of individuals who engage in deviance. More specifically, one learns deviant behavior by directly and indirectly acquiring opportunities, skills, or attitudes; by observing others engaged in the behavior; and by being rewarded for such behavior.

Whether a behavior is defined as deviant or not may change over time, as legal or moral values and norms change. It often depends on the group evaluating the behavior and enforcing the norms. What is viewed as deviance by outsiders, is often more likely to be considered *sanctioned deviance* by those within the subculture, especially within sport. That is, sport insiders often tolerate a wider range of deviation from the norms of the wider culture.

For example, tripping or pushing an opponent who is about to score violates the norm of fair play and the formal norms of the game yet may be sanctioned by coaches, players, and spectators as a necessary act. In fact, it may become established as an informal norm within a particular sport subculture (e.g., in basketball and hockey the act is perceived to be a *good* foul or penalty, respectively). Similarly, fighting in hockey, hustling in pool, or drinking at sport events are viewed by outsiders as deviant behaviors unique to specific subcultures.

Individuals learn deviant behavior in subcultures that value and reinforce certain behavioral patterns. For example, the use of violence, however defined, results from learning values that support violence. Similarly, hustling is an art acquired by hanging out in pool rooms, golf courses, and other places where one can hustle and be hustled.

Deviant Sport Acts

Within sport, deviance involves violating the rules of a game or organization, going beyond the commonly accepted definitions of fair play and sportsmanship, and intentionally using illegal means to intimidate or injure an opponent (Eitzen, 1981, 1988). Deviance occurs both on and off the playing field and involves players, coaches, administrators, and college alumni. Much of this deviance has arisen because of the increased bureaucratization and commercialization of sport—more rules, more pressure to win and earn a profit—and because league officials are unable or unwilling to penalize deviant acts.

Increasingly, athletes seem to be engaging in deviant behavior off the field (e.g., recreational drug use, which most consider legally or morally unacceptable) (Chass & Goodwin, 1986; Smith, G. 1983). Although the acts may not have serious consequences, they cause concern because sport figures are considered role models for youth.

We could cite numerous incidents of deviant acts off the field, but the social life of the rugby subculture alone provides an excellent example. A unique feature of rugby is that its behavioral patterns are highly similar in many cultures, and they are considered normative within the subculture. Sheard & Dunning (1973) noted the rugby subculture allows its players

> to behave with impunity in a manner which would bring immediate condemnation and punishment were it to occur among other social strata or even among members of the upper and middle classes in a different social setting. (p. 7)

Deviant behavior has become a ritualized and integral facet of rugby players' lifestyles. Off the field, rugby players violate societal norms regarding fighting, obscene language and songs, nakedness (a male striptease is a ritual at rugby parties), drunkenness, and vandalism against property.

Sheard and Dunning (1973) argue that rugby historically has been a male preserve, and the deviance began as a response to the threatened masculinity of middle- and upper-class males during the suffragette movement. Rugby filled men's need for a private refuge away from women.

However, recent excursions of women into the rugby subculture have not been perceived as a threat to men. Women occupy obscure positions and continue to be abused verbally (e.g., in songs) or physically (e.g., the "butt bite" is a traditional initiation rite for a woman entering the rugby social world).

Thomson (1977) suggests that this antisocial behavior is underreported or ignored, because the sport does not conflict with the values of the dominant ideology. In contrast, similar behavior by a motorcycle gang might be condemned, because most of their values *do* appear to conflict with those of society. A second explanation is that traditions of deviance in sport have led to the behavior being viewed as legitimate deviance, which is condoned and perhaps even encouraged as a safety valve for releasing tension. Highlight 10.2 illustrates how there is socially sanctioned deviance, as well, in the subculture of women's rugby teams.

Some behavior is perceived as deviant—but not negative—because the activity is pursued with an intensity beyond the bounds deemed appropriate or normal. Some recent examples include excessive involvement in long-distance running and bodybuilding (Ewald & Jiobu, 1985), to a level of addiction.

CHEATING IN SPORT SUBCULTURES

Cheating involves bending the interpretation or breaking the rules of a game or organization. People cheat to change or control the outcome of a contest. It happens more often when the rewards are high, when there are many rules (e.g., the NCAA), where technology is an important element of the game (e.g., auto or bicycle racing) or when the outcome is highly uncertain, either because of the element of chance or the perceived equal-

ity of the competition (Eitzen, 1981; Luschen, 1976; Wertz, 1981).

The subcultures of many sports call for the practice of what outsiders would call cheating. Athletes, coaches, administrators, and even officials, sometimes engage in unfair practices in a sport contest. But often this behavior is expected by the norms of the subculture. Violations are usually penalized but may be considered necessary and good by those in the game setting. Some examples include intentionally tripping or pushing a player on a breakaway in hockey or basketball or tackling a receiver before the football arrives. These examples of intentional cheating become part of the tactics and strategy of a game.

Routinized and Deviant Cheating

Some forms of cheating have become *routinized* or *institutionalized* (Eitzen, 1981) and generally are accepted as part of a game. "Everyone does it; we can do it" is a common argument to justify the act. Some examples of this type of cheating are intentionally falling in hockey, faking an injury to pressure the official into awarding a penalty or foul, interference (i.e., picks) in football or basketball, and hitting an opponent after the whistle to intimidate or to draw a retaliatory penalty. These incidents are taught and encouraged by coaches and fans. Often they are used to test the interpretation of gray areas in the rules or to gain a psychological advantage over an opponent.

By contrast, *deviant* cheating is seldom accepted and, if detected, usually generates severe punishment. Covert and often undetected cheating could include, for example, improving one's lie in golf; playing below one's level of ability to fix games or hustle an opponent; violating academic rules (falsifying transcripts, awarding unearned cred-

Highlight 10.2
Deviance in Women's Rugby

In contrast to Sheard and Dunning's (1973) portrayal of rugby as a "male preserve," Wheatley's (1986) subcultural examination of female rugby teams shows that women can achieve positions of power and control in sport. Where male rugby players view women as sex objects or as people to ridicule and abuse physically, women in the female rugby subculture turn men into the victims of abuse or neglect. As marginal or peripheral participants, men are usually surprised and shocked by the profanity, drinking habits, absence of modesty, and apparent approval of homosexuality that is demonstrated in this female sport subculture, and cannot understand why they are ignored by the female participants.

Participation in rugby is usually perceived as an atypical leisure behavior for women. This view is compounded by postgame behavior, which, like that of male rugby players, runs counter to common social norms—singing lewd songs, holding drinking contests, using profanity, and exhibiting bruises acquired in a match. This behavior violates accepted notions of what is feminine. Thus, the female rugby subculture acquires a different identity from both mainstream society and from other women's sports. In this way, female rugby players challenge our assumptions about what constitutes feminine behavior, about which leisure activities are appropriate for women, and about women's views on alternative forms of sexuality. Clearly women create somewhat different meanings, values, and lifestyles within the female rugby subculture. As Wheatley (1986) concludes:

> In rejecting the socially constructed feminine identity dictated by patriarchal society, the female rugby subculture assumes a different identity, one which allows for more flexibility and freedom. In assuming this identity, they effectively challenge the constraining ideologies imposed through oppressive patriarchal domination. (pp. 16-17)

its, playing ineligible athletes); not negotiating with free agents as required by the collective bargaining agreement; stealing play books from opponents; altering the playing surface (e.g., watering the base paths to slow a team that has the ability to steal bases); and using illegal equipment (e.g., a racket, bat, or stick that exceeds the legal size).

Cheating may occur less in sport than in other social institutions, for a variety of reasons. First, officials and viewers watch for such behavior, and an elaborate set of rules and by-laws restrict, inhibit, or prevent cheating. Second, cheating by an individual or team breeds cheating by opponents. In tennis, for example, the player who constantly awards close calls in his favor can expect similar behavior from his opponent. Players and officials thus often agree, within a specific game or for a given sport, on what

Intentional cheating, such as holding in basketball, has become part of the tactics and strategy of many sports.

forms of cheating will be allowed. This is how interference, holding, and fouling from behind (all against the *formal* rules) have become routinized forms of cheating in football, hockey, soccer, and basketball; kicking or hitting an opponent with a bat or stick remain severe violations that are not tolerated.

Drugs

In recent years, sport authorities have had to detect and punish athletes' use of drugs to enhance performance (Stuck, 1988; Luschen, 1984). The use of drugs to improve performance beyond one's natural ability violates both the sense of fair play and the formal rules of most sports. Through doping techniques, an individual can gain advantage over others in strength (e.g., anabolic steroids), endurance (e.g., blood doping), speed, con-

centration, and the ability to continue play while injured or experiencing pain.

Previously, drug use most commonly was associated with such sports as boxing, horse racing, and professional bicycle racing. Today, athletes in a number of sports use drugs to enhance performance—often arguing that they must to remain competitive with other athletes using drugs. But the blame cannot be placed totally on the athlete. The perceived importance of gold medals and championships has encouraged fans, coaches, and sport officials to ignore this deviant behavior for many years. Similarly, the economic advantages of success for an athlete, team, and sponsor have encouraged the use of drugs to reap the benefits of endorsements and appearance fees.

Despite knowledge of later side-effects and an occasional death of an athlete from overdose, drug use was ignored in sport until the issue became a more widely known problem throughout society. Drug testing has now been introduced in many sports, along with drug-education programs. The practice persists, however, and athletes search for alternative drugs not yet detectable by existing tests. Athletes and coaches sometimes try to switch urine samples to escape detection and punishment.

Hustling

When an individual misrepresents his or her ability to manipulate the outcome of a game, the practice is called *hustling* (Bradshaw, 1987). To succeed, the hustler must enter the contest on even or favorable terms and sustain it long enough to maximize success or profit. Some of the better-known studies of hustlers focus on bowling (Steele, 1976), cards (Mahigel & Stone, 1976; Martinez & La Franchi, 1972; Prus & Sharper, 1979), and pool (Polsky, 1972).

To succeed, hustlers must spend most of their free time in the social milieu of their activity (e.g., bowling alley, pool room, card parlor, golf course), where they perfect both their game and their image. This is especially important in games where the hustler must deceive on the basis of his performance (e.g., miss shots, leave himself in a bad position, deliberately lose a game). Playing poorly cons the *mark* into entering or continuing a game. As Polsky (1972) notes, hustlers must never show their *real speed* (unless they find themselves being hustled), because they will exhaust the potential of that scene and be forced to move to another.

From the perspective of the dominant society, a hustler violates morally correct behavior toward one's fellow man and distorts a legitimate occupation. As a result, the hustler is often stigmatized and branded as a criminal who victimizes people. But many people engage in various forms of hustling. For example, some workers hustle their supervisors by constantly stressing how busy and overworked they are. In reality, they may be inefficient and underworked, with lots of time for long lunches, idle conversation with co-workers, and numerous coffee breaks.

A SUBCULTURE OF VIOLENCE IN SPORT?

Using street gangs as an example, some have argued that violence is a product of a subculture that encourages and rewards violence. Here, the toughest member usually has the highest status. Often these subcultures form among the lower class or in lower-status ethnic communities as a protest against the dominance of mainstream society.

Some scholars have argued that sports such as hockey and boxing comprise violent subcultures. Fighting, toughness, and demonstration of one's masculinity are encouraged

and rewarded in these sports because they were initially organized in this way. Certainly, less skilled boxers or hockey players often advance beyond their expected level of achievement because they act as "street fighters," "brawlers," or "goons." Other scholars have wondered whether the values and norms of athletes really differ from those of mainstream society and whether a violent subculture exists. Are the athletes merely adhering to an occupational norm that requires violence in certain situations? One test is whether the athletes engage in violent behavior away from the playing field to a greater extent than nonathletes.

Highlight 10.3 shows that on-ice behavior of hockey players is a poor predictor of off-ice behavior. There appears to be an occupational subculture that encourages and permits certain levels of violent behavior (fighting, but not stick-work) at some points in a game and at certain levels of competition. It seems clear that although isolated incidents of violence occur within some sports, these sports do not create an environment where violence is the norm. Also, the notion of a subculture of violence existing within all sports has little research support.

Institutionalized Interpersonal Violence

The learning of how and when to use violent forms of aggressive behavior begins early in the sport socialization process. The process involves observing the behavior of role models and the reactions of significant others (i.e., parents, fans, coaches) to the assaultive behavior. Once involved in community or school sport teams, the athlete is directly taught, and both formally and informally encouraged, to engage in aggressive acts. The behavior becomes a learned moral lesson that legitimates rule-violating behavior in specific

Highlight 10.3
A Subculture of Violence in Hockey: Myth or Fact?

It is frequently observed that organized youth hockey in Canada promotes an orientation toward fighting and other types of aggressive behavior that involve the hockey stick. It is alleged that these behaviors become important criteria for evaluation, and that players, coaches, and parents give approval for on-ice assaultive behavior against an opponent.

Does hockey attract and recruit players from a violent-prone subculture of society? Or do players learn to engage in violent behavior while progressing through the preprofessional occupational subculture of minor hockey? Based on extensive interviews with, and questionnaires completed by, hockey players aged 12 to 21, Smith (1983) found that players who receive more fighting and assaultive type of penalties also report higher scores, and therefore place more importance on values that promote the use of violence. This pattern increased for boys in progressively older age groups—that is, violent hockey

players share a subculture, and the values and behaviors characteristic of this violent subculture increase at higher levels of competition, where professional standards of conduct are more likely in force. Thus, violence becomes more legitimated as cultural values regarding the use of violence increase within the hockey subculture.

Smith found that contrary to conventional wisdom, violent hockey players are not more likely to engage in street fighting than other players or nonplayers. The violence expressed in hockey is an outcome, then, of the values and norms acquired within the hockey subculture in Canada. Further anecdotal evidence to support this subcultural theme of violence is shown by the lack of learned violent behavior on the part of European and Soviet hockey players. Pro-violent norms and values have not been inculcated within these hockey subcultures, as they have in Canada.

---

sport situations (Bredemeier, 1985; Mugno & Feltz, 1985; Silva, 1983; Smith, M.D., 1983). Highlight 10.4 illustrates how rule-violating behavior is learned and legitimated among young athletes.

Intentional assaults to injure or intimidate an opponent have been found, in some situations, to have a positive effect on performance (Widmeyer, 1984). For example, Widmeyer and Birch (1984) studied the types of penalties assessed during four seasons of play in the National Hockey League. They found

a positive relationship between the incidence of aggressive penalties (e.g., slashing, spearing, highsticking, boarding, charging, fighting) early in the game and winning the contest.

A number of authors have reported that assaults by players serve other more subtle functions (Bredemeier, 1985; Colburn, 1985; Goldstein, 1983; Silva, 1984). Some of these functions are acquiring honor and respect among peers; protecting nonaggressive star players; fostering team unity; enhancing one's

Highlight 10.4
Learning and Legitimation of Rule-Violating Behavior in Sport

To increase their chances of success, players periodically use excessive and unnecessary aggression in sports such as football, basketball, and hockey. Their strategy involves flagrant violation of the formal rules of the game, a behavior that is often learned and legitimated at an early age. Aggression, which involves a physical or verbal act designed to injure one's self or another physically or psychologically, is a learned form of behavior. Much of this learning occurs by observing and then imitating models who are rewarded for this type of behavior. Indeed, aggression in sport, whether legal or illegal, is judged as legitimate and expected behavior.

Studies of soccer, football, hockey, and basketball have found that specific acts of illegal assault observed in the play of college or professional players leads to similar behavior by youth and high school players (Bredemeier, 1985; Mugno & Feltz, 1985; Silva, 1983; Smith, 1983). Moreover, there appears to be a relationship between the number of illegal acts observed by players and the number of those acts used in their own games. These relationships generally are stronger with increasing levels of competition.

When players are asked if rule-violating behavior (e.g., spearing or a high-arm tackle in football; fighting or cross-checking in hockey; an elbow to the head or upper body in soccer or basketball; a brushback pitch in baseball; or a trip from behind in any sport) is legitimate or normative sport behavior, they have given some interesting responses. Specifically, males more than females, and males playing the sport longer and at higher levels of competition, perceived rule-violating behavior to be more legitimate, normal, and expected (Bredemeier, 1985).

In effect, in order to remain involved in progressively higher levels of sport competition, rule-violating behaviors must be learned and used. As a result, the perceived legitimacy of rule-violating behavior is increasingly internalized and accepted as normative behavior within the sport setting.

status and moral worth; entertaining the fans; and serving as a form of social control to inhibit more serious violent incidents (e.g., fighting in hockey instead of swinging sticks or spearing an opponent).

Hockey is unique among all sports in its fostering and legitimation of fistfighting. The meaning of this type of behavior is threefold. First, as noted above, violence is believed to influence the outcome of a game. Second, fighting attracts some fans and is encouraged and reinforced by spectators and the league. This view is supported by the high sales volume of hockey videotapes that feature fights between players. Beyond these direct purposes, fighting has become the modern equivalent of a ritualistic duel where a player, when challenged, must defend his honor and moral worth (Colburn, 1985). Thus, when an opponent drops gloves and stick, the informal norms of the game require the challenged player to behave likewise and fight. Players that back off or stall until an official intervenes run the risk of losing status and of having their moral worth and honor questioned.

It is interesting that only a small proportion of hockey players are socialized into fighting regularly. It has been estimated that in the National Hockey League, 2% of the players receive more than 20% of the penalty minutes. It seems that only a few players on each team are designated "hitmen".

Interpersonal Violence by Female Athletes

Once it was assumed that interpersonal violence on the playing field was unique to males, but increasingly the same behaviors are observed among female athletes (Bredemeier, 1985; Silva, 1983; Smith, 1983). Consider some examples from recent years.

- In an intramural championship basketball game, a female player threw the ball at the referee, and her coach punched the referee (Smith, 1983).
- The executive of a women's hockey league, at a meeting in 1982, suspended four female players for (a) spearing a referee with a stick; (b) kicking an opponent; (c) pushing an official; and (d) in retaliation for a punch from behind, swinging the stick like a baseball bat and hitting an opponent across the face mask.
- During the handshaking ritual following a college basketball game, a visiting coach confronted an opposing player who had thrown a ball in the face of one of her players after being fouled. The confronted player pushed the coach, and one of the coach's players grabbed the opposing player from behind, setting off a brawl. The confronted player sustained

a broken nose and bruised ribs; the visiting coach, who was knocked down and kicked in the ribs, allegedly defended herself by kicking opposing players (Kirkpatrick, 1987).
- A 24-year-old female hockey player was placed on probation for 18 months by a district court judge after being found guilty of assaulting an official during a hockey tournament. The player, after receiving a penalty, put a headlock on the female official and flipped her to the ice, causing a separated shoulder.

To some extent, this increase in verbal harassment, intimidation, and physical assault by female athletes and coaches reflects greater opportunities for women to participate in contact and combat sports. A number of other reasons have been identified as well, including

- an increased value on winning as women's sport has become more competitive and professionalized;
- women becoming socialized into sport by a process similar to males and learning similar values, norms, and behaviors;
- women wanting to be preceived as equal to male athletes and thereby demonstrating valued males behaviors; and
- increased crime and violence by women in the general society, which may spill over into sport.

Although the anecdotal evidence suggests that interpersonal violence is becoming an integral behavioral and value component of some women's sport, the level of violence in women's sport has probably not yet reached that of men's sport.

DELINQUENCY AND SPORT

Sport has been portrayed as a legitimate part of the high school, college, and community social worlds, in part because of its alleged deterrent effect on juvenile delinquency. Most of the research that has examined the relationship between rates of delinquency and athletic involvement has found that there is a *negative* association (Donnelly, 1981b; Hastad, Segrave, Pangrazi, & Petersen, 1984; Purdy & Richard, 1983; Segrave, 1983). That is, delinquency is less likely to occur among athletes.

The relationship seems to be stronger among lower-class youth, where delinquency tends to be more prevalent and to involve more serious types of offenses. Thus, relative to others in their social world, lower-class athletes are less involved in delinquent behavior and, in general, are less involved in criminal offenses like vandalism, robbery, and assault.

Most delinquent acts by athletes in recent years have involved college or professional athletes. They have been charged with offenses such as drunk driving, buying or selling illegal drugs, point-shaving, assault on police officers or women, murder, breaking and entering, and theft (Johnson, 1983).

Interestingly, a study of 15- and 16-year-old hockey players found that the higher the level of play the lower the involvement in delinquent behavior (Segrave, Hastad, & Moreau, 1985). It may be that adults who coach at the higher level of play exert more social control (e.g., curfews, supervised study). However, violent forms of delinquency appeared to be prevalent at all levels of play.

Investigators trying to explain the negative association between involvement in sport and rates of delinquency have noted that the relationship may be explained by factors other than the assumed positive influence of sport (Segrave, 1983; Segrave & Hastad, 1984a, 1984b). For example, delinquent-prone youth may be less attracted to sport as a leisure activity, or they may have been removed from sport teams. Notwithstanding these caveats,

Segrave and Hastad (1984b) found that among male and female high school athletes delinquent behavior was less likely to occur. They believe this occurs because athletes associate with peers and adults who tend toward conformity, stress adherence to social norms, and stress conventional values. And even for delinquent youth, interscholastic athletic participation was cited as a compelling reason to stay in school.

ARE TEAMS SUBCULTURES?

As a result of frequent interaction and shared experiences among its members, every sport team develops its own **idioculture**. Included are customs, values, beliefs, norms, language, a status hierarchy, and artifacts—all unique to that team. These go beyond characteristics common to the subculture associated with the specific sport. Most sociologists would not define these team cultures as subcultures, because they depart only minimally from the sport subculture. Whether we should label teams *subcultures* depends on how much uniqueness is required.

Some of the most and least successful teams have been observed to have a unique idioculture (e.g., the Oakland [now Los Angeles] Raiders, the Montreal Canadiens, the Boston Celtics, the Notre Dame football team, and the New York Mets, when they were perennial losers). Members understand the shared meanings and experiences that evolve in these settings and use them to relieve tension, develop cohesion, and isolate their group from outsiders, often including family and coaches. Some of these elements become visible and known to outsiders and represent the image and style of a particular team. Indeed, they become part of the tradition associated with that team. In some cases, elements of this idioculture persist from season to season; sometimes the elements disappear as personnel or the experiences of the team change (e.g., winning vs. losing seasons).

A good example of team idiocultures is provided by recent evidence that North American professional hockey and football teams with black uniforms receive more penalties than teams with lighter garb (Horn, 1988). In the National Football League, the Los Angeles Raiders, New Orleans Saints, Pittsburgh Steelers, Cincinnati Bengals, and Chicago Bears (the Bears actually wear navy blue uniforms that appear black) showed higher total numbers-of-yards-penalized compared with other teams for all but one year in the 1970-1986 period. The Philadelphia Flyers, Boston Bruins, and Chicago Black Hawks had higher total penalty-minutes than other National Hockey League teams over the same period. Moreover, teams that changed their uniform to black—the Vancouver Canucks and the Pittsburgh Penguins in the National Hockey League—received more penalties after they changed color.

Two processes probably operate to produce these differences. First, the black-uniformed teams probably have idiocultures that emphasize aggressive behavior more; the self-images of the players and the norms of game behavior are more violent for the black-uniformed teams. These differences may have come about through conscious efforts of management and coaches. The teams may have deliberately recruited aggressive players and dressed them in black to intimidate opponents. But the changes in penalty behavior for the Penguins and Canucks after changing their colors suggest that there is more to it. More or less the same personnel were in the game, but the penalties changed. A second possibility is that referees view teams differently if they wear black; the color may mean "evil" and "bad" to the officials, and they may respond accordingly in calling penalties. Recent laboratory studies suggest

that both of these processes occur (Horn, 1988).

To understand how an idioculture is created, Fine initiated a 3-year observational study of Little League baseball teams in five leagues (Fine, 1979, 1987). He identified five characteristics that affect which cultural items will become part of a team's idioculture. First, the element must be *known* to members of the team. Thus, one team referred to a foul ball over the backstop as a "Polish Home Run." This was based on the presence of Polish people as a minority group in the community and represented an ethnic slur about potential opponents. The cultural form must also be *usable* and *functional* during group interaction. If the form cannot be used because a coach or high-status player opposes its use, the element will not become part of the idioculture. In some instances, use of the element may function to support group goals or serve as an integrating or cohesive mechanism against other teams—or even against a coach unpopular with the players.

A fourth characteristic is that the cultural form must be *appropriate* for support of the status hierarchy within a team. Elements therefore change over time, either within a season or from season to season. A derogatory nickname will be dropped if the player acquires higher status or persist if it is introduced and perpetuated by a high-status player.

To illustrate, a first-year, smaller player on a youth soccer team was nicknamed "munchkin" by one of the star players during the preseason tryouts. As the season began and the rookie played only part of each game, the name persisted. However, as the player improved his play and effort, he acquired the status of starter and playmaker and regained his proper name. Similarly, nicknames develop over the course of a season to symbolize status and ability or to recall particularly memorable plays or events. If not derogatory, these may remain with the player or team for many seasons. Halfway through the season on the same youth soccer team, the first-string goalie was labeled "The Animal" after he was given a chance to play forward. This nickname appropriately depicted his style of play when he was unleashed from the goal area.

Finally, the element must be *triggered* by some significant event or experience that is unique to the team at a particular time (e.g., an error, an outstanding play, a new haircut, a type of clothing worn to or at the game, a humorous or tragic event). Thus, while the element may appear randomly, it is not likely to be adopted unless it has some unique meaning to the group at a specific point in a game or season.

OPPOSITION AND SOCIAL CHANGE THROUGH SPORT

Thus far we have discussed the unique beliefs, values, and lifestyles of sport subcultures. These appear to have few consequences for the wider society, save for the development and popularizing of new words and meanings, the types of clothing, and the avenues of spectatorship. Creation of new sport subcultures really brings little fundamental change in the wider society. We have also discussed forms of deviance that occur in subcultures. We may argue that increased violence in sport gives greater legitimacy to violence in the wider society, but, again, this violence does not significantly transform society. Sometimes, though, sport brings about major changes in the wider society. Two examples are especially compelling.

Negro baseball leagues survived in the U.S. for years before sport broke the *color line*, when the Brooklyn Dodgers signed Jackie Robinson to a National League contract. These leagues allowed blacks to acquire the skills of baseball and served as an avenue of sport mobility for blacks. Most important, though, they provided graphic and continual evidence of the high levels of ability and talent held by many blacks when they were thought inferior in every way, including athletically. The leagues helped change the cultural definition of blacks. This definition was further modified for many people when blacks began to participate with a high degree of success in professional, college, and Olympic sport.

Interestingly, there seems to have been a parallel development with women and sport. It was not long ago (Theberge, in press) that

> women's smaller bodies, allegedly fragile structures and weak constitutions were thought to make them unsuited for strenuous activity, including sport. The general argument against women's participation in sport was captured in a specific allegation that physical activity posed unacceptable risks to women's reproductive systems.

The movement of women into sport in the 1970s marked a new era of women's athletics. The importance of these developments extend beyond sport to the condition of women in the broader society. "Historically, the exclusion of women from sport or their acceptance as unwelcome intruders has provided powerful confirmation of their weakness and frailty. In a vicious circle of illogic and discrimination, women were excluded from sport, and their exclusion was interpreted as evidence of their weakness" (Theberge, in press).

The myth of the fragile woman has been seriously questioned now that women have partially broken the *gender line* in sport. The performance level of women in traditional sports such as tennis, swimming, and figure

Women have recently countered the myth of frailty by competing in endurance events such as marathons.

skating has increased markedly in the last two decades, and their involvement in endurance events has been especially noteworthy. What better way for women to counter the charge of frailty than through marathoning, for example, and by recording better times than many men. Sport has provided a visible setting within which to redefine the role of woman from that of a passive, fragile person to that of a competent, active person with high levels of achievement, strength, and endurance.

There is potential for further transformation of society's views on women; the redefinition is far from complete. Women still have much farther to go to attain equality, power, and control in sport settings.

WRAP-UP

Sport encompasses many subcultures. These subgroups are characterized by somewhat different beliefs, values, and lifestyles (i.e., different ways of thinking and behaving) compared with others in the wider society. But these subgroups also reflect many aspects of the wider culture, because members have been and are involved in *both* the wider society and the subculture.

Three basic types of subcultures exist in sport: avocational, occupational, and deviant. Avocational subcultures provide a social milieu in which individuals can intensively pursue a valued interest not easily found in the worlds of work and family. The subculture becomes a major source of the identity and satisfaction of the individual. Occupational subcultures have similar characteristics but involve paid "work" roles. Deviant sport subcultures provide important sources of identity and satisfaction for participants, but they do not have the same strong legitimacy in the wider society as avocational and occupational subcultures. Indeed, members of deviant subcultures are often abhorred by other society members, as with those (including athletes) who attempt to "fix" games for the purpose of winning at gambling and those who use drugs to enhance their performance.

Subcultures affect the wider culture. First, different ways of thinking and behaving in the subculture expose those in the wider society to alternative lifestyles.

Second, members of sport subcultures may find a sanctuary from which to resist the influences of the wider society. Some of this resistance may come through behavior that is clearly defined as deviant in the wider society.

In some instances, subcultures strongly oppose and initiate fundamental changes in the wider society. Although there are not many instances of large-scale change, we must accept the proposition that sport may both resist and help transform culture and society.

REFERENCES

Albert, E. (1984). Equipment as a feature of social control in the sport of bicycle racing. In N. Theberge & P. Donnelly (Eds.), *Sport and the sociological imagination* (pp. 318–333). Fort Worth: Texas Christian University Press.

Arnold, D.O. (1970). *The sociology of subcultures*. Berkeley, CA: Glendessary Press.

Birrell, S., & Turowetz, A. (1979). Character work-up and display: Collegiate gymnastics and professional wrestling. *Urban Life*, **8**, 219–246.

Bouton, J. (1970). *Ball Four: My life and hard times throwing the knuckleball in the big leagues*. New York: World.

Bradshaw, J. (1987). *Fast Company*. New York: Vintage.

Brandmeyer, G.A., & Alexander, L.K. (1982). Some sociological clues to baseball as the national pastime. In A.O. Dunleavy, A.W. Miracle, & C.R. Rees (Eds.), *Studies in the sociology of sport* (pp. 3–12). Fort Worth: Texas Christian University Press.

Bredemeier, B.J. (1985). Moral reasoning and the perceived legitimacy of intentionally injurious sport acts. *Journal of Sport Psychology*, **7**(2), 110–124.

Brislin, J. (1982). On becoming a college football player. In A.G. Ingham & E.F. Broom (Eds.), *Career patterns and career contingencies in sport* (pp. 334–368). Vancouver: University of British Columbia.

Brown, B.A., & Curtis, J.E. (1984). Does running go against the family grain? National survey results of marital status and running. In N. Theberge & P. Donnelly (Eds.), *Sport and the sociological imagi-*

nation (pp. 352–367). Fort Worth: Texas Christian University Press.

Charnofsky, H. (1968). The major league professional player: Self conception versus the popular image. *International Review of Sport Sociology*, **3**, 39–55.

Chass, M., & Goodwin, M. (1986). Drug abuse in baseball. In R. Lapchick (Ed.), *Fractured focus: Sport as a reflection of society* (pp. 277–309). Lexington, MA: Lexington Books.

Colburn, K. (1985). Honor, ritual and violence in ice hockey. *Canadian Journal of Sociology*, **10**(2), 153–170.

Donnelly, P. (1981a). Toward a definition of sport sub-cultures. In M. Hart & S. Birrell (Eds.), *Sport in the sociocultural process* (3rd ed., pp. 565–587). Dubuque, IA: Wm. C. Brown.

Donnelly, P. (1981b). Athletes and juvenile delinquents: A comparative analysis based on a review of the literature. *Adolescence*, **16**, 415–431.

Donnelly, P. (1984). Resistance through sports: Sport and cultural hegemony. In *Sports et societes contemporaines* (pp. 397–406). Paris: Societe Francaise de Sociologie du Sport.

Donnelly, P. (1985). Sport subcultures. In R. Terjung (Ed.), *Exercise and Sport Sciences Review* (pp. 539–578). New York: Macmillan.

Donnelly, P., & Young, K. (1988). The construction and confirmation of identity in sport subcultures. *Sociology of Sport Journal*, **5**, 223–240.

Eitzen, D.S. (1981). Sport and deviance. In G.R.F. Luschen & G.H. Gage (Eds.), *Handbook of social science of sport* (pp. 400–414). Champaign, IL: Stipes.

Eitzen, D.S. (1988). Conflict theory and deviance in sport. *International Review for the Sociology of Sport*, **23**, 193–203.

Ewald, K., & Jiobu, R.M. (1985). Explaining positive deviance: Becker's model and the case of runners and bodybuilders. *Sociology of Sport Journal, 2,* 144–156.

Faulkner, R.R. (1974). Making violence by doing work: Selves, situations and the world of professional hockey. *Sociology of Work and Occupations, 1,* 288–312.

Faulkner, R.R. (1975). Coming of age in organizations: A comparative study of career contingencies of musicians and hockey players. In D.W. Ball & J.W. Loy (Eds.), *Sport and social order: Contributions to the sociology of sport.* (pp. 521–558). Reading, MA: Addison-Wesley.

Featherston, M., & Hepworth, M. (1984). Fitness, body maintenance and lifestyle within consumer culture. In *Sports et societes contemporaines* (pp. 441–447). Paris: Societe Francaise de Sociologie du Sport.

Fine, G.A. (1979). Small groups and culture creation: The idioculture of Little League baseball teams. *American Sociological Review, 44,* 733–745.

Fine, G.A. (1987). *With the boys: Little League baseball and preadolescent culture.* Chicago: University of Chicago Press.

Gallmeier, C.P. (1987). Putting on the game face: The staging of emotions in professional hockey. *Sociology of Sport Journal, 4,* 347–362.

Gans, H.J. (1974). *Popular culture and high culture: An analysis and evaluation of taste.* New York: Basic Books.

Goffman, E. (1959). *The presentation of self in everyday life.* Garden City, NY: Doubleday.

Goldstein, J.H. (Ed.) (1983). *Sports violence.* New York: Springer-Verlag.

Hastad, D.N., Segrave, J.O., Pangrazi, R., & Petersen, G. (1984). Youth sport participation and deviant behavior. *Sociology of Sport Journal, 1,* 366–373.

Horn, J.C. (1988). Do black shirts make bad guys? *Psychology Today, 22*(11), 19–21.

Irwin, J. (1973). Surfing: The natural history of an urban scene. *Urban Life and Culture, 2*(2), 131–160.

Jacobs, G. (1976). Urban samurai: The karate dojo. In A. Yiannakis, T. McIntyre, M. Melnick, & D. Hart (Eds.), *Sport sociology: Contemporary themes* (2nd ed., pp. 134–142). Dubuque, IA: Kendall/Hunt.

Jarka, H. (1963). The language of skiers. *American Speech, 33,* 202–207.

Johnson, W. (1983, August 15). What's happened to our heroes? *Sports Illustrated,* pp. 32–42.

Kirkpatrick, C. (1987, February 2). College basketball. *Sports Illustrated,* pp. 52–59.

Klein, A.M. (1986). Pumping irony: Crisis and contradiction in bodybuilding. *Sociology of Sport Journal, 3,* 112–133.

Luschen, G. (1976). Cheating in sport. In D.M. Landers (Ed.), *Social problems in athletics: Essays in the sociology of sport* (pp. 67–77). Urbana, IL: University of Illinois Press.

Luschen, G. (1984). Before and after Caracas: Drug abuse and doping as deviant behavior in sport. In K. Olin (Ed.), *Contribution of sociology to the study of sport* (pp. 53–67). Jyvaskyla, Finland: University of Jyvaskyla.

Mahigel, E.L., & Stone, G.P. (1976). Hustling as a career. In D.M. Landers (Ed.), *Social problems in athletics: Essays in the sociology of sport* (pp. 78–85). Urbana, IL: University of Illinois Press.

Martinez, T.M., & La Franchi, R. (1972). Why people play poker. In G.P. Stone (Ed.), *Games, sport and power* (pp. 55–73). New Brunswick, NJ: Transaction Books.

McTeer, W., & Curtis, J.E. (1984). Sociological profiles of marathoners. In N. Theberge & P. Donnelly (Eds.), *Sport and the sociological imagination* (pp. 368–384). Fort Worth: Texas Christian University Press.

Mugno, D.A., & Feltz, D.L. (1985). The social learning of aggression in youth football in the United States. *Canadian Journal of Applied Sport Sciences,* **10**(1), 26–35.

Pearson, K. (1978). The concept subculture: A basic tool in defining and understanding sports phenomena. In F. Landry & W. Orban (Eds.), *Physical activity and human well-being* (Vol. 2, pp. 535–571). Miami: Symposia Specialists.

Pearson, K. (1979). *Surfing subcultures of Australia and New Zealand.* St. Lucia, Australia: University of Queensland Press.

Pearson, K. (1980). Cultural interpretation in sport: The outside world and pictures inside heads. *International Review of Sport Sociology,* **15**(3/4), 19–40.

Polsky, N. (1972). Of pool playing and poolrooms. In G.P. Stone (Ed.), *Games, sport and power* (pp. 19–54). New Brunswick, NJ: E.P. Dutton.

Prus, R., & Sharper, C.R.D. (1979). *Road hustler: The career contingencies of professional card and dice handlers.* Toronto: Lexington Books.

Purdy, D.A., & Richard, S.F. (1983). Sport and juvenile delinquency: An examination and assessment of four major theories. *Journal of Sport Behavior,* **6**, 179–193.

Rains, P. (1984). The production of fairness: The hidden world of officiating in the National Hockey League. *Sociology of Sport Journal,* **1**, 150–162.

Ralbovsky, M. (1974a). *Destiny's darlings.* New York: Hawthorn.

Ralbovsky, M. (1974b). *Lords of the locker room.* New York: Peter H. Wyden.

Renson, R. (1976). Social status symbolism of sport stratification. *Hermes,* **10**, 433–443.

Renson, R. (1978). Social status symbolism of sport stratification. In F. Landry & W. Orban (Eds.), *Sociology of sport* (pp. 191–200). Miami: Symposia Specialists.

Rosenberg, M.M., & Turowetz, A. (1975). The wrestler and the physician: Identity workup and organizational arrangements. In D.W. Ball & J.W. Loy (Eds.), *Sport and social order: Contributions to the sociology of sport* (pp. 559–574). Reading, MA: Addison-Wesley.

Scott, M.B. (1968). *The racing game.* Chicago: Aldine.

Segrave, J.O. (1983). Sport and juvenile delinquency. In R. Terjung (Ed.), *Exercise and sport sciences review* (Vol. 2, pp. 161–209). Philadelphia: Franklin Institute Press.

Segrave, J.O., & Hastad, D.N. (1984a). Future directions in sport and juvenile delinquency research. *Quest,* **36**, 37–47.

Segrave, J.O., & Hastad, D. (1984b). Interscholastic participation and delinquent behavior: An empirical assessment of relevant variables. *Sociology of Sport Journal,* **1**, 117–137.

Segrave, J.O., Hastad, D.N., & Moreau, C. (1985). An investigation into the relationship between ice hockey participation and delinquency. *Sociology of Sport Journal,* **2**, 281–298.

Sheard, K., & Dunning, E. (1973). The rugby football club as a type of "male preserve": Some sociological notes. *International Review of Sport Sociology,* **8** (3/4), 5–24.

Shibutani, T. (1955). Reference groups as perspectives. *American Journal of Sociology,* **60**, 562–569.

Silva, J.M. (1983). The perceived legitimacy of rule violating behavior in sport. *Journal of Sport Psychology,* **5**, 438–448.

Silva, J.M. (1984). Factors related to the acquisition and exhibition of aggressive sport behavior. In J.M. Silva & R.S. Weinberg (Eds.), *Psychological foundations of sport* (pp. 261–273). Champaign, IL: Human Kinetics.

Smith, G. (1983). Recreational drugs in sport. *Physician and Sports Medicine*, **11**(9), 75–82.

Smith, M.D. (1983). *Violence and sport*. Toronto: Butterworths.

Snyder, E.E., & Purdy, D.A. (1987). Social control in sport: An analysis of basketball officiating. *Sociology of Sport Journal*, **4**, 394–402.

Stebbins, R. (1987). *Canadian football: A view from the helmet*. London, ON: Centre for Social and Humanistic Studies.

Steele, P.D. (1976). The bowling hustler: A study of deviance in sport. In D. Landers (Ed.), *Social problems in athletics: Essays in the sociology of sport* (pp. 86–92). Urbana, IL: University of Illinois Press.

Steele, P.D., & Zurcher, L. (1973). Leisure sports as ephemeral roles. *Pacific Sociological Review*, **16**, 345–356.

Stone, G.P. (1972). Wrestling: The great American passion play. In E. Dunning (Ed.), *Sport: Readings from a sociological perspective* (pp. 301–335). Toronto: University of Toronto Press.

Stuck, M.F. (Ed.) (1988, May). Drugs and sport [entire issue]. *Arena Review*.

Theberge, N. (1977). *An occupational analysis of women's professional golf*. Unpublished doctoral dissertation, University of Massachusetts, Amherst.

Theberge, N. (in press). Women's athletics and the myth of female frailty. In J. Freeman (Ed.), *Women: A feminist perspective* (4th ed.). Palo Alto, CA: Mayfield.

Thomson, R. (1977). *Sport and deviance: A subcultural analysis*. Unpublished doctoral dissertation, University of Alberta, Edmonton, Canada.

Vaz, E.W. (1972). The culture of young hockey players: Some initial observations. In A.W. Taylor & M.L. Howell (Eds.), *Training: Scientific basis and application* (pp. 222–234). Springfield, IL: Charles C Thomas.

Vaz, E.W. (1982). *The professionalization of young hockey players*. Lincoln, NE: University of Nebraska Press.

Vaz, E.W., & Thomas, D. (1974). What price victory? An analysis of minor hockey players' attitudes towards winning. *International Review of Sport Sociology*, **9**(2), 33–56.

Voigt, D.Q. (1974). *A Little League journal*. Bowling Green, OH: Bowling Green University Popular Press.

Weinberg, S.K., & Arond, H. (1952). The occupational culture of the boxer. *American Journal of Sociology*, **57**, 460–469.

Wertz, S.K. (1981). The varieties of cheating. *Journal of the Philosophy of Sport*, **8**, 19–40.

Wheatley, E. (1986, October/November). *Playing, partying, and the process of culture creation: A subcultural examination of women's rugby groups*. Paper presented at the Seventh Annual Meeting of the North American Society for the Sociology of Sport, Las Vegas.

Widmeyer, W.N. (1984). Aggression: Performance relationships in sport. In J.M. Silva & R.S. Weinberg (Eds.), *Psychological foundations of sport* (pp. 274–285). Champaign, IL: Human Kinetics.

Widmeyer, W.N. & Birch, J.S. (1984). Aggression in professional ice hockey: A strategy for success or a reaction to failure? *Journal of Psychology*, **117**(1), 77–84.

Williams, T., & Donnelly, P. (1985). Subcultural production, reproduction and transformation in climbing. *International Review for the Sociology of Sport*, **20**, 3–15.

C H A P T E R   11

Sport, Collective Behavior, and Social Movements

Even the most casual observer of professional and amateur sport has seen or heard about violent incidents on the playing field. Some examples include brawls (*rhubarbs*) at the pitcher's mound or second base in baseball, bench-clearing brawls in hockey, and fights under the basket in basketball. Increasingly, spectators emulate this violent behavior, both inside and outside the stadium and before, during, and after games. There are fights in the stands at hockey, baseball, and football games; spectators throw debris onto the play-ing surface to protest the calls of officials; tennis spectators yell abuse at players; and normally sedate citizens are ejected from are-nas for irrational behavior directed against other fans, players, coaches, or officials. Most frequently, violence among spectators begins as enthusiastic support for a team and then escalates.

This collective and frequently deviant be-havior is aptly illustrated by soccer hooli-ganism in Great Britain. The most serious in-cident was on May 29, 1985, when Liverpool

(Great Britain) fans attacked Juventus (Italy) fans at the European Cup soccer championship in Brussels. The violence occurred one hour *before* the kickoff; part of the stadium wall was destroyed, 39 people were killed, and hundreds were hospitalized. In the end, 26 British fans were charged with involuntary manslaughter, and a Belgian soccer official and 2 state police officers were charged with failing to implement adequate security measures.

The number of deaths in the incident and the fact that it took place in supposedly neutral territory stimulated considerable news coverage and comment throughout the world. Indeed, the violence (with graphic pictures of the deceased) received much more media coverage than the soccer match. Stations replayed footage of the violence frequently, and scores of journalists analyzed and editorialized about the event for up to a month afterwards (Young, 1986). One indication of the importance attached to this event is that it received more coverage than a cyclone in Bangladash—which happened at the same time and killed thousands of people.

Violence among spectators seems to be increasing, although hard evidence is difficult to obtain. At the same time sport violence seems to have become more newsworthy, perhaps because its unexpectedness increases the sale of newspapers and generates higher television ratings. It is also possible that the two issues interact with each other. Spectators may be imitating behaviors learned from the media coverage of aggressive behavior.

Sociologists are intrigued with these occurrences of spectator behavior and are developing some understanding of why and how such behavior occurs. In this chapter we describe the types of **collective behavior** that have occurred in and around sport settings; introduce theories that help explain why this type of behavior occurs; identify some of the

consequences of collective behavior in sport settings; and consider how and why some forms of collective behavior result in social movements and social change.

THE CONCEPTS OF COLLECTIVE BEHAVIOR AND SOCIAL MOVEMENTS

Unlike most other forms of social behavior, collective behavior is usually spontaneous, unstructured, unorganized, and transitory. Some social movements (e.g., gay rights, antiabortion, civil rights, women's liberation) that originally were noninstitutionalized have become formal organizations and enhanced the strength and permanency of the movement. For example, hooliganism in England has become highly organized and is now a subcultural element of the British soccer structure.

The concept of collective behavior encompasses many social phenomena, social fads, and fashion crazes (e.g., the hoola hoop, punk hairstyles, preppy clothes, styles in sport uniforms), crowd panics (e.g., during a fire or a riot in a stadium), hostile outbursts (e.g., prison riots or rampages by fans of a losing team), spontaneous celebrations (e.g., when a government is overthrown or defeated in an election or among fans after a team wins a championship), and celebrations at regular holidays and festivals.

Collective behavior does *not* represent group behavior in the sense of behavior in a family, a sport team, or a work setting. It occurs when a number of persons in a particular setting spontaneously respond to a common stimulus. The behavior of these individuals is not subject to well-defined, shared norms because there is not enough interaction among the individuals for them to be considered a permanent group. In many instances of collective behavior, only a few of those present are involved. Many remain on the fringe as passive observers or as vocal supporters of the actual participants.

Researchers are at a real disadvantage in trying to study collective behavior. Unlike other forms of behavior, we are unable to predict precisely when an incident will occur. Often a collective behavior event is over within hours or days and the leaders, participants, and passive observers have dispersed.

In addition, the spontaneity of this behavior inhibits observation and interviews. Researchers must rely on media accounts or on-the-scene interviews with those still present after the event. Unfortunately, those at the center of the action have often fled or been arrested. Moreover, participants have only their recall to offer, and this may be of limited use because not all will know how or why an event started. They may have changed their perceptions because of participating, because of the outcome of the event (e.g., arrests, damage, physical beatings), or because of reading about or viewing media accounts of the event.

In some instances, a collective event occurs as a new, continuing form of social behavior known as a **social movement**. Social movements differ from collective behavior in that they are sustained attempts, through social interaction, to initiate or inhibit social change. For example, hooliganism approximates a social movement to the extent that it occurs repeatedly and sometimes involves the same leaders and participants. Other examples involve still more sustained social activity. They include efforts to promote acceptance of new or alternative ideas or lifestyles (e.g., the fitness or wellness movement, the feminist movement, the gay rights movement) or to enhance the quality of life (e.g., antismoking activism, environmental protection efforts, or campaigns for animal rights). Few social movements have originated within sport, although movements from the wider society have had considerable influence on the structure, form, and meaning of sport. Sport has often been a domain for the expression of social and economic discontent by both athletes and spectators.

PERSPECTIVES ON COLLECTIVE BEHAVIOR

The study of collective behavior attracted the interest of social philosophers as early as classical Greek and Roman times. Classical intellectuals often asked why the masses engaged repeatedly in disruptive and disorderly behavior. It was not until after the French Revolution that we found the first detailed study of crowd or *mob psychology*. This perspective was best represented by Le Bon (1960) in *La Foule* (*The Crowd*), first published in 1895. He reduced the explanation of crowd behavior to psychological tendencies that emerged in all individuals in a crowd situation. According to Le Bon, a crowd member becomes the victim of *mental contagion*, which replaces rational behavior with irrationality. The emotional crowd makes inferior beings out of those who come under its influence. By joining the **crowd**, individuals acquire a feeling of power and a sense that they are not responsible for their behavior.

This psychological explanation of crowd behavior was accepted for many decades. But there gradually developed a recognition that dynamic social processes within specific social settings could more fully explain crowd behavior and other collective events. As a result, four sociological perspectives on collective behavior have been proposed. Each has a different emphasis, but each helps explain the origin of collective behavior.

Contagion Perspective

Early sociologists modified Le Bon's work and proposed the **contagion theory of collective**

behavior. This explanation argues that the anonymity given to individuals in a crowd, coupled with a process of emotional inter-stimulation or hypnotism, compels them to feel and act as one. The result has been called *herding behavior*. It is argued that individuals milling around in a group become emotionally aroused and are susceptible to suggestions for behavior from any model or leader.

This approach has some support in the research literature. We know that once riots begin, emotional contagion often increases the number of active participants. We also know that crowd behavior results from precipitating events; how certain models respond influences the behavior of others. This perspective does *not* explain why some models behave in ways that result in a riot. Moreover, there are many instances of milling crowds (e.g., at a trade show, fall fair, market, or racetrack) that do not become riots.

Convergence Perspective

The **convergence theory of collective behavior** holds that if people with the same beliefs and feelings come together in the same setting, they can be easily stimulated to act by some precipitating event. This view is often combined with the *frustration-aggression hypothesis* which predicts that similar underlying frustrations among individuals will lead to aggressive behavior in a crowd setting. The behavior may be stimulated by the actions of one or more informal leaders, especially if these persons have charisma.

Given the transitory nature of most collective behavior, it is generally not possible to reassemble the crowd to determine whether most participants shared common frustrations or beliefs. Again, many crowds may consist of members with similar sociodemographic characteristics and yet never engage in disruptive crowd behavior. Although the convergence of individuals with common concerns may be an important factor in some crowd behavior, it does not seem to be the *only* factor.

Emergent Norm Perspective

Most often a crowd is a diverse group of individuals. As noted earlier, some crowd members are merely passive observers, who may strongly disapprove of the others' actions. Within a heterogeneous crowd, it has been argued that a shared understanding of expected behavior emerges to stimulate certain types of behavior and to impose sanctions on those who deviate from the norms (Turner & Killian, 1957). This view has been called the **emergent norm theory of collective behavior**.

The norms involved are specific and unique to the social situation and may determine, for example, whether an audience is emotional and loud, or quiet and passive. This shared understanding can emerge as the result of a few words, a prevailing mood, or the behavior of one or two models. When the crowd disperses, the norms usually cease to influence individual behavior, unless the individuals again find themselves in a similar situation.

To illustrate, tennis spectators have traditionally sat quietly and applauded performances at appropriate times. Verbal sparring on the court, both between players and with the umpire and spectators has encouraged audiences to more aggressively express their dissatisfaction with the performance of the umpire, linesman, or player. Similarly, in European soccer it has become more common to throw bottles or fireworks at opposing players or officials.

Value-Added Perspective

Another approach to studying sport and collective behavior is the **value-added theory**

of collective behavior of Smelser (1962). He sought to explain "Why . . . collective behavior episodes occur where they do, when they do, and in the ways they do" (p. 1). He argued that a number of determinants in the social setting must be present before a specific collective event occurs. Like the baking of a cake, the ingredients must be added together, often in a certain sequence, to lead to a certain outcome.

The first required element is *structural strain*. Perceived or real conflicts, deprivations, or ambiguities must be present to create a generalized tension or dissatisfaction. Some common underlying strains that have contributed to collective behavior in sport are antagonisms among social classes or among religious, political, ethnic, or racial groups. But these preexisting conflicts are not sufficient to create collective behavior. *Structural conduciveness* must also be present. That is, the crowd must agree that its grievances cannot be resolved successfully through normal channels.

In the presence of strain and conduciveness, other elements occurring in an added sequence can precipitate collective behavior. This is more likely if social-control agents are lacking (e.g., ushers, police, physical barriers). Among the social dynamics that can lead to a collective episode are

- a *generalized belief* that accounts for the strain (e.g., the referee appears to be prejudiced or incompetent) or indicates how the crowd should respond (e.g., throw debris at the officials or players on the field);
- *precipitating factors*, which often confirm generalized beliefs (e.g., player argues with the official or the official makes an unpopular decision, especially a ruling against the home team); and
- a *mobilization* of the participants to action by leaders and communication among the crowd (e.g., the coach is ejected, a few fans attempt to enter the playing area to express their dissatisfaction, or radio announcers or newspaper reporters comment negatively on the caliber of the officiating).

This perspective offers a more complete explanation of how and why collective behavior occurs and seems to be the best model to predict when social situations might lead to collective outbursts. But this perspective is not sufficient by itself and should be seen as complementing the others. For example, a generalized belief is probably *not* necessary for collective behavior. Certainly it is a relatively insignificant factor in riots that have no purpose; other theories are more useful in examining these incidents. Highlight 11.1 helps explain the dynamics of the Brussels soccer riot by using Smelser's value-added perspective.

HISTORY OF COLLECTIVE BEHAVIOR IN SPORT AUDIENCES

We know from historical accounts (Cameron, 1976; Guttmann, 1981, 1986) that riots in sport settings are not a recent event. Rival spectators at the chariot races in Rome fought regularly in the 4th, 5th, and 6th centuries A.D. Disgruntled spectators set Constantinople's Hippodrome on fire four times between 491 and 532 A.D.; in the Nitka riot of 532 A.D., about 30,000 citizens died. Later, in the Medieval and Renaissance periods in Europe, there was much concern about crowd control at tournaments; horse-racing, cricket, and cockfighting crowds periodically invaded the field or attacked officials (Guttmann, 1981, 1986; Lang, 1981; Smith, 1983; Vamplew, 1980).

Highlight 11.1
A Value-Added Perspective on the Riot at the European Championship Between Liverpool and Turin (Brussels, Belgium—May 30, 1985)

Background

- British soccer fans have been known for hooliganism at European stadiums for more than 15 years; they are seldom punished severely.
- In 1985 there were three major soccer riots in Britain, and Prime Minister Thatcher established a commission to consider the installation of steel fences to separate rival fans, and discuss a ban on alcohol sales.
- The European Cup soccer final is a major championship at the highest level of play; it takes place at a "neutral" site.

Structural Strain

- British and Italian teams have had a longstanding rivalry, with many hostile beliefs generated about the character and play of opposing players.
- 20,000 Liverpool fans descended on Brussels; about 10,000 of the remaining 38,000 spectators were from Italy, although many of Italian descent lived in or near Brussels and purchased tickets.

Precipitating Events

- Liverpool fans, drinking en route to the game, rioted in the streets from early in the morning, causing property damage and stealing.
- En route to the stadium, Liverpool fans verbally attacked Italian supporters.

- Some Italian fans pulled knives to defend themselves.
- Fans were not searched for bottles or knives before entering the stadium.
- Although seating was supposed to be segregated for those who purchased tickets from their home team, black market ticket sales for supposedly neutral fans resulted in sections of mixed fans and the presence of known political activists and hooligans.
- The British section became overcrowded.
- Insults were hurled back and forth between sections separated by a fence.
- A rumor, unfounded, spread that a British fan had been stabbed.

Mobilization for Action

- Liverpool fans threw bottles and pieces of concrete into the Italian section.
- When the Italian supporters retreated, the Liverpool fans charged and pushed down the fence, crushing some Italian supporters.
- Italian fans from other parts of the stadium rushed to the area.
- The pressure of the mob caused a large retaining wall to collapse, leaving 38 dead, mostly by suffocation, and almost 400 injured.

Social Control

- The structure of the stadium was inadequate for security.

(Cont.)

Highlight 11.1 Continued

- Spectators were not searched before entry.
- Few police were on duty inside the stadium; most were outside to control the postgame crowd, when trouble was expected depending on the outcome of the game.
- When the attack by the crowd began, there was an inadequate number of police inside the stadium to quell the mob, and those who were present were overrun, trampled, or retreated to safety.

Aftermath

- Following a 90-minute delay, play resumed; more rioting was feared if the game had been postponed.
- Turin Juventus won the championship, 1-0, on a penalty kick.
- The Belgium government banned all British teams from playing in their country.
- Twenty-six British soccer fans were charged with involuntary manslaughter; one Belgian soccer official and two police officers were charged with failing to provide adequate security measures.

Throughout history, no other sport has been so plagued with violence as soccer. The *Birmingham Daily Mail* reported on May 6, 1889, that "the lower element not infrequently molest strangers" (Maguire, 1986). Early in this century (April 17, 1909) an estimated 600 spectators invaded the field at the end of a Celtics-Rangers soccer match in Glasgow. These unruly fans tore down the goalposts, smashed fencing, and lit bonfires on the field. Maguire reports a shift between 1919 and 1939 toward respectability in the game when spectators' disorderly conduct grew less serious and declined in frequency. This respite was short-lived.

Soccer hooliganism did not really reemerge until the late 1950s and early 1960s, when large numbers of fans began to travel by bus or train to watch their team play in other cities. Contact with rival fans increased,

as did media coverage. In this same period, working-class youth known as *skinheads* became more rebellious against society. They began to use soccer matches as an arena for demonstrating their views (Williams, Dunning, & Murphy, 1986). As a result of the events in England since the 1960s, soccer hooliganism, once a form of collective behavior, has become more institutionalized and is almost predictable in its occurrence.

It has generally been assumed that North America and other parts of the world have not experienced disruptive sport crowds to the same degree as Europe, Great Britain, and South America. But Metcalfe (1978) and Dunstan (1973) document, respectively, a spectator invasion of a lacrosse field in Canada in the late 1800s and a similar event at a cricket match in Australia. In South America, many stadiums have moats around the

---

Highlight 11.2
An 1886 View of the Baseball Umpire

Mother, may I slug the umpire,
May I slug him right away,
So he cannot be here, Mother
When the clubs begin to play?

Let me clasp his throat, dear Mother
In a dear delightful grip
With one hand, and with the other
Bat him several on the lip.

Let me climb his frame, dear Mother
While the happy people shout
I'll not kill him, dearest Mother,
I will only knock him out.

Let me mop the ground up, Mother
With his person, dearest do,
If the ground can stand it, Mother
I don't see why you can't too.

Note. From *Washington Critic* (1886) as cited in "America's Manufactured Villain: The Baseball Umpire" by D.Q. Voigt, 1970. *Journal of Popular Culture*, **4**, (Summer), pp. 1-29. Copyright 1970 by Ray B. Browne. Reprinted by permission.

---

playing fields and detention centers for disruptive spectators. A civil judge may be present at the stadium to deal immediately with spectators charged with disorderly conduct (Lever, 1983).

In the United States, verbal harassment of baseball umpires by the public has long been encouraged. This normative behavior has occasionally been the impetus for spectators to invade the field and attack the umpire or the opposing team. It sometimes has escalated to the physical harassment of visiting teams on their way to or from the stadium (Kutcher, 1983). The role of the press in encouraging this behavior against officials is illustrated in Highlight 11.2, a poem published in the *Washington Critic* in 1886.

As spectator sport has become more popular in North America, disorders have occurred more frequently. Most of the widely reported incidents concern violent crowds. But collective behavior can also be nonviolent, at least initially, when it involves celebrations of a championship victory or is associated with an annual or periodic sport festival (e.g., the Super Bowl, the Kentucky Derby, the Indianapolis 500, the Grey Cup in Canada, the World Cup of soccer). Riots, with some property damage and arrests, have occurred in recent years in Detroit, Pittsburgh, and Montreal, following championship victories in baseball, football, and hockey, respectively. Police on horseback are increasingly being used to control celebration riots (e.g., in Shea Stadium following the 1986 World Series victory by the New York Mets).

Highlight 11.3 illustrates that although soccer is the most frequent setting, a variety of sports in a variety of countries have experienced disruptive behavior by spectators since the 1940s.

WHY IS SPORT A SETTING FOR COLLECTIVE BEHAVIOR?

Collective behavior appears to be almost unique to sport crowds compared with other types of leisure crowds. This difference warrants our close attention. A simple explanation is that the set of factors identified in the value-added perspective described earlier are most often present in sport settings.

The Rise of Spectator Sport as Popular Leisure Behavior

Sport spectating as a form of valued leisure behavior did not begin to spread to a large percentage of the population until the late 1800s and early 1900s (Bale, 1984; Jobling, 1970; Shergold, 1979; Twombly, 1976). This pattern was influenced by a shorter work-day and work-week, large numbers living in urban centers, an increased standard of living, the availability of interurban modes of transportation, and the increasing attention given by the mass media to sport events.

These developments and the increasing commercialization and advertising of sport led to the construction of more stadiums. Spectating offered an escape from mundane lifestyles and allowed citizens to identify positively with their community's or their nation's team. Psychologists have referred to this identification process as the *BIRG Phenomenon*—Basking In Reflected Glory (Cialdini et al., 1976). Moreover, in several countries, one team sport has emerged as a national pastime or mania: soccer, in England, Europe, and South America; baseball, in the United States and Japan; and hockey, in Canada. These *identity* sports become part of the culture and set the traditions for heavy spectator behavior in other sports as they emerge.

Part of the increased popularity of sport spectating is that many events have become festivals or carnivals. That is, the game itself is only one part, and sometimes a relatively small part, of a larger social event having additional meanings.

One meaning of *carnival* is a scheduled celebration, a vacation from everyday roles, rules, and status hierarchies (Listiak, 1976; Manning, 1983). In these settings there is often sanctioned deviance against individuals or property, at least within a range of tolerable behavior. Sport events are often promoted as festivals, with pre- and postgame parties, pep rallies, half-time spectacles, and the consumption of alcohol at the game (i.e., the party continues while the game is in progress). Another carnival aspect is the peaceful interaction of people from different racial or class backgrounds supporting a common team (Harris, 1983; Kutcher, 1983; Loy, 1981). Other forms of leisure activity are much less likely to feature such a strong emotional atmosphere or such strong identity with a locale (or team).

Viewing sport events as festive occasions encourages expressive behavior. Fans wear team colors or masquerade (e.g., paint faces, thematic costumes); cheer and boo; post banners and signs in stadiums; and travel to other cities to support their home team. In extreme cases, these expressive activities prompt sport

Highlight 11.3
The Pervasiveness of Sport Disorders

1946   Bolton, England—33 killed and more than 500 injured when barriers broke as spectators surged forward to seek a better viewing position of a soccer game.

1955   Montreal, Canada—Following the suspension of superstar Rocket Richard for a stick-swinging incident, the president of the NHL, Clarence Campbell, attended the next home game of the Montreal Canadiens. He was the object of physical and verbal abuse during the game. Following the explosion of a smoke bomb, the crowd spilled outside and joined those who had been peacefully demonstrating against the suspension. The two crowds merged, became a violent mob, and did more than $40,000 damage along 15 blocks of the main street.

1964   Lima, Peru—300 dead and 500 injured after Argentina beat Peru in an Olympic qualifying soccer game.

1966   Vancouver, Canada—5,000 fans rioted for 5 hours in the evening *prior to* the Grey Cup Football Championship game.

1968   Kingston, Jamaica—Following a cricket test match between England and Jamaica, a battle erupted between police and spectators.

1968   Kavseri, Turkey—40 dead and more than 600 injured at a second division soccer match when fights broke out over a controversial goal.

1969   Honduras and El Salvador—After a soccer match, rival fans, angered by their countries' boundary dispute, battled and ignited a formal war between the two countries, which led to the loss of more than 2,000 lives.

1971   Glasgow, Scotland—65 killed at a local soccer match between Glasgow Rangers (Protestants) and Glasgow Celtics (Catholics).

1974   Cairo, Egypt—48 killed and 47 injured when spectators jostled for better positions to see an exhibition soccer match with a visiting Czechoslovakian team.

1975   Leeds, England—Leeds United Soccer team was banned from European Cup competition for 4 years after rioting by their fans in Paris.

1975   Pittsburgh, United States—About 20,000 Pittsburgh Steeler fans engaged in drunk and disorderly conduct in the downtown area following the team's Super Bowl victory. At least 70 were injured and more than 200 were arrested.

1979   Lagos, Nigeria—24 killed and 27 injured in a soccer riot when officials switched off the lights before spectators had left the stadium.

(Cont.)

Highlight 11.3 Continued

1980   Calcutta, India—16 killed and more than 100 injured after the ejection of soccer players ignited a fight in the stands.

1980   Detroit, United States—A section of Tiger Stadium was temporarily closed to eliminate chronically violent behavior at baseball games.

1981   Basel, Switzerland—English soccer fans caused $75,600 damage to local property following a soccer match.

1982   Moscow, Soviet Union—20 killed in a stampede of soccer fans after Spartak defeated a team from the Netherlands.

1984   Paris, France—English soccer fans caused $886,200 damage in and around a Paris stadium following an *exhibition* match in which France defeated England.

1985   Mexico City, Mexico—8 dead when soccer fans stampeded to enter a stadium for a local match.

1985   Beijing, China—Following China's loss to Hong Kong in World Cup elimination play, a 30-minute riot outside the stadium injured at least 10 foreigners and police and caused physical damage to cars. Subsequently, two participants were sentenced to 2 years in prison for breaking a truck window and for helping to overturn a taxi; 120 others were held in custody for up to 3 weeks and publicly branded as troublemakers.

1985   Brussels, Belgium—Attending the European Cup Soccer Championship, British fans, having been taunted by Italian fans in the streets outside, attacked Italian fans inside the stadium 45 minutes before the match began. A concrete wall collapsed under the pressure; 38 were killed and 425 injured.

1985   London, England—25 Cambridge United soccer fans were sentenced from 5 months to 5 years in jail for attacking the visiting Chelsea fans. The individual who admitted inciting the riot was imprisoned for 5 years.

1985   Brazil—At an amateur soccer game in a small remote town, a center forward murdered an opponent on the field with a double-barreled gun. He, in turn, was lynched by enraged fans.

1987   Kiev, Russia—Angered by their team's loss, soccer fans attacked a train carrying Moscow players and fans.

1987   Milan, Italy—Fireworks thrown from the soccer terrace exploded on the Roma goalkeeper's leg and shoulder, causing him to lose consciousness; his heart stopped beating until revived by massage.

1987   Przysiersk, Poland—In a third division soccer match, all three officials were beaten by fans after Sporta, the home team, lost.

(Cont.)

Highlight 11.3 Continued

1987   Seville, Spain—A bottle thrown from the soccer terrace hit a linesman, and a champagne bottle cut a player, requiring 11 stitches.

1988   Nanchong, China—Thousands of Chinese soccer fans attacked police and besieged a rival team's hotel during a night-long riot in which 135 people were injured and more than 40 arrested. The incident started following a draw between two youth teams, which eliminated the home team from a national competition.

1988   Frankfurt, West Germany—One week before the European sport governing body met to reconsider the ban of English clubs, drunken English fans spent 4 days fighting inside and outside bars and damaging cars and furniture as they gathered for a potential final match between England and the Soviet Union later in the week. As a result, England's Football Association withdrew its application for readmission to European Cup soccer tournaments and declared their decision "a victory for the hooligan."

1989   Sheffield, England—Police allowed 3,000 to 4,000 late-arriving spectators—many of whom had no ticket—to enter the soccer stadium terraces unchecked. More than 200 were injured and 95 crushed to death when the surging crowd pressed against the fans already in the stands. Ironically, the fans in the terraces could not escape because a 2-1/2 meter steel fence ringed the field to keep "hooligans" in the stands.

riots (Dewar, 1979; Dunning, Murphy, & Williams, 1986; Roadburg, 1980; Smith, 1975, 1978). Moreover, in social situations where usual norms are suspended and where emergent, temporary norms are activated (Kutcher, 1983),

    . . . those who refuse to accept the definition of revelry are the deviants. It is a huge party that does not tolerate easily the party-pooper, who may be the unfortunate policeman whose job it is to curb excess. In many stadia, the most frequent problem is the inebriated fan who . . . feels this is a carnival, and he has a right to behave any way he wishes. . . . Other fans observing the arrest will often see the police as the deviant, violating the spirit of carnival. (p. 39)

It should be noted that most sport spectators do not exceed the bounds of carnival behavior. They are vocal or passive observers, who remain in the stands and do not invade the field. They also disperse in an orderly manner after the contest. But the increasing number of violent incidents can partly be attributed to the promotion of sporting events as carnivals and the associated spectator emotion and involvement in

As evidenced by these fireworks, sport events are more than leisure games—they are spectator events.

the contest. Owners and marketing personnel encourage greater fan involvement with cheerleaders, computerized messages on scoreboards, fireworks, large-screen replays of controversial or sensational plays, liquor sales, hat or T-shirt days, and so on. More and more, the contests have grown beyond simple games or leisure-time diversions. They are intended to be important episodes in the spectators' lives and identities. This heightened importance helps to catalyze outbreaks of collective behavior.

Social Patterns of Sport Fans

Modern spectators are knowledgeable, committed sport fans who demand and support sport spectacles at the amateur, college, professional, and Olympic levels. These fans pay to consume sport and often have an emotional investment in the event. This may help explain why some spectators have become active and periodically destructive. Do they perhaps feel cheated when highly paid athletes produce what appears to be a subpar performance?

Sport spectators at one time attended an event and then quickly forgot about it. Modern sport fans have a continuing and consuming interest in sport news. They can be expected to (McPherson, 1975)

- invest time and money in various forms of sport involvement;
- have some knowledge of sport performers, statistics, and strategies;
- have an emotional attachment or commitment to one or more athletes or sport teams;
- experience feelings and mood states while consuming a sport event;
- discuss sport frequently with friends and strangers; and
- arrange leisure time around attending or consuming amateur and professional sport events.

Some of these characteristics are illustrated, empirically, by a study of 52 males preidentified as having a deep commitment to consuming sport. Smith and his colleagues (1981) found that the typical respondent

- watched an average of 9.6 hours per week of sport on television in the summer and 11.9 hours in the winter;
- listened to sport on the radio an average of 3.1 hours per week;
- read three sport magazines per month and read about sport every day in the newspaper;
- followed two or three teams with special interest and followed at least one team they especially disliked;

- identified sport heroes they admired, primarily based on skill and other qualities valued in society, or athletes they disliked, primarily because they were perceived to be unsportsmanlike, immodest, or undisciplined;
- experienced significant, temporary emotional shifts when their favorite team lost (e.g., they became mildly depressed for a few hours);
- arranged leisure time to coincide with watching or attending sport events (e.g., holidays planned around home games, a wedding day postponed so as not to conflict with a football game);
- thought sport enhanced their quality of life by allowing them to socialize with friends, escape daily pressures and routines, or cope with boredom; and
- felt guilty about the time they spent on sport.

In short, for some fans sport consumes a significant part of their daily lives, including thought and conversation at work. Highlight 11.4 further illustrates the behavioral extremes to which fans may go to indulge their passion for sport.

Early research suggested that spectator involvement in sport helps release aggressive combative instincts (Brill, 1929). Similarly, Gerth and Mills (1954) reported that many mass audience situations, with their "vicarious components" (p. 63), serve the unintended psychological function of channeling and releasing emotions. Theoretically, great amounts of aggression are released cathartically by crowds of spectators cheering for their favorite stars and jeering the umpire.

Some believe, however, that sport events may make people more aggressive in a crowd situation, both during and after the event. Beisser (1979), a psychiatrist, argued that the need for excitement and stimulation can lead to aberrant forms of behavior, where the

"beast in the stadium becomes the insatiable crowd" (p. 78). Research findings on this topic are not at all clear (Bandura & Walters, 1963; Berkowitz, 1969; Goldstein & Arms, 1971). One possibility is that the individual's reaction to sport contests are specific to the sport or person.

Spinrad (1981) has suggested that spectator sport

- serves as a form of vicarious combat;
- provides psychological gratification through identification with sport heroes;
- enables the individual to participate in a subcultural folklore through the accumulation of knowledge about a particular sport or team;
- enables the individual to accumulate a set of individual or team statistics, and thereby retain and express a continuing interest in standards of excellence within a specific domain;
- stimulates dialogue and arguments about current and past players and teams; and
- allows individuals to play the roles of owner, manager, or coach by making appropriate strategy decisions (e.g., armchair quarterbacks, predicting the order of player selection in the NFL draft, or choosing players for an all-star game).

The emotional, behavioral, and cognitive commitments that fans bring to sport events may predispose them to disruptive, irrational behavior.

Sport Reflects Social Conflict in the Wider Society

Underlying tensions based on religious, racial, social-class, ethnic, or national-identity differences have spilled over into sport and have been a factor in disruptive sport crowds. Some examples include racially based fights at high school football games in the United

Highlight 11.4
The Deeply Committed Male Sport Fan

The following anecdotal examples of the bizarre behavior of sport fans are but a few of many that have stimulated scholars to try to find explanations for why the consumption of sport is so important in the lives of so many adults, especially males. If this could be known, we might better understand why collective episodes of a disruptive nature occur in sport settings.

Case Study 1

Charles Winkler (see Roberts, 1976), a middle-aged Nebraskan, makes a 210-mile round trip to the University of Nebraska stadium an average of four times per week to watch practices, scrimmages, and freshman and varsity games. En route he listens to audio tapes of great games in the past. He sometimes travels to the empty stadium to sit alone and reminisce about highlights he has witnessed in past games.

Case Study 2

Jonathan Schwartz (1979), a disc jockey and ardent Boston Red Sox fan, became despondent after the Red Sox lost four home games. Impulsively, he left town with $50 and a credit card and flew to Los Angeles to support the Red Sox in their next series. Not until he arrived did he remember to telephone and inform his wife where he was. He estimates that he spent over $15,000 between 1970 and 1977 listening to Red Sox broadcasts over long-distance telephone connections.

Case Study 3

Daniel Okrent (1980), in September, 1979, traveled to 13 different baseball stadiums on 13 consecutive days to watch 13 games involving *all* major league teams (he did not see one team play twice). This type of sport orgy has been fostered more recently by travel agents who promote annual excursions to satiate the committed baseball fan.

Case Study 4

Jonathan Yardley (1980), in his 40s, had his lifestyle dramatically altered by becoming addicted to the Baltimore Orioles. After attending a few games his behavior at games became that of a "passionate, irrational, screaming, bonkers Orioles fan." When the Orioles were on the road he couldn't get to sleep until he knew the outcome, often listening to games on the radio until 2:00 or 3:00 a.m. He thought and talked mostly about baseball, he read at least six daily newspapers for items about the Orioles, and he regularly calculated up-to-date player averages.

States; the El Salvador-Honduras political boundary dispute and subsequent soccer "war" (Lever, 1983); the French-English conflict in the 1955 Rocket Richard hockey riot in Quebec; the roots of hooliganism in the class struggle in Great Britain (Dunning, 1975;

Dunning, Murphy, Williams, & Maguire, 1984; Pearton, 1986); the longstanding religious battles between the Protestant Glasgow Rangers and the Catholic Glasgow Celtics; and refusal to compete against South African sport teams to protest the country's system of apartheid.

Along with these underlying social conflicts, ongoing social movements within the larger society can catalyze collective behavior. Some recent examples include the civil rights movement of the 1960s and 1970s and the protest movement of the 1970s, when individuals sought more freedom in a liberal, tolerant society and used and tolerated a degree of violence to demonstrate their point of view. Again, these changing values and behavioral patterns have spilled over into sport settings. Where the baseball fan once yelled, "Kill the umpire," the modern fan tries to *do* it, by hurling objects or invading the field.

Fans seem to have encouraged both the increased violence on the field and its spilling over into the stands and areas adjacent to the stadiums (Smith, 1983). The Miller Lite Study (Miller Brewing Company, 1983) reported, for example, that 14% of adult respondents in the United States indicate they "enjoy violence in sporting events" (p. 93). Similarly, Bryant and Zillmann (1983) report that television viewers enjoy NFL plays more when they are rough and violent.

The Role of the Mass Media

Although a cause and effect relationship has not been established between mass media coverage of sport and the occurrence of disruptive events, many suspect such a relationship. First, the major components of the mass media (newspapers, radio, and television) often selectively present distorted images of the situation that may help cause collective outbursts. These include controversial headlines, interviews with key players, frequent or excessive coverage of hostile sport events, slow-motion replays with repeated analyses, and exaggerated language used in sport stories. As an aside, in recent years one of the best-selling videos in parts of the Northeastern United States has been a collection of "the best fights in the NHL." The videos often feature slow-motion replays of particularly spectacular punches or highlight the glee on spectators' faces as they watch players fighting.

The press in Great Britain, partly to sell newspapers, emphasizes football hooligan stories, which may reinforce the behavior. Whannel (1979) analyzed the content of newspaper reports and identified four main ways of describing football hooligans: (a) mindless, senseless, or brainless; (b) maniacs, lunatics, mentally disturbed, or psychopathic; (c) foul, subhuman, animals, or criminals; and (d) a minority of nonfans or nonsupporters, who don't enjoy football. All of these characteristics are summarized in an apt phrase, attributed to a former star player named Bobby Moore. He described hooliganism (Whannel, 1979) as "the mindless mentality of the moronic minority" (p. 332).

Finally, the media promotes excitement and interest in sport to generate profits. They increase the level of serious commitment to a sport by suggesting it reflects one's own values and is a measure of one's personal worth. They thus become an indirect cause of increased violence, by both players and spectators (Weis, 1986). In fact, media handling of violence in professional sport settings may indirectly increase the incidence and severity of violent events in amateur sport, including youth sport.

The Physical and Social Environment of Sport

The nature of physical settings can influence the onset or severity of collective sport episodes (Semyonov & Farbstein, 1989). To illustrate, in amateur football or soccer matches spectators may stand dispersed along the sidelines, usually on opposing sides of the field. This distance tends to prevent opposing factions from direct physical contact, at least until the game is over. Somewhat similarly, many soccer stadiums in Great Britain and Europe require most spectators to stand in crowded terraces throughout the match, usually at opposite ends of the stadium. Similarly, where there is a price difference in tickets, seating areas of the stadium tend to attract individuals with similar characteristics.

In North America, most spectators sit in reserved or assigned seats. Typically, the seating sections furthest from the action (e.g., the bleachers in baseball, end zone in football, and upper tier in hockey) witness more disruptive events. Most problems with spectators in baseball, for example, emanate from the bleacher sections (the areas surrounding the outfield, which face home plate and are the farthest from the infield, where most of the action is). In some cases the bleacher arrangement seats spectators close to at least three players. When outfielders retreat to the fence to catch or retrieve balls, they easily can be hit by thrown objects or experience an unexpected beer shower.

In Europe and Great Britain, most stadiums are located in the inner city, and spectators from both teams arrive by train and walk to the stadium as a crowd. This heightens pregame excitement and provides the opportunity for opposing fans to engage in taunts and physical aggression before the game. (This occurred in the streets of Brussels before the soccer riot in May 1985).

North American spectators usually arrive at the suburban stadium by car in small groups or at the inner-city stadium by bus or car. Moreover, few fans from visiting teams attend, because generally they can remain at home and watch the event on television.

The composition of the audience may also contribute to the potential for disruptive behavior. Outside North America, few women and children attend games. This seems to encourage more drinking, obscene vocal behavior, and fighting in the audience. Crowds in North America also tend toward a mix of class backgrounds. European soccer spectators, alternatively, tend to be primarily male; many are from the working class, especially those who sit in the terraces. Hence, working class and male values of aggression and territorial protection prevail.

TYPOLOGIES OF SPORT CROWD BEHAVIOR

Although violent episodes of collective sport behavior tend to dominate the news and research literature, sport has also been the stimulus for nonviolent collective behavior. Celebrations of sport victories, for example, generally are peaceful and reasonably orderly.

The key point is that not all collective behavior is violent, nor can it all be classified as riotous. This recognition has led to the search for classification systems, or typologies, to describe and explain the basic types of events that occur. For example, Smith (1983) derived a classification scheme based on the extent to which there is a *legitimating belief* or *issue* present that ties the episode to some perceived problem in society. Participants can thus justify their behavior. Smith derives a typology in which riots are placed along a continuum ranging from the **issue-oriented riot** to the **issueless riot**. Depending on the issue involved, the sport or event may have varying degrees of importance as a catalyst. Highlight 11.5 presents Smith's typology.

Highlight 11.5
Smith's Typology of Sport Crowd Riots

Issue-Oriented Riots

Structural Sources

1. Demonstrations—a sport event is disrupted to draw attention to a political cause (e.g., the apartheid policy of South Africa; hooliganism incited by political factions).
2. Confrontations—traditional racial, class, religious, or national rivalries on the field are represented in the stands (e.g., some soccer riots have their basis in class or religious differences between two opposing factions).

Situational Sources

1. Denial of entry or disappointments—within a specific setting fans are denied entry, performers fail to appear, or the event is delayed without explanation.
2. Imminent or actual defeat—disappointed fans react to an unpopular or perceived incorrect decision by an official that guarantees a loss by the home team, or the crowd reacts to an unexpected or humiliating defeat.

Issueless Riots

Situational Sources

1. Time-out celebrations—an institutionalized carnival or festival where traditional moral norms are temporarily suspended, often prior to the actual game itself. Again, this may or may not get out of control. Some incidents of soccer hooliganism, especially in smaller towns in Great Britain, are examples of time-out behavior rather than of religious, class, or regional conflict.
2. Victory celebrations—a semi-institutionalized celebration in the presence of minimal or overlooked social control. This may or may not get out of control and attain the status of *riot*.

Note. Adapted from Smith (1983).

Issue-Oriented Protests and Riots

Clearly there are different types and degrees of protests and riots. These range from relatively peaceful protests to hostile attacks. It seems the setting, game structure, rules, ethos, and participants, all of which vary from sport to sport, influence the propensity to riot. Most riots, for example, occur in sports that are highly valued in a culture or community (Lee, 1985) and incorporate some element of physical contact on the playing field.

Underlying Tensions. In most riots, there seems to be an underlying, preexisting tension. Social differences among groups and accompanying prejudices, for example, can lead to hostility. This preexisting tension combined with the high in-group identification and solidarity typical of a sport event increases the potential for a riot. To illustrate, in the 1985 Brussels riot there were long-standing hostile beliefs about the style of play exhibited by players from each country. Italians have traditionally viewed British players as aggressive and physical; the British view Italian players (Davies, 1972) as "hysterical" (p. 268) and find distasteful the tantrums, emotion, and cheap tricks they use to gain advantage.

Hostilities are often perpetuated by the mass media to promote or heighten the level of excitement at a specific sport event. Or sometimes rumors begin to spread within the crowd and individuals become more responsive to external cues. This can occur particularly at half-time or other periods of inactivity on the field. The spreading of rumors or beliefs through communication channels can be an important factor in precipitating violence.

Specific Events. Sometimes a specific event, or series of events, sparks the violent outburst. Often this act involves violence on the field (especially if it is perceived as illegitimate, occurs against a player on the home team, and is not penalized) or in the stands (e.g., the police eject a spectator). Smith (1978), based on an analysis of 68 newspaper reports over a 10-year period, found that 74% of crowd violence was ignited by player violence. Other major precipitants were unpopular decisions by officials and spectators' verbal assaulting of players, who subsequently invaded the seating area.

Other Precipitating Factors. Dewar (1979), after viewing 40 professional baseball games, concluded that spectator fights are more likely to occur

- at evening games;
- when the audience nearly fills the stadium;
- late in the season, when a team is involved in a pennant race;
- in the less expensive seating sections;
- as the temperature increases; and
- late in a game.

Moreover, a fight between two spectators may escalate to large-scale brawls when others take sides or when ushers or police intervene. Outside intervention may create a *we* (spectators) versus *they* (agents of control) situation.

A second factor is the ecology of the stadium. Can the fans invade the field to attack property or humans, or are they restricted to throwing objects onto the playing surface? In soccer, examples abound of referees being attacked—and sometimes killed—on the field, in their dressing rooms, or when they leave the stadium. If anger or frustration cannot be released inside the stadium, nearby streets and buildings can become the objects of attack, as in the Rocket Richard riot in Montreal. Merchants located near the arena became the victims of a rampaging crowd that broke windows and vandalized property or stole goods.

Objects of attack outside the stadium may also have symbolic meaning. For example, in some racial riots a primarily white mob may ransack only businesses owned by blacks, or vice versa.

A final factor influencing whether a crowd explodes into action is the degree to which police and agents of social control are present. Strain can be reduced and precipitating factors isolated or controlled if there is a moat or screening around the playing area, if alcohol is forbidden or strictly controlled, and if many security personnel are visible and located in potential trouble areas. To illustrate, police appearing on the field with dogs and on horses during the last inning of the final 1986 World Series game in New York inhibited and prevented the onset of a celebration riot.

Influence of Leaders.   Again, we must remember that many riots are not ignited by on-field fights, unpopular decisions by officials, or emotional combatants in the stands. Other forces or factors can mobilize spectators to become an unruly mob. Frequently one or more leaders, by personal actions or verbal encouragement, serve as behavioral models and increase the likelihood of more in the crowd becoming active participants.

Recent inquiries into soccer hooliganism have found that political dissidents are infiltrating soccer crowds to create social unrest. In Great Britain, members of the radical National Front allegedly use soccer crowds to create incidents that will draw attention to their grievances. Gabler (1984) described a similar development in West Germany, where a lower middle-class juvenile subculture has been created around First Division Soccer. These organizations, like those in England, are being used to promote radical, right-wing interests.

Issueless Riots

Major sport events, as noted earlier, have become major festivals on the yearly calendar, where the usual constraints on behavioral and moral norms are relaxed and ignored. It is as if the representatives of the law and the host city say, "Within this geographical region [often clearly defined], we encourage you to participate in a large street party where you are free to break some of our minor laws, mingle with strangers, and enjoy all the stimulation or excitement you need, but then return peacefully to your routinized, unexciting life."

To illustrate, civic leaders in Mexico City are alleged to have deliberately permitted a wild celebration in the streets after Mexico won a soccer game in 1970 to enter the quarter-finals of the World Cup Tournament; the government, it is said, hoped to distract the public from social issues and other problems. Similarly, Lever (1983) argues that the unofficial government policy in Brazil "seems to include the notion that soccer can be used to distract workers from their serious grievances" (p. 61).

This view harkens back to the early Romans use of "bread and circuses" to control the masses. Similarly, some scholars have argued that major sport festivals are modern bread and circuses, which serve as safety valves to maintain order and stability and enhance community integration.

Some would argue that the lower classes suffer more strain and deprivation and therefore benefit and participate more in these sport festivals. However, most studies find that the middle class participates most heavily in these periods of legitimate deviance, perhaps because they are generally more constrained by daily legal, moral, and social norms. They are also more likely to be able to pay for air travel, game tickets, hotels, and meals.

Milling.   Large sport events provide opportunities for milling, a process analyzed by the sociologist, Erving Goffman (1967). He argued that individuals gather at any sport or social scene to seek "action" that "a tightly packed gathering of reveling persons can bring or create" (p. 197). The collective behavior that results normally is unstructured, unpredictable, and lacks clearly defined limits on how far and in what way societal laws can be stretched.

Pregame milling can occur in the lobbies of major hotels, in downtown streets, in bars and restaurants that promote fan involvement, and at the tailgate parties in stadium parking lots. (If you are interested in experiencing a tightly packed gathering, visit Bourbon Street in New Orleans any night during Mardi Gras. This social setting draws a fine line between excitement and panic, as one is literally swept along with the crowd.)

Membership in these settings is semipermanent over a given period of time, as people enter and leave. However, there are no real leaders and there is little sustained social interaction as participants "mill" around. Many remain at the periphery as passive spectators, at least initially. It is this type of "milling" celebration that has the potential to erupt into what Smith (1983) calls a "time-out" (p. 151) riot. Others call this an issueless riot. That is, condoned events before the sport event provide the excuse for large-scale uninhibited street parties. Smith (1983) cites the example of the Grey Cup riot the evening before the 1966 championship game in Vancouver. This episode involved an estimated 5,000 celebrants in the downtown hotel district, many of them male youths, who "smashed store windows, destroyed street decorations, lit fires in trash cans, and skirmished with police" (p. 152). This "celebration," which became an issueless riot, required 150 police and 12 dogs to disperse the crowd, and 260 participants were arrested for unlawful assembly and alcohol-related offenses. Earlier in the evening, when it was still viewed as a "time-out" celebration, police had ignored this type of behavior.

A similar issueless riot occurred on "Beer Night" at Cleveland Stadium on June 4, 1974. An estimated 60,000 cups of beer (at 10 cents each) were consumed; many were poured onto the outfielders of the visiting team. Eventually, spectators poured themselves onto the field, injuring four players and one umpire. Surprisingly, only nine spectators were arrested before the violence ended.

Celebration riots often begin with simple rowdiness, as demonstrated by these fun-loving goalpost climbers.

Celebrations. By far the most frequent incidents of disruptive celebrations are those following a major sport victory. In North America this type of celebration was introduced by fans in the late 1960s. One of the earliest celebrations followed the 1969 New York Mets World Series victory in Shea Stadium. Fans ran onto the field and into the dugout, where they stole pieces of sod and tore seats apart for souvenirs; security personnel watched with amusement. By the 1970s these victory celebrations spilled over into the streets outside the stadium; police remained passive until they thought events threatened public safety and order. Highlight 11.6 describes two sport celebrations that turned into issueless riots.

The potential for a celebration to escalate to a riot is increased, because of what McPhail and Miller (1973) call the *assembling*

Highlight 11.6
Two Examples of Celebration Riots

May 26, 1986

Montreal, Canada

Following the 23rd Stanley Cup victory in the history of the Montreal Canadiens (the game was played in Calgary), several thousand fans gathered and milled about in downtown Montreal. Most watched and shouted encouragement to a minority who overturned cars, lit a huge bonfire, and looted and vandalized over 20 stores. Several people suffered minor injuries, but only six young people were arrested. The police didn't arrive on the scene until about 3:30 a.m., almost 2 hours after the street celebrations began. The damage was estimated at more than $1 million.

June 16, 1986

Mexico City, Mexico

Mexico defeated Bulgaria to advance to the quarter-finals of the World Cup. A night of celebration exceeded that of June

3, when 200 people were injured and more than 80 arrested after Mexico's first World Cup victory.

Police blocked off central avenues to cars and allowed a crowd to celebrate. Women bared their breasts, youths danced in the streets, and alcohol was consumed openly and in great quantities. About 100 people were arrested for being drunk or disorderly.

Beyond the central area, criminals took advantage of the distracted police to commit more than 150 robberies; 11 people were killed in car accidents as they returned to Mexico City from celebrations in other parts of Mexico; scores of people were injured when they fell from moving cars as they raced through the city waving flags; and 2 people were shot in a slow-moving convoy of cars as noncelebrants lost tempers when stuck among the celebrants.

---

process. In this collective situation, people converge at a common downtown location or at an airport. Sometimes they were already present in the area; more likely, they received formal or informal suggestions from the media to meet at a specific location. Often the motivation is to greet and reward the winning team as they arrive at the airport or to attend a victory parade. Regardless of the instructions, large numbers of celebrants assemble and begin drinking and engaging in deviance. This setting often explodes into a riot. Today, the police are much better pre-

pared for the possibility of such celebration riots. Participants are either discouraged by a show of force (e.g., police on horses, police dogs present) or confined to a specific area by barricades. Any deviance outside these predefined boundaries is not tolerated.

Hooliganism

Hooliganism is the term describing the unique type of sport crowd behavior of some young soccer spectators in England. The term is thought to be derived from an antisocial family named Houlighan, who lived in East London during the 19th century (Taylor, 1971). The word was not used until the early 1960s, when journalists and magistrates began paying more attention to the actions of young soccer fans at games. Their behavior, which may have had a recreational or political motive, ranged from general rowdyism on trains to and from the matches, to disruptions outside the stadium, to disturbances that affected the game. While it is difficult to document the onset of hooligan behavior at soccer matches, it seems to have begun in the late 1950s when fans began to travel by train to other towns to support their teams.

In the 1960s and 1970s a new set of values and beliefs emerged within the youth subculture. These included challenges of authority, less adherence to social constraints, socializing mainly with age-peers, and the search for a unique identity. The changes in the youth subculture changed the purpose of attending soccer matches. No longer was the game as important as socializing with one's own type and establishing status within the group. As a result, young working-class males began to congregate and dominate the "ends" of the stadiums. A subculture began to evolve in these end zones, as fans chanted, waved scarves, and informally agreed to defend "their territory" against others. Moreover, the gangs traveled to and from games together, "took over" railway cars, and challenged opposing fans and players. Many of those seriously engaged in hooliganism were unemployed or underemployed, and for some, at least initially, being part of the gang expressed their perceptions of relative deprivation in society.

At first the forms of disruptive behavior were relatively minor—swearing, chanting team songs, taunting opponents, or running through the streets of an opponent's town. In time, perhaps reinforced and encouraged by media coverage, the disruptive behavior escalated to more serious acts such as invading the field, perhaps to influence the outcome of the game or to intimidate officials and opponents; physically assaulting opposing fans in the terraces and outside the stadium; destroying town and stadium property; and overtly challenging the police. As Pearton (1986) noted, soccer hooliganism came to represent "a form of affective violence of the kind against which taboos have been developed" (p. 83).

Much of this increased violence can be attributed to the "skinhead" movement that emerged in London. This subculture of highly aggressive males (especially against foreigners, hippies, and gays) found soccer crowds a useful setting in which to demonstrate their toughness. They infiltrated the "ends" and were largely responsible for spreading the violence from the terrace "ends" to the streets, stations, and trains. They also adopted the strategy of infiltrating their opponents' "end" with the goal of "taking it over." By the middle 1970s, hooliganism spread to matches in Europe that involved local or national British teams.

By the early and middle 1980s hooliganism was viewed as a national social problem and a political concern in Great Britain (Carroll, 1980; Taylor, 1987; White, 1982). At about this time, the hooligan movement was itself infiltrated by members of far right-wing political parties, such as the National Front. It has been alleged that National Front members instigated the tragedy in Brussels. Today, one group of analysts (Williams et al., 1986) suggests that 5,000 policemen per week, at a cost of more than $5 million per nine-month soccer season, is needed to control and isolate the disruptive segment of soccer in Great Britain.

To combat the growth of hooliganism, law enforcement agencies have used undercover agents and made arrests away from the soccer pitch. On January 20, 1987, in London, undercover police arrested 26 men alleged to be the most dangerous leaders of soccer hooliganism in Great Britain. The arrests, made by more than 250 police officers at 30 addresses, ended four months of undercover work in and around soccer matches. Those arrested were supporters of the two London soccer clubs (Millwall and West Ham) with a predisposition to be lawless and to fight. During the arrests, police confiscated a number of knives, loaded air rifles, and blackjacks from these "fans"!

Hooliganism occurs with sufficient regularity that it merits analysis as a form of collective behavior in England and elsewhere. However, we lack a definitive explanation of the cause of this antisocial behavior. Many myths and false beliefs still surround the phenomenon, largely because of a lack of valid research evidence (Melnick, 1986). For information we depend on media views and headlines, on government rhetoric, or on selective studies by scholars. These incomplete and inconsistent sources of information create and perpetuate myths. To illustrate, Melnick (1986) questions the validity of the following myths, many of which have already been discussed.

- Hooliganism is a modern phenomenon.
- Hooliganism is unique to Great Britain.
- Hooliganism in Great Britain constitutes a national social problem.
- Hooliganism is responsible for the declining attendance at soccer matches in Great Britain since World War II.
- Hooligans are thugs, criminals, animals, and the like.
- Hooligans have no interest in, or knowledge of, the game per se.
- Hooliganism represents a loss of self-control and can be prevented by harsher punishments.

SOCIAL CONTROL POLICIES AND LEGISLATION

Whatever the causes, the rise of modern sport has led to an apparent increase in the number and severity of collective sport outbursts. It is not surprising to find correspondingly strong measures of **social control**. These acts have sought to inhibit or divert the crowd by creating legislation or social policies; altering the physical structure of the playing and viewing milieu; punishing convicted celebrants; or showing force (e.g., uniformed police, dogs, horses, antiterrorist squads, firefighters with hoses).

To illustrate, the Popplewell Report, published in 1985, noted that in Great Britain in 1969, 1 police officer was assigned to a soccer match for every 1,000 spectators. In 1985, the ratio was 1 for every 75 spectators. Ironically, there have been few attempts to alleviate the larger underlying social strains (e.g., economic, racial, religious, or political inequities) that help lead to riots. Sport and law officials *have* shown more sensitivity and understanding of these elements in the social context of a specific game. Highlight 11.7 presents many recently suggested methods of preventing spectator violence.

Control measures do seem to be acting as a deterrent in recent years. Yet, as numerous authors have reported, many of the attempts to control the crowd are really short-term deterrents and not a real solution. As long as the underlying strains or predispositions persist, some elements of society will find an environment to express their discontent. Sport officials and politicians may need to work more closely to eliminate the underlying social strains that are often manifested in a sport setting.

COLLECTIVE IMITATION OF SPORT AGGRESSION

What is at issue here is not behavior in face-to-face interactions but collective behavior in

---

Highlight 11.7
Proposed Social-Control Mechanisms to Prevent Spectator Violence

Physical Alterations

- Moats around the playing field
- Higher screens or glass around the hockey rink or baseball field to keep players enclosed, and spectators out
- Canopies to protect players from being showered with debris when entering or leaving the playing area
- Seats installed to replace standing in terraces
- Barricades in the streets to confine the crowd to one area
- Segregated entrances and seating for opposing groups

Policies and Legislation

- High school football games played during daylight
- Spectators and teams banned from a country or town
- Parents prohibited from watching sons play Little League hockey
- Alcohol banned or sales rigorously controlled

- Spectators searched for alcohol at entry
- Penalty assessed to the home team if fans misbehave
- More stringent rules to eliminate or control on-field player violence
- Identity cards supplied by the home club shown to gain entrance to British soccer matches
- Obscene and racist chants outlawed

Law Enforcement Strategies

- Mounted policemen
- Police with riot gear
- Undercover police present
- Stringent revision and enforcement of fire and safety regulations in stadiums
- Armed military personnel
- Detention centers and courts in the stadium
- Undercover criminal investigations
- Increased security personnel (ushers) in each section
- Closed-circuit television to spot trouble-makers

---

a widely dispersed media audience. A sobering example of a collective response to aggression in sport events has come to light in the research of Phillips (1983). Phillips has demonstrated that the aggressive behavior portrayed in major televised boxing matches is imitated by spectators later—to the extreme of increasing the society's murder rate!

Phillips studied 18 heavyweight prize fights televised between 1973 and 1978 in the U.S.

and asked if the U.S. homicide rate increased beyond the expected rate immediately following the presentation of the fight. He found that this was indeed the case for 13 of the 18 fights. Moreover, he found that the most widely watched fights (e.g., the "Thrilla in Manila" between Ali and Frazier, which is said to be the most watched prize fight ever) showed the most marked effect on the homicide rate.

Some of Phillips's findings are presented in Table 11.1. Fights from locations both inside and outside the country showed an effect on the homicide rate. In the fights held outside the country, there is little chance that the murderers watched the fights live. The effect of the fights must have come through watching the televised portrayals.

Phillips' research also showed that the race (black vs. white) of murder victims in the days immediately following the presentation of the fights was correlated with the race of the fight loser. That is, murders of blacks increased when a black boxer lost, and murders of whites increased when a white boxer lost. Phillips interpreted this set of findings as showing that imitation was taking place.

This same research project did *not* show similar increases in murders following major football games, which also contain examples of aggression and violence. Phillips hypothesized that the difference between the sports is that no *individual* is singled out as a target for aggression in football. He believes that the dramatic presentation of the legitimacy of violence and aggression against individuals in boxing makes for homicidal behavior. By this logic, there could also be an increase in other forms of aggressive behavior. Perhaps further research will answer these questions.

Another collective response to sport events may be a reduction in the suicide rate. Curtis, Loy, and Karnilowicz (1986) have reported

Table 11.1   U.S. Homicides in Three Days Following 18 Heavyweight Prizefights, 1973–1978

Name of fight	Observed no. of homicides	Expected no. of homicides	Observed minus expected	Fight held outside U.S.	On network evening news?
Foreman/Frazier	55	42	13	Y	Y
Foreman/Roman	46	49	−3	Y	N
Foreman/Norton	55	54	1	Y	N
Ali/Foreman	102	82	20	Y	Y
Ali/Wepner	44	47	−3	N	Y
Ali/Lyle	54	47	7	N	Y
Ali/Bugner	106	83	23	Y	N
Ali/Frazier	108	82	26	Y	Y
Ali/Coopman	54	45	9	Y	N
Ali/Young	41	44	−3	N	N
Ali/Dunn	50	41	9	Y	Y
Ali/Norton	64	53	11	N	Y
Ali/Evangelista	36	42	−6	N	N
Ali/Shavers	66	67	−1	N	N
Spinks/Ali	89	79	10	N	Y
Holmes/Norton	53	49	4	N	N
Ali/Spinks	59	52	7	N	Y
Holmes/Evangelista	52	50	2	N	N

Note. From "Mass Media Violence and U.S. Homicides" by D. Phillips, 1983, *American Sociological Review*, **48**, pp. 560–568. Copyright 1983 by American Sociological Association. Adapted by permission.

that the Super Bowl and the World Series apparently *reduce* suicide rates slightly. The rates appear to be lower than expected on the day or two before the event, the day of the event, and on the day immediately afterward. In the next few days, the suicide rate is higher than expected. The net result is an apparent *saving* of lives. It is as if some people wait to kill themselves until the game is over. Similar, but much more marked, patterns were shown to hold for major holidays (July 4, Thanksgiving). In data collected from 1972 to 1978, there was a net gain of 16 fewer suicides than expected for the 7-day periods around the two sport events. Comparable data on the two major holidays showed 189 fewer suicides than expected.

SOCIAL MOVEMENTS AND SOCIAL CHANGE

As both history and an analysis of contemporary social life reveal, change is an inevitable process (Allison, 1987; Arbena, 1988; Bale, 1984). In this section we analyze different forms of **social change** that occur because of collective attempts in social movements to initiate, maintain, or resist social change. Some of these changes permeate parts of society and are reflected in unique lifestyles, perhaps becoming part of a subculture. Others represent a reformist or radical social movement. Some social movements have a later impact on sport after affecting the wider society; others occur at the same time inside and outside sport; others occur within sport first and then have an impact on society; while still others occur within sport and never affect other societal institutions.

Sources of Social Change

Social change usually occurs when a group of individuals acquires some degree of shared goals, beliefs, values, and actions that meet unfulfilled needs. Their collective action may be loosely or highly organized, spontaneous or the result of deliberate plans. In most instances, the attempt to initiate change is not irrational behavior. Rather, it results from a conflict of interests or values; a change in policy, program, or legislation; a need to cope with a societal problem; or a search for alternatives to some aspects of a social organization. Achieving the desired goals seldom involves deviant or revolutionary behavior. The change often occurs slowly and randomly over time rather than at a single, traumatic crisis. The result of a major change may be the emergence of new norms, an acceptance of new values, and the creation of new social groups.

Much social change, especially in the leisure domain, involves a temporary attraction to subcultural lifestyles (e.g., wearing biking shirts and pants, using the hoola hoop, skateboarding) rather than a revolutionary social movement. In leisure, as in art, there are cycles of perspectives. Thus, particular styles, forms, or artifacts temporarily become important and have symbolic meaning in an ever-changing quest for excitement, meaning, and variety. Sometimes fads and fashions alternate between generations, that is, a fad popular with one generation will be rejected by the following generation but reappear later.

Skateboarding illustrates the cyclical nature of fads. It was popular in 1964-65; by 1966 the fad was over. But in the 1970s with quieter, faster, and more durable polyurethane wheels, the craze once again spread from California across North America and to Europe, Japan, and New Zealand. By the early 1980s the fad had virtually disappeared again, only to reappear in the middle 1980s (Davidson, 1981).

How Social Change Occurs

Attitudes of participants range along a scale from *no change desired*, to a *reformist per-*

Sport, as well as society, is constantly changing.

spective, which seeks adjustments in the existing society (e.g., the fitness movement), to a *radical perspective*, where many changes are sought, often immediately and often of such a degree that the existing system must be destroyed or altered dramatically (e.g., a political revolution).

Radical and reformist individuals clearly view change positively and believe that it is necessary and of value to the social group. Those in the *no change desired* camp prefer the status quo and view any change as unnecessary, harmful, and disruptive to the social group. They resist change by collectively creating counter-movements (e.g., pro-choice groups oppose pro-life groups). In the long term, the rate and amount of change and the number of people affected may determine the permanency of the change; the extent to which changes are diffused within an institution, organization, or society; and the extent to which the change is introduced and accepted into other societies.

Social Change in Sport

Throughout this book, we have suggested that sport has undergone changes over the sweep of history. It is appropriate to close this chapter with a section on this topic, because a major social movement is implicated in many of the changes that have taken place in sport. Indeed, the only thing that has been constant about sport is that it has changed.

The best way we know to summarize the direction of the changes is to draw on Ingham's (1979) portrayal of the *ideal* types of organized sport in premodern and modern times. He discusses how changes have taken place in seven aspects of sport: (a) locales; (b) form of organization; (c) regulations; (d) recruitment processes; (e) action orientations; (f) normative framework; and (g) use of technology. These differences are described in detail in Highlight 11.8. You will have to agree from this list of differences that people from modern times would hardly recognize premodern sport as sport.

Ingham argues that the change in trends from premodern to modern sport is largely a

Highlight 11.8
An Ideal-Typical Portrayal
of "Organized" Sport in Two Historical Time-Frames

Pre-Modern

1. Locales—spas, resorts, social clubs, taverns, natural sites, and designated sites maintained by subscription fees (i.e., jockey club courses).

2. Organization—local, regional, and, in some sports, intersectional; events often the result of challenges; tavern keeper sponsorship, fetes, and fairs. . . . Club organization with a collegial pattern of decision-making. No player associations or "organized" labor.

3. Regulation—rules quite complex and attuned to conventional standards of etiquette, fashion, and style. Local in scope and oftentimes based upon the mutual consent of parties involved. Sometimes intentionally esoteric.

4. Recruitment—based on interest, subscription, invitation, challenge, cultural and peer pressure; not generally tied to ability; for life.

5. Action Orientations—eustress seeking [sensation seeking], conviviality, festivity, display, social approbation, exhibit skill and prowess, social solidarity; tradition, affectual, and when tied to the status order, value-rational.

6. Normative Framework—traditional conceptions of elite and popular culture; amateurism; when intellectualized, sport viewed as a means to health and fitness, to character development and, by a few religious leaders, as a means to spiritual fulfillment; some politicization; "organic" connection to collectivity.

7. Technicization—non-scientific; some instructional discourses; some "expert" opinions; use of communications media in the form of journals, magazines, newspapers; few technological props; . . . few professional specialists in the "support" services.

Modern

1. Locales—principally "enclosed" arenas, stadia, pavilions, "athletic/sport" clubs and publicly sponsored "playing fields."

2. Organization—centralized with local, regional, or geographic devolution of administrative routine; central regulatory agencies, international committees and sport federations; representational or collegial policy-making with bureaucratic administration; central administrative organs have supra-local meta-power. Events are "sanctioned" by respective sport federations. Players are organized into "associations." Key principle: the league and/or circuit.

3. Regulation—rules quite complex and attuned to manipulation-avoidance; standardized and exoteric; systematized; manipulated and, hence, calculative and conditional; imperative control and enforcement; as much of the "spirit" converted into the "letter" as is possible so as to avoid ambiguity; extra-institutional

(Cont.)

Highlight 11.8 Continued

intervention (i.e., courts and congress now involved).

4. Recruitment—feeder-system apprenticeship; based upon universalistic criteria; cultural, peer, community, and economic inducements; longevity tied to potential gate and performance values; key principle: career.

5. Action Orientations—profit and performance, professionalism, instrumentally rational or calculative, conditional means to an end, unitary value—meritocracy.

6. Normative Framework—modern mass society conceptions of work, service, and entertainment; commercialism; sport sanctioned by rhetorical claims to fitness and health, character development, intellectual growth, responsibility training, self-discipline, etc., "politicized"; estranged.

7. Technicization—"scientific" rationality pervasive; major emphasis on technique; much technological tinkering with both props and the human body; intellectualized strategically and intellectualization evident in the growth of the "sport sciences"; much use, indeed financial dependence on, the mass media; much mensuration re records and productivity/performance increments; para-medical and medical support services; business management orientation in administrative personnel; proliferation of experts, pseudo-experts/specialists.

Note. From "Methodology in the Sociology of Sport: From Symptoms of Malaise to Weber for a Cure" by A.G. Ingham, 1973, Quest, 31, pp. 206-208. Copyright 1979 by the National Association for Physical Education in Higher Education. Reprinted by permission.

function of the development of capitalism and its effects outside the economy in the larger society, including sport. Capitalism—with its highly rational calculation of profit-making and reinvestment of profit for bigger and more successful firms—is so commonplace to us in North America that we can easily take its effects for granted. But a major consequence of the influence of capitalism, according to Ingham, has been athletes' loss of control of (and estrangement from) sport. Control has shifted to owners, managers, and coaches. This point aptly illustrates the "good news, bad news" character of social change in sport. The level of sport performance has escalated rapidly in the past 30 years, from the rational calculations now applied to sport; but the changes have also had undesirable side ef-

fects, including alienated athletes, the use of steroids, life-threatening or crippling injuries, scandals, and abuses in college sport.

Guttmann (1978) has documented how increasing tendencies toward secularism, democratization, specialization, rationalization, bureaucratization, quantification, and record-seeking all were diffused into the world of sport from the wider society. To illustrate, specialized roles have appeared in sport (e.g., the designated hitter in baseball, the penalty-killer in hockey, the field-goal kicker in football) and elaborate records are now maintained by increasingly bureaucratic sport organizations. Perhaps the best recent illustration is the changing world of sport in the People's Republic of China since the Cultural Revolution ended in 1976 (Hoberman,

1987). Two of the most pronounced changes have been the increased emphasis on high-performance sport, as evidenced by China's success in the 1984 and 1988 Summer Olympics, and the increasingly scientific approach toward the development of athletes.

The Interactive Process of Change in Society and Sport

In some instances, changes in society and sport occur at about the same time and rate, with each reinforcing and supporting change in the other. In the desegregation movement, sport has been a model of change; blacks have also been integrated, at least to a degree, into societal institutions. Similarly, sport has provided greater opportunities for members of the working class, as they have acquired more leisure time and income. Sport has changed the makeup of Sunday and other religious events through the scheduling of sport events. And sport has fostered and heightened nationalism, primarily through the Olympic movement.

In contrast, some social movements have appeared later in sport than in the wider society. Two examples include the gay rights and women's liberation movement. Another example is the involvement of immigrant ethnic groups in sport or fitness activities. High levels of sport involvement often do not occur until the second generation, when offspring have been socialized from childhood to the norms of sport activity in the host society.

Some specific social changes within sport have led to significant changes in other aspects of our cultural life. The clothes, language, and lifestyles of athletes have become diffused and accepted in other social domains. Just count the number of T-shirts and athletic shoes worn to classes, work, church, and school. Many of these items, designed for athletic participation, have never been used in a sporting context—except perhaps by spectators or viewers. Similarly, many examples of sport technology, developed to enhance television production of a sport event or increase the safety of an athlete, have subsequently resulted in changes in other domains. Some examples from television include the use of the instant replay, slow motion, the split screen, and remote broadcasts via satellite for news events.

Finally, in recent years sport has experienced dramatic technological and structural change as advanced technology has developed and entrepreneurs have sought to make sport a more marketable product, especially on television. Some examples include the following:

- New sports have been created or invented (e.g., indoor soccer, arena football, triathlons, master's competition).
- Technological changes in equipment and facilities have led to higher performance levels (e.g., fiberglass pole vault, artificial turf, composite tennis rackets).
- New sport techniques have evolved (e.g., the Fosbury flop, the Wishbone T formation, the slam dunk);
- New rules have been created (e.g., the 24-second clock, the tiebreaker in tennis).
- Social movements unique to sport have appeared (e.g., jogging or running has evolved into a competitive activity with road races; the fitness and wellness movements have become a way of life for many North Americans).

WRAP-UP

Collective behavior is spontaneous, unstructured, unorganized, and transitory. It occurs frequently in sport, just as it does elsewhere in society. An example of collective behavior in sport is riots by crowds of spectators. Such riots have occurred across the recorded history of sport and in various societies.

Sport probably has become a more fertile ground for collective behavior in recent years. Among the reasons for this are increased opportunities for large audiences to get together at sport events, with many events having a "carnival" atmosphere; social conflicts among groups in the wider society, which can easily be represented at a sport event because members of the various subgroups often attend; the mass media's frequently publicizing sport riots, thereby providing a role model for future spectators; the physical environments of sport arenas, which often make it easy for precipitating events to set off a riot; and aspects of the contemporary spectator, who typically invests a great deal of commitment, interest, and emotion in the sport.

There are two basic types of collective behavior in sport: issue-oriented riots and issueless riots. In the former, some issue provides an impetus for the crowd's unruly behavior. Examples are a fight between athletes during the contest, an unpopular decision by an official, or an altercation among fans in the audience. In the issueless riot, with no discernable starting event, a crowd erupts, as when a victory celebration turns to collective acts of vandalism.

Because collective behavior is transitional, it changes sport only to the extent that it (a) ceases to be collective behavior and becomes the ritualized, repetitive behavior of a social movement or a subcultural form, as with hooliganism or (b) leads to changes in how a sport is organized, as with changes in social-control procedures.

Much of the collective behavior within sport is rooted in social strains that come to sport from the wider society. Contrary to common beliefs, conflicts of race, class, and politics are *not* excluded from sport settings and often contribute to collective behavior.

Collective behavior in sport generates interest, particularly in the media, and thus affects the wider society. Dramatic, short-term public reactions to sport are seen in the changes in homicide and suicide rates during and following major sport events. And some social movements within sport have changed lifestyles throughout the wider society.

Few social movements have begun in sport, although sport has reflected movements begun in the wider society. Many of the transformations sport has undergone in the last few centuries may be attributed to the social movement of capitalism. This led to major changes in the economy that affected other areas inside and outside the world of sport. Similarly, many of the evolving changes in women's sport may be attributed to the feminist movement.

REFERENCES

Allison, M.T. (1987). Kaleidoscope and prism: The study of social change in play, sport, and leisure. *Sociology of Sport Journal*, **4**, 144–155.

Arbena, J. (1988). *Sport and society in Latin America: Diffusion, dependency and the rise of mass culture*. Westport, CT: Greenwood.

Bale, J. (1984). International sports history as innovation diffusion. *Canadian Journal of History of Sport*, **15**(1), 39–63.

Bandura, A., & Walters, R.H. (1963). *Social learning and personablity development*. New York: Holt, Rinehart & Winston.

Beisser, A.R. (1979). The plight of the American sports fan. *Psychiatric Annals*, **9**(3), 70–77.

Berkowitz, L. (1969). The frustration-aggression hypothesis revisited. In L. Berkowitz (Ed.), *Roots of aggression: A re-exam-*

ination of the frustration-aggression hypothesis (pp. 1–28). New York: Atherton.

Brill, A.A. (1929). The way of the fan. North American Review. 228, 427–434.

Bryant, J., & Zillmann, D. (1983). Sports violence and the media. In J.H. Goldstein (Ed.), Sports violence (pp. 197–211). New York: Springer-Verlag.

Cameron, A. (1976). Circus factions: Blues and greens at Tome and Byzantium. Oxford: Clarendon.

Carroll, R. (1980). Football hooliganism in England. International Review of Sport Sociology, 15(2), 77–92.

Cialdini, R.B., Borden, K.J., Thorne, A., Walker, M.R., Freeman, S., & Sloan, L.R. (1976). Basking in reflected glory: Three (football) field studies. Journal of Personality and Social Psychology, 34, 366–375.

Curtis, J.E., Loy, J.W., & Karnilowicz, W. (1986). A comparison of suicide-dip effects of major sport events and civil holidays. Sociology of Sport Journal, 3, 1–14.

Davidson, J.A. (1981, May). A celebration of modern technology: The rise of skateboarding, 1963–1978. Paper presented at the Ninth Annual Convention of the North American Society for Sport History, Hamilton, ON.

Davies, H. (1972). The glory game. London: Weidenfeld and Nicolson.

Dewar, C.K. (1979). Spectator fights at professional baseball games. Review of Sport and Leisure, 4(1), 12–25.

Dunning, E. (1975). Industrialization and the incipient modernization of football. Stadion, 1, 103–139.

Dunning, E., Murphy, P., Williams, J., & Maguire, J.A. (1984). Football hooliganism in Britain before the first World War. International Review for the Sociology of Sport, 19, 215–240.

Dunning, E., Murphy, P., & Williams, J. (1986). Spectator violence at football matches: Towards a sociological explanation. The British Journal of Sociology, 37, 221–244.

Dunstan, K. (1973). Sports. Melbourne, Australia: Cassell.

Gabler, H. (1984, July). On the problem of soccer spectators' aggressions. Paper presented at the Olympic Scientific Congress, Eugene, OH.

Gerth, H.H., & Mills, C.W. (1954). Character and social structure: The psychology of social institutions. London: Routledge and Kegan Paul.

Goffman, E. (1967). Interaction ritual: Essays in face-to-face behavior. Chicago: Aldine.

Goldstein, J.H., & Arms, R.L. (1971). Effects of observing athletic contests on hostility. Sociometry, 34(1), 83–90.

Guttmann, A. (1978). From ritual to record: The nature of modern sports. New York: Columbia University Press.

Guttmann, A. (1981). Sports spectators from antiquity to the renaissance. Journal of Sport History, 8(2), 5–27.

Guttmann, A. (1986). Sports spectators. New York: Columbia University Press.

Harris, J.C. (1983). Pride and fever: Two university sport promotion themes. In F.E. Manning (Ed.), The world of play (pp. 25–37). Champaign, IL: Leisure Press.

Hoberman, J.M. (1987). Sport and social change: The transformation of Maoist sport. Sociology of Sport Journal, 4, 156–170.

Ingham, A.G. (1979). Methodology in the sociology of sport: From symptoms of malaise to Weber for a cure. Quest, 31, 187–215.

Jobling, I.F. (1970). Sport in nineteenth century Canada: The effects of technological changes on its development. Unpublished doctoral dissertation, University of Alberta, Department of Physical Education, Edmonton.

Kutcher, L. (1983). The American sport event as carnival: An emergent norm approach to crowd behavior. *Journal of Popular Culture*, **16**(4), 34–41.

Lang, G.E. (1981). Riotous outbursts at sport events. In G.R.F. Luschen & G.H. Sage (Eds.), *Handbook of social science of sport* (pp. 415–436). Champaign, IL: Stipes.

Le Bon, G. (1960). *The crowd.* New York: Viking. [Original work published 1895]

Lee, M.J. (1985). From revelry to hostility among sports fans. *Quest*, **37**, 38–49.

Lever, J. (1983). *Soccer madness.* Chicago: University of Chicago Press.

Listiak, A. (1976). "Legitimate deviance" and social class: Bar behavior during Grey Cup week. In R.S. Gruneau & J.G. Albinson (Eds.), *Canadian sport: Sociological perspectives* (pp. 404–433). Don Mills, ON: Addison-Wesley.

Loy, J.W. (1981). An emerging theory of sport spectatorship: Implications for the Olympic games. In J. Segrave & D. Chu (Eds.), *Olympism* (pp. 262–294). Champaign, IL: Human Kinetics.

Maguire, J. (1986). The emergence of football spectating as a social problem, 1880-1985: A sociogenetic and developmental perspective. *Sociology of Sport Journal*, **3**, 217–244.

Manning, F. (Ed.) (1983). *The celebration of society: Perspectives on contemporary cultural performance.* Bowling Green, OH: Bowling Green State University Press.

McPhail, C., & Miller, D. (1973). The assembling process: A theoretical and empirical examination. *American Sociological Review*, **38**, 721–735.

McPherson, B.D. (1975). Sport consumption and the economics of consumerism. In D.W. Ball & J.W. Loy (Eds.), *Sport and social order: Contributions to the sociology of sport* (pp. 243–275). Reading, MA: Addison-Wesley.

Melnick, M. (1986). The mythology of football hooliganism: A closer look at the British experience. *International Review for the Sociology of Sport*, **21**, 1–19.

Metcalfe, A. (1978). Working class physical recreation in Montreal, 1860-1895. In H. Cantelon & R. Gruneau (Eds.), *Working papers in the sociological study of sport and leisure* [Monograph 1]. Kingston, ON: Queen's University.

Miller Brewing Company. (1983). *The Miller Lite report on American attitudes toward sports.* Milwaukee: Author.

Okrent, D. (1980, April 28). Twenty-six teams in thirteen days. *Sports Illustrated*, pp. 62–76.

Pearton, R. (1986). Violence in sport and the special case of soccer hooliganism in the United Kingdom. In C.R. Rees & A.W. Miracle (Eds.), *Sport and social theory* (pp. 67–83). Champaign, IL: Human Kinetics.

Phillips, D.P. (1983). The impact of mass media violence on U.S. homicides. *American Sociological Review*, **48**, 560–568.

Roadburg, A. (1980). Factors precipitating fan violence: A comparison of professional soccer in Britain and North America. *British Journal of Sociology*, **31**, 265–276.

Roberts, M. (1976). *Fans! How we go crazy over sports.* Washington, DC: New Republic Book Co.

Schwartz, J. (1979, February 26). A day of light and shadows. *Sports Illustrated*, pp. 56–68.

Semyonov, M., & Farbstein, M. (1989). Ecology of sports violence: The case of Israeli soccer. *Sociology of Sport Journal*, **6**(1), 50–59.

Shergold, P.R. (1979). The growth of American spectator sport: A technological perspective. In R.I. Cashman & M. McKernan (Eds.), *Sport in history: The making of modern sporting history* (pp. 21–42). St.

Lucia, Australia: University of Queensland Press.

Smelser, N.J. (1962). *Theory of collective behavior*. New York: Free Press of Glencoe.

Smith, G.J., Patterson, B., Williams, T., & Gogy, J.M. (1981). A profile of the deeply committed male sports fan. *Arena Review*, **5**(2), 26–44.

Smith, M.D. (1975). Sport and collective violence. In D.W. Ball & J.W. Loy (Eds.), *Sport and social order: Contributions to the sociology of sport* (pp. 277-330). Reading, MA: Addison-Wesley.

Smith, M. (1978). Precipitants of crowd violence. *Sociological Inquiry*, **48**(2), 121–131.

Smith, M. (1983). *Violence and sport*. Toronto: Butterworths.

Spinrad, W. (1981). The function of spectator sports. In G.R.F. Luschen & G.J. Sage (Eds.), *Handbook of social science of sport* (pp. 354–365). Champaign, IL: Stipes.

Taylor, I. (1987). Putting the boot into a working-class sport: British soccer after Bradford and Brussels. *Sociology of Sport Journal*, **4**, 171–191.

Taylor, I.R. (1971). "Football mad": A speculative sociology of football hooliganism. In E. Dunning (Ed.), *Sport: Readings from a sociological perspective* (pp. 352–377). Toronto: University of Toronto Press.

Turner, R.H., & Killian, L.M. (1957). *Collective behavior*. Englewood Cliffs, NJ: Prentice-Hall.

Twombly, W. (1976). *Two hundred years of sport in America: A pageant of a nation at play*. New York: McGraw-Hill.

Vamplew, W. (1980). Sports crowd disorder in Britain, 1870–1914: Causes and controls. *Journal of Sport History*, **7**(1), 5–20.

Voigt, D.Q. (1970). America's manufactured villain: The baseball umpire. *Journal of Popular Culture*, **4**(Summer), 1–29.

Weis, K. (1986). How the print media affect sports and violence: The problems of sport journalism. *International Review for the Sociology of Sport*, **21**, 239–250.

Whannel, G. (1979). Football, crowd behaviour and the press. *Media, Culture and Society*, **1**, 327–342.

White, A. (1982). Soccer hooliganism in Britain. *Quest*, **34**, 154–164.

Williams, J., Dunning, E., & Murphy, P. (1986). The rise of the English soccer hooligan. *Youth and Society*, **17**, 362–380.

Yardley, J. (1980, April 7). Gimme an O. *Sports Illustrated*, pp. 92–108.

Young, K. (1986). The killing field: Themes in mass media responses to the Heysel Stadium riot. *International Review for the Sociology of Sport*, **21**, 253-264.

Glossary

Each definition lists the chapter where the term is first used in a sustained discussion.

Affective sport involvement—Emotional involvement in sport; compare with *cognitive sport involvement, primary behavioral involvement,* and *secondary behavioral involvement.* (Chapter 1)

Ageism—Beliefs about the inherent superiority of a particular age group over another, and discrimination based on these beliefs. (Chapter 9)

Agonal contests—Ritualized contests involving physical prowess that offer a means of determining social rank, recognizing excellence, and according honor. (Chapter 1)

Apartheid—A discriminatory system of restricted contact between races, as in the segregation of different groups of nonwhites in South Africa. (Chapter 4)

Avocational sport subculture—A group of people pursuing a central sport interest that they value highly, but not as an occupation; compare with *occupational sport subculture* and *deviant sport subculture.* (Chapter 10)

Back region—The private arena of a social organization that is not normally accessible to the public (e.g., locker room, hotel room); compare with *front region.* (Chapter 1)

Beliefs—Socially constructed and shared views about what should or should not be (e.g., "Don't cheat at sports") or what is, was,

or will be (e.g., "In baseball, three strikes and you're out"). (Chapter 1)

Bourgeoisie—Members of the capitalist class, who are owners of corporations, factories, and other major business organizations (e.g., the owners of professional sport teams). They control the means of production and accumulate wealth from surplus value provided by workers' labor; compare with *petite bourgeoisie* and *proletariat.* (Chapter 7)

Capitalism—An economic system supposedly based on free enterprise that effectively concentrates large investments, technology, and human resources in businesses controlled by the bourgeoisie, who purchase the labor power of workers. (Chapters 7 and 11)

Cartel—A group of firms (such as professional sport teams in a league) who agree to operate under procedures that restrict competition between them. These procedures eliminate competition from outsiders as well. (Chapter 5)

Cognitive sport involvement—The process of thinking and knowing about sport (e.g., knowing the history, organization, or strategies of a particular sport); compare with *affective sport involvement, primary behavioral involvement,* and *secondary behavioral involvement.* (Chapter 1)

Collective behavior—The spontaneous social actions of loosely structured groups of people in response to precipitating events. (Chapter 11)

Conflict perspective on social inequality—The perspective that argues that social inequalities result from the actions of dominant groups pursuing their self-interests, with social conflict and power seen as central features of social life; compare with the *functionalist perspective on social inequality*. (Chapter 7)

Contagion theory of collective behavior—The theory that crowds act out because emotional contagion occurs when people mill around together. (Chapter 11)

Contest mobility—A process whereby higher social status is earned through the personal motivation, effort, and ability of an individual competing against others in an open contest; compare with *sponsored mobility*. (Chapter 7)

Convergence theory of collective behavior—The theory that much crowd behavior is the result of people with similar interests coming together and acting upon those interests (e.g., people at a sporting event often have similar class, racial, or residence backgrounds and identify strongly with their class, race, or community). (Chapter 11)

Cross-sectional design—A research technique involving people from different age groups, all interviewed during the same period; compare with *longitudinal design*. (Chapter 9)

Crowd—A loosely structured mass of people who get together in a given area in a relatively spontaneous way for a short time in response to some stimulus, such as a sport event. (Chapter 11)

Cultural diffusion—The process whereby beliefs, values, and social activities (e.g., games or sports) are transferred from one society to another, in contrast to the independent development of similar activities. (Chapter 1)

Culture—A society's shared set of symbols and their meanings, embodied in beliefs, values, and norms. (Chapter 1)

Democratization—The process whereby a sport or other social activity becomes more accessible to, and popular among, different segments of a society, such as across age groups, social classes, or gender. (Chapter 1)

Desocialization—The process whereby an individual experiences role loss and an accompanying loss of associated power or prestige (e.g., retirement from a sport occupation). (Chapter 2)

Deviant behavior—The conduct of those who act contrary to the established norms or values of the wider society. (Chapter 10)

Deviant sport subculture—A sport group whose members' behaviors are contrary to some of the norms or values of the wider society; compare with *occupational sport subculture* and *avocational sport subculture*. (Chapter 10)

Discrimination—Differential and therefore unequal treatment of a group of persons; can apply to race or ethnic group (racism), gender (sexism), or age (ageism). (Chapters 8 and 9)

Economy—The organizations and practices within a society that lead to the production and distribution of material goods so as to promote the basic sustenance of life. (Chapter 5)

Education—The process by which the young learn about their culture and receive training in its values, knowledge, and skills in a classroom. (Chapter 3)

Emergent norm theory of collective behavior—The theory that even in a violent crowd, social interaction takes place that defines the situation and establishes norms for guiding behavior. (Chapter 11)

Enculturation—The process of learning and internalizing the prevailing values and accepted behavioral patterns of a culture; the same as *socialization*. (Chapter 3)

Ethnic group—A group of individuals with a shared sense of belonging based on a common heritage and sociocultural background; the individuals in an ethnic group are often visibly different from other individuals by virtue of unique lifestyle or appearance. (Chapter 8)

Family—A kinship group that legitimizes mating and provides care and socialization of children. (Chapter 2)

Free agency—A procedure in sport leagues whereby, after a certain number of years in the league, players are permitted to try to sell their services to teams other than the one that originally had them under contract; teams may bid against each other (in salary offers) for players' services. (Chapter 5)

Front region—The public arena of a social organization where its members are viewed by many others (e.g., athletes on the playing field or during television interviews); compare with *back region*. (Chapter 1)

Functionalist perspective on social inequality—The perspective that argues that social inequalities are based on the societal need to fill important positions with the most talented people and assumes that there is consensus among society's members on what positions are more important and, therefore, should receive greater rewards; compare with the *conflict perspective on social inequality*. (Chapter 7)

Gender—The cultural, or social psychological, definition of what it is to be male and female; compare with *sex*. (Chapter 9)

Generation—An age-based subgroup (people in adjacent birth cohorts) in which most members have experienced a significant sociohistorical event in a similar manner (e.g.,

the baby boom generation); this event often influences life chances and lifestyle across the life cycle. (Chapter 2)

Hooliganism—A form of deviant subcultural behavior engaged in by youths in Great Britain before, during, and after soccer games. (Chapter 11)

Ideologies—Emotionally charged beliefs and values that either explain and justify the status quo or, in the case of opposing ideologies, call for and justify alternatives. (Chapter 1)

Idioculture—A group that creates norms and behavior patterns (e.g., nicknames, inside jokes, rituals) that are different than those in the subculture of which it is a part (e.g., the norms and behaviors of a particular sport team, which are a result of traditions developed around that team). (Chapter 10)

Institution—Any enduring activity by groups and organizations, which addresses some important and persistent societal problem faced by a society (e.g., the family, educational system, law, polity, economy, or religion). (Chapter 1)

Institutional discrimination—Control of social institutions by one social group to the disadvantage of another; applies to race, gender, and age. (Chapter 8 and 9)

Institutionalization—A process whereby social groups, organizations, and activities become organized on an enduring basis to address some important and persistent problem; in other words, the process by which *institutions* develop. (Chapter 1)

Issueless riot—Spontaneous collective behavior that does not appear to be rooted in a specific issue, as when a crowd celebrating a home team victory produces large-scale property damage; compare with *issue-oriented riot*. (Chapter 11)

Issue-oriented riot—Spontaneous collective behavior resulting from an initiating event, as in a sport crowd rioting after a disputed call by a game official; compare with *issueless riot*. (Chapter 11)

Law—A norm passed by a legislative body, often specifying the punishment for a violation. (Chapter 4)

Legal system—The social activities and organizations, including courts, lawyers, and police, charged with maintaining and implementing a society's many legislated norms. (Chapter 4)

Legitimation—The process by which a social activity (such as a certain sport) comes to be considered respectable by the public at large (e.g., compare tennis, which is a respected sport in North America, and cockfighting, which is not an acceptable or legal sport in North America). (Chapter 1)

Longitudinal design—A research technique that collects data from the same sample of individuals at different times; compare with *cross-sectional design*. (Chapter 9)

Ludic activity—Social interaction based in play or games. (Chapter 1)

Mass media—Rapid and simultaneous communication to a large population, narrowing physical, temporal, and social distances; major examples are radio, television, and newspapers. (Chapter 6)

Minority groups—Subgroups whose members are blocked from full and equal participation in all phases of social life because of their race, ethnicity, age, or gender. (Chapter 8)

Norms—Formal or informal rules prescribing how categories of people are expected to act in particular situations, the violation of which is subject to sanction. (Chapter 1)

Nuclear family—A family group comprised of a couple and their children, a single parent and dependent children, or a couple without children. (Chapter 2)

Occupational sport subculture—A group of people who earn a livelihood from a partic-

ular sport; includes athletes and other roles, such as all types of sport producers; compare with *deviant sport subculture* and *avocational sport subculture*. (Chapter 10)

Petite bourgeoisie—People who own small businesses but do not employ others; compare with *bourgeoisie* and *proletariat*. (Chapter 7)

Politics—The process by which power and authority are exercised in making decisions and exercising influence in society. (Chapter 4)

Power—The ability of a person or group to influence (control or manipulate) the behavior of others. (Chapter 4)

Prejudice—Negative attitudes held toward people because of their race, ethnicity, gender, or age. (Chapters 8 and 9)

Primary behavioral involvement—Participation in a sport as a contestant or player; compare with *affective sport involvement*, *cognitive sport involvement*, and *secondary behavioral involvement*. (Chapter 1)

Proletariat—Members of the working class, who do not own the means of production and who sell their labor power for wages, such as professional athletes; compare with *bourgeoisie* and *petite bourgeoisie*. (Chapter 7)

Race (racial group)—An ethnic group whose membership is defined by perceptions of inherited biological traits. (Chapter 8)

Racism—Beliefs about the inherent superiority of one race over another, and discriminatory practices based on such beliefs. (Chapter 8)

Rationalization—The process whereby social organizations increasingly emphasize efficient means and calculated planning in order to achieve their goals (e.g., large-scale bureaucratic work organizations). (Chapter 1)

Reflection thesis—A theory that sport mirrors the beliefs, values, and norms of the wider society (e.g., achievement values and winning are emphasized in the workplace and in sport). (Chapter 1)

Reinforcement thesis—A theory that sport strengthens social inequities of the wider society (e.g., involvement in sport is perceived by the socially disadvantaged as an avenue for social mobility, thus lessening their frustration and inducing some element of social control). (Chapter 1)

Resistance thesis—A theory that sport provides an arena for opposition to the interests, values, and norms of the wider society (e.g., hooliganism). (Chapter 1)

Resocialization—A process of socialization that makes a sharp break with one's prior socialization. (Chapter 2)

Science—Activity geared toward the careful description of the real world, and the testing and validation of theories concerning the real world. (Chapter 1)

Secondary behavioral involvement—Involvement in sport as other than a player or contestant (i.e., as a producer or consumer); compare with *affective sport involvement, cognitive sport involvement*, and *primary behavioral involvement*. (Chapter 1)

Sex—The dichotomous physiological differences between males and females; compare with *gender*. (Chapter 9)

Sexism—Values, beliefs, and norms that define one gender as inferior to the other, and discriminatory practices based on these views. (Chapter 9)

Siblings—Brothers and sisters. (Chapter 2)

Significant others—Important people in one's life, such as family members and close friends, likely to influence one's values, beliefs, and behavior. (Chapter 1)

Social change—Any major alteration in the patterns of social relationships in society. (Chapter 11)

Social class—A group of people that differs from another in relationship to the means of production and whether it sells or purchases labor power, as in the differences among the *bourgeoisie, proletariat*, and *petite bourgeoisie* in contemporary society; compare the definitions of these three concepts. (Chapter 7)

Social conflict—A struggle over values or scarce resources in which two contesting groups seek to improve their situations. (Chapters 7–11)

Social control—The use of negative and positive sanctions (punishment and reward) by control agents to enforce conformity with their norms and expectations. (Chapter 11)

Social identity (social self)—The self-image derived from membership and interaction in social groups. (Chapter 2)

Social imitation theory—The theory that an individual learns by observing and modeling the behavior and perceived values, beliefs, and norms of significant others. (Chapter 2)

Socialization—A complex developmental learning process by which an individual acquires cultural knowledge, values, and norms; the same as *enculturation*. (Chapter 2)

Socialization into sport—The learning of appropriate sport behavior; includes such issues as who gets involved in sport and how and when people learn sport roles. (Chapter 2)

Socialization via sport—The process of acquiring in sport situations beliefs, values, and norms that are applicable in other social situations. (Chapter 2)

Social mobility—The process by which people move between social classes or socioeconomic status levels; requires that access to valued positions is somewhat open, rather than simply transmitted through a system of inheritance. (Chapter 7)

Social movement—A collective action to promote or resist change; participants have shared values, a sense of membership, shared understandings, and an organization with leaders and followers. (Chapter 11)

Social problem—A social situation that causes suffering for a significant number of society's members. (Chapter 9)

Social relationships—Interactions between people with consequences for every participant. (Chapter 1)

Social stratification—The process whereby people are assigned different social ranks based on the differential allocation of power, prestige, and privilege. (Chapter 7)

Society—A very large-scale collection of social relationships. (Chapter 1)

Socioeconomic status (social status)—One's relative position in society, determined by such factors as income and occupational prestige. (Chapter 7)

Sociology—The science that describes and constructs theories and explanations about the social relationships comprising a society. (Chapter 1)

Sponsored mobility—A process whereby higher social status is achieved through the efforts or assistance of others, especially members of the elite; compare with *contest mobility*. (Chapter 7)

Sport—A physical activity that is structured, goal-oriented, competitive, contest-based, and ludic. (Chapter 1)

Sport consumers—People who consume sport either directly (by attending sport events) or indirectly (via mass media). (Chapter 1)

Sport producers—Those responsible for staging a sport event (excluding competitors); includes coaches, managers, game officials,

health personnel, owners, promoters, and sporting goods manufacturers. (Chapter 1)

Stacking (positional segregation)—The assignment of athletes to positions on a sport team on the basis of ascribed (e.g., racial or ethnic) rather than achieved (performance) characteristics. (Chapter 8)

Subculture—A subgroup of society with distinctive beliefs, norms, and values. (Chapter 10)

Symbolic interaction—Interaction between persons based on the communication of symbols and meanings, as in the use of language. (Chapter 2)

Symbolic interaction perspective—The sociological view that emphasizes interpersonal interaction and its basis in the communication of symbols and shared meanings. (Chapter 2)

Theory—A tentative explanation of observable reality and the basis for predicting future events. (Chapter 1)

Value-added theory of collective behavior—The theory that collective behavior develops only when several elements are present in a social situation. Those elements are *structural strains* (social conflict), *structural conduciveness* (the lack of channels for resolving the conflict), a *generalized belief* (a shared belief about how to respond), *precipitating factors*, and *mobilization of the participants for action*. Each element adds to the likelihood of collective behavior occurring, but all must be present for it to occur. (Chapter 11)

Values—Ideas one holds about desirable goals to pursue. (Chapter 1)

Author Index

Subject Index